DEATH IN VENICE

A NEW TRANSLATION
BACKGROUNDS AND CONTEXTS
CRITICISM

Norton Critical Editions in the History of Ideas

For a complete list of Norton Critical Editions, visit
www.norton.com/college/English/nce_home.htm

A NORTON CRITICAL EDITION

Thomas Mann

DEATH IN VENICE

A NEW TRANSLATION
BACKGROUNDS AND CONTEXTS
CRITICISM

Translated and Edited by
CLAYTON KOELB
UNIVERSITY OF NORTH CAROLINA AT CHAPEL HILL

W · W · NORTON & COMPANY · *New York* · *London*

Copyright © 1994 by W. W. Norton & Company, Inc.

Printed in the United States of America

First Edition

The text of this book is composed in Electra
with the display set in Bernhard Modern
Composition by Vail
Manufacturing by Maple-Vail
Book design by Antonina Krass

Library of Congress Cataloging-in-Publication Data
Mann, Thomas, 1875–1955.
[Tod in Venedig.   English]
Death in Venice : a new translation, backgrounds and contexts,
criticism / Thomas Mann ; translated and edited by Clayton Koelb.
p.   cm.—(A Norton critical edition)
Includes bibliographical references.
I. Koelb, Clayton, 1942–   . II. Title.
PT2625.A44T62   1994
833'.912—dc20   93-4570

ISBN 0-393-96013-7

W. W. Norton & Company, Inc., 500 Fifth Avenue, New York, N.Y. 10110
www.wwnorton.com

W. W. Norton & Company Ltd., Castle House, 75/76 Wells Street,
London W1T 3QT

4 5 6 7 8 9 0

Contents

Preface

It seems almost impertinent to offer a new translation of Mann's most famous story. Other English versions exist, and some of them, such as that of David Luke, set a high standard of excellence. The aim here is not to supplant or even compete with those others but to offer North American students a text that strives to stay as close to Mann's German as one can without straining the norms of American English. This text does not attempt to be "poetic" in the sense of offering the translator's notion of high style. But it does reproduce, when appropriate, peculiarities of vocabulary and style—including metrical passages in dactylic hexameter—that are an integral part of Mann's intention.

Since the goal has always been to stay as close to the letter of the original as possible without sacrificing fluency, the reader can thus have some degree of assurance that variations in the style of the English translation bear a reliable relation to analogous variations in the German. That the English will not measure up to the German goes without saying—that is the fate of all translations.

The apparatus has deliberately been kept to a minimum so as not to burden the story with large numbers of footnotes. Notes are provided only to clarify matters that might otherwise remain obscure to the average well-informed reader. Nothing in the way of critical commentary has been attempted by the editor.

Mann's working notes are published here in English for the first time. They offer not only a wealth of information about the genesis of this particular story but also a window onto Mann's typical methods of work. I am grateful to Lynda Hoffmann Jeep for undertaking to do the translation of T. J. Reed's edition of the notes and also for compiling and translating the extracts from Mann's essays and letters.

Only a few essays out of the vast critical literature on *Death in Venice* could be offered here, and they were chosen with the primary aim of helping the student. Though they are all excellent examples of sophisticated Mann scholarship, they are not intended to be representative of the field or to be in any sense the cream of the crop. Some are long-acknowledged classics of interpretation, like André von Gronica's "Myth

Plus Psychology"; others are newer and offer perhaps controversial revisions of accepted views. Robert Tobin's essay treats a vitally important topic that has only recently emerged from the twilight of taboo. Unlike the others, it was specially commissioned for this volume. Manfred Dierks's piece has not appeared before in English, and I thank John Jeep for his substantial efforts in providing a translation. Considerations of space permitted the publication of only the most relevant portion of the Dierks/Jeep text.

I owe a special debt of gratitude to Julian Wuerth, who served as my research assistant during the most intense period of work on the volume and whose efforts went far beyond the call of duty. I must also thank Peter Jansen—the most perfectly bilingual person I know—who read the translation with extraordinary care and sensitivity. His comments saved me from many gaffs and infelicities (those that remain being entirely my own fault) and improved the final product immeasurably. Thanks are due as well to Katie Trumpener, who likewise offered valuable advice on the translation; to David Schabes, who helped on the bibliography; to George Kennedy, who clarified for me the puzzling matter of the *motus animi continuus*; and to David Luke, who generously encouraged and cooperated with this project from beginning to end.

The Text of
DEATH IN VENICE

Chapter 1

On a spring afternoon in 19—, a year that for months glowered threateningly over our continent,[1] Gustav Aschenbach—or von Aschenbach, as he had been known officially since his fiftieth birthday[2]—set off alone from his dwelling in Prinzregentenstrasse[3] in Munich on a rather long walk. He had been overstrained by the difficult and dangerous morning's work, which just now required particular discretion, caution, penetration, and precision of will: even after his midday meal the writer had not been able to halt the running on of the productive machinery within him, that "motus animi continuus" which Cicero claims is the essence of eloquence,[4] nor had he been able to obtain the relaxing slumber so necessary to him once a day to relieve the increasing demands on his resources. Thus, he sought the open air right after tea, hoping that fresh air and exercise would restore him and help him to have a profitable evening.

It was early May, and after weeks of cold, wet weather a premature summer had set in. The Englischer Garten, although only beginning to come into leaf, was as muggy as in August and at the end near the city was full of vehicles and people out for a stroll. Increasingly quiet paths led Aschenbach toward Aumeister, where he spent a moment surveying the lively crowd in the beer garden, next to which several hackneys and carriages were lingering; but then as the sun went down he took a route homeward outside the park over the open fields and, since he felt tired and thunder clouds now threatened over Föhring, he waited at the North Cemetery stop for the tram that would take him directly back into the city.

As it happened he found the tram stop and the surrounding area deserted. Neither on the paved Ungererstrasse, whose streetcar-tracks stretched in glistening solitude toward Schwabing, nor on the Föhringer Chaussee was there a vehicle to be seen;[5] nothing stirred behind the fences of the stonemasons' shops, where the crosses, headstones, and monuments for sale formed a second, untenanted graveyard, and the Byzantine architecture of the mortuary chapel across the way lay silent

1. In 1911, when the story was written, a number of diplomatic crises occurred that would eventually lead to World War I.
2. The word *von* ("from" or "of") appears only in the names of the nobility. Aschenbach was made an honorary nobleman on his fiftieth birthday.
3. See map of Munich, p. 67. Prinzregentenstrasse (J6) forms the southern boundary of the Englischer Garten. Mann lived in various apartments in this neighborhood—while writing *Death in Venice*, at 13 Mauerkirchestrasse (L5)—and often took walks similar to the one described here.
4. "Continuous motion of the spirit": Mann did not find this phrase in Cicero but gleaned it from Flaubert's letter to Louise Colet, dated July 15, 1853. (See T. J. Reed, *"Der Tod in Venedig,"* [Munich: Carl Hansen Verlag, 1983], p. 128.) The original source is probably Quintilian, who attributes it to Cicero, either in error or in reference to a work now lost.
5. See map of Munich, p. 67: the Englischer Garten is in area J6; Aumeister—M1; Föhring and Schwabing (districts in Munich)—M3 and J4; the North Cemetery—K2. Mann once lived on Ungererstrasse, which runs past the cemetery southwards into the city.

in the glow of the departing day. Its facade was decorated with Greek crosses and hieratic paintings in soft colors; in addition it displayed symmetrically arranged scriptural quotations in gold letters, such as, "They are entering the house of God," or, "May the eternal light shine upon them." Waiting, he found a few moments' solemn diversion in reading these formulations and letting his mind's eye bask in their radiant mysticism, when, returning from his reveries, he noticed a man in the portico, above the two apocalyptic beasts guarding the front steps. The man's not altogether ordinary appearance took his thoughts in a completely different direction.

It was not clear whether the man had emerged from the chapel through the bronze door or had climbed the steps up to the entry from the outside without being noticed. Aschenbach, without entering too deeply into the question, inclined to the first assumption. Moderately tall, thin, clean-shaven, and strikingly snub-nosed, the man belonged to the red-haired type and possessed a redhead's milky and freckled complexion. He was clearly not of Bavarian stock, and in any case the wide and straight-brimmed straw hat that covered his head lent him the appearance of a foreigner, of a traveler from afar. To be sure, he also wore the familiar native rucksack strapped to his shoulders and a yellowish Norfolk suit apparently of loden cloth. He had a gray mackintosh over his left forearm, which he held supported against his side, and in his right hand he held a stick with an iron tip, which he propped obliquely against the ground, leaning his hip against its handle and crossing his ankles. With his head held up, so that his Adam's apple protruded nakedly from the thin neck that emerged from his loose sport shirt, he gazed intently into the distance with colorless, red-lashed eyes, between which stood two stark vertical furrows that went rather oddly with his short, turned-up nose. It may be that his elevated and elevating location had something to do with it, but his posture conveyed an impression of imperious surveillance, fortitude, even wildness. His lips seemed insufficient, perhaps because he was squinting, blinded, toward the setting sun or maybe because he was afflicted by a facial deformity— in any case they were retracted to such an extent that his teeth, revealed as far as the gums, menacingly displayed their entire white length.

It is entirely possible that Aschenbach had been somewhat indiscreet in his half-distracted, half-inquisitive survey of the stranger, for he suddenly realized that his gaze was being returned, and indeed returned so belligerently, so directly eye to eye, with such a clear intent to bring matters to a head and force the other to avert his eyes, that Aschenbach, with an awkward sense of embarrassment, turned away and began to walk along the fence, intending for the time being to pay no more attention to the fellow. In a moment he had forgotten about him. But perhaps because the man had the look of the traveler about him, or perhaps because he exercised some physical or spiritual influence, Aschenbach's imagination was set working. He felt a sudden, strange expansion of his inner space, a rambling unrest, a youthful thirst for faraway places, a feeling so intense, so new—or rather so long unused and forgotten—that he stood rooted to the spot, his hands behind his back and his gaze to the ground, pondering the essence and direction of his emotion.

It was wanderlust and nothing more, but it was an overwhelming wanderlust that rose to a passion and even to a delusion. His desire acquired vision, and his imagination, not yet calmed down from the morning's work, created its own version of the manifold marvels and terrors of the earth, all of them at once now seeking to take shape within him. He saw, saw a landscape, a tropical swamp under a vaporous sky, moist, luxuriant, and monstrous, a sort of primitive wilderness of islands, morasses, and alluvial estuaries; saw hairy palm trunks rise up near and far out of rank fern brakes, out of thick, swollen, wildly blooming vegetation; saw wondrously formless trees sink their aerial roots into the earth through stagnant, green-shadowed pools, where exotic birds, their shoulders high and their bills shaped weirdly, stood motionless in the shallows looking askance amidst floating flowers that were white as milk and big as platters; saw the eyes of a lurking tiger sparkle between the gnarled stems of a bamboo thicket; and felt his heart pound with horror and mysterious desire. Then the vision faded, and with a shake of his head Aschenbach resumed his promenade along the fences bordering the headstone-makers' yard.

He had regarded travel, at least since he had commanded the financial resources to enjoy the advantages of global transportation at will, as nothing more than a measure he had to take for his health, no matter how much it went against his inclination. Too much taken up with the tasks that his problematic self and the European soul posed for him, too burdened with the obligation of productivity, too averse to distraction to be a success as a lover of the world's motley show, he had quite contented himself with the view of the earth's surface anyone could get without stirring very far from home. He had never even been tempted to leave Europe. Especially now that his life was slowly waning, now that his artist's fear of never getting finished—his concern that the sands might run out of the glass before he had done his utmost and given his all—could no longer be dismissed as pure fancy, his external existence had confined itself almost exclusively to the lovely city that had become his home and to the rustic country house he had built in the mountains where he spent the rainy summers.

Besides, even this impulse that had come over him so suddenly and so late in life was quickly moderated and set right by reason and a self-discipline practiced since early youth. He had intended to keep at the work to which he now devoted his life until he reached a certain point and then move out to the country. The thought of sauntering about the world, of thereby being seduced away from months of work, seemed all

too frivolous, too contrary to plan, and ultimately impermissible. And
yet he knew all too well why this temptation had assailed him so unexpectedly. He had to admit it to himself: it was the urge to escape that
was behind this yearning for the far away and the new, this desire for
release, freedom, and forgetfulness. It was the urge to get away from his
work, from the daily scene of an inflexible, cold, and passionate service.
Of course he loved this service and almost loved the enervating struggle,
renewed each day, between his stubborn, proud, so-often-tested will and
his growing lassitude, about which no one could be allowed to know
and which the product of his toil could not be permitted to reveal in any
way, by any sign of failure or of negligence. Yet it seemed reasonable
not to overbend the bow and not to stifle obstinately the outbreak of
such a vital need. He thought about his work, thought about the place
where once again, today as yesterday, he had been forced to abandon it,
a passage that would submit, it seemed, neither to patient care nor to
surprise attack. He considered it again, sought once more to break
through or untangle the logjam, then broke off the effort with a shudder
of repugnance. The passage presented no extraordinary difficulty; what
disabled him was the malaise of scrupulousness confronting him in the
guise of an insatiable perfectionism. Even as a young man, to be sure,
he had considered perfectionism the basis and most intimate essence of
his talent, and for its sake he had curbed and cooled his emotions,
because he knew that emotion inclines one to satisfaction with a comfortable approximation, a half of perfection. Was his enslaved sensitivity
now avenging itself by leaving him, refusing to advance his project and
give wings to his art, taking with it all his joy, all his delight in form and
expression? It was not that he was producing bad work—that at least was
the advantage of his advanced years; he felt every moment comfortably
secure in his mastery. But, though the nation honored it, he himself
was not pleased with his mastery, and indeed it seemed to him that his
work lacked those earmarks of a fiery, playful fancy that, stemming from
joy, gave more joy to his appreciative audience than did any inner content or weighty excellence. He was fearful of the summer in the country,
all alone in the little house with the maid who prepared his meals and
the servant who waited on him at table, fearful too of the familiar moun-
taintops and mountainsides that once more would surround him in his
discontented, slow progress. And so what he needed was a respite, a kind
of spur-of-the-moment existence, a way to waste some time, foreign air
and an infusion of new blood, to make the summer bearable and productive. Travel it would be then—it was all right with him. Not too far,
though, not quite all the way to the tigers. One night in a sleeping car
and a siesta for three or maybe four weeks in some fashionable vacation
spot in the charming south . . .

Such were his thoughts as the noise of the electric tram approached
along the Ungererstrasse, and he decided as he got on to devote this

evening to studying maps and time tables. Once aboard it occurred to him to look around for the man in the straw hat, his comrade in this excursion that had been, in spite of all, so consequential. But he could get no clear idea of the man's whereabouts; neither his previous location, nor the next stop, nor the tram car itself revealed any signs of his presence.

Chapter 2   *biographical chapter*

Gustav Aschenbach, the author of the clear and vigorous prose epic on the life of Frederick the Great;[1] the patient artist who wove together with enduring diligence the novelistic tapestry *Maia*, a work rich in characters and eminently successful in gathering together many human destinies under the shadow of a single idea; the creator of that powerful story bearing the title "A Man of Misery," which had earned the gratitude of an entire young generation by showing it the possibility for a moral resolution that passed through and beyond the deepest knowledge; the author, finally (and this completes the short list of his mature works), of the passionate treatment of the topic "Art and Intellect," an essay whose power of organization and antithetical eloquence had prompted serious observers to rank it alongside Schiller's "On Naïve and Sentimental Poetry";[2] Gustav Aschenbach, then, was born the son of a career civil servant in the justice ministry in L., a district capital in the province of Silesia.[3] His ancestors had been officers, judges, and government functionaries, men who had led upright lives of austere decency devoted to the service of king and country. A more ardent spirituality had expressed itself once among them in the person of a preacher; more impetuous and sensuous blood had entered the family line in the previous generation through the writer's mother, the daughter of a Bohemian music director. It was from her that he had in his features the traits of a foreign race. The marriage of sober conscientiousness devoted to service with darker, more fiery impulses engendered an artist and indeed this very special artist.

Since his entire being was bent on fame, he emerged early on as, perhaps not exactly precocious, but nonetheless, thanks to the decisiveness and peculiar terseness of his style, surprisingly mature and ready to go before the public. He was practically still in high school when he made a name for himself. Ten years later he learned how to keep up

1. King Frederick II (or Frederick the Great, 1712–1786) started Prussia on its rise to domination of Germany and made his court a prominent European cultural center.
2. *Frederick*, *Maia*, "A Man of Misery," and "Art and Intellect" are all titles of projects Mann himself had worked on and abandoned. Friedrich Schiller (1759–1805) was one of the most famous German writers of his day, producing poems, plays, and many works of philosophy and history. The essay mentioned here is a work of literary criticism.
3. The "L." might be a reference to Lübeck, the city of Mann's birth, though it is not in Silesia.

appearances, to manage his fame from his writing desk, to produce gracious and significant sentences for his necessarily brief letters (for many demands are made on such a successful and reliable man). By the age of forty, exhausted by the tortures and vicissitudes of his real work, he had to deal with a daily flood of mail bearing stamps from countries in every corner of the globe.

Tending neither to the banal nor to the eccentric, his talent was such as to win for his stories both the acceptance of the general public and an admiring, challenging interest from a more discerning audience. Thus he found himself even as a young man obliged in every way to achieve and indeed to achieve extraordinary things. He had therefore never known sloth, never known the carefree, laissez-faire attitude of youth. When he got sick in Vienna around the age of thirty-five, a canny observer remarked about him to friends, "You see, Aschenbach has always lived like this"—and the speaker closed the fingers of his left hand into a fist—"never like this"—and he let his open hand dangle comfortably from the arm of the chair. How right he was! And the morally courageous aspect of it was that, possessing anything but a naturally robust constitution, he was not so much born for constant exertion as he was called to it.

Medical concerns had prevented him from attending school as a child and compelled the employment of private instruction at home. He had grown up alone and without companions, and yet he must have realized early on that he belonged to a tribe in which talent was not so much a rarity as was the bodily frame talent needs to find its fulfillment, a tribe known for giving their best early in life but not for longevity. His watchword, however, was "Endure," and he saw in his novel about Frederick the Great precisely the apotheosis of this commandment, which seemed to him the essence of a selflessly active virtue. He harbored, moreover, a keen desire to live to a ripe old age, for he had long believed that an artistic career could be called truly great, encompassing, indeed truly worthy of honor only if the artist were allotted sufficient years to be fruitful in his own way at all stages of human life.

Since he thus bore the burdens of his talent on slender shoulders and wished to carry those burdens far, he was in great need of discipline. Fortunately for him discipline was his heritage at birth from his paternal side. At forty, at fifty, even at an age when others squander and stray, content to put their great plans aside for the time being, he started his day at an early hour by dousing his chest and back with cold water. Then, placing two tall wax candles in silver candlesticks at the head of his manuscript, he would spend two or three fervently conscientious morning hours sacrificing on the altar of art the powers he had assembled during his sleep. It was forgivable—indeed it even indicated the victory of his moral force—that uninformed readers mistook the Maia-world or the epic scroll on which unrolled Frederick's heroic life for the products of single sustained bursts of energy, whereas they actually grew into grandeur layer by layer, out of small daily doses of work and countless individual flashes of inspiration. These works were thoroughly excellent in every detail solely because their creator had endured for years under the pressure of a single project, bringing to bear a tenacity and perseverance similar to that which had conquered his home province,[4] and because he had devoted only his freshest and worthiest hours to actual composition.

If a work of the intellect is to have an immediate, broad, and deep effect, there must be a mysterious affinity, a correspondence between the personal fate of its originator and the more general fate of his contemporaries. People do not know why they accord fame to a particular work. Far from being experts, they suppose they see in it a hundred virtues that would justify their interest; but the real reason for their approval is something imponderable—it is sympathy. Aschenbach had actually stated forthrightly, though in a relatively inconspicuous passage, that nearly everything achieving greatness did so under the banner of "Despite"—despite grief and suffering, despite poverty, destitution, infirmity, affliction, passion, and a thousand obstacles. But this was more than an observation, it was the fruit of experience; no, it was the very formula for his life and his fame, the key to his work. Was it any wonder, then, that it was also the basis for the moral disposition and outward demeanor of his most original fictional characters?

Early on an observant critic had described the new type of hero that this writer preferred, a figure returning over and over again in manifold variation: it was based on the concept of "an intellectual and youthful manliness which grits its teeth in proud modesty and calmly endures the swords and spears as they pass through its body." It was a nice description, ingenious and precise, despite its seemingly excessive emphasis on passivity. For meeting one's fate with dignity, grace under pressure of pain, is not simply a matter of sufferance; it is an active achievement, a positive triumph, and the figure of St. Sebastian[5] is thus the most beautiful image, if not of art in general, then surely of the art under discussion here. Having looked at the characters in Aschenbach's narrated world, having seen the elegant self-discipline that managed right up to the last moment to hide from the eyes of the world the undermining process, the biological decline, taking place within; having seen the yellow, physically handicapped ugliness that nonetheless managed to kindle its smoldering ardor into a pure flame, managed even to catapult

underdog hero

4. As a result of the Seven Years' War (1756–1763), Frederick the Great wrested Silesia from Austria. Now the part of Silesia once in German hands has become a region in southwestern Poland.

5. An early Christian martyr, whose legendary sufferings were frequently depicted by Renaissance painters.

itself to mastery in the realm of beauty; or having seen the pale impotence that pulls out of the glowing depths of the spirit enough power to
force a whole frivolous people to fall at the feet of the cross, at the feet
of that very impotence; or the lovable charm that survives even the
empty and rigorous service of pure form; or the false, dangerous life of
the born deceiver, with the quick enervation of its longing and with
its artfulness[6]—having seen all these human destinies and many more
besides, it was easy enough to doubt that there could be any other sort
of heroism than that of weakness. In any case, what kind of heroism was
more appropriate to the times than this? Gustav Aschenbach was the
poet of all those who work on the edge of exhaustion, of the overburdened, worn down moralists of achievement who nonetheless still stand
tall, those who, stunted in growth and short of means, use ecstatic feats
of will and clever management to extract from themselves at least for a
period of time the effects of greatness. Their names are legion, and they
are the heroes of the age. And all of them recognized themselves in his
work; they saw themselves justified, exalted, their praises sung. And they
were grateful; they heralded his name.

He had been once as young and rough as the times and, seduced
by them, had made public blunders and mistakes, had made himself
vulnerable, had committed errors against tact and good sense in word
and deed. But he had won the dignity toward which, in his opinion,
every great talent feels an inborn urge and spur. One could say in fact
that his entire development had been a conscious and defiant rise to
dignity, beyond any twinge of doubt and of irony that might have stood
in his way.

Pleasing the great mass of middle-class readers depends mainly on
offering vividly depicted, intellectually undemanding characterizations,
but passionately uncompromising youth is smitten only with what is
problematic; and Aschenbach had been as problematic and uncompromising as any young man can be. He had pandered to the intellect,
exhausted the soil of knowledge, milled flour from his seed corn,
revealed secrets, put talent under suspicion, betrayed art. Indeed, while
his portrayals entertained, elevated, invigorated the blissfully credulous
among his readers, as a youthful artist it was his cynical observations on
the questionable nature of art and of the artist's calling that had kept the
twenty-year-old element fascinated.

But it seems that nothing so quickly or so thoroughly blunts a high-
minded and capable spirit as the sharp and bitter charm of knowledge;
and it is certain that the melancholy, scrupulous thoroughness charac-

---

6. The five characters described here as belonging to "Aschenbach's narrated world" are very
similar to figures in Mann's own works: Thomas Buddenbrook in the novel *Buddenbrooks*;
Lorenzo de' Medici in the drama *Fiorenza*; Girolamo Savonarola, also in *Fiorenza*; Klaus
Heinrich in *Royal Highness*; and Felix Krull in the novel of the same name—the very project
Mann had been working on long and diligently when he stopped to take a vacation in Venice.
Mann did not return to work on *Felix Krull* until forty years later.

teristic of the young seems shallow in comparison with the solemn decision of masterful maturity to disavow knowledge, to reject it, to move
beyond it with head held high, to forestall the least possibility that it
could cripple, dishearten, or dishonor his will, his capacity for action
and feeling, or even his passion. How else could one interpret the
famous story "A Man of Misery" save as an outbreak of disgust at the
indecent psychologism then current? This disgust was embodied in the
figure of that soft and foolish semi-villain who, out of weakness,
viciousness, and moral impotence, buys a black-market destiny for himself by driving his wife into the arms of a beardless boy, who imagines
profundity can justify committing the basest acts. The weight of the
words with which the writer of that work reviled the vile announced a
decisive turn away from all moral skepticism, from all sympathy with the
abyss, a rejection of the laxity inherent in the supposedly compassionate
maxim that to understand everything is to forgive everything. What was
coming into play here—or rather, what was already in full swing—was
that "miracle of ingenuousness reborn" about which there was explicit
discussion, not without a certain mysterious emphasis, in one of the
author's dialogues published only slightly later. Strange relationships!
Was it an intellectual consequence of this "rebirth," of this new dignity
and rigor, that just then readers began to notice an almost excessive
increase in his sense of beauty, a noble purity, simplicity, and sense of
proportion that henceforth gave his works such a palpable, one might
say deliberately classical and masterful quality? But moral determination
that goes beyond knowledge, beyond analytic and inhibiting perception—would that not also be a reduction, a moral simplification of the
world and of the human soul and therefore also a growing potential for
what is evil, forbidden, and morally unacceptable? And does form not
have two faces? Is it not moral and amoral at the same time—moral
insofar as form is the product and expression of discipline, but amoral
and indeed immoral insofar as it harbors within itself by nature a certain
moral indifference and indeed is essentially bent on forcing the moral
realm to stoop under its proud and absolute scepter?

   That is as may be. Since human development is human destiny, how
could a life led in public, accompanied by the accolades and confidence
of thousands, develop as does one led without the glory and the obligations of fame? Only those committed to eternal bohemianism would be
bored and inclined to ridicule when a great talent emerges from its libertine chrysalis, accustoms itself to recognizing emphatically the dignity
of the spirit, takes on the courtly airs of solitude, a solitude full of unas-
sisted, defiantly independent suffering and struggle, and ultimately
achieves power and honor in the public sphere. And how much playfulness, defiance, and indulgence there is in the way talent develops! A
kind of official, educative element began in time to appear in Aschenbach's productions. His style in later years dispensed with the sheer

audacity, the subtle and innovative shadings of his younger days, and moved toward the paradigmatic, the polished and traditional, the conservative and formal, even formulaic. Like Louis XIV[7]—as report would have it—the aging writer banished from his vocabulary every base expression. About this time it came to pass that the educational authorities began using selected passages from his works in their prescribed textbooks. He seemed to sense the inner appropriateness of it, and he did not refuse when a German prince, newly ascended to the throne, bestowed on the author of *Frederick*, on his fiftieth birthday, a nonhereditary title.

Relatively early on, after a few years of moving about, a few tries at living here and there, he chose Munich as his permanent residence and lived there in bourgeois respectability such as comes to intellectuals sometimes, in exceptional cases. His marriage to a girl from a learned family, entered upon when still a young man, was terminated after only a short term of happiness by her death. A daughter, already married, remained to him. He never had a son.

Gustav Aschenbach was a man of slightly less than middle height, dark-haired and clean shaven. His head seemed a little too big for a body that was almost dainty. His hair, combed back, receding at the top, still very full at the temples, though quite gray, framed a high, furrowed, and almost embossed-looking brow. The gold frame of his rimless glasses cut into the bridge of his full, nobly curved nose. His mouth was large, sometimes relaxed and full, sometimes thin and tense; his cheeks were lean and hollow, and his well-proportioned chin was marked by a slight cleft. Important destinies seemed to have played themselves out on this long-suffering face, which he often held tilted somewhat to one side.[8] And yet it was art alone, not a difficult and troubled life, that had taken over the task of chiseling these features. Behind this brow was born the scintillating repartee between Voltaire and King Frederick on the subject of war; these eyes, looking tiredly but piercingly through the glasses, had seen the bloody inferno of the field hospitals during the Seven Years' War.[9] Indeed, even on the personal level art provides an intensified version of life. Art offers a deeper happiness, but it consumes one more quickly. It engraves upon the faces of its servants the traces of imaginary, mental adventures and over the long term, even given an external existence of cloistered quietude, engenders in them a nervous sensitivity, an over-refinement, a weariness and an inquisitiveness such as are scarcely ever produced by a life full of extravagant passions and pleasures.

7. King of France from 1643 until his death in 1715.
8. Compare this description to the newspaper photograph of Gustav Mahler (page 86) that Mann put in his working notes.
9. Frederick the Great invited Voltaire (1694–1778), the most famous French writer of the time, to live at his palace; the Seven Years' War was fought by Prussia against an alliance of Saxony, Austria, and Russia. (See 9, n. 4.)

Chapter 3

Several obligations of both a practical and a literary nature forced the eager traveler to remain in Munich for about two weeks after his walk in the park. Finally he gave instructions for his country house to be prepared for his moving in within a month's time and, on a day sometime between the middle and end of May, he took the night train to Trieste, where he remained only twenty-four hours and where he boarded the boat to Pola[1] on the morning of the next day.

What he sought was someplace foreign, someplace isolated, but someplace nonetheless easy to get to. He thus took up residence on an Adriatic island, a destination that had been highly spoken of in recent years and lay not far from the Istrian coast. It was populated by locals dressed in colorful rags who spoke in wildly exotic accents, and the landscape was graced by rugged cliffs on the coast facing the open sea. But the rain and oppressive air, the provincial, exclusively Austrian clientele at the hotel, and the lack of the peaceful, intimate relation with the sea that only a soft sandy beach can offer—these things irritated him, denied him a sense of having found the place he was looking for; he was troubled by a pressure within him pushing in a direction he could not quite grasp; he studied ship schedules, he sought about for something; and suddenly the surprising but obvious destination came to him. If you wanted to reach in a single night someplace incomparable, someplace as out of the ordinary as a fairy tale, where did you go? The answer was clear. What was he doing here? He had gone astray. It was over there that he had wanted to go all along. He did not hesitate a moment in remedying his error and gave notice of his departure. A week and a half after his arrival on the island a swift motorboat carried him and his baggage through the early morning mist across the water to the military port, where he landed only long enough to find the gangway leading him onto the damp deck of a ship that was already getting up steam for a trip to Venice.

It was an aged vessel, long past its prime, sooty, and gloomy, sailing under the Italian flag. In a cavernous, artificially lit cabin in the ship's interior—to which Aschenbach had been conducted with smirking politeness by a hunchbacked, scruffy sailor the moment he embarked— sat a goateed man behind a desk. With his hat cocked over his brow and a cigarette butt hanging from the corner of his mouth, his facial features were reminiscent of an old time ringmaster. He took down the passengers' personal information and doled out tickets with the grimacing, easy

1. Trieste: an Italian port city at the northern end of the Adriatic; Pola: (now called Pula) an industrial port on the Adriatic, about thirty miles south of Trieste and seventy-five miles southeast of Venice.

demeanor of the professional. "To Venice!" He repeated Aschenbach's request, stretching his arm to dip his pen in the congealed remains at the bottom of his slightly tilted inkwell. "To Venice, first class! There, sir, you're all taken care of." He inscribed great letters like crane's feet on a piece of paper, poured blue sand out of a box onto them, poured it back into an earthenware bowl, folded the paper with his yellow, bony fingers, and resumed writing. "What a fine choice for your destination!" he babbled in the meantime. "Ah, Venice, a wonderful city! A city that is irresistible to cultured people both for its history and for its modern charm!" The smooth swiftness of his movements and the empty chatter with which he accompanied them had an anesthetic and diversionary effect, as if he were concerned that the traveler should change his mind about his decision to go to Venice. He hastily took the money and dropped the change on the stained cloth covering the table with the practiced swiftness of a croupier. "Enjoy yourself, sir!" he said with a theatrical bow. "It is an honor to be of service to you. . . . Next, please!" he cried with his arm raised, acting as if he were still doing a brisk business, though in fact there was no one else there to do business with. Aschenbach returned above deck.

With one arm resting on the rail, he observed the passengers on board and the idle crowd loitering on the pier to watch the ship depart. The second-class passengers, both men and women, crouched on the forward deck using boxes and bundles as seats. A group of young people, apparently employees of businesses in Pola, who had banded together in great excitement for an excursion to Italy, formed the social set of the first upper deck. They made no little fuss over themselves and their plans, chattered, laughed, and took complacent enjoyment in their own continual gesturing. Leaning over the railing they called out in fluent and mocking phrases to various friends going about their business, briefcases under their arms, along the dockside street below, while the latter in turn made mock-threatening gestures with their walking sticks at the celebrants above. One of the merrymakers, wearing a bright yellow, overly fashionable summer suit, red tie, and a panama hat with a cockily turned-up brim, outdid all the others in his screeching gaiety. But scarcely had Aschenbach gotten a closer look at him when he realized with something like horror that this youth was not genuine. He was old, no doubt about it. There were wrinkles around his eyes and mouth. The faint carmine of his cheeks was rouge; the brown hair beneath the colorfully banded hat was a wig; his neck was shrunken and sinewy; his clipped mustache and goatee were dyed; the full, yellowish set of teeth he exposed when he laughed was a cheap set of dentures; and his hands, bedecked with signet rings on both forefingers, were those of an old man. With a shudder Aschenbach watched him and his interaction with his friends. Did they not know, had they not noticed that he was old, that he had no right to wear their foppish and colorful clothes, had no right to pretend to be one of their own? They apparently tolerated him in their midst as a matter of course, out of habit, and treated him as an equal, answering in kind without reluctance when he teasingly poked one of them in the ribs. But how could this be? Aschenbach covered his brow with his hand and closed his eyes, which were feeling inflamed from not getting enough sleep. It seemed to him that things were starting to take a turn away from the ordinary, as if a dreamy estrangement, a bizarre distortion of the world were setting in and would spread if he did not put a stop to it by shading his eyes a bit and taking another look around him. Just at this moment he experienced a sensation of motion and, looking up with an unreasoning terror, realized that the heavy and gloomy hulk of the ship was slowly parting company with the stone pier. The engines ran alternately forward and reverse, and inch by inch the band of oily, iridescent water between the pier and the hull of the ship widened. After a set of cumbersome maneuvers the steamer managed to point its bowsprit toward the open sea. Aschenbach went over to the starboard side, where the hunchback had set up a deck chair for him and a steward dressed in a stained tailcoat offered him service.

The sky was gray and the wind was moist. The harbor and the island were left behind, and soon all sight of land vanished beyond the misty horizon. Flakes of coal soot saturated with moisture fell on the scrubbed, never drying deck. No more than an hour later a canvas canopy was put up, since it had started to rain.

Wrapped in his cloak, a book on his lap, the traveler rested, and the hours passed by unnoticed. It stopped raining; the linen canopy was removed. The horizon was unobstructed. Beneath the overcast dome of the sky the immense disk of the desolate sea stretched into the distance all around. But in empty, undivided space our sense of time fails us, and we lose ourselves in the immeasurable. Strange and shadowy figures—the old fop, the goat-beard from below deck—invaded Aschenbach's mind as he rested. They gestured obscurely and spoke the confused speech of dreams. He fell asleep.

At noon they called him to lunch down in the corridorlike dining hall onto which opened the doors of all the sleeping quarters and in which stood a long table. He dined at one end, while at the other the business employees from Pola, including the old fop, had been carousing since ten o'clock with the jolly captain. The meal was wretched and he soon got up. He felt an urgent need to get out, to look at the sky, to see if it might not be brightening over Venice.

It had never occurred to him that anything else could happen, for the city had always received him in shining glory. But the sky and the sea remained overcast and leaden. From time to time a misty rain fell, and he came to the realization that he would approach a very different Venice by sea than the one he had previously reached by land. He stood by the foremast, gazing into the distance, awaiting the sight of land.

He remembered the melancholy, enthusiastic poet of long ago who had furnished his dreams with the domes and bell towers rising from these waters. He softly repeated to himself some of those verses in which the awe, joy, and sadness of a former time had taken stately shape[2] and, easily moved by sensations thus already formed, looked into his earnest and weary heart to see if some new enthusiasm or entanglement, some late adventure of feeling might be in store for him, the idle traveler.

Then the flat coastline emerged on the right; the sea became populated with fishing boats; the barrier island with its beach appeared. The steamer soon left the island behind to the left, slipping at reduced speed through the narrow harbor named after it.[3] They came to a full stop in the lagoon in view of rows of colorfully wretched dwellings and awaited the arrival of the launch belonging to the health service.

An hour passed before it appeared. One had arrived and yet had not arrived; there was no great hurry and yet one felt driven by impatience. The young people from Pola had come up on deck, apparently yielding to a patriotic attraction to the military trumpet calls resounding across the water from the public garden.[4] Full of excitement and Asti, they shouted cheers at the *bersaglieri*[5] conducting drills over there. It was disgusting, however, to see the state into which the made-up old coot's false fellowship with the young people had brought him. His aged brain had not been able to put up the same resistance to the wine as the younger and more vigorous heads, and he was wretchedly drunk. His vision blurred; a cigarette dangled from his shaking fingers; he stood swaying tipsily in place, pulled to and fro by intoxication, barely able to maintain his balance. Since he would have fallen over at the first step, he dared not move from the spot. Yet he maintained a woeful bravado, buttonholing everyone who came near; he stammered, blinked, giggled, raised his beringed, wrinkled forefinger in fatuous banter, and ran the tip of his tongue around the corners of his mouth in an obscenely suggestive manner. Aschenbach watched him from under a darkened brow and was once again seized by a feeling of giddiness, as if the world were displaying a slight but uncontrollable tendency to distort, to take on a bizarre and sneering aspect. It was a feeling, to be sure, that conditions prevented him from indulging, for just then the engine began anew its pounding, and the ship, interrupted so close to its destination, resumed its course through the canal of San Marco.[6]

Once more, then, it lay before him, that most astounding of landing places, that dazzling grouping of fantastic buildings that the republic

2. August Graf von Platen, author of a series of sonnets about Venice. The lines Aschenbach recites to himself are probably those that open the first sonnet: "My eye left the high seas behind/as the temples of [the architect Andrea] Palladio rose from the waters."
3. Both the barrier island and the harbor are called "Lido." See the inset on map of Venice, p. 68.
4. See map of Venice, L-M7 (p. 68).
5. Asti spumante: a sweet, sparkling Italian wine; *bersaglieri*: elite Italian troops.
6. See map of Venice, H-K 6-7, p. 68.

presented to the awed gaze of approaching mariners: the airy splendor
of the palace and the Bridge of Sighs; the pillars on the water's edge
bearing the lion and the saint; the showy projecting flank of the fairy tale
cathedral; the view toward the gate and the great clock. It occurred to
him as he raised his eyes that to arrive in Venice by land, at the railway
station, was like entering a palace by a back door; that one ought not to
approach this most improbable of cities save as he now did, by ship,
over the high seas.

The engine stopped, gondolas swarmed about, the gangway was lowered, customs officials boarded and haughtily went about their duties;
disembarkation could begin. Aschenbach let it be known that he desired
a gondola to take him and his luggage over to the landing where he
could get one of the little steamboats that ran between the city and the
Lido;[7] for it was his intention to take up residence by the sea. His wishes
met with acquiescence; a call went down with his request to the water's
surface where the gondoliers were quarreling with each other in dialect.
He was still prevented from disembarking; his trunk presented problems;
only with considerable difficulty could it be pulled and tugged down
the ladderlike gangway. He therefore found himself unable for several
moments to escape from the importunities of the ghastly old impostor,
who, driven by some dark drunken impulse, was determined to bid elaborate farewell to the foreign traveler. "We wish you the happiest of
stays," he bleated, bowing and scraping. "Keep a fond memory of us!
Au revoir, excusez, and bonjour, your excellency!" He drooled, he bat-
ted his eyes, he licked the corners of his mouth, and the dyed goatee on
his elderly chin bristled. "Our compliments," he babbled, two fingertips
at his mouth, "our compliments to your beloved, your dearly beloved,
your lovely beloved . . ." And suddenly his uppers fell out of his jaw
onto his lower lip. Aschenbach took his chance to escape. "Your
beloved, your sweet beloved . . ." He heard the cooing, hollow,
obstructed sounds behind his back as he descended the gangway, clutch-
ing at the rope handrail as he went.

Who would not need to fight off a fleeting shiver, a secret aversion
and anxiety, at the prospect of boarding a Venetian gondola for the
first time or after a long absence? This strange conveyance, surviving
unchanged since legendary times and painted the particular sort of black
ordinarily reserved for coffins, makes one think of silent, criminal
adventures in a darkness full of splashing sounds; makes one think even
more of death itself, of biers and gloomy funerals, and of that final,
silent journey. And has anyone noticed that the seat of one of these
boats, this armchair painted coffin-black and upholstered in dull black
cloth, is one of the softest, most luxurious, most sleep-inducing seats

---

7. The large ocean-going steamship would have docked along the Riva d. Schiavoni (see map of
   Venice, H-15, p. 68), but the little boats that ply the lagoon would dock at San Marco (G-
   H5-6).

in the world? Aschenbach certainly realized this as he sat down at the gondolier's feet, opposite his luggage lying in a copious pile in the bow. The oarsmen were still quarreling in a rough, incomprehensible language punctuated by threatening gestures. The peculiar quiet of this city of water, however, seemed to soften their voices, to disembody them, to disperse them over the sea. It was warm here in the harbor. Stroked by the mild breath of the sirocco,[8] leaning back into the cushions as the yielding element carried him, the traveler closed his eyes in the pleasure of indulging in an indolence both unaccustomed and sweet. The trip will be short, he thought; if only it could last forever! The gondola rocked softly, and he felt himself slip away from the crowded ship and the clamoring voices.

How quiet, ever more quiet it grew around him! Nothing could be heard but the splashing of the oar, the hollow slap of the waves against the gondola's prow, rising rigid and black above the water with its halberdlike beak—and then a third thing, a voice, a whisper. It was the murmur of the gondolier, who was talking to himself through his clenched teeth in fits and starts, emitting sounds that were squeezed out of him by the labor of his arms. Aschenbach looked up and realized with some astonishment that the lagoon was widening about him and that he was traveling in the direction of the open sea. It seemed, then, that he ought not to rest quite so peacefully but instead make sure his wishes were carried out.

"I told you to take me to the steamer landing," he said with a half turn toward the stern. The murmur ceased. He received no answer.

"I told you to take me to the steamer landing!" he repeated, turning around completely and looking up into the face of the gondolier, whose figure, perched on the high deck and silhouetted against the dun sky, towered behind him. The man had a disagreeable, indeed brutal-looking appearance; he wore a blue sailor suit belted with a yellow sash, and a shapeless straw hat that was beginning to come unraveled and was tilted rakishly on his head. His facial features and the blond, curly mustache under his short, turned-up nose marked him as clearly not of Italian stock. Although rather slender of build, so that one would not have thought him particularly well suited to his profession, he plied his oar with great energy, putting his whole body into every stroke. Several times he pulled his lips back with the strain, baring his white teeth. His reddish eyebrows puckered, he looked out over his passenger's head and replied in a decisive, almost curt tone of voice: "You are going to the Lido."

Aschenbach responded, "Indeed. But I took the gondola only to get over to San Marco. I want to use the vaporetto."[9]

8. A hot wind originating in the Sahara, becoming humid as it picks up moisture over the Mediterranean.
9. "Little steamboat."

"You cannot use the vaporetto, sir."

"And why not?"

"Because the vaporetto does not accept luggage."

He was right about that; Aschenbach remembered. He said nothing. But the gruff, presumptuous manner of the man, so unlike the normal way of treating foreigners in this country, was not to be endured. He said, "That is my business. Perhaps I intend to put my luggage in storage. You will kindly turn back."

There was silence. The oar splashed, the waves slapped dully against the bow. And the murmuring and whispering began anew: the gondolier was talking to himself through his clenched teeth.

What to do? Alone at sea with this strangely insubordinate, uncannily resolute person, the traveler saw no way to enforce his wishes. And anyway, if he could just avoid getting angry, what a lovely rest he could have! Had he not wished the trip could last longer, could last forever? The smartest thing to do was to let matters take their course; more important, it was also the most pleasant thing to do. A magic circle of indolence seemed to surround the place where he sat, this low armchair upholstered in black, so gently rocked by the rowing of the autocratic gondolier behind him. The idea that he might have fallen into the hands of a criminal rambled about dreamily in Aschenbach's mind, but it was incapable of rousing his thoughts to active resistance. More annoying was the possibility that all this was simply a device by which to extort money from him. A sense of duty or of pride, the memory, as it were, that one must prevent such things, induced him once more to pull himself together. He asked, "What do you want for the trip?"

And the gondolier, looking out over him, answered, "You will pay."

It was clear what reply was necessary here. Aschenbach said mechanically, "I will pay nothing, absolutely nothing, if you take me where I do not want to go."

"You want to go to the Lido."

"But not with you."

"I row you well."

True enough, thought Aschenbach, and relaxed. True enough, you row me well. Even if you are just after my money, even if you send me to the house of Aides[1] with a stroke of your oar from behind, you will have rowed me well.

But no such thing occurred. In fact, some company even happened by in the form of a boat filled with musicians, both men and women, who waylaid the gondola, sailing obtrusively right alongside. They sang to the accompaniment of guitars and mandolins and filled the quiet air over the lagoon with the strains of their mercenary tourist lyrics. Aschenbach threw some money in the hat they held out to him, where-

---

1. A Greek spelling of "Hades."

upon they fell silent and sailed off. The murmur of the gondolier became perceptible once again as he talked to himself in fits and starts.

And so they arrived, bobbing in the wake of a steamer sailing back to the city. Two municipal officials walked up and down along the landing, their hands behind their backs and their faces turned to the lagoon. Aschenbach stepped from the gondola onto the dock assisted by one of those old men who seemed on hand, armed with a boathook, at every pier in Venice. Since he had no small coins with him, he crossed over to the hotel next to the steamer wharf to get change with which to pay the boatman an appropriate fee. His needs met in the lobby, he returned to find his baggage stowed on a cart on the dock. Gondola and gondolier had disappeared.

"He took off," said the old man with the boathook. "A bad man he was, sir, a man without a license. He's the only gondolier who doesn't have a license. The others telephoned over. He saw that we were on the lookout for him, so he took off."

Aschenbach shrugged his shoulders.

"You had a free ride, sir," the old man said, holding out his hat. Aschenbach threw some coins in it. He gave instructions that his luggage be taken to the Hotel des Bains[2] and then followed the cart along the boulevard of white blossoms, lined on both sides by taverns, shops, and boarding houses, that runs straight across the island to the beach.

He entered the spacious hotel from behind, from the garden terrace, and crossed the great lobby to reach the vestibule where the office was. Since he had a reservation, he was received with officious courtesy. A manager, a quiet, flatteringly polite little man with a black mustache and a French-style frock coat, accompanied him in the elevator to the third floor and showed him to his room. It was a pleasant place, furnished in cherry wood, decorated with highly fragrant flowers, and offering a view of the open sea through a set of tall windows. After the manager had withdrawn and while his luggage was being brought up and put in place in his room, he went up to one of the windows and looked out on the beach. It was nearly deserted in the afternoon lull, and the ocean, at high tide and bereft of sunshine, was sending long, low waves against the shore in a peaceful rhythm.

A lonely, quiet person has observations and experiences that are at once both more indistinct and more penetrating than those of one more gregarious; his thoughts are weightier, stranger, and never without a tinge of sadness. Images and perceptions that others might shrug off with a glance, a laugh, or a brief conversation occupy him unduly, become profound in his silence, become significant, become experience, adven-

2. "Hotel des Bains": French for bathing hotel, i.e. a hotel in front of which one may bathe in the ocean. One of the most famous resort hotels in Europe, it is designated "b" and can be found in area C2 on the map of the Lido (p. 69).

ture, emotion. <u>Loneliness fosters that which is original, daringly and bewilderingly beautiful, poetic.</u> But loneliness also fosters that which is perverse, incongruous, absurd, forbidden. Thus the events of the journey that brought him here—the ghastly old fop with his drivel about a beloved, the outlaw gondolier who was cheated of his reward—continued to trouble the traveler's mind. Though they did not appear contrary to reason, did not really give cause for second thoughts, the paradox was that they were nonetheless fundamentally and essentially odd, or so it seemed to him, and therefore troubling precisely because of this paradox. In the meantime his eyes greeted the sea, and he felt joy in knowing Venice to be in such comfortable proximity. He turned away at last, went to wash his face, gave some instructions to the maid with regard to completing arrangements to insure his comfort, and then put himself in the hands of the green-uniformed elevator operator, who took him down to the ground floor.

He took his tea on the terrace facing the sea, then went down to the shore and walked along the boardwalk for a good distance toward the Hotel Excelsior.[3] When he got back it seemed about time to change for dinner. He did so slowly and precisely, the way he did everything, because he was used to working as he got dressed. Still, he found himself in the lobby a bit on the early side for dinner. There he found many of the hotel's guests gathered, unfamiliar with and affecting indifference to each other, sharing only the wait for the dinner bell. He picked up a newspaper from a table, sat down in a leather chair, and looked over the assembled company. It differed from that of his previous sojourn in a way that pleased him.

A broad horizon, tolerant and comprehensive, opened up before him. All the great languages of Europe melded together in subdued tones. Evening dress, the universal uniform of cultured society, provided a decorous external unity to the variety of humanity assembled here. There was the dry, long face of an American, a Russian extended family, English ladies, German children with French nannies. The Slavic component seemed to predominate. Polish was being spoken nearby.

It came from a group of adolescents and young adults gathered around a little wicker table under the supervision of a governess or companion. There were three young girls who looked to be fifteen to seventeen years old and a long-haired boy of maybe fourteen. Aschenbach noted with astonishment that the boy was perfectly beautiful. His face, pale and gracefully reserved, was framed by honey-colored curls. He had a straight nose and a lovely mouth and wore an expression of exquisite, divine solemnity. It was a face reminiscent of Greek statues from the noblest period of antiquity; it combined perfection of form with a unique personal charm that caused the onlooker to doubt ever having met with

3. The Hotel Excelsior (marked "a") and its canal can be found on map of the Lido, A-B4, p. 69.

anything in nature or in art that could match its perfection. One could not help noticing, furthermore, that widely differing views on child-rearing had evidently directed the dress and general treatment of the siblings. The three girls, the eldest of whom was for all intents an adult, were got up in a way that was almost disfiguringly chaste and austere. Every grace of figure was suppressed and obscured by their uniformly habitlike half-length dresses, sober and slate-gray in color, tailored as if to be deliberately unflattering, relieved by no decoration save white, turned-down collars. Their smooth hair, combed tightly against their heads, made their faces appear nunnishly vacant and expressionless. It could only be a mother who was in charge here, one who never once considered applying to the boy the severity of upbringing that seemed required of her when it came to the girls. Softness and tenderness were the obvious conditions of the boy's existence. No one had yet been so bold as to take the scissors to his lovely hair, which curled about his brows, over his ears, and even further down the back of his neck—as it does on the statue of the "Boy Pulling a Thorn from his Foot."[4] His English sailor suit had puffy sleeves that narrowed at the cuff to embrace snugly the delicate wrists of his still childlike yet delicate hands. The suit made his slim figure seem somehow opulent and pampered with all its decoration, its bow, braidwork, and embroidery. He sat so that the observer saw him in profile. His feet were clad in black patent leather and arranged one in front of the other; one elbow was propped on the arm of his wicker chair with his cheek resting on his closed hand; his demeanor was one of careless refinement, quite without the almost sub-missive stiffness that seemed to be the norm for his sisters. Was he in poor health? Perhaps, for the skin of his face was white as ivory and stood out in sharp contrast to the darker gold of the surrounding curls. Or was he simply a coddled favorite, the object of a biased and capri-cious affection? Aschenbach was inclined to suppose the latter. There is inborn in every artistic disposition an indulgent and treacherous ten-dency to accept injustice when it produces beauty and to respond with complicity and even admiration when the aristocrats of this world get preferential treatment.

A waiter went about and announced in English that dinner was ready. Most of the company gradually disappeared through the glass door into the dining room. Latecomers passed by, arriving from the vestibule or from the elevators. Dinner was beginning to be served inside, but the young Poles still lingered by their wicker table. Aschenbach, comfort-ably seated in his deep armchair, his eyes captivated by the beautiful vision before him, waited with them.

The governess, a short, corpulent, rather unladylike woman with a

4. A famous Greco-Roman statue admired for the graceful pose and handsome appearance of the boy it depicts.

red face, finally gave the sign to get up. With her brows raised she pushed back her chair and bowed as a tall lady, dressed in gray and white and richly bejeweled with pearls, entered the lobby. The demeanor of this woman was cool and measured; the arrangement of her lightly powdered hair and the cut of her clothes displayed the taste for simplicity favored by those who regard piety as an essential component of good breeding. She could have been the wife of a highly placed German official. Her jewelry was the only thing about her appearance that suggested fabulous luxury; it was priceless, consisting of earrings and a very long, triple strand of softly shimmering pearls, each as big as a cherry.

The boy and the girls had risen quickly. They bent to kiss their mother's hand while she, with a restrained smile on her well-preserved but slightly tired and rather pointy-nosed face, looked across the tops of their heads at the governess, to whom she directed a few words in French. Then she walked to the glass door. The young ones followed her, the girls in the order of their ages, behind them the governess, the boy last of all. For some reason he turned around before crossing the threshold. Since there was no one else left in the lobby, his strangely misty gray eyes met those of Aschenbach, who was sunk deep in contemplation of the departing group, his newspaper on his knees.

What he had seen was, to be sure, in none of its particulars remarkable. They did not go in to dinner before their mother; they had waited for her, greeted her respectfully when she came, and then observed perfectly normal manners going into the dining room. It was just that it had all happened so deliberately, with such a sense of discipline, responsibility, and self-respect, that Aschenbach felt strangely moved. He lingered a few moments more, then went along into the dining room himself. He was shown to his table, which, he noted with a brief twinge of regret, was very far away from that of the Polish family.

Tired but nonetheless mentally stimulated, he entertained himself during the tedious meal with abstract, even transcendent matters. He pondered the mysterious combination of regularity and individuality that is necessary to produce human beauty; proceeded then to the general problem of form and of art; and ultimately concluded that his thoughts and discoveries resembled those inspirations that come in dreams: they seem wonderful at the time, but in the sober light of day they show up as utterly shallow and useless. After dinner he spent some time smoking, sitting, and wandering about in the park, which was fragrant in the evening air. He went to bed early and passed the night in a sleep uninterruptedly deep but frequently enlivened by all sorts of dreams.

The next day the weather had gotten no better. There was a steady wind off the land. Under a pale overcast sky the sea lay in a dull calm, almost as if it had shriveled up, with a soberingly contracted horizon; it had receded so far from the beach that it uncovered several rows of long sandbars. When Aschenbach opened his window, he thought he could detect the stagnant smell of the lagoon.

He was beset by ill humor. He was already having thoughts of leaving. Once years ago, after several lovely weeks here in springtime, just such weather had been visited upon him and had made him feel so poorly that he had had to take flight from Venice like a fugitive. Was he not feeling once again the onset of the feverish listlessness he had felt then, the throbbing of his temples, the heaviness in his eyelids? To change his vacation spot yet again would be a nuisance; but if the wind did not shift soon, he simply could not remain here. He did not unpack everything, just in case. He ate at nine in the special breakfast room between the lobby and the dining room.

In this room prevailed the solemn stillness that great hotels aspire to. The waiters went about on tip-toe. The clink of the tea service and a half-whispered word were all one could hear. Aschenbach noticed the Polish girls and their governess at a table in the corner diagonally across from the door, two tables away. They sat very straight, their ash-blond hair newly smoothed down flat, their eyes red. They wore starched blue linen dresses with little white turned-down collars and cuffs, and they passed a jar of preserves to each other. They had almost finished their breakfast. The boy was not there.

Aschenbach smiled. Well, little Phaeacian, he thought. It seems you, and not they, have the privilege of sleeping to your heart's content. Suddenly cheered, he recited to himself the line:

"Changes of dress, warm baths, and downy beds."[5]

He ate his breakfast at a leisurely pace, received some mail that had been forwarded—delivered personally by the doorman, who entered the room with his braided hat in hand—and opened a few letters while he smoked a cigarette. Thus it happened that he was present for the entrance of the late sleeper they were waiting for over there in the corner.

He came through the glass door and traversed the silent room diagonally over to the table where his sisters sat. His carriage was extraordinarily graceful, not only in the way he held his torso but also in the way he moved his knees and set one white-shod foot in front of the other. He moved lightly, in a manner both gentle and proud, made more lovely still by the childlike bashfulness with which he twice lifted and lowered his eyelids as he went by, turning his face out toward the room. Smiling, he murmured a word in his soft, indistinct speech and took his place, showing his full profile to the observer. The latter was once more,

5. The Phaeacians were an island people who sheltered Odysseus and to whom he related many of his adventures. Alcinous, the king of the Phaeacians, tells Odysseus: "we set great store by feasting,/harpers, and the grace of dancing choirs,/changes of dress, warm baths, and downy beds" (*The Odyssey*, Bk. 8, ll. 248–49; trans. Robert Fitzgerald).

and now especially, struck with amazement, indeed even alarm, at the truly godlike beauty possessed by this mortal child. Today the boy wore a lightweight sailor suit of blue and white striped cotton with a red silk bow on the chest, finished at the neck with a simple white upright collar. And above this collar, which did not even fit in very elegantly with the character of the costume, rose up that blossom, his face, a sight unforgettably charming.[6] It was the face of Eros, with the yellowish glaze of Parian marble, with delicate and serious brows, the temples and ears richly and rectangularly framed by soft, dusky curls.[7]

Fine, very fine, thought Aschenbach with that professional, cool air of appraisal artists sometimes use to cover their delight, their enthusiasm when they encounter a masterpiece. He thought further: Really, if the sea and the sand were not waiting for me, I would stay here as long as you stay. With that, however, he departed, walking past the attentive employees through the lobby, down the terrace steps, and straight across the wooden walkway to the hotel's private beach. There he let a barefoot old man in linen pants, sailor shirt, and straw hat who managed affairs on the beach show him to his rented beach cabana and arrange a table and chair on its sandy, wooden platform. Then he made himself comfortable in his beach chair, which he had pulled through the pale yellow sand closer to the sea.

The beach scene, this view of a carefree society engaged in purely sensual enjoyment on the edge of the watery element, entertained and cheered him as it always did. The gray, smooth ocean was already full of wading children, swimmers, and colorful figures lying on the sandbars with their arms crossed behind their heads. Others were rowing about in little flat-bottomed boats painted red and blue, capsizing to gales of laughter. People sat on the platforms of the cabanas, arranged in a long neat row along the beach, as if they were little verandas. In front of them people played games, lounged lazily, visited and chatted, some dressed in elegant morning clothes and others enjoying the nakedness sanctioned by the bold and easy freedom of the place. Down on the moist, hard sand there were a few individuals strolling about in white beach robes or in loose, brightly colored bathing dresses. To the right some children had built an elaborate sand castle and bedecked it with little flags in the colors of every country. Vendors of mussels, cakes, and fruit knelt and spread their wares before them. On the left, a Russian family was encamped in front of one of the cabanas that were set at a

6. The words "rūhtē dīe / Blūtē dēs / Hāuptēs iñ / ūnvēr / glēichlīchēm / Līebreīz ("rōse ūp thāt / blōssōm, hīs / fāce, ā / sīght ūnfōr/gēttāblȳ / chārmīng") form a Homeric hexameter (largely dactylic in meter, but with spondees substituted for dactylic feet at will, except in the fifth foot, which requires a dactyl, and the sixth, which requires a spondee. In German and English imitations of Homer's meter, trochees are often substituted for spondees). Mann embedded a number of such lines in the prose of his story.
7. Eros was the Greek god of love. Parian marble, quarried on the Greek island of Paros, was highly prized in antiquity as a material for sculpture.

right angle between the others and the sea, thus closing that end of the beach. The family included men with beards and huge teeth; languid women past their prime; a young lady from a Baltic country, sitting at an easel and painting the ocean to the accompaniment of cries of frustration; two affable, ugly children; and an old maid in a babushka, displaying the affectionately servile demeanor of a slave. They resided there in grateful enjoyment, called out endlessly the names of their unruly, giddy children, exchanged pleasantries at surprising length in their few words of Italian with the jocular old man from whom they bought candy, kissed each other on the cheeks, and cared not a whit for anyone who might witness their scene of shared humanity.

Well, then, I will stay, thought Aschenbach. Where could things be better? His hands folded in his lap, he let his eyes roam the ocean's distances, let his gaze slip out of focus, grow hazy, blur in the uniform mistiness of empty space. He loved the sea from the depth of his being: first of all because a hardworking artist needs his rest from the demanding variety of phenomena he works with and longs to take refuge in the bosom of simplicity and enormity; and, second, because he harbors an affinity for the undivided, the immeasurable, the eternal, the void. It was a forbidden affinity, directly contrary to his calling, and seductive precisely for that reason. To rest in the arms of perfection is what all those who struggle for excellence long to do; and is the void not a form of perfection? But while he was thus dreaming away toward the depths of emptiness, the horizontal line of the sea's edge was crossed by a human figure. When he had retrieved his gaze from the boundless realms and refocused his eyes, he saw it was the lovely boy who, coming from the left, was passing before him across the sand. He went barefoot, ready to go in wading, his slim legs bare from the knees down. He walked slowly but with a light, proud step, as if he were used to going about without shoes, and looked around at the row of cabanas that closed the end of the beach. The Russian family was still there, gratefully leading its harmonious existence, but no sooner had he laid eyes on them than a storm cloud of angry contempt crossed his face. His brow darkened, his lips began to curl, and from one side of his mouth emerged a bitter grimace that gouged a furrow in his cheek. He frowned so deeply that his eyes seemed pressed inward and sunken, seemed to speak dark and evil volumes of hatred from their depths. He looked down at the ground, cast one more threatening glance backward, and then, shrugging his shoulders as if to discard something and get away from it, he left his enemies behind.

A sort of delicacy or fright, something like a mixture of respect and shame, caused Aschenbach to turn away as if he had not seen anything; for it is repugnant to a chance witness, if he is a serious person, to make use of his observations, even to himself. But Aschenbach felt cheered and shaken at the same time—that is, happiness overwhelmed him.

This childish fanaticism directed against the most harmless, good-natured target imaginable put into a human perspective something that otherwise seemed divinely indeterminate. It transformed a precious creation of nature that had before been no more than a feast for the eyes into a worthy object of deeper sympathy. It endowed the figure of the youngster, who had already shone with significance because of his beauty, with an aura that allowed him to be taken seriously beyond his years.

Still turned away, Aschenbach listened to the boy's voice, his clear, somewhat weak voice, by means of which he was trying to hail from afar his playmates at work on the sand castle. They answered him, calling again and again his name or an affectionate variation on his name. Aschenbach listened with a certain curiosity, unable to distinguish anything more than two melodious syllables—something like Adgio or more frequently Adgiu, with a drawn-out *u* at the end of the cry. The sound made him glad, it seemed to him that its harmony suited its object, and he repeated it softly to himself as he turned back with satisfaction to his letters and papers.

With his small traveling briefcase on his knees, he took his fountain pen and began to attend to various matters of correspondence. But after a mere quarter of an hour he was feeling regret that he should thus take leave in spirit and miss out on this, the most charming set of circumstances he knew of, for the sake of an activity he carried on with indifference. He cast his writing materials aside and turned his attention back to the sea; and not long after, distracted by the voices of the youngsters at the sand castle, he turned his head to the right and let it rest comfortably on the back of his chair, where he could once more observe the comings and goings of the exquisite Adgio.

His first glance found him; the red bow on his breast could not be missed. He was engaged with some others in setting up an old board as a bridge over the moat around the sand castle, calling out advice on proper procedure and nodding his head. There were about ten companions with him, boys and girls, most of an age with him but a few younger, chattering in a confusion of tongues—Polish, French, and even some Balkan languages. But it was his name that most often resounded through it all. He was evidently popular, sought after, admired. One companion, likewise a Pole, a sturdy boy called something like Yashu, who wore a belted linen suit and had black hair slicked down with pomade, seemed to be his closest friend and vassal. With the work on the sand castle finished for the time being, they went off together along the beach, arms about each other, and the one called Yashu gave his beautiful partner a kiss.

Aschenbach was tempted to shake his finger at him. "Let me give you a piece of advice, Kritobulos," he thought and smiled to himself. "Take a year's journey. You will need at least that much time for your recovery."[8] And then he breakfasted on large, fully ripe strawberries that he obtained from a peddler. It had gotten very warm, although the sun had not managed to pierce the layer of mist that covered the sky. Lassitude seized his spirit, while his senses enjoyed the enormous, lulling entertainment afforded by the quiet sea. The task of puzzling out what name it was that sounded like Adgio struck the serious man as a fitting, entirely satisfying occupation. With the help of a few Polish memories he determined that it was probably Tadzio he had heard, the nickname for Tadeusz. It was pronounced Tadziu in the form used for direct address.[9]

Tadzio was taking a swim. Aschenbach, who had lost sight of him for a moment, spotted his head and then his arm, which rose as it stroked. He was very far out; the water apparently stayed shallow for a long way. But already his family seemed to be getting concerned about him, already women's voices were calling to him from the cabanas, shouting out once more this name that ruled over the beach almost like a watchword and that possessed something both sweet and wild in its soft consonants and drawn-out cry of *uuu* at the end. "Tadziu! Tadziu!" He turned back; he ran through the sea with his head thrown back, beating the resisting water into a foam with his legs. The sight of this lively adolescent figure, seductive and chaste, lovely as a tender young god, emerging from the depths of the sky and the sea with dripping locks and escaping the clutches of the elements—it all gave rise to mythic images. It was a sight belonging to poetic legends from the beginning of time that tell of the origins of form and of the birth of the gods. Aschenbach listened with his eyes closed to this mythic song reverberating within him, and once again he thought about how good it was here and how he wanted to stay.

Later on Tadzio lay on the sand, resting from his swim, wrapped in a white beach towel that was drawn up under his right shoulder, his head resting on his bare arm. Even when Aschenbach refrained from looking at him, instead reading a few pages in his book, he almost never forgot who was lying nearby or forgot that it would cost him only a slight turn of his head to the right to bring the adorable sight back into view. It almost seemed to him that he was sitting here with the express purpose of keeping watch over the resting boy. Busy as he might be with his own affairs, he maintained his vigilant care for the noble human figure not far away on his right. A paternal kindness, an emotional attachment filled and moved his heart, the attachment that someone who produces beauty at the cost of intellectual self-sacrifice feels toward someone who naturally possesses beauty.

After midday he left the beach, returned to the hotel, and took the elevator up to his room. There he spent a considerable length of time in

---

8. This is the advice Socrates gave to Kritobulos, who had kissed the handsome son of Alcibiades, according to Xenophon's *Memorabilia* (Bk. 1, ch. 3).
9. See Mann's working notes, p. 70.

front of the mirror looking at his gray hair and his severe, tired face. At the same time he thought about his fame and about the fact that many people recognized him on the street and looked at him with respect, all on account of those graceful, unerringly accurate words of his. He called the roll of the long list of successes his talent had brought him, as many as he could think of, and even recalled his elevation to the nobility. He then retired to the dining room for lunch and ate at his little table. As he was entering the elevator when the meal was over, a throng of young people likewise coming from lunch crowded him to the back of the swaying little chamber. Tadzio was among them. He stood very close by, so close in fact that for the first time Aschenbach had the opportunity to view him not from a distance like a picture but minutely, scrutinizing every detail of his human form. Someone was talking to the boy, and while he was answering with his indescribably sweet smile they reached the second floor, where he got off, backing out, his eyes cast down. Beauty breeds modesty, Aschenbach thought and gave urgent consideration as to why. He had had occasion to notice, however, that Tadzio's teeth were not a very pleasing sight. They were rather jagged and pale and had no luster of health but rather a peculiar brittle transparency such as one sometimes sees in anemics. He is very sensitive, he is sickly, thought Aschenbach. He will probably not live long. And he refrained from trying to account for the feeling of satisfaction and reassurance that accompanied this thought.

He passed a couple of hours in his room and in the afternoon took the vaporetto across the stagnant-smelling lagoon to Venice. He got off at San Marco, took tea in the piazza, and then, following his habitual routine in Venice, set off on a walk through the streets. It was this walk, however, that initiated a complete reversal of his mood and his plans.

The air in the little streets was odiously oppressive, so thick that the smells surging out of the dwellings, shops, and restaurants, a suffocating vapor of oil, perfume, and more, all hung about and failed to disperse. Cigarette smoke hovered in place and only slowly disappeared. The press of people in the small spaces annoyed rather than entertained him as he walked. The longer he went on, the more it became a torture. He was overwhelmed by that horrible condition produced by the sea air in combination with the sirocco, a state of both nervousness and debility at once. He began to sweat uncomfortably. His eyes ceased to function, his breathing was labored, he felt feverish, the blood pounded in his head. He fled from the crowded shop-lined streets across bridges into the poor quarter. There beggars molested him, and the evil emanations from the canals hindered his breathing. In a quiet piazza, one of those forgotten, seemingly enchanted little places in the interior of the city, he rested on the edge of a well, dried his forehead, and reached the conclusion that he would have to leave Venice.

For the second time, and this time definitively, it became clear that this city in this weather was particularly harmful to his health. To remain stubbornly in place obviously went against all reason, and the prospect of a change in the direction of the wind was highly uncertain. A quick decision had to be made. To return home this soon was out of the question. Neither his summer nor his winter quarters were prepared for his arrival. But this was not the only place with beaches on the ocean, and those other places did not have the noxious extra of the lagoon and its fever-inducing vapors. He recalled a little beach resort not far from Trieste that had been enthusiastically recommended to him. Why not go there and, indeed, without delay, so that yet another change of location would still be worthwhile? He declared himself resolved and stood up. At the next gondola stop he boarded a boat to take him to San Marco through the dim labyrinth of canals, under graceful marble balconies flanked by stone lions, around corners of slippery masonry, past mournful palace facades affixed with business insignia reflected in the garbage-strewn water. He had trouble getting to his destination, since the gondolier was in league with lace and glass factories and made constant efforts to induce him to stop at them to sightsee and buy; and so whenever the bizarre journey through Venice began to weave its magic, the mercenary lust for booty afflicting this sunken queen of cities did what it could to bring the enchanted spirit back to unpleasant reality.

Upon returning to the hotel he did not even wait for dinner but went right to the office and declared that unforeseen circumstances compelled him to depart the next morning. With many expressions of regret the staff acknowledged the payment of his bill. He dined and then passed the mild evening reading magazines in a rocking chair on the rear terrace. Before going to bed he did all his packing for the morning's departure.

He did not sleep especially well, as the impending move made him restless. When he opened the windows the next morning the sky was still overcast, but the air seemed fresher and . . . he already started to have second thoughts. Had he been hasty or wrong to give notice thus? Was it a result of his sick and unreliable condition? If he had just put it off a bit, if he had just made an attempt to get used to the Venetian air or to hold out for an improvement in the weather instead of losing heart so quickly! Then, instead of this hustle and bustle, he would have a morning on the beach like the one yesterday to look forward to. Too late. Now he would have to go ahead with it, to wish today what he wished for yesterday. He got dressed and at eight o'clock took the elevator down to breakfast on the ground floor.

The breakfast room was still empty when he entered. A number of individual guests arrived while he sat waiting for his order. With his teacup at his lips he watched the Polish girls and their attendant come in. Severe and morning-fresh, eyes still red, they proceeded to their table in the corner by the window. Immediately thereafter the doorman approached him with hat in hand to tell him it was time to leave. The car was ready, he said, to take him and some other travelers to the Hotel Excelsior, and from there a motor boat would convey them through the company's private canal to the railroad station. Time was pressing, he said. Aschenbach found it not at all pressing. There was more than an hour until the departure of his train. He was annoyed at the habitual hotel practice of packing departing guests off earlier than necessary and informed the doorman that he wanted to finish his breakfast in peace. The man withdrew hesitatingly only to show up again five minutes later. The car simply could not wait longer, he said. Very well, let it go and take his trunks with it, Aschenbach replied with annoyance. As for himself, he preferred to take the public steamer at the proper time and asked that they let him take care of his own arrangements. The employee bowed. Aschenbach, happy to have fended off this nuisance, finished his meal without haste and even had the waiter bring him a newspaper. Time had become short indeed when at last he got up to leave. And it just so happened that at that very moment Tadzio came in through the glass door.

He crossed the path of the departing traveler on his way to his family's table. He lowered his eyes modestly before the gray-haired, high-browed gentleman, only to raise them again immediately in his own charming way, displaying their soft fullness to him. Then he was past. Adieu, Tadzio, thought Aschenbach. I saw you for such a short time. And enunciating his thought as it occurred to him, contrary to his every habit, he added under his breath the words: "Blessings on you." He then made his departure, dispensed tips, received a parting greeting from the quiet little manager in the French frock coat, and left the hotel on foot, as he had arrived. Followed by a servant with his hand luggage, he traversed the island along the boulevard, white with flowers, that led to the steamer landing. He arrived, he took his seat—and what followed was a journey of pain and sorrow through the uttermost depths of regret.

It was the familiar trip across the lagoon, past San Marco, up the Grand Canal.[1] Aschenbach sat on the curved bench in the bow, his arm resting on the railing, his hand shading his eyes. They left the public gardens behind them; the Piazzetta once more revealed its princely splendor, and soon it too was left behind. Then came the great line of palaces, and as the waterway turned there appeared the magnificent marble arch of the Rialto.[2] The traveler looked, and his heart was torn. He breathed the atmosphere of the city, this slightly stagnant smell of

1. See map of Venice, C-F3-6, p. 68. One can follow Aschenbach's journey through the lagoon, past the public gardens (Giardini Pubblici, L-M7), the Piazzetta ("little plaza," H5), and San Marco, up the Grand Canal ("Canal Grande," C-F3-6), under the Rialto (G4), to the railroad station ("Stazione Ferroviaria," C3).
2. A famous, highly arched bridge over the Grand Canal, pictured on the front cover of this edition.

sea and of swamp from which he had felt so strongly compelled to flee, breathed it now deeply, in tenderly painful draughts. Was it possible that he had not known, had not considered how desperately he was attached to all this? What this morning had been a partial regret, a slight doubt as to the rightness of his decision, now became affliction, genuine pain, a suffering in his soul so bitter that it brought tears to his eyes more than once. He told himself he could not possibly have foreseen such a reaction. What was so hard to take, actually sometimes downright impossible to endure, was the thought that he would never see Venice again, that this was a parting forever. Since it had become evident for the second time that the city made him sick, since for the second time he had been forced to run head over heels away, he would have to regard it henceforth as an impossible destination, forbidden to him, something he simply was not up to, something it would be pointless for him to try for again. Yes, he felt that, should he go away now, shame and spite would certainly prevent him from ever seeing the beloved city again, now that it had twice forced him to admit physical defeat. This conflict between the inclination of his soul and the capacity of his body seemed to the aging traveler suddenly so weighty and so important, his physical defeat so ignominious, so much to be resisted at all cost, that he could no longer grasp the ease with which he had reached the decision yesterday, without serious struggle, to acquiesce.

Meanwhile, the steamer was approaching the railway station, and his pain and helplessness were rising to the level of total disorientation. His tortured mind found the thought of departure impossible, the thought of return no less so. In such a state of acute inner strife he entered the station. It was already very late, he had not a moment to lose if he was to catch his train. He wanted to, and he did not want to. But time was pressing, it goaded him onward; he made haste to obtain his ticket and looked about in the bustle of the station for the hotel employee stationed here. This person appeared and announced that the large trunk was already checked and on its way. Already on its way? Yes indeed—to Como. To Como? After a frantic exchange, after angry questions and embarrassed answers, the fact emerged that the trunk had been put together with the baggage of other, unknown travelers in the luggage office at the Hotel Excelsior and sent off in precisely the wrong direction.

Aschenbach had difficulty maintaining the facial expression expected under such circumstances. An adventurous joy, an unbelievable cheerfulness seized his breast from within like a spasm. The hotel employee sped off to see if he could retrieve the trunk and returned, as one might have expected, with no success whatever. Only then did Aschenbach declare that he did not wish to travel without his luggage and that he had decided to return and await the recovery of the trunk at the Hotel des Bains. Was the company boat still here at the station? The man assured him it was waiting right at the door. With an impressive display of Italian cajolery he persuaded the agent to take back Aschenbach's ticket. He swore he would telegraph ahead, that no effort would be spared to get the trunk back with all due speed, and . . . thus came to pass something very odd indeed. The traveler, not twenty minutes after his arrival at the station, found himself once again on the Grand Canal on his way back to the Lido.

What a wondrous, incredible, embarrassing, odd and dreamlike adventure! Thanks to a sudden reversal of destiny, he was to see once again, within the very hour, places that he had thought in deepest melancholy he was leaving forever. The speedy little vessel shot toward its destination, foam flying before its bow, maneuvering with droll agility between gondolas and steamers, while its single passenger hid beneath a mask of annoyed resignation the anxious excitement of a boy playing hooky. Still from time to time his frame was shaken with laughter over this mischance, which he told himself could not have worked out better for the luckiest person in the world. Explanations would have to be made, amazed faces confronted, but then—so he told himself—all would be well again, a great disaster averted, a terrible error made right, and everything he thought he had left behind would be open to him once more, would be his to enjoy at his leisure. . . . And by the way, was it just the rapid movement of the boat, or could it really be that he felt a strong breeze off the ocean to complete his bliss?

The waves slapped against the concrete walls of the narrow canal that cut through the island to the Hotel Excelsior. A motor bus was waiting there for the returning traveler and conveyed him alongside the curling waves down the straight road to the Hotel des Bains. The little manager with the mustache and the cutaway frock coat came down the broad flight of steps to meet him.

With quiet cajolery the manager expressed his regret over the incident, declared it extremely embarrassing for himself personally and for the establishment, but expressed his emphatic approval of Aschenbach's decision to wait here for the return of his luggage. To be sure, his room was already taken, but another, by no means worse, stood ready. "Pas de chance, monsieur,"[3] said the elevator man with a smile as they glided upwards. And so the fugitive was billeted once again, and in a room that matched almost exactly his previous one in orientation and furnishings.

Tired, numb from the whirl of this strange morning, he distributed the contents of his small suitcase in his room and then sank down in an armchair by the open window. The sea had taken on a light green coloration, the air seemed thinner and purer, the beach with its cabanas and boats seemed more colorful, although the sky was still gray. Aschenbach looked out, his hands folded in his lap, content to be here once more,

---

3. "No luck, sir."

but shaking his head in reproach at his own fickle mood, his lack of knowledge of his own desires. He sat thus for perhaps an hour, resting and thoughtlessly dreaming. At noon he spied Tadzio, dressed in his striped linen suit with red bow, returning from the shore through the beach barrier and along the wooden walkway to the hotel. Aschenbach recognized him at once from his high vantage point even before he got a good look at him, and he was just about to form a thought something like: Look, Tadzio, you too have returned! But at that very moment he felt the casual greeting collapse and fall silent before the truth of his heart. He felt the excitement in his blood, the joy and pain in his soul, and recognized that it was because of Tadzio that his departure had been so difficult.

He sat quite still, quite unseen in his elevated location and looked into himself. His features were active; his brows rose; an alert, curious, witty smile crossed his lips. Then he raised his head and with both his arms, which were hanging limp over the arms of his chair, he made a slow circling and lifting movement that turned his palms forward, as if to signify an opening and extending of his embrace. It was a gesture of readiness, of welcome, and of relaxed acceptance.

Chapter 4

The god with fiery cheeks now, naked, directed his horses,[1] four-abreast, fire-breathing, day by day through the chambers of heaven, and his yellow curls fluttered along with the blast of the east wind. A silky-white sheen lay on the Pontos,[2] its broad stretches undulating languidly. The sands burned. Under the silvery shimmering blue of the ether there were rustcolored canvas awnings spread out in front of the beach cabanas, and one passed the morning hours in the sharply framed patch of shade they offered. But the evening was also delightful, when the plants in the park wafted balsamic perfumes, the stars above paced out their circuits, and the murmur of the night-shrouded sea, softly penetrating, cast a spell on the soul. Such an evening bore the joyful promise of another festive day of loosely ordered leisure, bejeweled with countless, thickly strewn possibilities of happy accidents.

The guest, whom accommodating mischance kept here, was far from disposed to see in the return of his belongings a reason to depart once more. He had been obliged to get along without a few things for a couple of days and to appear at meals in the great dining room wearing his traveling clothes. Then, when the errant baggage was finally set down

---

1. This chapter opens with another dactylic hexameter: "[Nun] lēnktĕ / Tāg fǖr / Tāg dĕr / Gŏtt mĭt dĕn / hĭtzĭgĕn / Wāngĕn . . ." ("[the] gŏd wĭth / fĭery / chĕeks nŏw, / nākĕd, dĭ/rĕctĕd hĭs / hŏrsĕs . . ."). See also p. 25, n6. The god with fiery cheeks is Helios, the sun god.
2. The Black Sea, but in Greek simply "the sea." Here—a figurative reference to the Adriatic.

once more in his room, he unpacked thoroughly and filled closets and drawers with his things, determined for the time being to stay indefinitely, happy to be able to pass the morning's hours on the beach in his silk suit and to present himself once more at his little table at dinner time wearing proper evening attire.

The benevolent regularity of this existence had at once drawn him into its power; the soft and splendid calm of this lifestyle had him quickly ensnared. What a fine place to stay, indeed, combining the charms of a refined southern beach resort with the cozy proximity of the wondrous, wonder-filled city! Aschenbach was no lover of pleasure. Whenever and wherever it seemed proper to celebrate, to take a rest, to take a few days off, he soon had to get back—it was especially so in his younger days— anxiously and reluctantly back to the affliction of his high calling, the sacred, sober service of his day-to-day life. This place alone enchanted him, relaxed his will, made him happy. Sometimes in the morning, under the canopy of his beach cabana, dreaming away across the blue of the southern sea, or sometimes as well on a balmy night, leaning back under the great starry sky on the cushions of a gondola taking him back home to the Lido from the Piazza San Marco, where he had tarried long—and the bright lights and the melting sounds of the serenade were left behind—he remembered his country home in the mountains, the site of his summertime struggles, where the clouds drifted through the garden, where in the evening fearful thunderstorms extinguished the lights in the house and the ravens he fed soared to the tops of the spruce trees. Then it might seem to him that he had been transported to the land of Elysium at the far ends of the earth, where a life of ease is bestowed upon mortals, where there is no snow, no winter, no storms or streaming rain, but rather always the cooling breath rising from Okeanos,[3] where the days run out in blissful leisure, trouble-free, struggle-free, dedicated only to the sun and its revels.

Aschenbach saw the boy Tadzio often, indeed almost continually; limited space and a regular schedule common to all the guests made it inevitable that the lovely boy was in his vicinity nearly all day, with brief interruptions. He saw, he met him everywhere: in the hotel's public places, on the cooling boat trips to the city and back, in the ostentation of the piazza itself;[4] and often too in the streets and byways a chance encounter would take place. Chiefly, however, it was the mornings on the beach that offered him with delightful regularity an extended opportunity to study and worship the charming apparition. Yes, it was this narrow and constrained happiness, this regularly recurring good fortune that filled him with contentment and joy in life, that made his stay all

---

3. According to Greek mythology, Okeanos was the river encircling the world; Elysium—located at the western edge of the earth—a pleasant otherworld for those heroes favored of the gods.
4. Piazza San Marco, the great plaza in front of the cathedral of Saint Mark. (See map of Venice, H5, p. 68).

the more dear to him and caused one sunny day after another to fall so agreeably in line.

He got up early, as he otherwise did under the relentless pressure of work, and was one of the first on the beach when the sun was still mild and the sea lay white in the glare of morning dreams. He gave a friendly greeting to the guard at the beach barrier, said a familiar hello to the barefoot old man who got his place ready, spreading the brown awning and arranging the cabana furniture on the platform, and settled in. Three hours or four were then his in which, as the sun rose to its zenith and grew fearsome in strength and the sea turned a deeper and deeper blue, he could watch Tadzio.

He would see him coming from the left along the edge of the sea, would see him from the back as he appeared from between the cabanas, or sometimes would suddenly discover, not without a happy shudder, that he had missed his arrival and that he was already there, already in the blue and white bathing suit that was now his only article of attire on the beach, that he was already up to his usual doings in sand and sun— his charmingly trivial, lazily irregular life that was both recreation and rest, filled with lounging, wading, digging, catching, resting, and swimming, watched over by the women on the platform who called to him, making his name resound with their high voices: "Tadziu! Tadziu!" He would come running to them gesturing excitedly and telling them what he had done, showing them what he had found or caught: mussels and sea horses, jelly fish, crabs that ran off going sideways.[5] Aschenbach understood not a single word he said, and though it may have been the most ordinary thing in the world it was all a vague harmony to his ear. Thus, foreignness raised the boy's speech to the level of music, a wanton sun poured unstinting splendor over him, and the sublime perspectives of the sea always formed the background and aura that set off his appearance.

Soon the observer knew every line and pose of this noble body that displayed itself so freely; he exulted in greeting anew every beauty, familiar though it had become, and his admiration, the discreet arousal of his senses, knew no end. They called the boy to pay his compliments to a guest who was attending the ladies at the cabana; he came running, still wet from the sea; he tossed his curls, and as he held out his hand he stood on one foot while holding the other up on tiptoe. His body was gracefully poised in the midst of a charming turning motion, while his face showed an embarrassed amiability, a desire to please that came from an aristocratic sense of duty. Sometimes he would lie stretched out with his beach towel wrapped about his chest, his delicately chiseled arm propped in the sand, his chin in the hollow of his hand. The one

5. Another Homeric hexameter: ("Mŭschĕln, / Sēepfērdchĕn, / Quallēn ŭnd / seĩtlĭch / lãufĕndē / Krēbsĕ" ("mussĕls aňd / sēa hŏrsĕs, / jēllȳ fĭsh, / crăbs thăt răn / ŏff gõiñg / sĩdewãys"). See also p. 25, n6 p. 34, n1.

called Yashu sat crouching by him, playing up to him, and nothing could have been more enchanting than the smiling eyes and lips with which the object of this flattery looked upon his inferior, his vassal. Or he would stand at the edge of the sea, alone, separated from his friends, very near Aschenbach, erect, his hands clasped behind his neck, slowly rocking on the balls of his feet and dreaming off into the blue yonder, while little waves that rolled in bathed his toes. His honey-colored hair clung in circles to his temples and his neck; the sun made the down shine on his upper back; the subtle definition of the ribs and the symmetry of his chest stood out through the tight-fitting material covering his torso; his armpits were still as smooth as those of a statue, the hollows behind his knees shone likewise, and the blue veins showing through made his body seem to be made of translucent material. What discipline, what precision of thought was expressed in the stretch of this youthfully perfect body! But was not the rigorous and pure will that had been darkly active in bringing this divine form into the clear light of day entirely familiar to the artist in him? Was this same will not active in him, too, when he, full of sober passion, freed a slender form from the marble mass of language, a form he had seen with his spiritual eye and that he presented to mortal men as image and mirror of spiritual beauty?

 almost creepy...

Image and mirror! His eyes embraced the noble figure there on the edge of the blue, and in a transport of delight he thought his gaze was grasping beauty itself, the pure form of divine thought, the universal and pure perfection that lives in the spirit and which here, graceful and lovely, presented itself for worship in the form of a human likeness and exemplar. Such was his intoxication; the aging artist welcomed the experience without reluctance, even greedily. His intellect was in labor, his educated mind set in motion. His memory dredged up ancient images passed on to him in the days of his youth, thoughts not until now touched by the spark of his personal involvement. Was it not written that the sun turns our attention from intellectual to sensuous matters? It was said that the sun numbs and enchants our reason and memory to such an extent that the soul in its pleasure forgets its ordinary condition; its amazed admiration remains fixed on the loveliest of sun-drenched objects. Indeed, only with the help of a body can the soul rise to the contemplation of still higher things. Amor[6] truly did as mathematicians have always done by assisting slow-learning children with concrete pictures of pure forms: so, too, did the god like to make use of the figure and coloration of human youth in order to make the spiritual visible to us, furnishing it with the reflected glory of beauty and thus making of it a tool of memory, so that seeing it we might then be set aflame with pain and hope.

Those, at any rate, were the thoughts of the impassioned onlooker.

6. The god of love.

He was capable of sustaining just such a high pitch of emotion. He spun himself a charming tapestry out of the roar of the sea and the glare of the sun. He saw the ancient plane tree not far from the walls of Athens, that sacred, shadowy place filled with the scent of willow blossoms, decorated with holy images and votive offerings in honor of the nymphs and of Achelous.[7] The stream flowed in crystal clarity over smooth pebbles past the foot of the wide-branched tree. The crickets sang. Two figures reclined on the grass that gently sloped so that you could lie with your head held up; they were sheltered here from the heat of the day—an older man and a younger, one ugly and one handsome, wisdom at the side of charm. Amidst polite banter and wooing wit Socrates taught Phaedrus about longing and virtue. He spoke to him of the searing terror that the sensitive man experiences when his eye lights on an image of eternal beauty; spoke to him of the appetites of the impious, bad man who cannot conceive of beauty when he sees beauty's image and is incapable of reverence; spoke of the holy fear that overcomes a noble heart when a godlike face or a perfect body appears before him—how he then trembles and is beside himself and scarcely dares turn his eyes upon the sight and honors him who has beauty, indeed would even sacrifice to him as to a holy image, if he did not fear looking foolish in the eyes of others. For beauty, my dear Phaedrus, beauty alone is both worthy of love and visible at the same time; beauty, mark me well, is the only form of spirit that our senses can both grasp and endure. For what should become of us if divinity itself, or reason and virtue and truth were to appear directly to our senses? Would we not be overcome and consumed in the flames of love, as Semele was at the sight of Zeus?[8] Thus beauty is the sensitive man's way to the spirit—just the way, just the means, little Phaedrus. . . . And then he said the subtlest thing of all, crafty wooer that he was: he said that the lover was more divine than the beloved, because the god was in the former and not in the latter—perhaps the tenderest, most mocking thought that ever was thought, a thought alive with all the guile and the most secret bliss of love's longing.

A writer's chief joy is that thought can become all feeling, that feeling can become all thought. The lonely author possessed and commanded at this moment just such a vibrant thought, such a precise feeling: namely, that nature herself would shiver with delight were intellect to bow in homage before beauty. He suddenly wanted to write. They say, to be sure, that Eros loves idleness; the god was made to engage in no other activity. But at this moment of crisis the excitement of the love-struck traveler drove him to productivity, and the occasion was almost a matter of indifference. The intellectual world had been challenged to

7. A brook or small river in ancient Athens, here personified as a god.
8. Semele, one of Zeus's many mortal loves, was the mother of Dionysus. She was burned alive when she insisted on seeing Zeus in his actual divine form.

profess its views on a certain great and burning problem of culture and of taste, and the challenge had reached him. The problem was well known to him, was part of his experience; the desire to illuminate it with the splendor of his eloquence was suddenly irresistible. And what is more, he wanted to work here in the presence of Tadzio, to use the boy's physical frame as the model for his writing, to let his style follow the lines of that body that seemed to him divine, to carry his beauty into the realm of intellect as once the eagle carried the Trojan shepherd into the ethereal heavens.[9] Never had his pleasure in the word seemed sweeter to him, never had he known so surely that Eros dwelt in the word as now in the dangerous and delightful hours he spent at his rough table under the awning. There with his idol's image in full view, the music of his voice resounding in his ear, he formed his little essay after the image of Tadzio's beauty—composed that page-and-a-half of choice prose that soon would amaze many a reader with its purity, nobility, and surging depth of feeling. It is surely for the best that the world knows only the lovely work and not also its origins, not the conditions under which it came into being; for knowledge of the origins from which flowed the artist's inspiration would surely often confuse the world, repel it, and thus vitiate the effects of excellence. Strange hours! Strangely enervating effort! Strangely fertile intercourse between a mind and a body! When Aschenbach folded up his work and left the beach, he felt exhausted, even unhinged, as if his conscience were indicting him after a debauch.

meta fiction

The next morning as he was about to leave the hotel he chanced to notice from the steps that Tadzio was already on his way to the shore, alone; he was just approaching the beach barrier. He felt first a suggestion, then a compulsion: the wish, the simple thought that he might make use of the opportunity to strike up a casual, cheerful acquaintanceship with this boy who unwittingly had caused such a stir in his mind and heart, speak with him and enjoy his answer and his gaze. The lovely lad sauntered along; he could be easily caught up with; Aschenbach quickened his steps. He reached him on the walkway behind the cabanas, was about to put his hand on his head or on his shoulder, was about to let some word pass his lips, some friendly French phrase. But then he felt his heart beating like a hammer, perhaps only because of his rapid walk, so that he was short of breath and could only have spoken in a trembling gasp. He hesitated, tried to master himself, then suddenly feared he had been walking too long right behind the handsome boy, feared he might notice, might turn around with an inquiring look. He took one more run at him, but then he gave up, renounced his goal, and hung his head as he went by.

Too late! he thought at that moment. Too late! But was it really too

---

9. Zeus took the form of an eagle to capture the lovely Trojan shepherd Ganymede and carry him up to Olympus, where the boy became Zeus's lover and cupbearer to the gods.

late? This step he had failed to take might very possibly have led to something good, to something easy and happy, to a salutary return to reality. But it may have been that the aging traveler did not wish to return to reality, that he was too much in love with his own intoxication. Who can untangle the riddle of the artist's essence and character? Who can understand the deep instinctive fusion of discipline and a desire for licentiousness upon which that character is based? For it is licentiousness to be unable to wish for a salutary return to reality. Aschenbach was no longer inclined to self-criticism. The taste, the intellectual constitution that came with his years, his self-esteem, maturity, and the simplicity of age made him disinclined to analyze the grounds for his behavior or to decide whether it was conscience or debauchery and weakness that caused him not to carry out his plan. He was confused; he feared that someone, if only the custodian on the beach, might have observed his accelerated gait and his defeat; he feared very much looking foolish. And all the while he made fun of himself, of his comically solemn anxiety. "We've been quite confounded," he thought, "and now we're as crestfallen as a gamecock that lets its wings droop during a fight. It must surely be the god himself who thus destroys our courage at the very sight of loveliness, who crushes our proud spirit so deeply in the dust. . . ." His thoughts roamed playfully: he was far too arrogant to be fearful of a mere emotion.

He had already ceased to pay much attention to the extent of time he was allowing himself for his holiday; the thought of returning home did not even cross his mind. He had had an ample amount of money sent to him by mail. His sole source of concern was the possible departure of the Polish family, but he had privately obtained information, thanks to casual inquiries at the hotel barber shop, that the Polish party had arrived only very shortly before he did. The sun tanned his face and hands, the bracing salt air stimulated his emotions. Just as he ordinarily used up all the resources he gathered from sleep, nourishment, or nature on literary work, so now he expended each contribution that sun, leisure, and sea air made to his daily increase in strength in a generous, extravagant burst of enthusiasm and sentiment.

He slept fitfully; the exquisitely uniform days were separated by short nights full of happy restlessness. To be sure he retired early, for at nine o'clock, when Tadzio had left the scene, the day was over as far as he was concerned. At the first glimmer of dawn, however, a softly penetrating pang of alarm awakened him, as his heart remembered its great adventure. No longer able to endure the pillow, he arose, wrapped himself in a light robe against the morning chill, and positioned himself at the open window to await the sunrise. This wonderful occurrence filled his sleep-blessed soul with reverence. Heaven, earth, and sea still lay in the ghostly, glassy pallor of dawn; a fading star still floated in the insubstantial distance. Then a breath of wind arose, a winged message from unapproachable abodes announcing that Eos was arising from the side of her spouse. There became visible on the furthest boundary between sea and sky that first sweet blush of red that reveals creation assuming perceptible form. The goddess was approaching, she who seduced young men, she who had stolen Kleitos and Kephalos and enjoyed the love of handsome Orion in defiance of all the envious Olympians.[1] A strewing of roses began there on the edge of the world, where all shone and blossomed in unspeakable purity. Childlike clouds, transfigured and luminous, hovered like attending Cupids in the rosy bluish fragrance. Purple light fell on the sea, then washed forward in waves. Golden spears shot up from below to the heights of the heavens, and the brilliance began to burn. Silently, with divine ascendancy, glow and heat and blazing flames spun upwards, as the brother-god's sacred chargers, hooves beating, mounted the heavens.[2] The lonely, wakeful watcher sat bathed in the splendor of the god's rays; he closed his eyes and let the glory kiss his eyelids. With a confused, wondering smile on his lips he recognized feelings from long ago, early, exquisite afflictions of the heart that had withered in the severe service that his life had become and now returned so strangely transformed. He meditated, he dreamed. Slowly his lips formed a name, and still smiling, his face turned upward, his hands folded in his lap, he fell asleep once more in his armchair.

The whole day that had thus begun in fiery celebration was strangely heightened and mythically transformed. Where did that breath of air come from, the one that suddenly played about his temples and ears so softly and significantly like a whisper from a higher realm? White feathery clouds stood in scattered flocks in the heavens like grazing herds that the gods tend.[3] A stronger wind blew up; Poseidon's steeds reared and ran, and the bulls obedient to the god with the blue-green locks lowered their horns and bellowed as they charged. But amid the boulders on the distant beach the waves hopped up like leaping goats. A magical world, sacred and animated by the spirit of Pan,[4] surrounded the beguiled traveler, and his heart dreamed tender fables. Often, as the sun set behind Venice, he would sit on a bench in the park to watch Tadzio, dressed

1. Eos: The Greek goddess of dawn, connected in many myths with seductions of handsome young men, including Kleitos and Kephalos. She also took the hunter Orion as her lover, making the goddess Artemis (who also loved him) so jealous that she killed Orion with her arrows.
2. "Glow" and "heat" are possibly a reference (in free translation from Greek into German) to the mythical horses Lampos and Phaethon (i.e., "Shiner" and "Bright"). These mythical horses draw the sun chariot of Eos's brother Helios; according to Greek mythology Helios drives this chariot through the heavens daily. The sentence closes with a Homeric hexameter: ". . . stiegen des / Bruders / heilige / Renner / über den / Erdkreis . . ." (". . . brother-god's / sacred / chargers,/ hooves beating, / mounted the / heavens").
3. Another hexameter: [ver]breiteten / Scharen am / Himmel gleich / weidenden / Herden du / Götter (". . . scattered / flocks in the / heavens like / grazing / herds that the / gods tend").
4. Poseidon, the god "with the blue-green locks," was the Greek god of the sea. The "steeds" and "bulls" mentioned here are the waves rolling in on the beach. Pan, a Greek god who was half man and half goat, is associated with fertility and sexuality.

in white with a colorful sash, delight in playing ball on the smooth, rolled gravel; and it was as if he were watching Hyacinthos, who had to die because two gods loved him. Indeed he felt the painful envy Zephyros felt toward his rival in love, the god who abandoned his oracle, his bow, and his cithara to spend all his time playing with the beautiful boy. He saw the discus, directed by cruel jealousy, strike the lovely head; he, too, turned pale as he received the stricken body; and the flower that sprang from that sweet blood bore the inscription of his unending lament. . . .[5]

There is nothing stranger or more precarious than the relationship between people who know each other only by sight, who meet and watch each other every day, even every hour, yet are compelled by convention or their own whim to maintain the appearance of indifference and unfamiliarity, to avoid any word or greeting. There arises between them a certain restlessness and frustrated curiosity, the hysteria of an unsatisfied, unnaturally suppressed urge for acquaintanceship and mutual exchange, and in point of fact also a kind of tense respect. For people tend to love and honor other people so long as they are not in a position to pass judgment on them; and longing is the result of insufficient knowledge.

Some sort of relationship or acquaintance necessarily had to develop between Aschenbach and the young Tadzio, and with a pang of joy the older man was able to ascertain that his involvement and attentions were not altogether unrequited. For example, what impelled the lovely boy no longer to use the boardwalk behind the cabanas when he appeared on the beach in the morning but instead to saunter by toward his family's cabana on the front path, through the sand, past Aschenbach's customary spot, sometimes unnecessarily close by him, almost touching his table, his chair? Did Aschenbach's superior emotional energy exercise such an attraction, such a fascination on the tender, unreflecting object of those emotions? The writer waited daily for Tadzio's appearance; sometimes he would act as if he were busy when this event took place and let the lovely one pass by without seeming to notice. Sometimes, though, he would look up, and their eyes would meet. Both of them were gravely serious when it happened. In the refined and respectable bearing of the older man nothing betrayed his inner tumult; but in Tadzio's eyes there was the hint of an inquiry, of a thoughtful question. A hesitation became visible in his gait, he looked at the ground, he looked up again in his charming way, and when he was past there seemed to

---

5. According to a Greek myth, Apollo and Zephyros (god of the west wind and son of Eos) were rivals for the love of Hyacinthos. In a fit of jealousy Zephyros caused a gust of wind to blow a discus off course so that it struck and killed the boy. In his grief Apollo made the hyacinth flower arise from the spilled blood. The Greeks thought they could see in the flower the letters alpha and iota written in rows, forming the Greek version of "Alas! Alas!" ("*Aiai! Aiai!*"). Apollo was associated with the oracle, bow, and cithara (an instrument similar to the lyre).

be something in his demeanor saying that only his good breeding prevented him from turning around.

One evening, however, something quite different happened. The Polish children and their governess were missing at the main meal in the large dining room. Aschenbach had taken note of it with alarm. Concerned about their absence, he was strolling in front of the hotel at the bottom of the terrace after dinner, dressed in his evening clothes and a straw hat, when he suddenly saw appear in the light of the arc lamps the nunlike sisters and their attendant, with Tadzio four steps behind. They were apparently returning from the steamer landing after having taken their meal for some reason in the city. It must have been cool on the water: Tadzio wore a dark blue sailor's coat with gold buttons and a sailor's hat to go with it. The sun and sea air had not browned him. His skin was the same marble-like yellow color.it had been from the beginning. But today he seemed paler than usual, whether because of the cool temperature or because of the pallid moonglow cast by the lamps. His even brows showed in starker contrast, his eyes darkened to an even deeper tone. He was more beautiful than words could ever tell, and Aschenbach felt as he often had before the painful truth that words are capable only of praising physical beauty, not of rendering it visible.

He had not been expecting the exquisite apparition: it had come on unhoped for. He had not had time to fortify himself in a peaceful, respectable demeanor. Joy, surprise, and admiration might have been clearly displayed in the gaze that met that of the one he had so missed—and in that very second, it came to pass that Tadzio smiled. He smiled at Aschenbach, smiled eloquently, intimately, charmingly, and without disguise, with lips that began to open only as he smiled. It was the smile of Narcissus leaning over the mirroring water, that deep, beguiled, unresisting smile that comes as he extends his arm toward the reflection of his own beauty—a very slightly distorted smile, distorted by the hopelessness of his desire to kiss the lovely lips of his shadow—a coquettish smile, curious and faintly pained, infatuated and infatuating.[6]

He who had been the recipient of this smile rushed away with it as if it were a gift heavy with destiny. He was so thoroughly shaken that he was forced to flee the light of the terrace and the front garden and to seek with a hasty tread the darkness of the park in the rear. Strangely indignant and tender exhortations broke forth from him: "You must not smile so! Listen, no one is allowed to smile that way at anyone!" He threw himself on a bench; he breathed in the nocturnal fragrance of the plants, beside himself. Leaning back with his arms hanging at his sides, overpowered and shivering uncontrollably, he whispered the eternal for-

6. For haughtily rejecting all lovers, Narcissus, a beautiful youth, was condemned by the gods of the ancient Greeks to fall in love with his own reflection. Having pined away for this reflection, he was turned into a narcissus flower.

mula of longing—impossible under these conditions, absurd, reviled, ridiculous, and yet holy and venerable even under these conditions—"I love you!"

Chapter 5

In the fourth week of his stay on the Lido Gustav Aschenbach made a number of disturbing discoveries regarding events in the outside world. In the first place it seemed to him that as the season progressed toward its height the number of guests at the hotel declined rather than increased. In particular it seemed that the German language ceased to be heard around him: lately his ear could detect only foreign sounds in the dining room and on the beach. He had taken to visiting the barber-shop frequently, and in a conversation there one day he heard something that startled him. The barber had mentioned a German family that had just left after staying only a short time; then he added by way of flattering small talk, "But you're staying, sir, aren't you. You're not afraid of the disease." Aschenbach looked at him. "The disease?" he repeated. The man broke off his chatter, acted busy, ignored the question. When Aschenbach pressed the issue, he explained that he knew nothing and tried to change the subject with a stream of embarrassed eloquence.

That was at noon. In the afternoon Aschenbach sailed across to Venice in a dead calm and under a burning sun. He was driven by his mania to pursue the Polish children, whom he had seen making for the steamer landing along with their attendant. He did not find his idol at San Marco. But at tea, sitting at his round wrought-iron table on the shady side of the piazza, he suddenly smelled a peculiar aroma in the air, one that he now felt had been lurking at the edge of his consciousness for several days without his becoming fully aware of it. It was a medicinally sweet smell that put in mind thoughts of misery and wounds and ominous cleanliness. After a few moments' reflection he recognized it; then he finished his snack and left the piazza on the side opposite the cathedral. The odor became stronger in the narrow streets. At the street corners there were affixed printed posters in which the city fathers warned the population about certain illnesses of the gastric system that could be expected under these atmospheric conditions, advising that they should not eat oysters and mussels or use the water in the canals. The euphemistic nature of the announcement was obvious. Groups of local people stood together silently on the bridges and in the piazzas, and the foreign traveler stood among them, sniffing and musing.

There was a shopkeeper leaning in the doorway of his little vaulted quarters among coral necklaces and imitation amethyst trinkets, and Aschenbach asked him for some information about the ominous odor.

The man took his measure with a heavy-lidded stare and then hastily put on a cheerful expression. "A precautionary measure, sir," he answered with many a gesture. "A police regulation that we must accept. The weather is oppressive, the sirocco is not conducive to good health. In short, you understand—perhaps they're being too careful. . . ." Aschenbach thanked him and went on. Even on the steamer that took him back to the Lido he could now detect the odor of disinfectant.

Once back at the hotel he went directly to the lobby to have a look at the newspapers. In the ones in foreign languages he found nothing. The German papers mentioned rumors, cited highly varying figures, quoted official denials, and offered doubts about their veracity. This explained the departure of the German and Austrian element. The citizens of other nations apparently knew nothing, suspected nothing, and were not yet concerned. "Best to keep quiet," thought Aschenbach anxiously, as he threw the papers back on the table. "Best to keep it under wraps." But at the same time his heart filled with a feeling of satisfaction over this adventure in which the outside world was becoming involved. For passion, like crime, does not sit well with the sure order and even course of everyday life; it welcomes every loosening of the social fabric, every confusion and affliction visited upon the world, for passion sees in such disorder a vague hope of finding an advantage for itself. Thus Aschenbach felt a dark satisfaction over the official cover-up of events in the dirty alleys of Venice. This heinous secret belonging to the city fused and became one with his own innermost secret, which he was likewise intent upon keeping. For the lovesick traveler had no concern other than that Tadzio might depart, and he recognized, not without a certain horror, that he would not know how to go on living were that to happen.

Recently he had not contented himself with allowing chance and the daily routine to determine his opportunities to see and be near the lovely lad; he pursued him, he lay in wait for him. On Sundays, for example, the Polish family never went to the beach. He guessed that they went to mass at San Marco. He followed speedily, entered the golden twilight of the sanctuary from the heat of the piazza, and found him, the one he had missed so, bent over a prie-dieu[1] taking part in the holy service. He stood in the background on the fissured mosaic floor, in the midst of a kneeling, murmuring crowd of people who kept crossing themselves, and felt the condensed grandeur of the oriental temple weigh voluptuously on his senses. Up in front the priest moved about, conducted his ritual, and chanted away, while incense billowed up and enshrouded the feeble flames of the altar candles. Mixed in with the sweet, heavy, ceremonial fragrance seemed to be another: the smell of the diseased city. But through all the haze and glitter Aschenbach saw how the lovely one up in front turned his head, looked for him, and found him.

1. A bench on which to kneel during prayer, with a raised shelf for elbows or book.

↲ the boy worships God, the man worships the boy

When at last the crowd streamed out of the open portals into the shining piazza with its flocks of pigeons, the infatuated lover hid in the vestibule where he lay in wait, staking out his quarry. He saw the Polish family leave the church, saw the children take leave of their mother with great ceremony, saw her make for the Piazzetta on her way home. He ascertained that the lovely one, his cloisterly sisters, and the governess were on their way off to the right, through the clock tower gate, and into the Merceria,[2] and after giving them a reasonable head start he followed. He followed like a thief as they strolled through Venice. He had to stop when they lingered somewhere, had to flee into restaurants or courtyards to avoid them when they turned back. He lost them, got hot and tired as he searched for them over bridges and in dirty cul-de-sacs, and suffered long moments of mortal pain when he saw them coming toward him in a narrow passage where no escape was possible. And yet one cannot really say he suffered. He was intoxicated in head and heart, and his steps followed the instructions of the demon whose pleasure it is to crush under foot human reason and dignity.

At some point or other Tadzio and his party would take a gondola, and Aschenbach, remaining hidden behind a portico or a fountain while they got in, did likewise shortly after they pulled away from the bank. He spoke quickly and in subdued tones to the gondolier, instructing him that a generous tip was in store for him if he would follow that gondola just now rounding the corner—but not too close, as unobtrusively as possible. Sweat trickled over his body as the gondolier, with the roguish willingness of a procurer, assured him in the same lowered tones that he would get service, that he would get conscientious service.

He leaned back in the soft black cushions and glided and rocked in pursuit of the other black, beak-prowed bark, to which his passion held him fastened as if by a chain. Sometimes he lost sight of it, and at those times he would feel worried and restless. But his boatman seemed entirely familiar with such assignments and always knew just how to bring the object of his desire back into view by means of clever maneuvers and quick passages and shortcuts. The air was still, and it smelled. The sun burned heavily through a haze that gave the sky the color of slate. Water gurgled against wood and stone. The cry of the gondolier, half warning and half greeting, received distant answer from out of the silent labyrinth as if by mysterious arrangement. Umbels of flowers hung down over crumbling walls from small gardens on higher ground. They were white and purple and smelled like almonds. Moorish window casings showed their forms in the haze. The marble steps of a church descended into the waters; a beggar crouching there and asserting his misery held out his hat and showed the whites of his eyes as if he were

---

2. Formerly a principal mercantile district just north of the Piazza San Marco. (See map of Venice, G-5, p. 68). Many shops are still located there.

blind; a dealer in antiques stood before his cavelike shop and with fawning gestures invited the passerby to stop, hoping for a chance to swindle
him. That was Venice, that coquettish, dubious beauty of a city, half
fairy tale and half tourist trap, in whose noisome air the fine arts once
thrived luxuriantly and where musicians were inspired to create sounds
that cradle the listener and seductively rock him to sleep.[3] To the traveler in the midst of his adventure it seemed as if his eyes were drinking
in just this luxury, as if his ears were wooed by just such melodies. He
remembered, too, that the city was sick and was keeping its secret out of
pure greed, and he cast an even more licentious leer toward the gondola
floating in the distance before him.

Entangled and besotted as he was, he no longer wished for anything
else than to pursue the beloved object that inflamed him, to dream
about him when he was absent and to speak amorous phrases, after the
manner of lovers, to his mere shadow. His solitary life, the foreign
locale, and his late but deep transport of ecstasy encouraged and persuaded him to allow himself the most bewildering transgressions without
timidity or embarrassment. That is how it happened that on his return
from Venice late in the evening he had stopped on the second floor of
the hotel in front of the lovely one's door, leaned his brow against the
hinge in complete intoxication, unable for a protracted period to drag
himself away, heedless of the danger of being caught in such an outrageous position.

Still, there were moments when he paused and half came to his
senses. How has this come to pass? he wondered in alarm. How did I
come to this? Like everyone who has achieved something thanks to his
natural talents, he had an aristocratic interest in his family background.
At times when his life brought him recognition and success he would
think about his ancestors and try to reassure himself that they would
approve, that they would be pleased, that they would have had to admire
him. Even here and now he thought about them, entangled as he was
in such an illicit experience, seized by such exotic emotional aberrations. He thought about their rigorous self-possession, their manly
respectability, and he smiled a melancholy smile. What would they say?
But then what would they have said about his whole life, a life that had
so diverged, one might say degenerated, from theirs, a life under the
spell of art that he himself had mocked in the precocity of his youth,
this life that yet so fundamentally resembled theirs? He too had done his
service, he too had practiced a strict discipline; he too had been a soldier
and a man of war, like many of them. For art was a war, a grinding
battle that one was just no longer up to fighting for very long these days.
It was a life of self-control and a life lived in despite, a harsh, steadfast,
abstemious existence that he had made the symbol of a tender and

3. Apparently a reference to Richard Wagner, who had composed in Venice.

timely heroism. He had every right to call it manly, call it courageous, and he wondered if the love-god who had taken possession of him might be particularly inclined and partial somehow to those who lived such a life. Had not that very god enjoyed the highest respect among the bravest nations of the earth? Did they not say that it was because of their courage that he had flourished in their cities? Numerous war heroes of ages past had willingly borne the yoke imposed by the god, for a humiliation imposed by the god did not count. Acts that would have been denounced as signs of cowardice when done in other circumstances and for other ends—prostrations, oaths, urgent pleas, and fawning behavior—none redounded to the shame of the lover, but rather he more likely reaped praise for them.[4]

Such was the infatuated thinker's train of thought; thus he sought to offer himself support; thus he attempted to preserve his dignity. But at the same time he stubbornly kept on the track of the dirty doings in the city's interior, that adventure of the outside world that darkly joined together with his heart's adventure and nourished his passion with vague, lawless hopes. Obsessed with finding out the latest and most reliable news about the status and progress of the disease, he went to the city's coffee houses and leafed through the German newspapers, which had long since disappeared from the table in the hotel lobby. He read alternating assertions and denials. The number of illnesses and deaths might be as high as twenty, forty, even a hundred or more; but then in the next article or next issue any outbreak of the epidemic, if not categorically denied, would be reported as limited to a few isolated cases brought in by foreigners. There were periodic doubts, warnings, and protests against the dangerous game being played by the Italian authorities. Reliable information was simply not available.

The solitary guest was nonetheless conscious of having a special claim on his share in the secret. Though he was excluded, he took a bizarre pleasure in pressing knowledgeable people with insidious questions and forcing those who were part of the conspiracy of silence to utter explicit lies. At breakfast one day in the main dining room, for example, he engaged the manager in conversation. This unobtrusive little person in his French frock coat was going about between the tables greeting everyone and supervising the help. He made a brief stop at Aschenbach's table, too, for a casual chat. Now then why, the guest just happened to ask very casually, why in the world had they been disinfecting Venice for all this time? "It's a police matter," the toady answered, "a measure intended to stop in due and timely fashion any and all unwholesome conditions, any disturbance of the public health that might come about owing to the brooding heat of this exceptionally warm weather." "The

4. A reference to the Athenian code of love as described by Pausanias in Plato's *Symposium*, sections 182d–e, 183b.

police are to be commended," replied Aschenbach. After the exchange of a few more meteorological observations the manager took his leave.

On that very same day, in the evening after dinner, it happened that a little band of street singers from the city performed in the hotel's front garden. They stood, two men and two women, next to the iron lamppost of an arc light and raised their faces, shining in the white illumination, toward the great terrace, where the guests were enjoying this traditional popular entertainment while drinking coffee and cooling beverages. Hotel employees—elevator boys, waiters, and office personnel—stood by listening at the entrances to the lobby. The Russian family, zealous and precise in taking their pleasure, had wicker chairs moved down into the garden so as to be nearer the performers. There they sat in a semicircle, in their characteristically grateful attitude. Behind the ladies and gentlemen stood the old slave woman in her turbanlike headdress.

The low-life virtuosos were extracting sounds from a mandolin, a guitar, a harmonica, and a squeaky violin. Interspersed among the instrumental numbers were vocals in which the younger of the women blended her sharp, quavering voice with the sweet falsetto of the tenor in a love duet full of yearning. But the chief talent and real leader of the group was clearly the other man, the guitar player, who sang a kind of buffo baritone while he played. Though his voice was weak, he was a gifted mime and projected remarkable comic energy. Often he would move away from the group, his great instrument under his arm, and advance toward the terrace with many a flourish. The audience rewarded his antics with rousing laughter. The Russians in particular, ensconced in their orchestra seats, displayed particular delight over all this southern vivacity and encouraged him with applause and cheers to ever bolder and more brazen behavior.

Aschenbach sat at the balustrade, cooling his lips from time to time with a mixture of pomegranate juice and soda that sparkled ruby-red in his glass. His nerves greedily consumed the piping sounds, the vulgar, pining melodies; for passion numbs good taste and succumbs in all seriousness to enticements that a sober spirit would receive with humor or even reject scornfully. His features, reacting to the antics of the buffoon, had become fixed in a rigid and almost painful smile. He sat in an apparently relaxed attitude, and all the while he was internally tense and sharply attentive, for Tadzio stood no more than six paces away, leaning against the stone railing.

He stood there in the white belted suit that he sometimes wore to dinner, a figure of inevitable and innate grace, his left forearm on the railing, his ankles crossed, his right hand supported on his hip. He wore an expression that was not quite a smile but more an air of distant curiosity or polite receptivity as he looked down toward the street musicians. Sometimes he straightened up and, with a lovely movement of both arms that lifted his chest, he would pull his white blouse down through his leather belt. Occasionally, though—as the aging observer noted with triumph and even with horror, his reason staggering—Tadzio would turn his head to look across his left shoulder in the direction of the one who loved him, sometimes with deliberate hesitation, sometimes with sudden swiftness as if to catch him unawares. Their eyes never met, for an ignominious caution forced the errant lover to keep his gaze fearfully in check. The women guarding Tadzio were sitting in the back of the terrace, and things had reached the point that the smitten traveler had to take care lest his behavior should become noticeable and he fall under suspicion. Indeed his blood had nearly frozen on a number of occasions when he had been compelled to notice on the beach, in the hotel lobby, or in the Piazza San Marco that Tadzio was called away from his vicinity, that they were intent on keeping the boy away from him. He felt horribly insulted, and his pride flinched from unfamiliar tortures that his conscience prevented him from dismissing.

In the meantime the guitar player had begun singing a solo to his own accompaniment, a popular ditty in many verses that was quite the hit just then all over Italy. He was adept at performing it in a highly histrionic manner, and his band joined in the refrain each time, both with their voices and all their instruments. He was of a lean build, and even his face was thin to the point of emaciation. He stood there on the gravel in an attitude of impertinent bravura, apart from his fellow performers, his shabby felt hat so far back on his head that a roll of red hair surged forth from beneath the brim, and as he thumped the guitar strings, he hurled his buffooneries toward the terrace above in an insistent recitative. The veins on his brow swelled in response to his exertions. He seemed not to be of Venetian stock, more likely a member of the race of Neapolitan comics, half pimp, half actor, brutal and daring, dangerous and entertaining. The lyrics of his song were as banal as could be, but in his mouth they acquired an ambiguous, vaguely offensive quality because of his facial expressions and his gestures, his suggestive winks and his manner of letting his tongue play lasciviously at the corner of his mouth. His strikingly large Adam's apple protruded nakedly from his scrawny neck, which emerged from the soft collar of a sport shirt worn in incongruous combination with more formal city clothes. His pale, snub-nosed face was beardless and did not permit an easy reckoning of his age; it seemed ravaged by grimaces and by vice. The two defiant, imperious, even wild-looking furrows that stood between his reddish eyebrows went rather oddly with the grin on his mobile lips. What particularly drew the attention of the lonely spectator, however, was his observation that this questionable figure seemed to carry with it its own questionable atmosphere. For every time the refrain began again the singer would commence a grotesque circular march, clowning and shaking the hands of his audience; every time his path would bring him directly underneath Aschenbach's spot, and every time that happened there wafted up to the terrace from his clothes and from his body a choking stench of carbolic acid.[5]

His song finished, he began collecting money. He started with the Russians, who produced a generous offering, and then ascended the steps. As bold as he had been during the performance, just so obsequious was he now. Bowing and scraping, he slithered about between the tables, a smile of crafty submissiveness laying bare his large teeth, and all the while the two furrows between his red eyebrows stood forth menacingly. The guests surveyed with curiosity and some revulsion this strange being who was gathering in his livelihood. They threw coins in his hat from a distance and were careful not to touch him. The elimination of the physical separation between the performer and his respectable audience always tends to produce a certain embarrassment, no matter how pleasurable the performance. The singer felt it and sought to excuse himself by acting servile. He came up to Aschenbach, and with him came the smell, though no one else in the vicinity seemed concerned about it.

"Listen," the lonely traveler said in lowered tones, almost mechanically. "They are disinfecting Venice. Why?" The jester answered hoarsely: "Because of the police. That, sir, is the procedure when it gets hot like this and when the sirocco comes. The sirocco is oppressive. It's not conducive to good health. . . ." He spoke as if he were amazed that anyone could ask such questions, and he demonstrated by pushing with his open palm just how oppressive the sirocco was. "So there is no disease in Venice?" Aschenbach asked very quietly through his closed teeth. The tense muscles in the comedian's face produced a grimace of comic perplexity. "A disease? What sort of disease? Is the sirocco a disease? Do you suppose our police force is a disease? You like to make fun, don't you? A disease! Why on earth? Some preventive measures, you understand. A police regulation to minimize the effects of the oppressive weather . . . ," he gesticulated. "Very well," Aschenbach said once again, briefly and quietly, and he dropped an indecently large coin into the hat. Then he indicated with a look that the man should go. He obeyed with a grin and a bow. But even before he reached the steps two hotel employees intercepted him and, putting their faces very close to his, cross-examined him in whispers. He shrugged, he protested, he swore that he had been circumspect. You could tell. Dismissed, he returned to the garden and, after making a few arrangements with his group by the light of the arc lamp, he stepped forward to offer one parting song.

It was a song the solitary traveler could not remember ever having heard before, an impudent Italian hit in an incomprehensible dialect

5. A chemical used as a disinfectant.

embellished with a laughing refrain in which the whole group regularly joined, fortissimo. The refrain had neither words nor instrumental accompaniment; nothing was left but a certain rhythmically structured but still very natural-sounding laughter, which the soloist in particular was capable of producing with great talent and deceptive realism. Having reestablished a proper artistic distance between himself and his audience, he had regained all his former impudence. His artfully artificial laughter, directed impertinently up to the terrace, was the laughter of scorn. Even before the part of the song with actual lyrics had come to a close, one could see him begin to battle an irresistible itch. He would hiccup, his voice would catch, he would put his hand up to his mouth, he would twist his shoulders, and at the proper moment the unruly laughter would break forth, exploding in a hoot, but with such realism that it was infectious. It spread among the listeners so that even on the terrace an unfounded mirth set in, feeding on nothing but itself. This appeared only to double the singer's exuberance. He bent his knees, slapped his thighs, held his sides, fairly split with laughter; but he was no longer laughing, he was howling. He pointed his finger upwards, as if to say that there could be nothing funnier than the laughing audience up there, and soon everyone in the garden and on the veranda was laughing, including the waiters, elevator boys, and servants lingering in the doorways.

Aschenbach no longer reclined in his chair; he sat upright as if trying to defend himself or to flee. But the laughter, the rising smell of hospital sanitation, and the nearness of the lovely boy—all blended to cast a dreamy spell about him that held his mind and his senses in an unbreakable, inescapable embrace. In the general confusion of the moment he made so bold as to cast a glance at Tadzio, and when he did so he was granted the opportunity to see that the lovely lad answered his gaze with a seriousness equal to his own. It was as if the boy were regulating his behavior and attitude according to that of the man, as if the general mood of gaiety had no power over the boy so long as the man kept apart from it. This childlike and meaningful docility was so disarming, so overwhelming, that the gray-haired traveler could only with difficulty refrain from hiding his face in his hands. It had also seemed to him that Tadzio's habit of straightening up and taking a deep sighing breath suggested an obstruction in his breathing. "He is sickly; he will probably not live long," he thought once again with that sobriety that sometimes frees itself in some strange manner from intoxication and longing. Ingenuous solicitude mixed with a dissolute satisfaction filled his heart.

The Venetian singers had meanwhile finished their number and left, accompanied by applause. Their leader did not fail to adorn even his departure with jests. He bowed and scraped and blew kisses so that everyone laughed, which made him redouble his efforts. When his fellow performers were already gone, he pretended to back hard into a lamppost at full speed, then crept toward the gate bent over in mock pain. There at last he cast off the mask of the comic loser, unbent or rather snapped up straight, stuck his tongue out impudently at the guests on the terrace, and slipped into the darkness. The audience dispersed; Tadzio was already long gone from his place at the balustrade. But the lonely traveler remained sitting for a long time at his little table, nursing his pomegranate drink much to the annoyance of the waiters. The night progressed; time crumbled away. Many years ago in his parents' house there had been an hourglass. He suddenly could see the fragile and portentous little device once more, as though it were standing right in front of him. The rust-colored fine sand ran silently through the glass neck, and as it began to run out of the upper vessel a rapid little vortex formed.

In the afternoon of the very next day the obstinate visitor took a further step in his probing of the outside world, and this time he met with all possible success. What he did was to enter the English travel agency in the Piazza San Marco and, having changed some money at the cash register and having assumed the demeanor of a diffident foreigner, he directed his fateful question to the clerk who was taking care of him. The clerk was a wool-clad Briton, still young, his hair parted in the middle and eyes set close together, possessed of that steady, trustworthy bearing that stands out as so foreign and so remarkable among the roguishly nimble southerners. He began: "No cause for concern, sir. A measure of no serious importance. Such regulations are frequently imposed to ward off the ill effects of the heat and the sirocco. . . ." But when he raised his blue eyes he met the foreigner's gaze. It was a tired and rather sad gaze, and it was directed with an air of mild contempt toward his lips. The Englishman blushed. "That is," he continued in a low voice, somewhat discomfited, "the official explanation, which they see fit to stick to hereabouts. I can tell you, though, that there's a good deal more to it." And then, in his candid and comfortable language, he told the truth.

For some years now Asiatic cholera had shown an increasing tendency to spread and roam. The pestilence originated in the warm swamps of the Ganges delta, rising on the foul-smelling air of that lushly uninhabitable primeval world, that wilderness of islands avoided by humankind where tigers lurk in bamboo thickets. It had raged persistently and with unusual ferocity throughout Hindustan; then it had spread eastwards to China and westwards to Afghanistan and Persia;[6] and, following the great caravan routes, it had brought its horrors as far as Astrakhan and even Moscow. But while Europe was shaking in fear lest the specter should progress by land from Russia westward, it had emerged simultaneously in several Mediterranean port cities, having

6. Hindustan: Persian name of India; Persia: now Iran.

been carried in on Syrian merchant ships. It had raised its grisly head in
Toulon and Malaga, shown its grim mask several times in Palermo and
Naples, and seemed now firmly ensconced throughout Calabria and
Apulia. The northern half of the peninsula had so far been spared. On
a single day in mid-May of this year, however, the terrible vibrioid bacteria had been found on two emaciated, blackening corpses, that of a
ship's hand and that of a woman who sold vegetables. These cases were
hushed up. A week later, though, there were ten more, twenty more,
thirty more, not localized but spread through various parts of the city. A
man from the Austrian hinterlands who had come for a pleasant holiday
of a few days in Venice died upon returning to his home town, exhib-
iting unmistakable symptoms. Thus it was that the first rumors of the
affliction visited upon the city on the lagoon appeared in German newspapers. In response the Venetian authorities promulgated the assertion
that matters of health had never been better in the city. They also immediately instituted the most urgent measures to counter the disease. But
apparently the food supply—vegetables, meat, and milk—had been
infected, for death, though denied and hushed up, devoured its way
through the narrow streets. The early arrival of summer's heat made a
lukewarm broth of the water in the canals and thus made conditions for
the disease's spread particularly favorable. It almost seemed as though
the pestilence had been reinvigorated, as if the tenacity and fecundity of
its microscopic agitators had been redoubled. Cures were rare; out of a
hundred infected eighty died, and in a particularly gruesome fashion,
for the evil raged here with extreme ferocity. Often it took on its most
dangerous form, commonly known as the "dry type." In such cases the
body is unable to rid itself of the massive amounts of water secreted by
the blood-vessels. In a few hours' time the patient dries up and suffo-
cates, his blood as viscous as pitch, crying out hoarsely in his convul-
sions. It sometimes happened that a few lucky ones suffered only a mild
discomfort followed by a loss of consciousness from which they would
never again, or only rarely, awaken. At the beginning of June the quarantine wards of the Ospedale Civico quietly filled up, space became
scarce in both of the orphanages, and a horrifyingly brisk traffic clogged
the routes between the docks at the Fondamenta Nuove and San
Michele, the cemetery island.[7] But the fear of adverse consequences to
the city, concern for the newly opened exhibit of paintings in the public
gardens, for the losses that the hotels, businesses, and the whole tourist
industry would suffer in case of a panic or a boycott—these matters
proved weightier in the city than the love of truth or respect for international agreements. They prompted the authorities stubbornly to maintain their policy of concealment and denial. The highest medical official
in Venice, a man of considerable attainments, had angrily resigned his

7. See map of Venice, p. 68: Ospedale Civico (H3-4)—city hospital; Fondamento Nuove (H3)—
   the new piers (lit. new footings); Cimitiero (I1)—San Michele, the cemetery island.

post and was surreptitiously replaced by a more pliable individual. The citizenry knew all about it, and the combination of corruption in high places with the prevailing uncertainty, the state of emergency in which the city was placed when death was striking all about, caused a certain demoralization of the lower levels of society. It encouraged those antisocial forces that shun the light, and they manifested themselves as immoderate, shameless, and increasingly criminal behavior. Contrary to the norm, one saw many drunks at evening time; people said that gangs of rogues made the streets unsafe at night; muggings and even murders multiplied. Already on two occasions it had come to light that alleged victims of the plague had in fact been robbed of their lives by their own relatives who administered poison. Prostitution and lasciviousness took on brazen and extravagant forms never before seen here and thought to be at home only in the southern parts of the country and in the seraglios of the orient.

The Englishman explained the salient points of these developments. "You would do well," he concluded, "to depart today rather than tomorrow. The imposition of a quarantine cannot be more than a few days off." "Thank you," said Aschenbach and left the agency.

The piazza was sunless and sultry. Unsuspecting foreigners sat in the sidewalk cafes or stood in front of the cathedral completely covered with pigeons. They watched as the swarming birds beat their wings and jostled each other for their chance to pick at the kernels of corn offered to them in an open palm. In feverish excitement, triumphant in his possession of the truth, but with a taste of gall in his mouth and a fantastic horror in his heart, the lonely traveler paced back and forth over the flagstones of the magnificent plaza. He considered doing the decent thing, the thing that would cleanse him. Tonight after dinner he could go up to the lady with the pearls and speak to her. He planned exactly what he would say: "Permit me, Madame, stranger though I may be, to be of service to you with a piece of advice, a word of warning concerning a matter that has been withheld from you by self-serving people. Depart at once, taking Tadzio and your daughters with you. There is an epidemic in Venice." He could then lay his hand in farewell on the head of that instrument of a scornful deity, turn away, and flee this swamp. But at the same time he sensed that he was infinitely far from seriously wanting to take such a step. It would bring him back to his senses, would make him himself again; but when one is beside oneself there is nothing more abhorrent than returning to one's senses. He remembered a white building decorated with inscriptions that gleamed in the evening light, inscriptions in whose radiant mysticism his mind's eye had become lost. He remembered too that strange figure of the wanderer who had awakened in the aging man a young man's longing to roam in faraway and exotic places. The thought of returning home, of returning to prudence and sobriety, toil and mastery, was so repugnant to him that his face broke out in an expression of physical disgust. "Let them keep quiet," he whispered vehemently. And: "I will keep quiet!" The consciousness of his guilty complicity intoxicated him, just as small amounts of wine will intoxicate a weary brain. The image of the afflicted and ravaged city hovered chaotically in his imagination, incited in him inconceivable hopes, beyond all reason, monstrously sweet. How could that tender happiness he had dreamed of a moment earlier compare with these expectations? What value did art and virtue hold for him when he could have chaos? He held his peace and stayed.

That night he had a terrifying dream—if indeed one can call "dream" an experience that was both physical and mental, one that visited him in the depths of his sleep, in complete isolation as well as sensuous immediacy, but yet such that he did not see himself as physically and spatially present apart from its action. Instead, its setting was in his soul itself, and its events burst in upon him from outside, violently crushing his resistance, his deep, intellectual resistance, passing through easily and leaving his whole being, the culmination of a lifetime of effort, ravaged and annihilated.

It began with fear, fear and desire and a horrified curiosity about what was to come. Night ruled, and his senses were attentive; for from afar there approached a tumult, a turmoil, a mixture of noises: rattling, clarion calls and muffled thunder, shrill cheering on top of it all, and a certain howl with a drawn-out *uuu* sound at the end. All this was accompanied and drowned out by the gruesomely sweet tones of a flute playing a cooing, recklessly persistent tune that penetrated to the very bowels, where it cast a shameless enchantment. But there was a phrase, darkly familiar, that named what was coming: *"The stranger god!"* [8] A smoky glow welled up, and he recognized a mountain landscape like the one around his summer house. And in the fragmented light he could see people, animals, a swarm, a roaring mob, all rolling and plunging and whirling down from the forested heights, past tree-trunks and great moss-covered fragments of rock, overflowing the slope with their bodies, flames, tumult, and reeling circular dance. Women, stumbling over the fur skirts that hung too long from their belts, moaned, threw their heads back, shook their tambourines on high, brandished naked daggers and torches that threw off sparks, held serpents with flickering tongues by the middle of their bodies, or cried out, lifting their breasts in both hands. Men with horns on their brows, girdled with hides, their own skins shaggy, bent their necks and raised their arms and thighs, clashed brazen cymbals and beat furiously on drums, while smooth-skinned boys used garlanded staves to prod their goats, clinging to the horns so they could be dragged along, shouting with joy, when the goats sprang. And the ecstatic band howled the cry with soft consonants in the middle and a

8. Dionysus, the god of intoxication and sexual license.

drawn-out *uuu* sound on the end, a cry that was sweet and wild at the same time, like none ever heard before: here it rang in the air like the bellowing of stags in rut; and there many voices echoed it back in anarchic triumph, using it to goad each other to dance and shake their limbs, never letting it fall silent. But it was all suffused and dominated by the deep, beckoning melody of the flute. Was it not also beckoning him, the resisting dreamer, with shameless persistence to the festival, to its excesses, and to its ultimate sacrifice? Great was his loathing, great his fear, sincere his resolve to defend his own against the foreign invader, the enemy of self-controlled and dignified intellect. But the noise and the howling, multiplied by the echoing mountainsides, grew, gained the upper hand, swelled to a madness that swept everything along with it. Fumes oppressed the senses: the acrid scent of the goats, the emanation of panting human bodies, a whiff as of stagnant water—and another smell perceptible through it all, a familiar reek of wounds and raging sickness. His heart pounded with the rhythm of the drum beats, his mind whirled, rage took hold of him and blinded him, he was overcome by a numbing lust, and his soul longed to join in the reeling dance of the god. Their obscene symbol,[9] gigantic, wooden, was uncovered and raised on high, and they howled out their watchword all the more licentiously. With foam on their lips they raved; they stimulated each other with lewd gestures and fondling hands; laughing and wheezing, they pierced each other's flesh with their pointed staves and then licked the bleeding limbs. Now among them, now a part of them, the dreamer belonged to the stranger god. Yes, they were he, and he was they, when they threw themselves on the animals, tearing and killing, devouring steaming gobbets of flesh, when on the trampled moss-covered ground there began an unfettered rite of copulation in sacrifice to the god. His soul tasted the lewdness and frenzy of surrender.

The afflicted dreamer awoke unnerved, shattered, a powerless victim of the demon. He no longer shunned the observant glances of people about him; he no longer cared if he was making himself a target of their suspicions. And in any case they were all departing, fleeing the sickness. Many cabanas now stood empty, the population of the dining room was seriously depleted, and in the city one only rarely saw a foreigner. The truth seemed to have leaked out, and in spite of the stubborn conniving of those with vested interests at stake, panic could no longer be averted. The lady with the pearls nonetheless remained with her family, perhaps because the rumors did not reach her or perhaps because she was too proud and fearless to succumb to them. Tadzio remained, and to Aschenbach, blind to all but his own concerns, it seemed at times that death and departure might very well remove all the distracting human life around them and leave him alone with the lovely one on this island.

9. The phallus.

Indeed, in the mornings on the beach when his gaze would rest heavily, irresponsibly, fixedly on the object of his desire; or at the close of day when he would take up his shameful pursuit of the boy through narrow streets where loathsome death did its hushed-up business; then everything monstrous seemed to him to have a prosperous future, the moral law to have none.

He wished, like any other lover, to please his beloved and felt a bitter concern that it would not be possible. He added youthfully cheerful touches to his dress, took to using jewelry and perfume. Several times a day he took lengthy care getting dressed and then came down to the dining room all bedecked, excited and expectant. His aging body disgusted him when he looked at the sweet youth with whom he was smitten; the sight of his gray hair and his sharp facial features overwhelmed him with shame and hopelessness. He felt a need to restore and revive his body. He visited the barbershop more and more frequently.

Leaning back in the chair under the protective cloth, letting the manicured hands of the chattering barber care for him, he confronted the tortured gaze of his image in the mirror.

"Gray," he said with his mouth twisted.

"A bit," the man replied. "It's all because of a slight neglect, an indifference to externals—quite understandable in the case of important people, but still not altogether praiseworthy, all the less so since just such people ought not to harbor prejudices in matters of the natural and the artificial. If certain people were to extend the moral qualms they have about the cosmetic arts to their teeth, as logic compels, they would give no little offense. And anyway, we're only as old as we feel in our hearts and minds. Gray hair can in certain circumstances give more of a false impression than the dye that some would scorn. In your case, sir, you have a right to your natural hair color. Will you allow me to give you back what is rightfully yours?"

"How?" Aschenbach inquired.

So the glib barber washed his customer's hair with two liquids, one clear and one dark, and it turned as black as it had been in youth. Then he rolled it with the curling iron into soft waves, stepped back and admired his handiwork.

"All that's left," he said, "is to freshen up the complexion a bit."

He went about, with ever renewed solicitude, moving from one task to another the way a person does who can never finish anything and is never satisfied. Aschenbach, resting comfortably, was in any case quite incapable of fending him off. Actually he was rather excited about what was happening, watching in the mirror as his brows took on a more decisive and symmetrical arch and his eyes grew in width and brilliance with the addition of a little shadow on the lids. A little further down he could see his skin, previously brown and leathery, perk up with a light application of delicate carmine rouge, his lips, pale and bloodless only a moment a ago, swell like raspberries, the furrows in his cheeks and mouth, the wrinkles around his eyes give way to a dab of cream and the glow of youth. His heart pounded as he saw in the mirror a young man in full bloom. The cosmetic artist finally pronounced himself satisfied and thanked the object of his ministrations with fawning politeness, the way such people do. "A minor repair job," he said as he put a final touch to Aschenbach's appearance. "Now, sir, you can go and fall in love without second thoughts." The beguiled lover went out, happy as in a dream, yet confused and timid. His tie was red, and his broad-brimmed straw hat was encircled by a band of many colors.

A tepid breeze had come up; it rained only seldom and then not hard, but the air was humid, thick, and full of the stench of decay. Rustling, rushing, and flapping sounds filled his ears. He burned with fever beneath his makeup, and it seemed to him that the air was filled with vile, evil wind-spirits, impure winged sea creatures who raked over, gnawed over, and defiled with garbage the meals of their victim.[1] For the sultry weather ruined one's appetite, and one could not suppress the idea that all the food was poisoned with infection.

Trailing the lovely boy one afternoon, Aschenbach had penetrated deep into the maze in the heart of the diseased city. He had lost his sense of direction, for the little streets, canals, bridges, and piazzas in the labyrinth all looked alike. He could no longer even tell east from west, since his only concern had been not to lose sight of the figure he pursued so ardently. He was compelled to a disgraceful sort of discretion that involved clinging to walls and seeking protection behind the backs of passersby, and so he did not for some time become conscious of the fatigue, the exhaustion which a high pitch of emotion and continual tension had inflicted on his body and spirit. Tadzio walked behind the rest of his family. In these narrow streets he would generally let the governess and the nunlike sisters go first, while he sauntered along by himself, occasionally turning his head to assure himself with a quick glance of his extraordinary dawn-gray eyes over his shoulder that his lover was still following. He saw him, and he did not betray him. Intoxicated by this discovery, lured onward by those eyes, tied to the apron string of his own passion, the lovesick traveler stole forth in pursuit of his unseemly hope—but ultimately found himself disappointed. The Polish family had gone across a tightly arched bridge, and the height of the arch had hidden them from their pursuer. When he was at last able to cross, he could no longer find them. He searched for them in three directions—straight ahead and to both sides along the narrow, dirty landing—but in vain. He finally had to give up, too debilitated and unnerved to go on.

1. The harpies, wind spirits, of classical legend, often described as snatching things. Mann refers here particularly to the legend of Phineus, whom the harpies plagued by stealing and defiling his food.

His head was burning hot, his body was sticky with sweat, the scruff of his neck was tingling, an unbearable thirst assaulted him, and he looked about for immediate refreshment of any sort. In front of a small greengrocer's shop he bought some fruit, strawberries that were overripe and soft, and he ate them while he walked. A little piazza that was quite deserted and seemed enchanted opened out before him. He recognized it, for it was here that weeks ago he had made his thwarted plan to flee the city. He collapsed on the steps of the well in the very middle of the plaza and rested his head on the stone rim. It was quiet, grass grew between the paving stones, refuse lay strewn about. Among the weathered buildings of varying heights around the periphery was one that looked rather palatial. It had Gothic-arched windows, now gaping emptily, and little balconies decorated with lions. On the ground floor of another there was a pharmacy. Warm gusts of wind from time to time carried the smell of carbolic acid.

He sat there, the master, the artist who had attained to dignity, the author of the "Man of Misery," that exemplary work which had with clarity of form renounced bohemianism and the gloomy murky depths, had condemned sympathy for the abyss, reviled the vile. There he sat, the great success who had overcome knowledge and outgrown every sort of irony, who had accustomed himself to the obligations imposed by the confidence of his large audience. There he sat, the author whose greatness had been officially recognized and whose name bore the title of nobility, the author whose style children were encouraged to emulate—sat there with his eyes shut, though from time to time a mocking and embarrassed look would slip sidelong out from underneath his lids, only to conceal itself again swiftly; and his slack, cosmetically enhanced lips formed occasional words that emerged out of the strange dream-logic engendered in his half-dozing brain.

"For beauty, Phaedrus—mark me well—only beauty is both divine and visible at the same time, and thus it is the way of the senses, the way of the artist, little Phaedrus, to the spirit.[2] But do you suppose, my dear boy, that anyone could ever attain to wisdom and genuine manly honor by taking a path to the spirit that leads through the senses? Or do you rather suppose (I leave the decision entirely up to you) that this is a dangerously delightful path, really a path of error and sin that necessarily leads astray? For you must know that we poets cannot walk the path of beauty without Eros joining our company and even making himself our leader; indeed, heroes though we may be after our own fashion, disciplined warriors though we may be, still we are as women, for passion is our exaltation, and our longing must ever be for love. That is our bliss and our shame. Do you see, then, that we poets can be neither wise

2. Aschenbach's fantasy is based on Plato's *Phaedrus*, esp. section 250d ff. Plato does not deal explicitly with the question of the artist in this passage, but in another (245a) Socrates argues that madness is necessary to enter the gates of poetry.

nor honorable, that we necessarily go astray, that we necessarily remain dissolute adventurers of emotion? The masterly demeanor of our style is a lie and a folly, our fame and our honor a sham, the confidence accorded us by our public utterly ridiculous, the education of the populace and of the young by means of art a risky enterprise that ought not to be allowed. For how can a person succeed in educating others who has an inborn, irremediable, and natural affinity for the abyss? We may well deny it and achieve a certain dignity, but wherever we may turn that affinity abides. Let us say we renounce analytical knowledge; for knowledge, Phaedrus, has neither dignity nor discipline; it is knowing, understanding, forgiving, formless and unrestrained; it has sympathy for the abyss; it *is* the abyss. Let us therefore resolutely reject it, and henceforth our efforts will be directed only toward beauty, that is to say toward simplicity, grandeur, and a new discipline, toward reborn ingenuousness and toward form. But form and ingenuousness, Phaedrus, lead to intoxication and to desire, might lead the noble soul to horrible emotional outrages that his own lovely discipline would reject as infamous, lead him to the abyss. Yes, they too lead to the abyss. They lead us poets there, I say, because we are capable not of resolution but only of dissolution. And now I shall depart, Phaedrus; but you stay here until you can no longer see me, and then you depart as well."

A few days afterwards Gustav von Aschenbach left the hotel at a later hour than usual, since he was feeling unwell. He was struggling with certain attacks of dizziness that were only partly physical and were accompanied by a powerfully escalating sense of anxiety and indecision, a 'feeling of having no prospects and no way out. He was not at all sure whether these feelings concerned the outside world or his own existence. He noticed in the lobby a great pile of luggage prepared for departure, and when he asked the doorman who was leaving, he received for an answer the aristocratic Polish name he had in his heart been expecting to hear all along. He took it in with no change in the expression on his ravaged face, briefly raising his head as people do to acknowledge casually the receipt of a piece of information they do not need, and asked, "When?" The answer came: "After lunch." He nodded and went to the beach.

It was dreary there. Rippling tremors crossed from near to far on the wide, flat stretch of water between the beach and the first extended sandbar. Where so recently there had been color, life, and joy, it was now almost deserted, and an autumnal mood prevailed, a feeling that the season was past its prime. The sand was no longer kept clean. A camera with no photographer to operate it stood on its tripod at the edge of the sea, a black cloth that covered it fluttering with a snapping noise in a wind that now blew colder.

Tadzio and three or four playmates that still remained were active in front of his family's cabana to Aschenbach's right; and, resting in his beach chair approximately halfway between the ocean and the row of cabanas, with a blanket over his legs, Aschenbach watched him once more. Their play was unsupervised, since the women must have been busy with preparations for their departure. The game seemed to have no rules and quickly degenerated. The sturdy boy with the belted suit and the black, slicked-down hair who was called Yashu, angered and blinded by sand thrown in his face, forced Tadzio into a wrestling match, which ended swiftly with the defeat of the weaker, lovely boy. It seemed as if in the last moments before leave-taking the subservient feelings of the underling turned to vindictive cruelty as he sought to take revenge for a long period of slavery. The winner would not release his defeated opponent but instead kneeled on his back and pushed his face in the sand, persisting for so long that Tadzio, already out of breath from the fight, seemed in danger of suffocating. He made spasmodic attempts to shake off his oppressor, lay still for whole moments, then tried again with no more than a twitch. Horrified, Aschenbach wanted to spring to the rescue, but then the bully finally released his victim. Tadzio was very pale; he got up halfway and sat motionless for several minutes supported on one arm, his hair disheveled and his eyes darkening. Then he rose to his feet and slowly walked away. They called to him, cheerfully at first but then with pleading timidity. He paid no attention. The black-haired boy, apparently instantly regretting his transgression, caught up with him and tried to make up. A jerk of a lovely shoulder put him off. Tadzio crossed diagonally down to the water. He was barefoot and wore his striped linen suit with the red bow.

He lingered at the edge of the sea with his head hung down, drawing figures in the wet sand with his toe. Then he went into the shallows, which at their deepest point did not wet his knees, strode through them, and progressed idly to the sandbar. Upon reaching it he stood for a moment, his face turned to the open sea, then began to walk slowly to the left along the narrow stretch of uncovered ground. Separated from the mainland by the broad expanse of water, separated from his mates by a proud mood, he strode forth, a highly remote and isolated apparition with wind-blown hair, wandering about out there in the sea, in the wind, on the edge of the misty boundlessness. Once more he stopped to gaze outward. Suddenly, as if prompted by a memory or an impulse, he rotated his upper body in a lovely turn out of its basic posture, his hand resting on his hip, and looked over his shoulder toward the shore. The observer sat there as he had sat once before, when for the first time he had met the gaze of those dawn-gray eyes cast back at him from that threshold. His head, resting on the back of the chair, had slowly followed the movements of the one who was striding about out there; now his head rose as if returning the gaze, then sank on his chest so that his eyes looked out from beneath. His face took on the slack, intimately

symbol of death

absorbed expression of deep sleep. It seemed to him, though, as if the pale and charming psychagogue[3] out there were smiling at him, beckoning to him; as if, lifting his hand from his hip, he were pointing outwards, hovering before him in an immensity full of promise. And, as so often before, he arose to follow him.

Minutes passed before anyone rushed to the aid of the man who had collapsed to one side in his chair. They carried him to his room. And later that same day a respectfully shaken world received the news of his death.

for narrator – like biography Ch. 2

---

3. Leader of souls (to the underworld), a title of the Greek god Hermes.

BACKGROUNDS AND CONTEXTS

A Map of Munich, ca. 1910 †

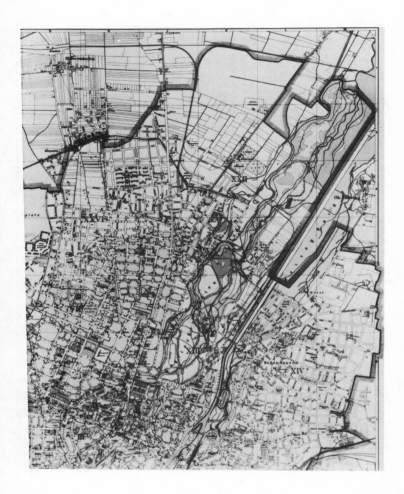

† Oscar Brunn's Plan von München, ca. 1910. Courtesy of the Geography and Map Division, Library of Congress.

A Map of Venice, ca. 1911 †

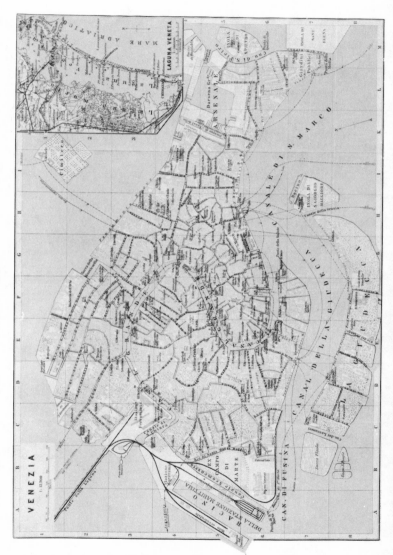

A Map of the Lido, ca. 1911 †

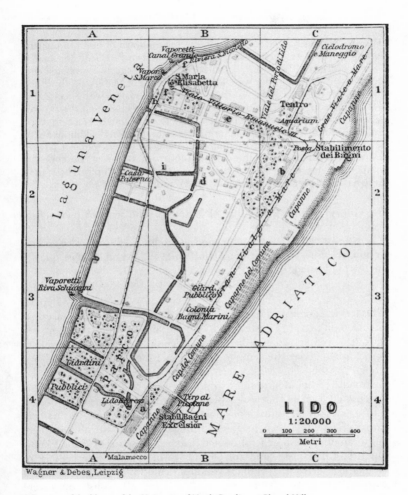

THOMAS MANN

Working Notes for *Death in Venice*†

[Thomas Mann's regular habit was to assemble a sheaf of notes in preparation for a major writing project, and he followed this habit in the case of *Death in Venice*. These working notes consist of 31 sheets, numbered consecutively in the order they were found at the time of Mann's death. (Sheet number 1 is simply a cover, so that the actual notes begin with sheet 2.)

The following conventions have been used in transcribing these notes: material added later by Mann himself is enclosed in square brackets; words underlined in the manuscript are printed in italics; editorial additions are set in angled brackets. Various marks were made by Mann (often a large X beside, or a diagonal line through, a line or lines) during the course of composition, usually to indicate that the material in question had been used; these have not been retained in this transcription.]

⟨2⟩   Tadzio's smile is like that of Narcissus who sees his own reflection—he sees it on the face of the other

he sees his beauty in the impressions it produces. There is also coquetry and tenderness in this reciprocating smile with which Narcissus kisses the lips of his shadow.

⟨3⟩   Paris, July 2, 1911
Dear Mr. Tommy, Please forgive me that the answer has taken so long. I didn't dare to write you a definite answer and wanted first to consult a well-known Polish woman. I could never reach the girl at home; finally today she came to me and said the same thing that I had thought myself. That which seemed to you to be "Adgu" is "Tadzio" (German "Tadschio"), a short form of a very beautiful Polish name: Tadeusch (German Tadeusch) vocative: "Tadziu."

In a work by the great Polish poet Adam Mickiewicz, the hero is named *"Tadeusz,"* then in 1794, during the Polish Revolution there was a famous Polish general named Tadeusz Kosciuzko. I don't know which German first name corresponds to or roughly translates it; in French it is "Thadée." Perhaps you also heard *"Wladzio"* being called (a short form of *Wladyslaw*, French *"Ladyslas"* ⟨⟩). Polish kings were given this name, but Tadeusz is much more beautiful. "Adgu" doesn't even exist, might be a short form of *Adam*, but is a very boring name. That's all that I can tell you. If you need any kind of information, I'm gladly at your disposal. Please excuse the mistakes in my German.

† From Thomas Mann, *"Der Tod in Venedig." Text, Materialen, Kommentar,* ed. T. J. Reed (Munich: Hanser, 1983) 86–120. Reprinted by permission of S. Fischer Verlag GmbH, Frankfurt am Main. Translated by Lynda Hoffman Jeep. Sheets 1 through 30 are preserved in the Thomas Mann Archive in Zurich; sheet 31 is part of the Mann collection of the Yale University library.

When am I coming to Munich? I would like to come soon, but I hope
not sooner than the fall because I have to go somewhere now, where I
can paint without being troubled. Greetings to you and Katia. Best
wishes to you both.

Sincerely yours,
Olga Meerson
3 rue Schoelcher

⟨4⟩   *References from Chapter II to V*
Ancestors, brave at work
Love of fame and *capacity* for fame
Endure. Training. Service as a soldier. Under the
stress of great works. The nevertheless.
Ascent from problems to dignity. And now! The conflict is: beginning
from "dignity," from an enmity to knowledge and second state of ease,
from an antianalytical state he falls into *this* passion. The form is the
sin. The surface is the abyss. How very much will art again become a
problem for the artist who has become worthy of dignity! Eros is [for the
artist] the guide to that which is intellectual, to spiritual beauty, the road
to the highest passes for him through the senses. But that is a dangerously charming road, a wrong [way] = and sinful way, even though
there is no other one. "Poets will always be denied such an impetus.
Their impetus is always tragedy. In *life* (and the artist is a man of life!)
longing must always remain *love*: that is longing's good fortune and tragedy." Understanding, that the artist *cannot* be worthy of dignity, [that
he necessarily goes the wrong way] remains a Bohemian [gypsy, liber-
tine] and an eternal adventurer of the emotions. The tone of his style
seems to him to be a lie and buffoonery; a most laughable order, honor
and nobility. Dignity is saved solely by death (the "tragedy," the
"ocean,"—counsel, [escape] and refuge from all higher forms of love. ⟨⟩⟩
    The fame of the artist a farce, the mass reliance on him stupidity,
education through

⟨5⟩   art a daring undertaking to be outlawed. Ironic that the boys read
him. Irony of officialdom, of ennoblement.

Finally: State of effeminacy, enervation, demoralization.

⟨6⟩   Myrrha

"only beauty is at once visible (sensually perceptible, sensually [as true]
bearable) *and* amiable, i.e., part of that which is godly, part of eternal
harmony. It is the only amiable thing that is visible, sensually perceptible, sensually tolerable. By the rest we would be sensually destroyed like
Semele. Therefore beauty is the way of the sensual person, of the artist

to "amiability," godliness, eternity, harmony, to the intellectual, the
pure, the ideal, the *moral:* the only way and—a dangerous way, that
almost necessarily leads one astray, that leads to confusion. Love of
beauty leads to morality, to a renunciation of sympathy with the abyss,
to psychology, analysis ⟨added below⟩ [i.e. to the affirmation of passion
and of life]; leads to simplicity, greatness and beautiful severity, to
reborn naturalness, to form, but just with this leads again to the abyss.

What is moral? *Analysis?* (The destruction of passion?) Passion does
not possess severity, it is knowing, understanding, forgiving, without
tone and form. Passion has sympathy for the abyss [it *is* the abyss]. Or
the *form?* The love of beauty? But it leads to intoxication, to desire, and
therefore likewise to the abyss.

⟨7⟩   *Harpies:* horribly gaunt. They quickly flew in, falling upon all the
food with insatiable gluttony, fed, unable to become satiated, and *defiled*
what they left behind with their ordure. Shriveled up and withered,
usually with the face of a girl, rough ears, the body of a bird and sharp
claws, also even with their head decorated with a crown and a tuft.
Poets give them long, thin hands with iron claws, a bird's head, wings,
feathered body, human legs and the feet of a chicken.

They devour the food out of the mouths of the condemned, or defile
it to such an extent as to make it unpalatable. It was in this manner that
King Phineus of Bithynia was plagued, because he had the eyes of his
children from his first marriage poked out and set them out for the wild
animals. Banished by his clan, they lived on the Strofadian Islands:

"Virginal, the birds' face————
————also the clawed hands, and full of hunger
   the countenance
Always pale."

"Suddenly with a horribly rushing plunge from the cliff
The Harpies approach and wave their wings with echoing
sounds,
And they plunder the feast and defile everything with ordure,
Ransacked; their shrieks sound monstrous to the last breath."

"Again from other expanses of the air and from hidden nooks
Sounds the swarm and encircles the prey with clawed talons,
And they desecrate the meal with their mouths.————
————The gruesome breed
————The malevolent birds of the sea.
————it thunders in speedy flight to the ether
Leaving gnawed-upon spoils and filthy tracks

⟨8⟩   *Elysian Fields,* on the border of the earth where "an easy life is
bestowed upon man," (It never snows there, there is never winter or

storm nor pouring rain, but rather the lightly breathing breath of the west rises from distant Oceanus, that he may bring freshness to man.)

Harpies, wind spirits.

Tithonus, husband of *Aurora:* from his side the goddess of the dawn arises, to bring the light of day to gods and men. The distant dwelling places on the Ocean river, from where she arises in the morning.

Idyll in Elysium. A state of delight under the mildest of heavens; care-free, life there is easy, in this respect similar to the life of the gods, but without aspiration or deed.

Insanity as a correlation of measure and form. Known to the Greeks: during the period of its fullest development *insanity* ($\mu\alpha\nu\iota\alpha$), a tempo-rary disturbance of psychological balance, a state of the overwhelming of the self-conscious spirit, a state of *possession* by foreign powers, achieved wide recognition as a religious phenomenon. Greek religious life corresponds to this overflowing of feeling as the opposite pole: the composure expressed in quiet measure, with which heart and vision lift themselves towards the gods.

The home of the Dionysian cult is in *Trace*. Here in mountain heights *at night, by torchlight*. Noisy music, *blaring bronze cymbals, thundering great handdrums and the deep sounding flutes, whose har-mony entices one to insanity*. The revelers dance with clear shouts of joy, in a raving, twirling, lurching circular dance; they dance enthusias-tically across the fields. Mostly women, in long flowing gowns, made of fox skins or covered with deer hides, with horns on their heads, too, with streaming hair, snakes in their hands, *and swinging daggers or thyr-sus staffs, that hide the points of the lances under the ivy. They rage to the utmost*, finally throwing themselves upon the animal that has been chosen as their victim, hashing and tearing and biting into the bloody flesh with their teeth, that they devour raw. Etcetera. The objective is mania, overexcitement of the being, ecstasy, overstimulation of percep-tion to the point of visionary states. Only by means of overexcitement and widening of his being can man enter into correspondence with the god and his swarm of spirits. *The god is invisibly present or at least near, and the din of the feast is supposed to pull him all the way in.*

Ecstasy. Hieromania, in which the soul, having escaped from the body, unites with the godly. The soul is now with and in the god, in the state of *enthusiasm*.

The mystic Dschelaleddin Rumi: "Whoever knows the power of the dance, lives in God; for he knows how love kills. Allah hu!"

Eos steals or kidnaps, besides *Tithonus* (offspring of the old Trojan royal family), also the handsome *Orion* and enjoys his love in spite of the envy of the other gods. Furthermore she also steals *Cleitus* because of his beauty, a young man from the line of the seer Melampus, in order to be able to live among the gods. Also *Cephalus* (King Deionus of Thessaly). She spied him while he was hunting in the early morning, fell in love with him and carried him off to some distant mountains.

⟨9⟩   *Ganymede*, Tros' son, king of Troy, a youth of such beauty that Zeus elected to place him among the heavenly gods. Once while Ganymede was pasturing his father's herds on Mount Ida, Zeus descended upon him in the form of a giant eagle and carried him, gently suspended, up to the clouds.

Hyacinth, Apollo's favorite. The god forgot because of him to tend to Delphi, to play the cithara and to span his bow. Zephyr, because he was jealous, directed the discus thrown by Apollo in such a way that it killed the young man. His blood becomes a flower.

Blissful liveliness of nature: Each gentle being reminds one of higher animation. The great and mighty daemonic powers are from the heavenly clouds, the woolly clouds become herds of cows, lambs and goats, which belong to gods. The ocean waves flowing in and carrying, are horses and bulls (roaring and bowing their horns), the goats leaping between the rocks and cliffs of surging waves.

Apollo [the Delish god] is the pure god of light, but at the same time the horrible sender of epidemics and a quick death. Poseidon, fortifier of the earth, but also shaker of the earth (Earthquake).

Demon, as a designation for the superior powers as a group, especially when one believed that the deity may be credited with anything detrimental, namely a *human infatuation with evil* even of a satanic kind.
     The demon who drives the one *striving for nobility in the direction of error* and offense is the deity itself.

Dionysius: His significance is not exhausted with ecstasy from wine and intoxication; he carries completely different excitations with him and therefore corresponds to a large facet of life in antiquity, even to human nature in general, concerning which the ancients never spoke clearly.
     In the mask of the Hellenistic fertility god a semi-foreign being is expressed. One of the personifications of the "suffering" (dying and reviving) god, whose cult was celebrated with excited laments and jubilation, had taken on an especially wild, intoxicating behavior in Asia Minor, and was substituted for the Greek Dionysus through repeated

contact with Hellas. The god is portrayed as a *foreigner, invading from without by force*. He is the son or escort of the Phrygian mother of the gods, who likewise had forced her way into Greece *(Cybele)*. "She likes the noise of the bells and handdrums and the sound of flutes and the howling of the wolves and the gleaming-eyed lions and echoing mountains and woody canyons" (Homer).—And with just as wild an army now even this Dionysus moves on, and like the goddess, *he also inflicts insanity*. Not only those who insult the servants of the mother of the gods (Corybantes), but also *whoever views the celebration of the mysteries* or enters (without being summoned) into her holy—

⟨10⟩   place. The wine god's *"swarm," joined by the inhabitants of an entire city*, may well be in a most enraptured state, whose festivities may (later) take on the richest form, the portrayal of his myth becoming the motive for tragedy and comedy:—*behind this looms an unearthly spirit*, who in the myth not only drives his blinded Maenads to all kinds of atrocities, but also in his time demanded human sacrifice here and there and sent insanity and fatal illnesses when he was not paid homage. It was told how at one time in Calydon *death and insanity* had begun to carry away all the inhabitants, because the love of a Dionysian priest had not been accepted. This only half-Greek Dionysus differs from all of the other gods first in that he appears as a newly arrived foreigner and second in that he demands fanatical homage and acknowledgment. Probably wild "swarms" were formed in an Anatolian manner that really murdered those who did not go along with them. In the myth everyone who defies this god suffers the most horrific punishments *(murderous frenzy)*. But even those who immediately paid homage suffered in the end, as though Dionysus' horrible side had to prevail again and again.

With this experience he gives up what remains of his power, ability to intoxicate, all at once. Runs off crazed.

⟨11⟩   *Plutarch*

Amor's temple in Thespiae.

"For Amor loves idleness; it is only that for which he is made—"

Mercury was supposed to lead the souls into the underworld and was then named psychagogos and psychopompos.

Amor, relative of Venus, the Muses and the Graces, who, as a poet said, "Scatter the early seeds of love in man's breast."

Enthusiasm: composed of en and theos, means the accommodation of the deity. *Types:*
  Insanity (Apollo)
  Bacchic
    Pertaining to the Muses
    Warlike
    Love

Frenzy of Love: When one is seized by this, then no Muse, no gentle song, no change of setting is capable of calming it. Such a person loves the object that sets him on fire when it is near and longs for him when he is gone. *During the day he follows him continuously, at night he keeps watch at his door.* One usually says the hallucinations of the poets are dreams of the waking, but because of their liveliness, this holds much truer for the hallucinations of lovers, who speak to, caress and *call their lovers by name* as though they were present.

⟨12⟩   In Chalcis at the market place the tomb of the [Pharsalian] Cleomachus, who won a victory against the Chalcidians and died, all this viewed by his lover (favorite). The Chalcidians, who previously abhorred pederasty, began after this incident to value it highly and to honor it. There they sing: "Charming boys, gallant nature's offspring, do not begrudge high-born men the pleasure of your blossoming." For it is through *gallantry* that Amor blossoms, the pleasure-giver in the cities of the Chalcidians.

The bravest peoples, the Boeotians, the Lacedaemonians, the Cretans were most devoted to love, in like manner many of the old heroes, for example Meleager, Achilles, Aristomenes, Cimon, Epaminondas. *The latter died with his favorite, Kaphisodorus, near Manineia and lies buried next to him there.*

Hercules had so many "love affairs" that it is difficult to list them all. Admetus loved his wife Alcestis and was his favorite at the same time. *Apollo, too, was supposed to have been one of Admetus' lovers and for this reason served him an entire year without payment.*

Amor teaches you
"Music and even if you were unskilled at it."
(Euripides)

  "Doesn't this testify to divine enthusiasm, that the lover, who practically disdains everything else, not only his friends and relatives, but also laws, authorities and kings, who fears nothing, admires or flatters no one, is even capable himself of "opposing the crashing bolt of lightening" (Pindar), ⟨doesn't it further testify⟩ that this same one, nevertheless, as soon as he views the object of his love, *"is thunderstruck, like the rooster who fearfully drops his wings in a fight,"* that his courage is broken and his proud bearing completely pushed to the ground?

Many still see the same body and the same beauty, but it is only the lover who is captivated by it and this necessitates a special disposition of the soul.—No, *the god himself is the cause,* who touches the one and leaves the other alone."

⟨13⟩ *"Crossing over the loudly raging Acheron."* (Poetic)

"As poorly as an inexperienced body can endure the sun, just as poorly can love tolerate an uneducated soul without discomfort."
The sun turns our power of thought from intellectual to sensual things. It bewitches us by the beauty and glow of its appearance and convinces us that everything, even truth itself, is not to be searched for anywhere else but in the sun itself. Ignorant and forgetful of another life. In the same manner that daylight causes one to forget nightly dreams, the sun bewitches and numbs memory and understanding, to such an extent that out of joy and admiration we forget everything intellectual. And nevertheless it is only in the intellectual world that the soul can come to know the true nature of things. As soon as it reaches this point it remains fixed, in a state of surprised admiration, on the beautiful and divine object. Then the soul believes that everything here below is beautiful and valuable, even if a divine, virtuous love does not serve her as physician and savior, who physically approaches her and guides her, as though out of the underworld, to truth and to the realm of truth, into *the sojourn of absolute, pure and guileless beauty,* whose *embrace and more familiar company* she has so long desired. Amor himself, like a *mystagogue,* leads the soul into the holy place and lifts it up to observe the elevated objects. *She can only approach these objects in life with the help of a physical body.* Just as the mathematicians make visible and touchable pictures of spheres, cubes and dodecahedrons to show to children who are not yet capable of understanding the abstract forms of incorporeal and immutable substance, so it is that the sensual Amor creates for us *beautiful mirrors* of *beautiful objects.* In order to make the divine and intellectual visible to us he makes use of mortal and mutable beings, especially the shapes, colors, and forms of young people, who are ornamented with the glow of beauty, achieving gradually, through these means, the most lively remembrance of objects once seen.—Only those who, through wise use of reason and with the help of modesty, take away the fire of all too intense ardour and leave the soul with only its glow, light and warmth, experience, as Epicure says, not the raging

impulse for coition,—but only an *admirable and fertile extension, like that of upward growing plants.*

"The mightiest of the gods bore the beautifully shod Iris, embraced by the golden curled Zephyr."

"The *rainbow* is nothing more than a refraction of our face when it is fixed upon a moist cloud, which touches the broken rays of the sun and upon viewing the shimmering light awakens in us the belief that the image exists in the cloud itself. The device that Amor employs for good-natured souls who love the beautiful is precisely of this kind. A person inspired by a respectable and virtuous love devotes all of his thoughts to that divine and *spiritual beauty* and uses the beauty of a visible body only as a tool of memory; in this way he loves and admires it, finds great pleasure in associating with it and becomes more and more inflamed for the spiritual through it."

"Just as it was of old in Rome that when a dictator was nominated all other town councillors were obliged to give up their positions, so it was with those for whom Amor had become master: they were then freed from the control of every other master and loved, *like the temple servants,* in complete independence."

⟨14⟩ *Plato*

says there is a kind of madness that does not arise without divine influence, a rapture and inversion of reason and judgment [this condition is referred to as enthusiasm], whose origin and movement is derived from a higher power.

Socrates to the beautiful Agathon: "I believe, being near you, that I can become full of your mature and beautiful wisdom. Because my wisdom is meager and uncertain, uncertain like a dream. Your wisdom, on the contrary, glows and has a light trajectory. You are still so young and your trajectory shown yesterday in front of more than thirty thousand Greeks!"

"For the friend is more divine than the lover. The friend carries the god within him."

"And so is Eros also and every act of love in itself, in general neither something noble nor worthy of being praised, but rather only he is worthy of praise, who knows how to love nobly."

In *Elis* and *Boeotia*, everywhere where people are not glib, the lover's submission to the friend is understood, because the lover doesn't first have to be cajoled, which is what the people there are incapable of. In Ionia, by contrast, and everywhere where there are barbarians our love is simply considered a disgrace. The tyrants condemn it, because they condemn philosophy and the physical education of the body. In both cases the baseness of the point of view is obvious. They are unrefined. In Athens they are, on the one hand, very lenient, so that one is supposed to believe that it is considered there to be extremely noble to love and to be loved.

Custom gives the lover certain freedoms to do that which is most amazing to everyone's applause, things, for example, that would disgrace him if they served another purpose: begging and imploring, taking oaths and lying down in front of doors, in other words behaving more bastardly than the last slave; one would accuse him of crawling and cowardliness. The lover is accompanied by everyone's goodwill, he can do anything, he even behaves especially audaciously.—On the other hand great severity and fatherly reserve of young people so that love appears to be a disgrace.

⟨15⟩   Custom wants to test fidelity and superior conviction; for this reason it demands that the lover should flee and demands that his friends should lie in wait for him. For this reason it is considered base to let oneself be caught easily and quickly. The superiority of the Athenians lies in knowing that in reality nothing is good or bad, but rather that it depends on whether one gives into the base, the adept student of physical love, or gives into that which is noble.

"For once was our nature thus: we were not whole, and the desire for the whole is Eros."

From Agathon's speech: "Thus the god is young and his figure is delicate. . . . Wherever he encounters an unyielding disposition Eros flees, and he will only while in a gentle soul. . . . [Eros] Therefore he must himself be *the most gentle being* . . . and Eros is also *supple.* . . . Eros is *well-proportioned,* and his beautiful deportment shows it, and this distinguishes, as we know, the god above all. . . . Eros has a beautiful color because he lives from blossoms. Wherever bodies and souls do not bloom or where they lose blossoms he does not go, and only where there is blooming and fragrance does Eros rest, there the god whiles.——And finally, do we not know *that also in the command of the arts only he shines and will be admired who has been taught by Eros,* and that everyone will remain in the shadows and without fame who the god has not enchanted?——*Where we will all meet again, to that place Eros leads the way.*——Eros is the creator of all human tenderness, richness, grace and longing.—In all labor, in every fear and every desire, *with each word*—he knows how to guide securely, there Eros is assistance and the savior."

From the teachings of Diotima from Mantineia to Socrates: Poverty thought, because I am poor I want to have a child by Wealth, and Poverty lay down with Wealth and bore Eros from him. This happened on Aphrodite's birthday, and therefore Eros is from

⟨16⟩ Nature in love with everything beautiful. But as the son of Wealth and Poverty he has the nature and mark of both. (*Symposium* 51–52)

". . . and so in view of this multiple beauty no longer desire, like a slave, the beauty of this one boy and require the beauty of this one individual and be vulgar and petty, . . . but *brought to the shore of the great ocean of beauty*, create here many noble words and thoughts with the *endless urge for wisdom*, until strong and mature he then views each individual bit of knowledge, that there is the knowledge of beauty. . . . Yes, Socrates, whoever from below begins to rise up and begins to view that eternal beauty, because he knew how to love the beloved correctly, *he has reached the end and is complete and blessed.*

"First he will learn beauty from everything and approach that eternal beauty in steps, Socrates, like climbing steps, steps. On the first step he sees the beauty of a body, on the second the beauty of two bodies, and then he sees the beauty of all bodies, and from the beautiful morals to the beautiful teachings the last step carries him to that single science, which encompasses there the eternal beauty. . . . When you view this it will not appear to you like gold or beautiful clothing or like those beautiful young boys or youths, *whose appearance shocks even you and the others, and with whom you want to remain forever, remain without eating or drinking, just gazing at them, only present in their minds . . .* And don't you believe that man will only achieve perfection where he sees beauty in his soul and no longer views the images of virtue— because his eye can no longer fix upon images—rather truth itself, because he views it there, creates . . . that in order to reach the highest good, no one could choose a better guide than Eros."

⟨17⟩ [Fame and Procreation]
". . . Don't wonder any longer why all of nature loves and honors its own blood: nature does so because of immortality, for which it strives!

When you think about man's ambition, you would have to marvel at his senselessness if you didn't think about my words and remember *how strongly man is possessed by the desire to become famous and to maintain fame into eternity. And how, for this reason, people do more for fame than for their children, seek danger, . . . endure pain, are even prepared to die.* Do you think that they would do it if they did not believe in the eternal memory of the great love that we still have for them today? Oh no. For the virtue of immortality and for glowing fame they and everyone else have done everything. For people love immortality more than anything else. *Whoever wants to procreate in the body is drawn to women,* and it is the children who should transport immortality, memory and luck into the future for him. Besides this one, however, are those others *who want to procreate in the soul that which the soul should conceive and bear, i.e., insight and virtue.* And in this sense *all poets are procreators,* and those who are considered in the trade to be inventors and who create the highest and most beautiful understanding, with that I mean the standard and justice in their souls, in this respect knowing how to maintain the state and the family. . . . Then he goes out and searches for the beautiful in which his seed will be fertilized . . . And who would prefer having his own biological children over this race, when he considers Homer and Hesiod and aspires to the other noble poets, who have left behind a race that provides them with eternal fame and continual remembrance. Or when one considers Lycurgus's children, the laws that he bequeathed . . . *All of the many men who have created virtue with their noble deeds are honored in Hellas and among the barbarians. And for the sake of these children the many altars have been erected in thanks to them and never because of the race of their blood and name.*

Phaedrus. Whenever a man sees an earthly beauty, then he remembers true beauty and his wings grow and he wants to ascend to it again. . . . *And this is true for he who is possessed.* But I'm telling you, this godliness is real like no other.

Whenever they see an *image of eternal beauty here below, then they are frightened and beside themselves;* they don't know what has happened because their eyes are stupid and blind.

He who is not ordained or who is depraved does not easily achieve a view of beauty when he sees an earthly image. He is blind and doesn't know how to *show reverence* . . . yes, he doesn't shy away from lechery and stands shameless in the face of his unnatural desire. If, however, one who is ordained sees one of those *who have seen much on high, a countenance liken to that of a god, that reflects that great beauty,* or he who views the beautiful figure of a body, he trembles and a holy fear overcomes him like before. It is then that he first sees it and honors the youngster like a god. Yes, if he didn't want to avoid looking like a fool he would make a sacrifice to his beloved—like to a statue, to a god.

. . . And longingly the soul desires to go there where she believes it will be able to see him, *he who possesses beauty.*

⟨18⟩ The infinite balled up into one, absolute beauty standing upon the face of the earth, banned in one human form.—

Intoxication and worship.—
    He sees the eternal forms, beauty itself, the single basis from which every beautiful form issues forth.

The field of truth, the abode of the perfect, pure and guileless beauty whose embrace and intimate company he has so long desired.
    Like the manner in which mathematicians show forms, beautiful mirrors of beautiful objects, Amor makes that which is pure and intellectual visible through young people.
    A person inspired by respectable and virtuous love, directs all of his thoughts back to that divine and *intellectual* beauty and needs the beauty of a visible body as memory's tool.

G—just seeing her alone frightens you and the others and those with whom you want to stay forever, stay without eating and drinking, just seeing her, being near them.

Ph. Whenever they see an *image of eternal beauty* here below, they are frightened and beside themselves; they don't know what's happening to themselves, because their eyes are stupid and blind.
    He who is not ordained or depraved cannot easily view beauty when he sees an earthly image. He is blind and knows

⟨On the back of the page⟩

        Breeding   Nobility
    Proportion sober
staunch and pure will

⟨19⟩ not to be honored. If, however, one who is ordained sees one of those who have seen much on high, a countenance liken to that of a god, *that reflects that great beauty*, or if he views the beautiful figure of a body he trembles, and a holy fear overcomes him. . . . It is then that he first sees beauty and honors the youngster like a god. Yes, if he didn't want to avoid the appearance of looking like a fool he would make a sacrifice to his beloved—

Ph only beauty is simultaneously visible and adorable, i.e., it is the only intellectual form that is perceptible to the senses, that is tolerable to the senses. [Where] Therefore beauty is the artist's path, a means. The lover is more divine than the beloved and his knowledge of this fact is the source of all of love's irony.

(A part of the divine. In the presence of the rest, the sensual image of rationality, virtue, truth or even in the presence of the collective divine we would pine away and burn for love like Semele burned for Zeus.)

⟨20⟩   He remembers his puritanical ancestors while his passion is rising. What would they say? But what would they have said about his entire life [which in principle for that] about which he himself, in their spirit, had said such skeptical and ironic things,—and which, to be perfectly frank, was so similar to their life. He too had done strict and warlike service, and in the eyes of the bravest peoples Eros stood in high esteem.

Eros and *the word*. (With words—with them he certainly knows how to exert influence. The relationship of the eloquent Athenians to him. Work on the beach. ⟨⟩)

Only he is successful in art whom Eros has instructed. Even his art was sober service at the temple in Thespis. Eros has always resided within him. Tadzio was always his king. Even his love of fame was Eros.

⟨21⟩   And is considered to be one who is possessed.

    The noble one who sees the image of eternal beauty here below is frightened and beside himself.
    A godlike countenance that mirrors that great beauty.

Eos

Ganymede. Hyacinth.
Blessed liveliness of nature.

On the verge of speaking to him.

The smile in front of the balcony.

⟨22⟩   *Cholera asiatica*
The rate of mortality varies according to the magnitude of the epidemic and age etc. It reaches 60–70 percent. About half of the population is immune.
    From time immemorial the pestilence has been native to certain parts of East India. Since 1817 it has shown a conspicuous tendency toward dispersion and migration. In 1816 scattered small pockets of cholera formed at the mouth of the Ganges. In the ensuing century the disease *spread* over the entire peninsula; by 1818 it had *wandered across* all of India, *caused great damage* to the Indian-Chinese archipelago, *spread* itself 1820–21 over all of China and *pressed forward* across Persia in

1823 to Astrakhan. Proceeding from a new epidemic that broke out in
1826 in Bengal the cholera reached the banks of the Volga again in
1829, appeared in Astrakhan in 1830 and two months later in Moscow
and *held the reins of pestilence* over Europe by spreading across all of
European Russia, in 1831 spreading across Germany for the first time
as a disastrous disease and penetrating through to England and France
in 1832. In the same year in emigrant ships to America. Up until 1838
many small epidemics in Europe, then a complete break until 1846
when again a train of pestilence formed *in India* traveling over *Persia
and Syria* reaching the German borders in 1848 spreading then over
most of Europe and North America and up until 1859 causing various
epidemics throughout the entire northern hemisphere. A fourth epidemic *1865–75, distinguished itself from all of the earlier ones by its
peculiar development and the rapidity with which it reached Europe from
Asia*. While it otherwise always advanced from India via Afganistan,
Persia and Asian Russia to Europe and took more than a year to reach
the European borders, *this time it reached southern Europe in only a few
days by sea over the Arabian coast and covered a great part of Europe in
only a few weeks.*—A further epidemic broke out in 1884 in Toulon and
Marseille, spread to Italy, especially Naples, infested Spain in 1885
where it also appeared in 1890. Summer 1892 from Persia to Baku and
Astrakhan, covered almost all of Russia and August 1892 spread to
Hamburg, simultaneously in France (Paris, Le Havre, Rouen) and Bel-
gium (Antwerp). 1893, 94, 95 only sporadic cases in Europe.

Agreement for international measures against the spread of cholera at
the Hygiene Convention held in Dresden in 1893 and the preparation
of the German law concerning infectious diseases [1893] that was issued
in 1900.

Course of the Asiatic epidemic or Indian cholera: for days on end
exhaustion, digestive trouble, painless watery diarrhea; often, however,
the warning signals don't appear; it begins in a flash. Suddenly, usually
at night, stormy evacuation, only at the beginning, of a colored substance, soon consisting only of a watery substance. (Alkaline, countless
epitheliums from the small intestine, beads of fat, blood corpuscles,
triple phosphate crystals and countless bacteria, among them those that
carry the specific virus.) In addition profuse vomiting, first the contents
of the stomach and bile, then likewise a fluid similar to rice water. *In
the case of the so-called dry cholera (cholera sicca), an especially dangerous strain that seldom appears, the watery excretion does not occur
because the intestinal canal is temporarily paralyzed and not able to
expel the particles it has exuded.* With the occurrence of the watery
excretion excruciating thirst, considerable reduction in body temperature and pulse. Weak heartbeat, blue limbs, nose, ears and cold as a
corpse, the face wastes away, the eyes hollow, the voice hoarse and mute
(vox cholerica.) No discharge of urine. Painful cramps in the calves

and feet. This is called the "algid phase" (stadium algidum). Finally, occasionally with the reduction of the previous excretions, pulse and heartbeat disappear completely, and usually death ensues evidenced by general inanition (asphyxial cholera).—During the period of convalescence a strange febrile illness often occurs that takes a course similar to typhoid. (So-called choleratyphoid) that sometimes lasts for weeks and often proves fatal for the infected person. With this the patients perish, after a brief improvement, from uremia or sepsis.

Results of the autopsy: A liquid similar to rice water in the intestinal canal, also in the stomach, consisting of [excreted] bloody water that has been perspired in great quantities and countless rejected intestinal epitheliums. Intestinal lining inflamed, partially suffused with blood and robbed of its protective covering. Blood dark blue-red, coagulated, almost tough with a consistency of tar or pitch, accumulated in the heart, lacking in the capillary vessels so that the cellular tissue, muscles etc. are anaemic, dry, tough, unelastic, skin gray and wrinkled, serous skin sticky. During the process protein in the urine. *Hence: Excessive excretion of water from the blood vessels into the cavity of the intestinal track. Therefore, this viscid, slow moving blood is no longer capable of penetrating the fine capillary vessels. Consequently, the respiratory process falters: difficulty in breathing and alarm when choking.* Symptoms associated with the brain, because the brain does not receive enough nourishment due to poor circulation. *The viscid blood has greatly reduced moisture,* therefore all parts of the skin are lacking their usual fullness. *Blue color as a result of deficient breathing, in need of oxygen.*

During epidemics vibrios were often also found in the intestines of apparently healthy people who had come into contact with cholera patients; however, due to a greater individual immunity (except for mild diarrhea) are protected. These individuals are, however, just as dangerous for the spread of the disease as the severely ill, perhaps even more so because the pathogenic agents are spread by them unchecked.

Actual home east India, endemic especially to the Ganges delta. The rapid increase and acceleration of transport since the introduction of steamboats explains the extensive spread of the disease since the nineteenth century. Hardly a country has been spared, only [countries] areas in the mountains that have sparse trade and in the arctic zone. [Only] two *paths* especially important *for the spread:* The first one through central Asia following the main roads of the caravan trade to European Russia. *The second by the sea route to Mediterranean harbors.* Danger from sea trade very much in the foreground.

Type of diffusion: Often direct infection from infected individuals to healthy ones. Indirect infection especially through drinking water into which cholera defecation and vomit have been dumped. In Hamburg *30 percent of the population fell ill* because (in contrast to Altona, where well-filtered water is used) in Hamburg, unfiltered water was directed into the city. Several public institutions that were serviced by wells were spared. Direct infection relatively unusual, because the excreted bacilli have to enter the intestine of a healthy individual in a relatively fresh state otherwise they die. It's much different when excrement gets into the drinking water. Then the pathogenic agents are taken in by many individuals at once and explosive spreading occurs like in Hamburg. A city with good, centrally located waterworks often

⟨23⟩   ⟨Newspaper clipping: Picture of Gustav Mahler⟩

⟨Bild-Archiv der Österreichischen Nationalbibliothek, Wien.⟩

⟨24⟩   less responsive to the epidemic than a poor water system, a well-planned system of canals offers more protection because the excrement, the water from the home and the wash which contains countless pathogenic agents is immediately carried off. Introduction of the disease: It is usually a poor person who doesn't consult a doctor and therefore doesn't take precautionary measures. If there is a vegetable salesman or a milk saleswoman among those taken ill then comma bacilli can infect the wares so that the pinnacle of the outbreak would usually be in late summer because the water temperature of the river the highest—good for the bacilli. During this time of year digestive problems are prevalent whereby people are susceptible to infection. Affluence and density of the residential area play a large role in the spread. Absolute cordon, even with vigorous quarantine measures, is not possible. In addition, great detriment to trade. Limitation of examining people who come from cholera-infested areas, isolating those infected, observing the healthy ones over a longer period of time.

Treatment: First ricinus oil or calomel [mercurious chloride] as a purgative. Then opium. Infusions of table salt under the skin, between muscles, into the blood vessels, doses of one to two liters repeated every day, frequently stimulate the heart and increase urine secretion. Alcohols for the heart are regurgitated in serious cases.

Hamburg. Outbreak August. With exceptional swiftness across the entire city: On August 16th two cases, on the 16th, 1,024, on September 2nd, 561 died. Three million ⟨deutsche marks⟩ were granted for the fight. Already by the end of October 16,956 people were fading of whom 8,605 died. Land trade, even after the expiration, very much reduced, even more so sea trade. Afterwards extensive measures to improve health conditions: establishment of an Institute for Hygiene, rapid completion of the sand filter for the waterworks, revision of the police building law in which in new housing to be built provisions are made for light and air, law concerning housing maintenance, whereby the inhabiting of older, unhealthy housing is prevented and the use of lobby space as living quarters limited.

Venice (approximately 160,000 inhabitants) (Hamburg circa 800,000)

A large hospital (ospedale civico) in the former School di San Marco. A military hospital, psychiatric hospital on the San Sereilio and San Clemente islands. Two orphanages. Institutions for the housing, rescue and care of children.

A water main leads from the mainland into the city. Every two years international art exhibitions in the Giardini Publici. *San Michele:* the cemetery island.

Cholera in Venice: 1848, while Prime Minister Martini forced the defense of the city against Austrian blockade. The population suffered terribly from the bombardment, famine and *cholera*.

Hygiene:

According to the law from 1865, departments of health in Italy are under the Home Office; in each province there is a department of health, in each county and in the municipalities a health commission.

International standards for quarantine measures: prepared for the cholera at conventions, among those, that in Venice 1892. The countries have pledged immediate mutual notification when herds of cholera appear; furthermore, the type and extent of surveillance of infected people has been regulated, especially of infested or suspicious ships.

Quarantines: If they exhibit symptoms typical of cholera, affected individuals may be detained, others only (according to the customs revision) examined by a doctor. When traveling from an infected area, travelers will be subject to a 5-day-long health inspection by the police.

The *Ganges* flows into the Bengali Gulf forming, together with the Brahmaputra, the largest delta in the world. The southern section of the delta, a luxuriantly overgrown, *very unhealthy swamp and island labyrinth*, is called the *Sunderban.*

$$
\begin{array}{ll}
1911 & \\
\underline{-\ 53} & \\
1858 \text{ born} & \quad 1858 \\
& \quad \underline{\ \ 30} \\
& \quad 1888
\end{array}
$$

Honey-colored hair (darker than golden blond)

$$
\begin{array}{l}
17000{:}7 = 2428 \\
\underline{14} \\
\ \ \underline{30} \\
\ \ \ \underline{20} \\
\ \ \ \ \underline{60} \\
\ \ \ \ \ \underline{56} \\
\ \ \ \ \ \ \underline{4}
\end{array}
$$

⟨25⟩ The form similar to those of the mortals

Like balsam

Beautifully curled

For as in unpleasant form appears . . .

"Jewelry changed frequently and warm baths and quiet"
    (Concerning the Phaeacians)

The blue-curled Poseidon

> blossom
Grow [rampant], luxuriant, lavish,
voluptuous, wanton, lulling

⟨Reverse side⟩

Anguish   Torture   Pain

  Need   Grief

Conformity
Proportionate   Accommodating
Obedient

⟨26⟩   Development of his *style*: established in the classical, traditional, academic, conservative.

  In the cloisterlike quiet of external life extreme fastidiousness and vanity of the nerves due to art. (Also due to actual adventure: something bloody in Friedrich.)

An equal distance from the banal and the eccentric.

"Nevertheless." His works came about not only against his delicate nature, but also against his *spirit*, against skepticism, suspicion, cynicism, which stands against art and the artist himself, the heroic Hamlet.

No ignoble word, like Louis XIV.

Under the enduring and high stress of a great work.

That's fate. How could a development with the participation of a large participating public not progress differently than one that is carried out alone, without the glow and favor of fame!

⟨27⟩   District court, county court, higher regional court.

Liegnitz 66,620 inhabitants. Garrison. County and district courts. High school.

  His heroic model

> [Common is everything that doesn't]
> Only at the beginning poetry then prose writer.

Problem of youth: skepticism concerning art and artistry. Knowledge, irony. Then growing dignity.

Turning away from skepticism and knowledge, prepared in "misery." Moral resolution beyond knowledge [and psychology]. *Simultaneously* strengthening formal perception. "Reborn unreservedness." But moral strength beyond knowing means likewise a simplification, *becoming morally naïve* concerning the world and the soul and therefore a stronger tendency toward vice, to that which is forbidden, to all possibilities and—impossibilities. Just as that which is formal is moral and immoral at the same time: chaste and amoral, even anti-moral.

⟨Reverse side⟩

1899
  10
1909

⟨28⟩   Amor's temple at Thespiae

For Amor loves idleness.

Enthusiasm.

During the day he follows him without pause, at night he keeps watch—

Eros and bravery

Thunderstruck like a rooster

Many actually saw the same body (intoxication)

The beautiful body (Platonic ecstasy) tool for the memory of intellectual beauty.

Autonomy of the temple servant.

Custom gives the lover the freedom—to become a slave.

Eros is: young and of delicate stature, supple, well proportioned and with beautiful posture.

Instruction from Eros in the command of the arts, without him no fame. Take pains in everything. . . . *In speech* he knows well how to guide. The Athenians and the word. (Work on the beach.) Even his art was sober service at the temple in Thespiae. Love of fame and the ability to achieve fame.

Upon seeing them even you and the others started and it was with them that you wanted to remain—

⟨Reverse side⟩
Departure May 22nd. At Br. ⟨Brioni⟩ 10 days. Departure from there June 2nd. The beginning of the cholera in the 4th week of his stay in Lido; about June 27th.

Affliction, adventure,

⟨29⟩ I demand spirit from the servant. Everything is common that doesn't speak to the spirit and arouses nothing other than sensual interest. (Schiller)

It is important to write well. And whoever writes the best has the right to the highest and most refined objects.

Intellectualism of the modern artist. ⟨Newspaper clipping⟩

Spirit = Christianity, Platonism. Sensuality, sculpture = heathenism. *Like Schiller:* naïve and sentimental. *Goethe* (naïve): the highest art is external. With both the opposition not expressed purely. Goethe a student of Spinoza, analytical, psychologist. Schiller possesses a good portion of sensual naïveté. The artist's weakness for Catholicism. The one strives for the other. The intellectual doesn't marvel at anything more than that which is physically formed. The born sculptor has spirtual ambition.

Every real comedian has a tendency toward the circus, to clowning, to the fun of parody; it is his peculiar talent and all the rest is ambition and childlike respect for that which is exalted, the spirit, literature.
    The art of acting, reduced to physical talent of Sonnenthal's talent as a prostitute and swindler. But the talent (somewhat animal-like, [to] chiefly apelike) has a craving for the exalted, has the ambition of giving his work dignity through high intellectual proportions. . . .
    The artists' talent for vaudeville, pertaining to that apelike talent, that for the artist is not only the spiritual basis of his artistry, this cross-breed of Lucifer and clown. The parody is the root. But strong talent is a thorn in dignity's side, a push toward higher spirtuality and performance. . . .

⟨30⟩ ⟨Newspaper clipping⟩
The cholera in Italy
    *Palermo, September 4th. the tourist association of Palermo sends us statistics concerning the cases of cholera reported there from which the following conclusions can be made. June: 772 cases, among them 393

deaths; July: 1,132 cases, 307 deaths; August: 531 cases, 95 deaths. The total mortality rate in the last days of August in Palermo varies between 40 and 20, with a downward trend, among them almost half children under six years of age. According to the available statistics the most severe days were reported in the first 10 days of July. Then the disease decreased unsteadily until it reached a low on August 27th of one case and one death. The standing on August 31st . . .
⟨End of the clipping⟩

⟨End of the report from the *Münchner Neuesten Nachrichten* September 5, 1911⟩
amounted to 4 new cases as opposed to no deaths. According to these statistics it seems that the situation in Palermo with its 350,000 inhabitants has greatly improved.

⟨31⟩   He begins to pursue him. (During the day he pursues him without pause, at night he keeps watch—) (Love gives the lover the freedom—to become a slave.)
    Lewd Venice.
In what ways!!—Trys to support himself morally. The memory of his ancestors, of his gallant life. Eros and gallantry. New impressions of "evil." The manager. The musician. Pursuit through diseased Venice. The strawberries, realization at the cistern. Last look and dissolution.

Ancestors: official, austere, respectable, miserly, sober, moralistic.
Jester, buffoon
Joker
Street minstrel

The lechery and frenzy of the fall.

THOMAS MANN

Extracts from Letters †

To Hans von Hülsen

Bad Tölz, July 3, 1911
I sent my study of Chamisso[1] out into the world today and notice a positive desire to undertake a difficult, if not impossible novella.

† As excerpted in *Dichter über ihre Dichtungen* [Writers on their writings]: *Thomas Mann*, ed. Hans Wysling, vol. 1 (Frankfurt: S. Fischer, 1975) 395, 396, 397, 401, 404, 406–7, 412–19, 421, 422, 435.
1. The essay "Chamisso" (1911).

To Philipp Witkop

Bad Tölz, July 18, 1911

I am in the midst of work: a really strange thing that I brought with me from Venice, a novella, serious and pure in tone, concerning a case of pederasty in an aging artist. You say, "Hum, hum!" but it is quite respectable.

To Ernst Bertram

Munich, October 16, 1911

I just returned from the country and am still in a confused state; in addition to that I am tormented by a work, which, in the process of its execution, has evermore proved itself to be an impossible conception to which I have already devoted too much care to give it up.

To Wilhelm Herzog

Munich, December 8, 1911

I had actually planned a longer letter, but cannot find the peace of mind for it, since I am occupied to the point of torment with a novella that is perhaps an impossible conception.

To Heinrich Mann [2]

Munich, April 2, 1912

My life is somewhat difficult at present, but I've never completely ceased working, with the exception of a few illnesses, and *Death in Venice* will, I hope, be finished by the time I go to Davos (at the beginning of May). It's at least something very strange, and if you're unable to approve of it in its entirety, at least you won't be able to deny some instances of its beauty. A classicizing chapter seems especially to be a success. For the time being the novella will appear as a "Hundertdruck" from Hans von Weber in an opulent edition. [3]

To Hedwig Fischer

Bad Tölz, October 14, 1912

I hope the second half will not disappoint you. It does not have a positive ending; the dignity of the "hero and poet" is completely destroyed. It is a real tragedy, * * * and that "descent onto the plains of optimism" for which I was so intensely reproached in *Royal Highness* will be found to have been strictly avoided here. I am going to be careful never to write a comedy again, at the end of which "they are united." Now, in this case, it was unlikely that they would be united from the beginning.

2. Thomas Mann's older brother and fellow writer.
3. "Hundertdruck": a short run; Hans von Weber: the volume's publisher.

To Philipp Witkop

Munich, March 12, 1913

Concerning my novella, I constantly hear approval, even admiration, from all sides. Never before has the immediate reaction been so lively— and thus to my great joy the voices that count are among those being raised. It seems that for once I have been completely successful—a happy coincidence, that goes without saying. For once everything is in harmony; it is whole; the crystal is pure.

To Heinrich Mann.

Bad Tölz, August 11, 1913

Tonio Kröger was merely lachrymose, *Royal Highness* vain, *Death in Venice* half-formed and false.

To Samuel Fischer

Bad Tölz, August 22, 1914

It is the German spirit, the German language and Weltanschauung, German culture and training that triumphs there, and thus someone like myself also does not now need to hold himself in contempt. A few days ago the Rhenish poet Schmidtbonn visited me. He said, "Soldierly spirit is in your *Death in Venice!*" I knew that, but I still enjoyed hearing it.

To Elisabeth Zimmer

Bad Tölz, September 6, 1915

Today I am hardly a competent interpreter of *Death in Venice*. I have almost forgotten the composition. Certainly the story is mainly a story about death and, to be sure, death as a seductive, immoral power—a story about the lasciviousness of ruin. But the problem that I especially had in mind was that of the dignity of the artist; I wanted to present something like the tragedy of mastership. This seems to have become clear to you, since you hold the speech to Phaedrus[4] to be the core of the whole thing. Originally I had not planned anything less than telling the story of Goethe's last love, the love of the seventy-year-old for that little girl, whom he still absolutely wanted to marry, but it was a marriage that she and also his relatives did not want.[5] A cruel, beautiful, grotesque, deeply moving story that I nevertheless may still sometime

---

4. A character in Plato's dialogue of the same name.
5. In 1822 the aging German poet, playwright, and novelist, Johann Wolfgang von Goethe (1749–1832) fell in love with Ulrike von Levetzow, a young girl; he proposed marriage, but his proposal was spurned.

tell, this is the story for the present out of which *Death in Venice* grew. I believe that this source of the novella also expresses the most correct thing about the original intention of the story. Beyond that such an artistic thing is indeed difficult to categorize, but rather represents a dense network of intentions and relationships that possesses something organic and, therefore, thoroughly ambiguous.

To Paul Amann

Bad Tölz, September 10, 1915

It is amazing with what certainty you characterize the main intellectual intention of my last story. I am all the more grateful to you for the formula because it pretty well coincides with the final thought of the new work that concerns me at present. It is too bad that the best critics do not criticize; those who write and judge are mainly riff-raff. As far as *Death in Venice* is concerned, I am hardly a competent interpreter today, I have almost forgotten the composition. But one thing I do know is that I have been misunderstood almost from the very beginning in the crudest manner. The embarrassing thing was that the "hieratic atmosphere" was interpreted as a personal claim, when it was nothing more than mimicry. (Even Greek education was taken to be an end in itself, and yet it was only an aid and spiritual refuge for the person experiencing it. The character of the whole thing is more Protestant than classical.)

*　*　*

When I talk about the artist or even the master craftsman, I do not mean myself; I do not pretend that I am a master craftsman or even an artist, but rather only that I *know* something about artistry and mastery. Nietzsche says somewhere: "In order to understand something about art one should produce a few works of art." And he names the warmth-conducting media of the living artists, whose actions serve to "achieve the consciousness of the great masters." When I examine myself carefully, it was this and nothing else that was the objective of my creative work: to achieve the consciousness of the masters. It was a game—like the way I played "prince" as a boy—of achieving princely consciousness. By working artistically, I gained an understanding of the artist's existence, even the existence of the great artist, and can say something about it. The path to insight into *princely* existence was not any different. In general: I am talking much less about myself than about that which my own existence allows me to *divine*.

To Joseph Ponten

Munich, June 6, 1919

And so it pleases me that *Death in Venice* met with your approval.
People like us are obviously too much the *humanist, let me use the
word*, to be able to acquire a taste for artistic bolshevism. Just between
us, the style of my novella is somewhat *parodic*. It is a question of a sort
of mimicry that I love and unintentionally exercise. I once tried to
define the style by saying that it was a secret adaptation of the personal
to the factual. The relationship of *Death in Venice* to *The Island* is
obvious; it was immediately striking to me. The third sibling is Hauptmann's *The Heretic from Soana*.[6]

To Carl Maria Weber

Munich, July 4, 1920

I have been reading many of your poems and have found ample opportunity for fondness, even admiration. It is certainly no accident that you
are at your best as an artist where your feelings reach the highest level
of freedom and unabashedness, as in "The Swimmers," which has
much of the humanity of the younger generation in it, and in "The
Pleasure of Words," an unquestionably beautiful poem. I say that,
although I wrote *Death in Venice*—to which you dedicate such friendly
words of defense in your letter—against objections and reproaches that
are likely too well-known to you yourself. I wish you had been able to
take part in a discussion that I recently had on a long, extended evening
with Willy Seidel and a third art enthusiast, Kurt Martens. For it would
be extremely unwelcome to me if you and others retained the impression that I would have wanted to deny or renounce a kind of feeling that
I honor because it is almost necessarily spiritual—with much more
spirit, at any rate, than "normal" feeling—and I may say that it's hardly
accessible to me in a limited way.

You cleverly and clearly recognized the *artistic* reason that it could
take on this appearance. It lies in the difference between the Dionysian
spirit of the irresponsible-individualistic lyric outpouring and the objec-
tivity-bound Apollonian, ethically and socially responsible epic. I strove
for the balance of sensuality and morality that I found ideally perfected
in *Elective Affinities*,[7] which I read five times during my work on *Death
in Venice*, if I remember correctly. But that the novella, in essence, is
of a hymnic nature, even of hymnic origin, cannot have eluded you.
The painful process of objectivization that had to develop out of the

6. *The Island*: a novella by Joseph Ponten (1918), *The Heretic from Soana*: a novella by Gerhart
   Hauptmann (1918).
7. A novel (1809) by Johann Wolfgang von Goethe.

necessities of my nature is portrayed in the introduction to the otherwise unsuccessful *Song of the Child*.

Do you still know? A most intense intoxication, an exceptional feeling
Even came over you once and hurled you down,
So that you lay, forehead in your hands. Like a hymn
Your soul arose there, the struggling spirit urged itself forth to the song
In tears. Unfortunately, nothing changed. For there began a laborious attempt at objectification.
Look, for you the *drunken song* became the *moral story*.

But the artistic occasion for misunderstanding is actually just one among others. The purely spiritual ones are in fact more important: for example, the *naturalistic* one, for you young people such a strange attitude of my generation, that forced me also to view the "case" pathologically and to allow this motif (climacteric) to change places with the symbolic (Tadzio as Hermes Psychopompos). Something still more spiritual because more personal must be added: the basic outlook, is by all means not "Greek," but rather Protestant-puritanical ("bourgeois"); not only the outlook of the experiencing hero, but also my outlook, in other words, our basically suspicious, thoroughly pessimistic relationship to passion itself and in general. Hans Bühler, whose writings absolutely captivate me—the idea of his "role of eroticism" etc. is definitely major and deeply Germanic— once defined eros as "the affirmation of a person disregarding his *value*." This definition includes all the irony of eros, one must say from the moralist's standpoint—obviously again a standpoint only to be taken ironically. "That really is a nice affirmation that 'leaves value out of consideration.' I thank you!" But on a more serious note: passion as confusion and degradation was actually the subject matter of my story. What I originally intended to tell was not homoerotic at all. It was the story— grotesquely seen—of the aged Goethe and a young girl in Marienbad,[8] whom he absolutely wanted to marry with the approval of her ambitious matchmaker-Mama and to the horror of his family. The young girl did not want to marry him at all. This was the story—with all of its horrible-comical, highly embarrassing situations inclining towards too-reverent laughter—this awkward, touching, and great story that I still might write some day. What also came up at that time was a personal, lyric travel experience that made me determined to carry things to the pinnacle by introducing the motif of "forbidden" love. . . .

* * *

The problem of the erotic, even the problem of beauty seems to me to be contained in the tense relationship between life and spirit. I had made allusions to this where one should not have expected it. "The

8. Ulrike von Levetzow.

relationship of life and intellect," I said in the *Reflections*,[9] "is an extremely delicate, difficult, exciting, and painful one, charged with irony and eroticism. . . ." And I continue talking about a "sly" longing that perhaps forms the actual philosophical and poetic relationship of the spirit toward life. "Longing namely goes back and forth between spirit and life. Life, too, longs for the spirit. Two worlds whose relationship is erotic, *without the sexual polarity being clear*, without the one representing the masculine, the other the feminine principle: that is life and spirit. *Therefore, there is no union between them, but rather only a short, intoxicated illusion of union and understanding, an eternal tension without solution. . . . It is the problem of beauty*, that the spirit finds life beautiful. . . . The spirit that loves is not fanatical, it is spiritual, it is political, it courts, and its courting is erotic irony. . . ."

Tell me if one can "betray" himself any better. My idea of the erotic, my *experience* of it, is completely expressed here. But finally, what do we have here other than the translation of one of the most beautiful love poems in the world into the critical-prosaic, of the poem whose final stanza begins: "Who the deepest has thought loves what is most alive."[1]

This wonderful poem contains the entire justification for the direction of feeling under discussion in the speech and the entire explanation for it, which is also my own. George did say that in *D. i. V.* the highest is pulled down into the sphere of decay, and he is right.[2] I did not go through the naturalist school unpunished. But renunciation, defamation? No.

To Carl Maria Weber

Munich, July 29, 1920

I wrote to you that this sphere of feelings[3] was "hardly accessible to me" in a conditional manner.[4] "Hardly, in a conditional manner," that means *almost absolutely*—you misunderstood that and praise me for my power of empathy. But that is not the way things are, and without a personal emotional adventure, *Death in Venice* would never have evolved out of the Goethe novella. I do not want to have lied after the fact—especially because it would hardly have been to my human advantage. [416–17]

9. *Reflections of an Unpolitical Man* (1918).
1. From Friedrich Hölderlin's "Socrates and Alcibiades," in *Friedrich Hölderlin: Poems and Fragments*, tr. Michael Hamburger (London: Cambridge UP, 1980), 67.
2. George: the German poet, Stephan George (1868–1933); *D.i.V.*: *Death in Venice*.
3. *In Death in Venice*.
4. See letter to Weber, dated July 4, 1920, above.

To Wolfgang Born

Munich, March 18, 1921

It is with pleasure that I'm inspecting your graphic fantasies for my story *Death in Venice*.

* * *

Just one more word about the last picture, entitled *Death*. That one strikes me as strange and almost mysterious because of a similarity. In the early summer of 1911 the news of Gustav Mahler's death played into the conception of my story. I was able to make his acquaintance earlier in Munich and his consumingly intense personality made the strongest impression upon me. From the island Brioni, where I was staying at the time of his death, I followed the bulletins in the Viennese press, written as if for a prince, concerning his last hours. And while later this shock[5] mingled with the impressions and ideas out of which the novella grew, I gave my hero, who had succumbed to orgiastic disso-lution, not only the first name of the great musician, but also in his physical description, Mahler's visage. Still, I wanted to be certain that in the case of such a casual and hidden correlation one would not be able to talk at all about recognition on the part of the readership. Even in your case as the illustrator no one spoke about it. For you neither knew Mahler personally, nor had I confided anything about that secret personal correlation to you. Nevertheless—and this is what startled me at first sight—Aschenbach's head portrayed in your picture unmistakably manifests the Mahler type. That really is strange. Is it not said (Goethe said it) that language cannot express the individual and specific, and therefore it is not possible to be understood, if the other person does not have the same view? The other person, it is said, has to pay more atten-tion to the intention of the speaker than to his words. But because you, the artist, as the result of my words were able to hit upon the individual, language must not only have a direct impact from one person to another, but, as a literary-artistic means, be able to retain the powers of intention, the suggestive powers that make a transfer of visual perception possible. This is so interesting to me that I did not, at this opportunity, want to be completely silent about it. Best wishes for your work and thanks for your noble effort concerning mine!

To Ernst Bertram

Munich, April 29, 1924

Death in Venice is appearing now in *The Dial*[6] and does not read poorly.

5. The shock of Mahler's death.
6. American literary magazine.

To Ernst Bertram

Munich, May 31, 1924

You should hear what the managing editor of *The Dial* wrote to me. "May I add," he wrote, "that every day fresh congratulations come to us over our good fortune in having been able to publish your *Death in Venice*, which has made *a real stir* in the American literary world."

To Bedrich Fucik

Munich, April 15, 1932

In the French interview I called *Tonio Kröger* and *Death in Venice* the works that I most believe in because I suspect that the novella's closed and terse form has a better chance of continued existence than the relaxed and drawn-out form of the novel.

To Erika and Klaus Mann[7]

Munich, May 25, 1932

After the "Bains"[8] in Lido I still want to write you a letter because the place is so important to me and I'm pleased to know you're there and I, in spirit, with you, living the life that otherwise can never be found, between the warm sea in the morning and the ambiguous city in the afternoon. Ambiguous is really the most modest adjective that one can give it (Simmel used it), but with all of its layers of meaning it fits Venice. And in spite of all of the silliness and corruption that have taken over and about which you are irritated, this musical ambivalent magic is still alive or at least there are hours when it triumphs. You say that in the middle of the last century it was beautiful. But Platen had already said: "Still, Venice only exists in the land of dreams." Nevertheless, he loved it boundlessly, the way it was back then, just as did Byron, and later Nietzsche.[9] Certain dispositions associate an incomparable melancholy with the name Venice, a melancholy full of the sense of "homeland," a nativeness that today is rather spoiled and stale—I admit that. (Godfather Bertram never got over it). But my heart would still pound, if I were there again.

7. Erika Mann (1905–1969), the eldest of Mann's six children; Klaus Mann (1906–1949), the second of Mann's children.
8. The Grand-Hôtel des Bains.
9. August Graf von Platen (1796–1835), German poet; Friedrich Nietzsche (1844–1900), German philosopher; George Gordon, Lord Byron (1788–1824), English Romantic poet.

THOMAS MANN

Extracts from Essays †

From "On Richard Wagner's Art"

Wagner[1] is nineteenth century through and through. Yes, he is the representative German artist of this epoch, who will perhaps live on as great and certainly as extremely unhappy in the memory of mankind. When I think of the twentieth-century masterpiece, I imagine something that differs very essentially from the Wagnerian and, I believe, differs favorably—something that is exceptionally logical, well-formed, and clear, something that is both rigid and serene, not of a lesser tension of the will than Wagner's, but of a cooler, nobler, and even healthier spirituality, something that does not seek its greatness in baroque immenseness nor its beauty in intoxication—a new classicism, it seems to me, must come.

But still, whenever a tone, a weighty phrase from Wagner's works unexpectedly reaches my ear, I am joyfully startled, a kind of homesickness and longing for youth comes over me and, as in times long past, my soul surrenders to the clever and ingenious, yearning and cunning charm.

Venice, late May 1911

From "Reflections during the War"

Are not the relationships that join art and war together completely allegorical? It has at least always seemed to me that it is not the worst artist who recognizes himself in the image of the soldier. That present-day victorious warring principle—organization—is after all the first principle, the essence of art. The interplay of enthusiasm and order; systematic representation; creating strategic bases, continuing to build, and surging forward with "lines of communication;" solidarity, preciseness, circumspection; courage, resoluteness in enduring drudgery, and defeats in battle against the tough opposition of the cause; contempt for that which is called "security" in burgherly life ("security" is the favorite term and the loudest claim of the burgher), becoming accustomed to an endangered, tense, circumspect life; mercilessness towards oneself, moral radicalism, self-denial to the limit, martyrdom, full engagement of all of the primary forces of body and soul, without which it seems laughable to attempt anything; as an expression of training and

† As excerpted in *Dichter über ihre Dichtungen [Writers on their writings]: Thomas Mann*, ed. Hans Wysling, vol. 1 (Frankfurt: S. Fischer, 1975) 394, 404–5, 407–8, 409–11, 423, 425–26, 428–30, 433–34, 438–42.
1. Richard Wagner (1813–1883), German composer.

honor finally a feeling for ornamentation and pomp: all of this is indeed
at once militarylike and artistic. With good reason art has been called a
war, a grueling battle: the very German word "duty" is even more beautifully suited to it, and to be sure the artist's duty is much more closely
related to that of the soldier than to that of the priest. The antithesis
between the artist and the burgher—which literature has gladly cultivated, has been characterized as a bequest of romanticism—is not easily
understood, as it seems to me. For we do not intend this opposition—
burgher and gypsy—but rather more precisely—civilian and
soldier. * * *

August–September 1914

From "Burgherly Nature" in Reflections of an Unpolitical Man

It was a youthful romantic illusion and youthful fancy if I ever imagined that I was sacrificing my life to "art" and that my burgherly nature
was a nihilistic mask; if I, to be sure with candid irony toward both
sides, gave art, the "work," precedence over life and declared that "to be
completely creative," one could not live, one had to die. In truth, "art"
is only a means of fulfilling my life ethically. My "work"—let me use the
word—is not the product, meaning, and purpose of an ascetic–orgiastic
denial of life, but an ethical form of expression of my life itself: my
tendency toward autobiography already testifies to this, a tendency that
has ethical origins, but that, to be sure, does not exclude the most lively
esthetic will to impartiality, distance, and objectification, a will, then,
that is again only the will to faithful workmanship and that, among other
things, produces that stylistic dilettantism that allows the subject to speak
and that led, in Death in Venice, for example, to the astounding public
misunderstanding: that "hieratic atmosphere," the "master style," of the
story, was personal ambition, something I wanted to surround and
express myself with, and that I now had ridiculous ambitions to attain—
when it was, in fact, a matter of accommodation, yes, of parody.

* * *

From the beginning, my insignificant prose has been so little able to
do without a critical admixture that for me the concepts "prose" and
"criticism" have seemed almost identical. But my critical attitude has
always been directed at life, not at any political misfortunes, and even
though to me writing, yes, fiction, has meant hardly anything other
than intellectual criticism of reality, I have still perhaps been too positively attuned to be creatively disposed toward a purely negative characterization, toward lampoons, toward satire that is without pity. I do not
believe that form can develop at all without sympathy—pure negation
produces flat caricature. If I have understood anything at all of my times
sympathetically, it is its type of heroism, the modern-heroic life form

and attitude of the overburdened, overdisciplined *moralist of accomplishment* "working on the brink of exhaustion," and here is my psychological contact with the character of the new burgher, my only contact, but one that is important and moving to me. I have never created him in real, political-economic form; I had neither enough sympathy nor understanding to do this. But fiction has always seemed to me to be symbolic, and I may say that I have hardly written anything that has not been symbolic of the heroism of this modern, neoburgherly character. Yes, seen in this way, Thomas Buddenbrook is not only a German burgher, but also a modern bourgeois; he is the first figure in whose formation this decisive experience participated; and this experience worked formatively, creating symbols in my work from the main characters of the Renaissance play, through all the figures in the novel about the prince,[2] all the way to Gustav Aschenbach.

Summer 1916

From "*Against Justice and Truth*" in Reflections of an Unpolitical Man

Intellectually, I belong to that race of writers throughout Europe who, coming from *décadence*, appointed to be chroniclers and analysts of *décadence*, at the same time have the emancipatory desire to reject it—let us say pessimistically: they bear the velleity of this rejection in their hearts and at least *experiment* with overcoming decadence and nihilism. Discerning people will find signs of this tendency, of this desire and attempt, everywhere in my works, and when a talented correspondent told me after my most recent work had been published that Maurice Barrés had written a story with almost exactly the same title—it is called *La mort de Venise*—he did not do so without allusion to a distant correlation. It is clear that Barrés' nationalism and Catholicism, his seizing and propagating of the idea of revenge as a means of *excitement*, meant nothing else than the attempt to overcome decadence; and it is just as clear what a strongly national origin this attempt had—and how a German version would have to be different. Of course, the latter would not be *political* (and lead to the president's chair in a patriotic league) but *moral*; nor would it be *Catholic*, expecting everything to come from the outside, from the cult of tradition, but *Protestant*, appealing to the inner sense of duty, Kantian-Prussian.

September 1916

From "*On Belief*" in Reflections of an Unpolitical Man

"Things are bad today," Nietzsche said, "with the higher artists: are they not almost all being destroyed by inner lack of discipline? No longer

2. Thomas Buddenbrook: from the novel *Buddenbrooks* (1901); Renaissance play: *Fiorenza* (1905); novel about the prince: *Royal Highness* (1909).

are they tyrannized from the outside by the *absolute table of values* of a church or of a court, nor do they learn any longer to rear their own, inner tyrant, their *will*." The longing, striving, seeking of the times, which definitely is *not* for freedom, but which is longing for an "inner tyrant," for an "absolute system of values," for constraint, for the moral return to certainty—it is a striving for *culture*, for dignity, for bearing, for form—and I may speak of this for I knew about it before many others did, I harkened to it and tried to present it: not as a prophet, not as a propagandist, but novelistically, that is, experimentally and without final commitment. I experimented in a story with the renunciation of the psychologism and relativism of the dying epoch; I had an artist say good-bye to "knowledge for its own sake," renounce sympathy for the "abyss," and turn to the will, to value judgment, to intolerance, to "resolution." I gave all this a catastrophic, that is, a skeptical-pessimistic ending. I cast doubt on the possibility of an artist's gaining *dignity*. I had my hero, who tried it, discover and admit that it was not possible. I know well that the "new will" that I had frustrated would never have become a problem for me at all, an object of my artistic instinct, if I had not had a part in it, for in the realm of art there is no objective knowledge, there is only an intuitive and lyrical one. But to frustrate it, this "new will," to give the experiment a skeptical-pessimistic ending: precisely this seemed *moral* to me—as it seemed artistic to me. For my nature is such that doubt, yes, despair, seems to me more moral, decent, and artistic than any kind of leader-optimism, let alone that politicizing optimism that would like to be saved at any cost by belief—by belief in what? In democracy!

October 1917

From "Irony and Radicalism" in Reflections of an Unpolitical Man

But irony is always irony toward both sides; it directs itself against life as well as against intellect, and this takes the grand gesture away from it, this makes it melancholy and modest. To the extent that it is ironic, art is also melancholy and modest—or let us say more correctly: the artist is so. For the area of morality is the personal one. The artist, then, to the extent that he is an ironist, is melancholy and modest; "passion," the grand gesture, the great word, are denied him, yes, intellectually he cannot even attain dignity. The ambivalence of his central position, his hybrid nature of intellect and sensuality, the "two souls in his breast," prevent it. An artist's life is no dignified life, the path of beauty no dignified path. Beauty, you see, is indeed intellectual, but also sensual ("divine and visible at the same time," Plato said), and therefore it is the artist's path to intellect. But whether anyone who tries to reach intellect through the senses can gain wisdom and a man's true dignity I once questioned in a story in which I had an artist who had "become dignified" realize that people like him must necessarily remain immoral and adventurers of feeling; that the magistral posture of his tale had been lies and foolishness, his noble attitude a trick, the confidence the masses had in him quite ridiculous, and educating the nation and youth through art a risky undertaking to be forbidden.

Having him realize this in a melancholy, ironic way, I remained true to myself—which is the point I am interested in.

December 1917–January 1918

From "On the Way"

I went on board in Venice. . . . My God, in what a state of emotion did I see the beloved city again after I had carried it around in my heart for thirteen years! I will always count among my most cherished and fantastic memories the slow ride in the gondola from the train station to the steamboat with strangers through the night and the wind. Again I heard the quiet, the secret splashing of the water against its silent palaces; Venice's deathly elegance surrounded me again. Church fronts, squares and steps, bridges and alleys with a few pedestrians appeared unexpectedly and floated away. The *gondolieri* exchanged their calls. I was home. . . . The steamboat, resting in front of the *piazetta*, did not depart until the next evening. During the morning I was in the city, at the square, in San Marco, the alleys. The entire afternoon I stood on deck and took in the beloved composition: the pillars with the lion, the saint, the enchanted Arabian gothic of the palace, the resplendently jutting flank of the fairy-tale temple; I was convinced that no face during the approaching cruise would be able to surpass this image in my soul]; I departed in real pain.

April 12, 1925

From "On Marriage"

Without a doubt homoeroticism, the man-to-man bond of love, the sexual comradeship, enjoys today a kind of favor due to the climate of the times and is viewed by the educated not solely in the light of a clinical monstrosity. It is no accident that even in France, the country of gallantry par excellence, a well-known author[3] has come forth with a dialectical and obviously passionate apology for this emotional sphere, after he had kept the work hidden for a long time. Indeed, it is not right to ridicule or make fun of an emotional zone that has inspired the

3. André Gide, who first published "Corydon," his work on homosexuality, anonymously.

Medicean tomb and the David, the Venetian sonnets and the *Pathétique* in B minor.[4]

*   *   *

The principle of beauty and form does not issue from the sphere of life; its relationship to life is at most strictly of a critical and corrective nature. It stands opposed to life in proud melancholy and is most deeply bound to the idea of death and infertility. Platen said:

> Whoever has seen beauty,
> Is already delivered over to death.

But these two lines form the original and basic formula of all aestheticism, and it is with full justification that homoeroticism should be called erotic aestheticism.

Who denies that this judgment has been pronounced morally? There is no blessing like that of beauty, and that is a fatal blessing. Lacking the blessing of nature and life may be its pride, a most melancholy pride, but it is condemned by this, spurned, marked with the sign of hopelessness and absurdity.

August 1925

From "Parisian Account"

Friday the twenty-second. Never in my life will I forget Mr. Marcus Arelius Goodrich, *Chicago Tribune*, from this morning. He did have competition; there was a lot going on—the telephone rang and whimpered continually—but Marcus Arelius beat everything far and near. I had never before encountered this type of monumental childlike innocence and cheerfulness, triumphant national freshness in general. Oh yes, the peoples, the races, the types of the world! It is something for me, I expand my horizon, I observe, and I like it. Marc. Aurel. contrasts most wonderfully with the French figures and figurines we see today. Hello and How are you and the shoulders of an athlete and a marvelous set of teeth in that wonderfully sculptured, shaved, well-rested face with the Celtic pale-grey eyes beneath the fashionably combed hair smoothed back from the forehead, and in those stubby-fingered, naïve, and strong hands the walking stick, through whose bony handle a piece of leather was drawn. He sat down and began talking and laughed with his vehement Anglo-Saxon boyish accent—he *is* too glad and he would so *very* much like to know—and asked *questions* . . . "What do you feel when you look back upon your life!!" And outbursts of radiant admiration about the most modest reply. And the story, that lovely thing, you know,

4. References to the work of Michelangelo (1475–1564), Italian Renaissance artist; August Graf von Platen (1796–1835), German poet; and Pyotr Ilich Tchaikovsky (1840–1893), Russian composer—all of whom were homosexual.

Death in Venice, please, tell me something about it! Stylistically, I said shyly, the story has, in contrast to other things, something more Latin about it. "I see!" he cried glowing. *"Boccaccio!"* [5] And how he laughed when the usual bothersome rumbling and stirring in the water heater next to which we were sitting only became significantly louder when the worm-worn wheel turned! This school-boy fun! A sense of humor remains the greatest advantage of this race and will never cease to tie me to it. . . . To be brief, Goodrich was a top-notch refreshment. The ash blond little German-Italian, Isenburg, although he is the translator of *Tonio Kröger* and is in general very polite, fell in my estimation; nothing could support him.

February–April 1926

From "Lübeck as an Intellectual Form of Life"

Now if one wants to vent his anger on me and deal me a sudden blow, then I can be sure that my Lübecker origins and Lübecker *marzipan* are going to come under discussion: if nothing else occurs to them, then this strange marzipan occurs to them in connection with me and I am portrayed as a Lübecker marzipan baker, which is then called literary satire. It does not bother me in the least; as far as Lübeck is concerned, one has to be from someplace and I do not see why Lübeck should be a more ridiculous place of origin than anywhere else. I count it, in fact, among the better places of origin. I cannot in any way feel offended because of the marzipan, because in the first place it is a very good tasting substance, and, secondly, it is not less than trivial but rather, in fact, curious and, as I said, mysterious. Marci-pan—that obviously means, or at least according to my theory, *panis Marci*, Marcus' bread, for St. Mark, who is the patron saint of Venice. And if you look at this confection more closely—this mixture of almonds, rosewater, and sugar—then the suspicion arises that the Orient is at the bottom of this, that we have a candy from the Harem to deal with, and that the recipe for this sumptuous, indigestible morsel came from the Orient via Venice to Lübeck with some old Mr. Niederegger. Venice and Lübeck: some of you can remember that I wrote a novella *Death in Venice* in which I show myself to be pretty much at home in the seductively death-bound city, the romantic city par excellence. I use the phrase "at home" in its full and true sense: in the sense namely of another poem, an idyllic poem, that half-jokingly intimates hexameters and talks about how the hometown exists twofold for me—on the one hand as a harbor on the Baltic Sea, gothic and grey, but still like a miracle of origin once again removed, the pointed arches in Arabian enchantment, in the lagoon,

5. Giovanni Boccaccio (1313–1375), medieval Italian author of *The Decameron* (1353), a collection of one hundred sometimes licentious tales set during an outbreak of the black plague.

most familiar inheritance from childhood and still

> Fable-foreign, an extravagant dream.—Oh the young man's terror,
> As the serious gondola carried him first, that reposing one glided
> Along the big canal, passing the palaces
> Incomparable flight, when for the first time his shy
> Foot trod the tiles of the splendid palace, which the dream structure
> Closed, golden motley, the Byzantine temple,
> Rich in pointed arches and pillars and little towers and domes,
> Under the silky tent of sea breeze inundated blue!
> Did he not find, smelling the native fragrance of water, the city
> hall arcades,
> Where they held the money exchange, the important citizens of the
> free city,
> Again at the ducal palace, with its low arched
> Hall, above which the lighter one hanging with delicate foliage?
> No, do not anyone deny me the secret relation
> Between the trade harbors, the aristocratic city republics,
> Not between the homeland and the fairy tale, the Eastern dream!

You see, ladies and gentlemen, here for once the image of Lübeck appears, flowing together with that of the southern sister, unveiled out of the subconscious, and it proves that those clowns are not all wrong when they themselves believe that *Death in Venice* is really marzipan, even if in a deeper manner than they intended, and that a certain way of living was produced in the novel *Buddenbrooks*, which itself was set in Lübeck. I do not want to talk about *Tonio Kröger*,[6] whose background is likewise Lübeck and whose entire theme develops out of the opposition between the northern homeland of the emotions and the southern sphere of art. * * *

May 1926

From "Biographical Notes"

Adhering very long to the tone of Krull's[7] memoirs was obviously difficult, a delicate balancing act, and the desire to rest after this task probably lent encouragement to the idea of interrupting its continuation in the spring of 1911. It was not the first time that my wife and I spent part of May in Lido. A series of curious circumstances and impressions had to combine with a secret search for new things so that a productive idea could emerge; this then found its realization under the name of *Death in Venice*. I had modest intentions with the novella as I had with all of my undertakings; I intended it to be an improvisation, quickly finished, and an interpolation in my work on the confidence-man

---

6. *Buddenbrooks* (1901) and the novella *Tonio Kröger* (1903)—both by Mann.
7. Title character from the novel *Confessions of Felix Krull, Confidence Man*, begun in 1910 and finally published in 1954.

novel, a story that, according to material and length, would be just about fitting for the *Simplicissimus*.[8] But things—or whatever could best be substituted for the term to express the orgiastic—have their own will, according to which they take form. *Buddenbrooks*, which was planned according to Kielland's model of a novel about a merchant of at most two hundred fifty pages, had its own will. *The Magic Mountain*[9] exerted its own will, and Aschenbach's story also showed itself to be "self-willed," going a good distance beyond the meaning that I had wanted to give it. In truth every work is of course fragmentary, yet contains an expression of our essence within itself. Such an expression is the only, difficult way by which to experience this essence, and it is no wonder that it does not occur without any surprises. Here much crystallized, in the true sense of the word "crystalline," to produce a structure that, playing in the light of many a facet, suspended in multiple relationships, is probably capable of inducing a dreamlike state in the one who is actively guarding its realization. I love this word: "relationship." For me the concept "relationship" coincides with the concept of "meaning," however relatively that is to be understood. That which has meaning is nothing more than that which is rich in relationships, and I remember well the grateful understanding with which I heard the name of my story mentioned by Ernst Betram as he read the deep Venice chapter from the manuscript of his Nietzsche mythology.

Nothing different was happening on the periphery of the story than was happening inside it. Everything was right in a certain way, and I was reminded of my experience with *Tonio Kröger* where the native symbolism and just composition of even insignificant details was dictated by reality. One would think that in a novella about young people scenes like the one in the public library or the one with the police are functionally conceived for the sake of the idea, the joke. They are not; they are just taken from reality. It is the same way in *Death in Venice*; nothing was invented. The traveler at the north cemetery in Munich, the gloomy Polesian ship, the old dandy, the suspicious gondolier, Tadzio and his family, the unsuccessful departure due to a mix-up with the luggage et cetera, et cetera—it was all there; the cholera, the honest clerk in the travel agency, the malicious itinerant singer, or whatever else mentioned—everything was given; it really needed only to be employed to demonstrate its remarkable ability to be interpreted compositionally. It may somehow be connected with this experience that, during the ever longer and more drawn-out work on the novella, I momentarily had the feeling of a certain absolute transformation, that I had achieved a certain sovereign precision that I had never known before. I was living alone with the children in Tölz * * * and the lively interest that our visiting friends showed at the evening readings in my

8. *Simplicissimus*: a literary magazine in which Mann occasionally published.
9. Mann's novel, published 1924.

small study might have prepared me for the almost stormy sensation that the public appearance of the novella was to excite. With the German public, who basically recognize only the seriously ponderous and not that which is light, it caused a certain moral rehabilitation of the author of *Royal Highness*[1] in spite of the questionable nature of the material.

January–February 1930

From "On Myself"

At that time I would not have dared conjure up the figure of Goethe; I did not believe I had the strength to do it and gave it up. I created a modern hero, a gentle type of hero, like those I had already fondly shaped in earlier works—Thomas Buddenbrooks and Girolamo Savonarola's brother[2]—hence a *hero of weakness*, who works on the brink of exhaustion, extracting from himself the maximum. In brief: a hero of the stamp so baptized by me as the "moralist of achievement."

*   *   *

Again my theme was the devastating invasion of passion, the destruction of a structured, apparently conclusively mastered life, which is degraded by the "foreign god," by Eros-Dionysus, and thrust into the absurd. The artist, imprisoned by passion, cannot really become dignified: this basic tendency of bitter, melancholy skepticism in the face of all artistic power (patterned upon Plato's dialogues) is expressed in the confession I place in the mouth of the hero, who is already marked by death.

This is a strange brand of moral self-discipline set forth in a book that, even with intentional irony, makes a display in its diction, in its prose, of that dignified and masterly pose, a pose that it then brands a lie and folly. The melancholy, skeptical criticism of artistic production in general—manifested already in *Tonio Kröger*, in *Tristan*,[3] in *Fiorenza*, from the moral and human point of view—is brought to a climax in *Death in Venice*. At the same time the pedagogical claims that are censured should actually have snuck into the artist's identity; these claims, ideas actually began to play a role in my life once I had gone beyond the youthful epoch of solitude and Bohemianism. I developed those ideas and claims in the essay "Goethe and Tolstoy," which brought the world of *autobiography*, of confession, into direct relation with that of *pedagogy*, of human formation, of education. I showed how the educational element already lives, consciously or unconsciously, in the autobiographical-confessional mode and grows out of it. "No one," I claimed,

1. Mann's novel, published 1909.
2. Thomas Buddenbrook: from *Buddenbrooks* (1901); Girolamo Savonarola's brother: in *Fiorenza* (1905), a verse drama.
3. *Tristan* (1903), a novella.

"has ever understood his own self as a cultural task and, in attending to this task, allowed himself to become troubled, without also attaining an apparently accidental educational influence in the world at large. And the moment of this insight, because it first occurs at the height of life, is the most intense moment in the life of a productive person."

Take this as an example of the strange, *double-track nature* of poetic thought: the same author who expressed something like this in an essay denies any pedagogical influence in the story, in all artistic and poetic production, with almost flagellating pessimism. But how deeply, nevertheless, the idea of education had taken root in my soul is demonstrated by the fact that the next material that I undertook became, in my hands and against all foresight and intention, a late form of the German Bildungsroman. I am talking about *The Magic Mountain** ***

*   *   *

The story or prose poem that we were last talking about and, by the way, was the first of all my works to appear in English (in America in the journal that has in the meantime disappeared, *The Dial*), *Death in Venice* possesses a strangely prominent double position in my personal life as an author and, at the same time, in the era to which this life belonged. The story appeared in 1913, just before the outbreak of the First World War, with which a period of European life ended and new fateful worlds opened up for the survivors. And, to my way of thinking, this position at a turning point in time was not accidental, corresponding exactly to the role that it played in my interior life insofar as it signified a finality and an extreme, a conclusion. It was the moral, formally most pointed, and most collected formulation of the decadence problem and the problem of the artist; that was the sign under which my work had been produced since *Buddenbrooks* and that, with *Death in Venice*, was finally fully realized. *Death in Venice* was executed in absolute accordance with the full realization of the bourgeois era's problem of individualism, a problem that was leading to catastrophe. Along the personal path that had lead to *Death in Venice* there was no more going forward, no over and beyond, and I understood completely when friends back then showed their concern about my work in respect to where I would go from there—but I countered this concern with the same apathy, the same mixture of fatalism and vital trust that was characteristic of my unproved youth. It is really a question of vitality whether or not one clears a critical hurdle, a hurdle of relative and limited perfection such as I had reached; whether one is capable of loosening up what has become *tight*, what has really taken on form, and keeping his productivity alive, of letting new content flow into it, of broadening the spiritual basis of one's life and extending it and building it higher—or whether, in the context of a new era, nothing but repetition or silence is our lot. This decision is not made by the will; it merely occurs; and if we at first are not even aware of having made the decision, then that is because growth never is a decisive abandonment of the old and worn out, which would not have known anything about the new and additional, but rather the result of the old already containing elements of the new and with the new taking up elements of the old again and leading them forth. This is the relationship of *Death in Venice* to *The Magic Mountain*. In Aschenbach's story some things are suggested that no longer belong to the old bourgeois world, but already have something to do with newer, post-bourgeois life, although it is taken ironically-pessimistically ad absurdum. *The Magic Mountain* is to a great extent a romantic book, a book of sympathy with death. And still it is a way out of an individual life of pain into a new, more social, and more humane morality, and in none of my earlier books could the sentence have stood that Hans Castorp dreams in the snow: "One should not concede death control over one's thoughts for the sake of love and goodness."

March–April 1940

CRITICISM

✱ ANDRÉ VON GRONICKA

"Myth Plus Psychology": A Style Analysis of *Death in Venice* †

I

In an exchange of letters with the Hungarian anthropologist Karl Kerényi, Thomas Mann has pointed to a basic quality of his writings by
revealing that he had early recognized "Mythos plus Psychologie" as his
natural "Element" and that he had been for a long time "a passionate
friend of this combination."[1] Mann's formula calls for a brief amplifi-
cation. "Myth" as used in it stands for rather more than the term con-
ventionally defines. It encompasses legend, history, and the literary
traditions of the more recent past; it calls for a language that is cleansed
of the colloquial and the commonplace, is marked by lyric pathos, or
evokes the monumental and the statuesque. "Psychology," on the other
hand, implies a penetrating analysis and a carefully controlled statement
in an all but naturalistic idiom, of the reality of the psycho-physical
world. The "plus" in the formula does not represent simple addition
but a most subtle combination and permutation of disparate elements
resulting in a unique "Steigerung" [enhancement].

When we examine Mann's *oeuvre* with this revealing statement in
mind, it is not difficult to detect this "combination" even in the very
early works in which the author time and again bursts through the pre-
dominantly realistic, even naturalistic theme and style, transcends psychology, and confronts the reader unexpectedly with the surreality of
the demonic and the diabolic by way of caricature and the grotesque
(Luischen),[2] with apocalyptic visions *(Gladius Dei; Fiorenza)*. Or else
he leads us in a manner at times reminiscent of Hoffmann, at times
of Andersen, into the magical fairy-tale world *(Kleiderschrank; Royal
Highness)*, only to bring us back to reality, rarely with a jolt, mostly by
way of gentle transition, or to leave us suspended in the ambivalence of
reality and make-believe inextricably fused. This bifocal view of life that
encompasses both the transcendent and the real develops steadily to

† From *Germanic Review* 31 (1956): 191–205. Reprinted with permission of the Helen Dwight
Reid Educational Foundation. Published by Heldref Publications, 1319 Eighteenth St., N.W.,
Washington, D.C. 20036-1802. Copyright © 1956. Clayton Koelb has translated German words,
phrases, and quotations unless their meaning is clear from the context or they have been absorbed
into English. Quotations from the Norton Critical Edition of *Death in Venice* have been substituted for those from the original German text, with bracketed page references to this edition following.

1. Karl Kerényi, *Romandichtung und Mythologie; ein Briefwechsel mit Thomas Mann* (Zürich:
Rheinverlag, 1945), p. 82.
2. An interesting corroboration of this early tendency is offered by Thomas Mann's sketches in
the *Bilderbuch für artige Kinder,* esp. the sketches "Rechtsanwalt Jacobi und Gattin," "Mutter
Natur," and "Das Läben," reproduced in V. Mann, *Wir waren fünf* (Konstanz: Südverlag,
1949), pp. 56ff.

reach, in the masterly novella *Death in Venice*, a degree of perfection which Mann has rarely if ever excelled.

To be sure, he coined the formula "myth plus psychology" with explicit reference to the *Joseph* tetralogy. However, in this relatively late work the effect of the "combination" though it has gained in sophistication and finesse, has lost something of its unbroken vitality and immediacy, and this for three basic reasons: first, because the very plot and locale of the tetralogy are drawn from myth, legend, and ancient history, not from the palpable reality of the "here and now" and their realization is a deliberate act of "deception," a "game";

> The precision and the realization are deceptions, a game, a counterfeit, a realization and actualization produced by edited investigation with all the tools of speech, psychology, and depiction, whose soul, though having a serious dimension, is humor.[3]

Secondly, because of a programmatical purposefulness of the rationalization and humanization, the "restructured functioning" of myth with the help of psychology:

> Too often, during the last decades, myth was misused as a tool of obscurantistic counterrevolution, so that a mythical novel such as *Joseph*, when it first appeared, would not necessarily have excited suspicion, as though its author were swimming with the current, murky as it was. One had to let it go, this suspicion, because under closer scrutiny one became aware of the changing function of myth, a type of change one had never thought possible. One observed a development, a development similar to that which takes place in battle when a captured artillery piece is turned around completely and redirected against the enemy. In this book myth was taken from the hands of fascism and, to the utmost degree, *humanized* into the language.[4]

And finally, because of a sharply increased irony, a playfulness in the author's attitude toward his material, his "Stoff":

> The discussion is a part of the game here, . . . is indirect, is a particular style and a jesting, a contribution to pseudoprecision. It is very close to satire and, in any case, to irony: for the scientific, applied to the entirely unscientific and fairy-tale–like, is pure irony.[5]

In the *Novelle*, on the other hand, everything springs with a surprisingly unbroken vitality and directness from that bifocal view of life: the locale,

---

3. Cf. Th. Mann, "Joseph und seine Bruder," *Neue Studien* (Berlin: Berman-Fischer, 1948), p. 165.
4. *Neue Studien*, pp. 169ff; cp. also *Romandichtung und Mythologie*, p. 82. The italics are Mann's.
5. *Neue Studien*, pp. 165ff.

the plot, and especially the characters. Here everything is rooted both in this-worldliness and in the realm of myth and legend. Here Thomas Mann lays hold of life in all its concrete outer-inner, psycho-physical reality, while reaching deep into the rich storehouse of myth, and legend, as well as of modern literature. He does this with an uninhibited creative energy that informs reality with myth's timeless grandeur, while rescuing myth from abstract remoteness and endowing it with a vibrant immediacy far removed from "Persiflage."

In the "Sketch of My Life," written in 1930, Mann recollects that he had never before or since the composition of *Death in Venice* experienced "such a splendid sensation of uplift."[6] Of the hero of the *Novelle*, of Gustav von Aschenbach he says: "His memory was active, and his mind conjured up ancient thoughts that had been passed down to him in his youth, which he had, until now, never instilled with his own vitality."[7] We are safe in reading this characterization of Aschenbach's creative state of mind as a fragment of self-revelation on the part of the author. It was surely in a similar state of supreme creative élan that Mann achieved the well-nigh miraculous, and could write both as the soberly meticulous analyst and delineator of physis and psyche[8] and as the inspired recreator of the world of myth. Thus, in this *Novelle* Mann's cultivated mind, oriented Janus-like toward the past as well as the present, becomes a potent synthesist of the meticulously observed and recorded world of contemporary, bourgeois civilization and the timeless and measureless vistas of man's cultural heritage. It creates a unique work of art, suspended in an unceasing tension between the poles of psychological realism and the symbolism of myth, which we now propose to examine in some detail.

II

We know from Mann's autobiographical sketch that a trip to the Lido in the spring of 1911 had furnished him "all the materials for his *Novelle*": "The traveler at the north cemetery in Munich, the gloomy ship from Pola, the old dandy, the suspicious gondolier, Tadzio and his family, the unsuccessful departure due to a mix-up with the luggage, the cholera, the honest clerk in the travel agency, the malicious itinerant singer, et cetera, et cetera—it was all there," and—significantly—"proved to have the most wonderful capacity for interpretation to be worked out in the course of composition."[9] The above enumeration is

---

6. "Lebensabriß," *Neue Rundschau*, XLI (June 1930), pp. 732ff.
7. Th. Mann, *Die schönsten Erzählungen*, Forum Bücher (Stockholm: Berman-Fischer, 1938), pp. 181f.
8. D. E. Oppenheim, *Dichtung und Menschenkenntnis* (München: Bergmann, 1926), p. 142: "In this work *[Death in Venice]* the psychological art of the poet rises to a proud self-sufficiency."
9. "Lebensabriß, p. 753.

its own best proof that the "capacity for interpretation" did not reside in
the raw materials *per se*, but rather was a characteristic of the artist, of
this particular artist, who seized upon them and had the intellectual
equipment and the genius to transform them into the stuff of art:

> The focus one directs, as an artist, on the inner and outer reality,
> differs from the one a normal person directs on the same: it is at
> once both colder and more passionate, . . . a dark impulse drives
> one to 'observe,' to perceive with lightning speed and painful mal-
> ice every last detail, every last aspect that, in a literary sense, is
> typical in meaning, widens perspectives, and characterizes the
> race, the social, the psychological. . . .[1]

and again, he asks, "But what is [the artist's] material?" to answer with
all possible emphasis, "The personal is everything. The only true material is the personal."[2]

> And sums up: "Whether he [the creative artist] fills an age-old fairy
> tale or a piece of living reality with his breath and his essence, the
> giving of soul to, the penetration and filling of the material with
> that which is the creative artist, transforms the material to make it
> his own," that is, to a unique work of art.[3]

The central locale of the *Novelle*, Venice, "the sunken queen" [30]
(167)[4] is caught by Mann's bifocal vision as the "flattering and suspiciously beautiful . . . half fairy tale, half tourist trap" [47], in its sordid
reality and mythical splendor. We are not spared the oppressive sultriness and fetid stench of its alleyways, nor the garbage floating on its
canals with their evil exhalations; yet above these very waters there rises
the "airy splendor" of its palaces, bridges, churches, of its "fairy tale
cathedral," rendered in a rhythmical prose of exquisite limpidity and
grace [17]. This *ambiente* is done with the most painstaking precision of
detail, yet not in order to produce a naturalistic picture of the city, but to
create, by way of an ever alert selectivity, a highly stylized composition
characterized by a tense equilibrium of realism and idealization. There
is modern Venice drawn in a decidedly up-to-date idiom, liberally sprinkled with technical terms and with foreign loan-words and entire
phrases, particularly French:

> The waves slapped against the concrete walls of the narrow canal
> that cut through the island to the Hotel Excelsior. A motor bus was
> waiting there for the returning traveler. . . . To be sure, his room
> was already taken, but another, by no means worse, stood ready.
> "Pas de chance, monsieur," said the elevator man with a smile as

1. "Bilse und ich," *Rede und Antwort* (Berlin: Fischer, 1922), pp. 13f.
2. *Pariser Rechenschaft* (Berlin: Fischer, 1926), p. 119.
3. *Rede und Antwort*, p. 23.
4. Numbers in parentheses indicate pages in *Die schönsten Erzählungen*.

they glided upwards. And so the fugitive was billeted once again. . . . [33]

And next to, superimposed upon, and integrated into this modern Venice is the timeless, exotic city *par excellence*, the "very seat of all dissoluteness,"[5] the perfect stage for the "silent, criminal adventures in a darkness full of splashing sounds" [17] as fashioned by the imagination of Elizabethan poets and dramatists and by the Italian novelists, Venice of Oriental "fairy-tale splendor," Romantic Venice risen from the dreams of Byron, Platen, Wagner, and Nietzsche, that magical city of ruthless passions, of passions-unto-death, of the *Liebestod* [love-death]. And on this complex *montage*,[6] this subtle composite of reality and literary tradition, Mann superimposes the world of classical antiquity,[7] its scenery, historical figures (Socrates, Phaedros, Critobolus[8]) and the gods of Olympus:

> The goddess was approaching, she who seduced young men, she who had stolen Kleitos and Kephalos and enjoyed the love of handsome Orion in defiance of all the envious Olympians. A strewing of roses began there on the edge of the world, where all shone and blossomed in unspeakable purity. Childlike clouds, transfigured and luminous, hovered like attending Cupids in the rosy bluish fragrance. Purple light fell on the sea, then washed forward in waves. Golden spears shot up from below to the heights of the heavens, and the brilliance began to burn. Silently, with divine ascendancy, glow and heat and blazing flames spun upwards, as the brother-god's sacred chargers, hooves beating, mounted the heavens. The lonely, wakeful watcher sat bathed in the splendor of the god's rays; he closed his eyes and let the glory kiss his eyelids. [41]

One need but compare the imagery and rhythm of this passage with the word-choice and general tone of Mann's description of modern Venice to be at once impressed by the amplitude of this style, by its skillful exploitation of the devices of contrast and counterpoint. This style has developed into a perfect vehicle of Mann's formula, of his "combination." From its wealth of realistic detail it extracts the maximum of

---

5. Cp. Lord Byron, as quoted by W. Pabst, "Satan and the Ancient Gods in Venice," *Euphorion*, XLIX (Jan. 1955), p. 337: "That is, been at Venice, which was much visited by the young English gentlemen of those times (Elizabethan), and was then what Paris is now—the seat of all dissoluteness."

6. Mann's definition of this "Montage-Technik": ". . . The fitting together of factual, historical, personal, yes literary realities, so that, hardly being different from the 'panoramas' shown me in my youth, the tangible reality of the panorama blends in, barely discernible, with the perspectives of a painting and the illusory." *Die Entstehung des Doktor Faustus* (Amsterdam: Beermann-Fischer, 1949), p. 33.

7. Cf. Fr. H. Mautner, "Die griechischen Anklänge in Th. Manns *Tod in Venedig*," *Monatshefte*, XLIV (Jan. 1952), pp. 20–26.

8. Cf. L. Gustafson, "Xenophon und der *Tod in Venedig*," *Germanic Review*, XXI (October 1946), pp. 209–214.

symbolical meaning, weaves a rich pattern of fact and fancy, modernity and myth and lends to the reality of life a new dimension in depth.

III

Turning from the locale of the *Novelle* to its characters, we shall limit ourselves to three prominent figures, to the "stranger" in his various guises, to Tadzio and to Gustav von Aschenbach. The bifocal vision of Thomas Mann is clearly at work when the stage is set for Aschenbach's fateful meeting with the stranger. Time and place are stated in an exact factual manner which could well serve to open a realistic, even naturalistic tale, yet the apparent realism of the "Englischer Garten" and the "beergarden, next to which several hackneys and carriages were lingering," of the Ungererstrasse with its streetcar tracks, is subtly modified by interwoven elements of description: the "increasingly quiet paths," the sinking sun, Aschenbach's "route homeward outside the park over the open fields[!]," his tiredness and the thunderstorm that broods threateningly over Föhring, are elements which charge this realism with a significant atmosphere and lend it a symbolical quality which gradually becomes dominant. Our attention is drawn to the desolate "stonemasons' shops, where the crosses, headstones, and monuments for sale formed a second, untenanted graveyard," to the "Byzantine architecture of the mortuary chapel . . . in the glow of the departing day," to a setting which causes Aschenbach's inner vision ("geistiges Auge") to lose itself "in their radiant mysticism" [4].

When the stage is set in this manner, the stranger makes his unobserved, uncanny entrance to stand—elevated—at the portals of the funeral hall: "It was not clear whether the man had emerged from the chapel through the bronze door or had climbed the steps up to the entry from the outside without being noticed" [4] Here, surely, is more than a suggestion of the mysterious and eery which, however, is at once counteracted by the very next sentence: "Aschenbach, without entering too deeply into the question, inclined to the first assumption" [4]. Both the content and tone of this sentence, especially the matter-of-fact, offhand phrase "inclined to the first assumption" are calculated to break or at least weaken the spell of spectral other-worldliness that might have been worked by the description of the cemetery, the funeral hall with its "hieratic paintings" and "apocalyptic beasts" and of the "not altogether ordinary appearance" of the stranger.

The manner in which the stranger's appearance is characterized reminds one at first of an official identification, abrupt, curt, exact in its phrasing: "moderately tall, thin, clean-shaven, and strikingly snub-nosed" [4]. Suddenly, however, we become aware that the figure is raised above commonplace reality, acquires a statuesque quality, a striking monumentality. No longer merely a Bavarian tourist, the stranger has grown to the stature of a mythical figure. He *is* the arch-tempter Satan, he *is* also the imperious, ruthless liberator from life's toil, Death with his characteristic mask: "his short, turned-up nose," with lips "retracted to such an extent that his teeth, revealed as far as the gums, menacingly displayed their entire white length" [4], the skull as it appears in many a *Totentanz* [dance of death]. To be sure, in this composite figure the hoof of Satan is decorously hidden. Yet the stranger's long, scrawny neck with its starkly protruding Adam's apple, red eyelashes over pale eyes would amply identify the Lord of Hell even if it were not for the two "stark vertical furrows" etched on his forehead and drawn down between his eyes, which—ever since Dante's day— have served to symbolize the devil's mythical horns.[9] But while shaping this mythical figure, Mann is ever intent to justify and explain its existence on realistic and psychological grounds. "It may be that his elevated and elevating location had something to do with it . . ." he ventures to suggest and again, in explanation of the mask of death and the marks of the devil, he offers as the realistic cause, the sun's blinding rays which may well have forced the stranger to grimace [4].

The effect of the stranger upon Aschenbach, though powerful, is rendered in a pointedly realistic manner. The bellicose gaze of the stranger, "so belligerent, so directly eye to eye, with such a clear intent to bring matters to a head . . ." [4] causes no sudden surrender, no petrefaction nor casting down upon bended knees with head thrown back and arms spread wide. To suggest such a typically expressionistic gesture is to point up the absurdity of all excess and eccentricity and sudden "breakthrough" within the context of Thomas Mann's world-view and corresponding style. His Aschenbach is merely "embarrassed," turns away and "in a moment . . . had forgotten about him" [4]. It is difficult to imagine a more sobering denouement of a highly charged situation.

But then the author switches to the psychological plane and here unfolds a masterful analysis of the effect of the meeting upon Aschenbach's psyche, his "imagination" shows how the indefinable "physical or spiritual influence [of the stranger]" releases a flood of long and ruthlessly repressed emotions[1] which crystallizes into a wake-dream of such poignancy as to leave Aschenbach shaken, his heart throbbing "with horror and mysterious desire" [5].

Yet is this transfer to the realistic plane of psychoanalysis complete? Does the mythical figure of the stranger vanish altogether in the light of this analysis? Are his "not altogether ordinary appearance" and enigmatical influence really "explained" on rational grounds? Can we agree with Aschenbach when he attempts to rationalize the encounter as the upshot

---

9. Cp. Pabst, op. cit., p. 348.
1. Cp H. Hatfield, *Thomas Mann* (Norfolk: New Directions Books, 1951), p. 61: "Too great a devotion to the Prussian ideals of duty and discipline brings him to the point of collapse; the 'death wish' rebels against the categorical imperative of his conscious mind."

of a sudden onset of "wanderlust and nothing more"? [5] By no means.
It is precisely the paradox of Mann's style that, despite its thorough realism, it leaves myth and legend in their very palpable existence. The
mythical figure of the stranger will return, to weave its enigmatical spell,
in the mythico-realistic forms of the Gondolier-Charon; of the lewd and
lascivious old fop; of the goatee'd captain of the "ship from Pola" to sell
Gustav von Aschenbach a first class ticket to Venice and, on the mythical level, to draw up a first rate devil's pact: "He inscribed great letters like
crane's feet on a piece of paper, poured blue sand out of a box onto them,
poured it back into an earthenware bowl, folded the paper with his yellow, bony fingers, and resumed writing" while his "empty chatter . . .
had an anesthetic and diversionary effect, as if he were concerned that
the traveler should change his mind about his decision to go to Venice"
[14]. The choice of vocabulary and the resultant slight but significant
exaggeration and "focusing" of reality are such as to make the suggestion
inescapable: Aschenbach is here being lured, hypnotised into a contract,
the terms of which are final and fatal.[2] And once again the stranger
appears as the mendicant singer of crude and vulgar ballads who is
marked by the self-same death-devil features and becomes, moreover,
associated in Aschenbach's mind with the symbol *par excellence* of death,
the hourglass. The "balladeer" had just made his grotesque exit amidst
diabolically derisive laughter of triumph over his victim:

> The night progressed; time crumbled away. Many years ago in his
> parents' house there had been an hourglass. He suddenly could see
> the fragile and portentous little device once more, as though it were
> standing right in front of him. The rust-colored fine sand ran
> silently through the glass neck, and as it began to run out of the
> upper vessel a rapid little vortex formed. [53]

The motif of the inexorably vanishing sand [life] acquires a particularly
ominous and sinister effect through the adroitly selected detail of the
"rapid little vortex," that down-sucking whirlpool of passion. The passage is a perfect example of a meticulously observed, realistic description
charged with an atmosphere of the numenous.

All these figures stand in the realm of the possible, do not strain
unduly our sense of the real, yet—at bottom—they are spectral.
"Though they did not appear contrary to reason, did not really give
cause for second thoughts, the paradox was that they were nonetheless
fundamentally and essentially odd" [21]. They are creatures both of this
world and not of it. Emissaries of the beyond, they move in the bright
light of day, upon the firm ground of reality. Their existence within

---

2. A theme which was to become central in *Dr. Faustus*. "It is the flight . . . into a pact with the
devil, the thirst of a proud spirit threatened by sterility, for the loss of self-restraint at any price
. . ." Th. Mann, *Die Entstehung des Doktor Faustus* (Amsterdam: Bermann-Fischer, 1949),
p. 31. Cp. also A. von Gronicka, "Th. Mann's Doktor Faustus," *Germanic Review*, XXIII
(October 1948), esp. pp. 211f.

space and time, in the here and now, is guaranteed, as it were, by the realism of their surroundings, yet they, in turn, impart to the world in which they move an air of mystery and magic, a strange and dreamlike quality: "It seemed to him that things were starting to take a turn away from the ordinary, as if a dreamy estrangement, a bizarre distortion of the world were setting in" [15] and "Aschenbach watched him [the old fop] from under a darkened brow and was once again seized by a feeling of giddiness, as if the world were displaying a slight but uncontrollable tendency to distort, to take on a bizarre and sneering aspect" [16]. Moreover, the surrealistic quality of these encounters is enhanced by their very repetition which soon impresses as being preordained, inexorable. Thomas Mann was to elaborate the view of human life as a repetition and recurrence of mythical constellations, of proto-patterns, "cosmic images in perpetual motion" into a life's philosophy and was to give this deeply romantic *Weltanschauung* its fullest artistic expression in the *Joseph* novels.[3] Yet already in this relatively early *Novelle* (1911) we find this view creating in Aschenbach's encounters with the life-death symbol, the stranger in his various guises, a striking prefiguration of the "mythical" of the "repetition and return of the original creation," of the "mythical recurrence" so basic to the tetralogy.

IV

The figure of Tadzio is also the creature of the two worlds of reality and myth, a creation of Mann's bifocal view. We see him, almost exclusively through Aschenbach's eyes, both from a distance "as if looking at a picture," "image and mirror of spiritual beauty," [37] as well as from close-range. We see him as the little Polish boy of pale complexion, with carious teeth, we hear his high-pitched voice, observe a fit of his high-strung temper. But we also behold him as the paragon of beauty whose flawless profile awakens in Aschenbach memories of "Greek statues from the noblest period of antiquity" [21], "poetic legends from the beginning of time that tell of the origins of form and of the birth of the gods" [28]. In fact, Tadzio's shortcomings serve to support rather than weaken in Aschenbach's mind the ideal qualities of his figure. The pallor of Tadzio's cheeks enhances the boy's resemblance to the "statue of the *Boy Pulling a Thorn from his Foot* [22]; the collar of his sailor suit, precisely because of its poor fit, serves to set off all the more effectively "that blossom, his face, a sight unforgettably charming . . . the face of Eros, with the yellowish glaze of Parian marble . . ." [25] and the fit of uncontrollable temper acquires, in Mann's carefully stylized description, the quality of myth, and calls to mind the image of a young god in

3. Cp. P. Heller, "Some Functions of the Leitmotif in Th. Mann's Joseph Tetralogy," *Germanic Review*, XXII (April 1947), pp. 126–141; also J. Lesser, *Thomas Mann in der Epoche seiner Vollendung* (München: Dresch, 1952), pp. 133 ff.

rage: ". . . a storm cloud of angry contempt crossed his face. His brow darkened, his lips began to curl, and from one side of his mouth emerged a bitter grimace that gouged a furrow in his cheek. He frowned so deeply that his eyes seemed pressed inward and sunken, seemed to speak dark and evil volumes of hatred from their depths" [26].

This "enhancement" of the realistic figure into a figure of myth is carried out with the greatest circumspection. Nowhere is the reader required to relinquish reality in favor of myth. To be sure, Tadzio is set apart from his sisters, he is "popular, sought after, admired" [27]. That in itself, however, would not lift him above the plane of reality. Only in Aschenbach's inflamed imagination is the figure likened to or identified with the immortal beings of Greek mythology. Even Tadzio's final appearance as Hermes in that impressive setting of complete isolation on the sea-encircled sand bar as a "highly remote and isolated apparition . . ." [62] is at once rationalized as a vision of the dying poet: "It seemed to him, though, as if the pale and charming psychagogue out there was smiling at him, beckoning to him; as if, lifting his hand from his hip, he were pointing outwards, hovering before him in an immensity full of promise" [63]. Analysis, then, proves psychological realism unbetrayed. Tadzio's identification with figures of myth can in every instance be explained on solidly rational grounds as a figment of Aschenbach's over-wrought imagination.

And yet, such is the vividness of Mann's evocation of the mythical figures and their identification with Tadzio that we experience their fusion as palpably real and must exert a conscious effort to disengage in our imagination the "real" boy from the mythical overlay of the divine figures. Here Mann achieved a truly perfect *montage*, a splendid example of what Vernon Venables aptly calls his "new technique for the exploitation of poetic meaning . . . in which no symbol is allowed unequivocal connotation or independent status, but refers to all the others and is bound rigorously to them by means of a highly intricate system of subtly developed associations." Neither Tadzio as the Polish boy, nor Tadzio-Hyacinthus [42] nor Tadzio-Narcissus [43],[4] nor even Tadzio-Hermes [63][5] are "allowed independent status" but they "are identified with each other and finally fused into the single, nuclear, paradoxical meaning which Mann wishes to emphasize":[6] Tadzio as the embodi- .

4. Cp. T. O. Brandt, "Narcissism in Thomas Mann's 'Der Erwahlte,' " *German Life and Letters*, N.S., VII (1954), 233–241; also H. Mitlacher, "Die Entwicklung des Narzissbegriffs," *Germanisch-Romanische Monatschrift*, XXI (1938), 373ff.
5. Cp. Th. Mann in *Romandichtung und Mythologie*, p. 83: "To see the egotistical designated as essentially childlike godliness had to give me joy: it reminded me of Tadzio in *Death in Venice!*"
6. Vernon Venable, "Death in Venice," *The Stature of Thomas Mann*, ed. Ch. Neider (New York: New Directions Press, 1947), p. 131. Unfortunately, Venable's interpretation of examples in support of his definition greatly weakens it. Thus, he maintains that ". . . in the first episode, the symbols were for the most part unambiguous: the stranger meant life and life only; the cemetery death and death only . . ." etc., certainly a simplistic interpretation in flat contradiction of his own theoretical position.

ment and symbol of beauty's fatal fascination for the endangered artist. And even this "single, nuclear . . . meaning" does, in fact, remain "paradoxical." For, while Tadzio *is* Aschenbach's tempter into the "boundless mixture," a "stranger god," another Dionysos who leads the "frenzy of surrender" [57],[7] even though he *is* Aschenbach's guide into the limitless, formless vastness of the sea, that symbol of the "perfection of nothingness," of the "undivided, the immeasurable, the eternal" [26], the guide into the bliss of Nirvana,[8] Tadzio *is*, at one and at the same time, the very antithesis of this rôle and this realm. For he is also the "image and mirror," the paragon of measured, perfectly articulated form. With the regularity of a *leitmotif* he is contraposed to the measureless, shapeless void of the ocean as the supreme articulation and embodiment of Apollinic plasticity, harmony, balance. A well-defined vertical, he cuts boldly across the sea's limitless horizontal: "But while he was thus dreaming away toward the depths of emptiness, the horizontal line of the sea's edge was crossed by a human figure. When he had retrieved his gaze from the boundless realms and refocused his eyes, he saw it was the lovely boy who, coming from the left, was passing before him across the sand" [26]. Thus Tadzio is, paradoxically, the inspiration and challenge to the artist's creative urge that measures and molds and bodies forth and is its nemesis, the tempter to lassitude, stupor, and final disintegration of body and mind.

When Aschenbach first catches sight of the youth, he is at once impressed by his beauty as a magical combination of a uniquely personal charm and of the "purest perfection of form" [21]. He is stimulated to musings on the secret of the "mysterious combination of regularity and individuality that is necessary to produce human beauty" [23]. It is this "mysterious synthesis" which Thomas Mann has achieved in his figure of Tadzio. He has created in him the human being of flesh and blood with its unique charm, with its flaws and failings that bring him close to us and rouse our compassion which goes out only toward our fellow men; and he has raised this "real" being into a complex symbol whose existence is beyond time and space in the realm of eternal myth. In sum, he has achieved in Tadzio a perfect combination of "psychology plus myth."

V

It is not at all surprising to find in Mann's portrayal of Gustav von Aschenbach his skill of psychological analysis and realistic description

7. Tadzio is identified with the "stranger God" by means of the orgiastic cry "with soft consonants in the middle and a drawn-out *uuu* sound on the end, a cry that was sweet and wild at the same time," which is the very sound pattern of Tadzio's name "that possessed something both sweet and wild in its soft consonants and drawn-out *uuu* at the end" [57,28].

8. Cp. Mann, "Lübeck as a Spiritual Existence," *Die Forderung des Tages* (Berlin: Fischer, 1929), p. 47: "The sea is no landscape; it is the experience of nothingness and death, a metaphysical dream."

at a high pitch of perfection,[9] for Aschenbach is, to a significant degree, a self-portrait and is the representative of a way of life, the artist's life, which Mann has explored with such uncompromising, sharp-eyed penetration. Rather, it is impressive to find the author able to maintain in his portraiture of _the protagonist the same subtle balance and tension between reality and symbol, psychology and myth_ which we had found in the other characters of the _Novelle._ Mann's delineation of Aschenbach oscillates tensely between the poles of apotheosis and deflation, of idealization and searching analysis touched with gentle irony, between grandiloquence and understatement, between rhetorical flourish and sober naturalistic prose,[1] without however ever quite touching either extreme.

This dialectical polarity of style is rooted in Mann's attitude toward his hero, which is at once detached and empathetic, marked by an urge to elevate to the prototypical and to deflate to the problematical, characterized by sincere admiration, even adulation and by that smiling irony that has discovered the Achilles' heel. This double-visioned manner of portrayal is also predicated upon _Mann's basic concept of the protagonist as an "unheroic" hero, as the "moralist of achievement" par excellence._ This heroism is a heroism of weakness, a heroism of the "despite," despite frailty of body, despite a problematical, overfastidious, quickly exhausted mind. Such heroism cannot be conveyed except by way of realistic description and searching psychoanalysis, while at the same time the urge to ennoble must also be operative. Thus, Mann's favorite combination of "psychology plus myth" proves to be the perfect means to body forth such a "heroic" figure. Gustav von Aschenbach is raised upon a pedestal as _the_ poet-laureate of exemplary achievement, but he is also examined as a "case" on the psychiatrist's couch. He is associated in the reader's mind with figures of the glorious Grecian past and of Christian legend, with Socrates and Saint Sebastian.[2] Yet these figures are themselves brought down from their lofty plane. To be sure, Socrates is shown as a man of mature wisdom [38] but he is also characterized with quite un-Grecian pathos as the all-too-human mark of youth's seductive beauty [38], and the figure of Saint Sebastian is introduced, significantly, by a "wise analyst"—none other, of course, than the "analyst" Thomas Mann himself—who proceeds to modernize the figure by way of an analysis which is both "precise" and "ingenious" into the representative of an "intellectual and youthful manliness, which grits its

9. Cp. D. E. Oppenheim, loc. cit.
1. Cp. the opening sonorous, gandiloquent sentences of the biographical section II: "the author of the clear and vigorous prose epic on the life of Frederick the Great . . ." [7] with such a sober, pointedly realistic description of Aschenbach as: "Gustav Aschenbach, then, was born the son of a career civil servant in the justice ministry in L., a district capitol in the province of Silesia . . ." [7] or again with the following passage: "Gustav Aschenbach was a man of slightly less than middle height, dark-haired and clean shaven. His head seemed a little too big for a body that was almost dainty" [12].
2. Also with Xenophon, as shown very convincingly by L. Gustafson, op. cit.

teeth in proud modesty and calmly endures the swords and spears as they pass through its body" [9]. It is interesting to note how this passage in its choice of descriptive vocabulary holds the finest balance between the elevated and the realistic style, moving closer to the former in such a traditionally "heroic" phrase as: "endures the swords and spears as they pass through its body"; tending toward the realistic in the expression: "grits its teeth," which serves to render a carefully observed physiological detail from the workaday world. Unquestionably, the sacrosanct figure of the Saint loses some of its patina in the hands of the "precise." In fact, it may be argued that the very opposite of "myth-building" is taking place, that it is not Aschenbach who is elevated, by the process of association and approximation, to the Saint's immortal plane, but rather that it is the figure of saintly legend that suffers a loss of imposing other-wordliness in changing into an "unheroic" hero of our times. The juster view would seem to be that of a well-nigh perfect ambivalence with the patina lost by the Saint's being transferred to the figure of Mann's hero.

Aschenbach's way to his doom is traced with extreme economy on the level of plot, in keeping with the demands of the *Novelle* genre and, more significantly, with Mann's view of the highest function of narrative art. With Schopenhauer he holds that the epic writer's aim should be to conjure up the richest possible inner life by means of a minimum of external action: "Art is found where, with the slightest use of outside life, one's inner life is moved most strongly; for it is the inner life, actually, which is the object of our interest."[3] Thus every detail of Aschenbach's outward life is so chosen as to illuminate the deepest recesses of his mind and to furnish the richest symbolical meaning. Aschenbach is drawn, on the psychological level, as the aging man whose rational, disciplined self is overwhelmed by a late and sudden eruption of emotional drives which had been all too long and ruthlessly suppressed; he is also the artist "who produces beauty at the cost of intellectual self-sacrifice" [28]. This delineation is most searching in its statement of the unique case, yet at the same time it is most effective in raising the unique to the typical. Aschenbach transcends the individual, he too is "image and mirror," his fate is set up as the symbol and mirror of the lot of creative man who follows the danger-beset path, that "path of error and sin" [60] which leads by way of the senses toward the goal of ultimate cognition and beauty. In fact, Aschenbach's figure gains its importance precisely by transcending the unique and individual "case" and rising to the typical and the eternal. Thus, *Death in Venice*, is once again seen to be an important step in Mann's reorientation, with growing maturity, from the "bourgeois-self" to timeless myth: "It would seem true as a rule that in certain years the taste for the merely individual and special, the exceptional case, the 'bourgeois' in the widest sense of the

3. "Kunst des Romans," *Altes und Neues* (Frankfurt: Fischer, 1953), p. 396.

word, has gradually been lost. Stepping to the forefront of interest, in its place, has been the common, the eternally-human, the eternally-recurring, the timeless, in short: the mythical."[4]

It is but natural that Aschenbach's figure and fate, being central to the *Novelle*, would have received extensive and intensive treatment. To enter upon a full-scale analysis would be to move along well-beaten paths. Nevertheless, one important theme seems to have received no more than passing mention[5] and deserves elaboration. It is the typically Romantic theme of the fatal fascination held by the sunlit, idyllic South for the denizen of the mist-shrouded North. The *locus classicus* of this theme in the *Novelle* is that seemingly realistic description of Aschenbach's summerplace in the mountains and the subsequent passage quoted all but verbatim from Homer's *Odyssey*.

Just prior to complete surrender to the lure of Venice and his long yearning for "freedom," Aschenbach thinks back to the place of his creative toil in the North: "he remembered his country home in the mountains, the site of his summertime struggles, where the clouds drifted through the garden, where in the evening fearful thunderstorms extinguished the lights in the house and the ravens he fed soared to the tops of the spruce trees" [35]. Surely, on the level of realism, it is rather startling to have Aschenbach keep "ravens" for pets. Yet this eccentricity of description with its attention-provoking "cue" is, of course, intentional. It serves to switch the mind of the reader attuned to the "combination" of realism and myth to the mythological plane. With a start one becomes aware of Aschenbach's approximation to Odin-Wodan whose mythological bird was, in fact, the raven. Now the other elements of the *montage* fall neatly into place and reveal their full significance: the mountainous setting, the low hanging clouds, the terrifying storms that extinguish the lights of the house, the ravens swinging in the wind-tossed "tops of the spruce trees." With what calculated effect the words are chosen to conjure up the mythological setting without entirely cancelling out reality! We see Aschenbach's "country home" but at the same time we see, as if superimposed upon it, mighty Thor in his ram-drawn chariot laying about him with hammer and lightning, threatening the home, extinguishing the hospitable fire of helpless mortals; we see the typical setting which Romantic imagination has formed into the timeless abode of the Nordic gods, especially stark and forbidding when contrasted with the idyllic shores of the Mediterranean and the sunlit heights of Olympus.

It is precisely this Romantic antithesis that patterns Aschenbach's feelings and thoughts. As he recalls his Northern home, his present surroundings turn into a veritable Elysium: "Then it might seem to him that he had been transported to the land of Elysium at the far ends of

4. *Neue Studien*, p. 166; cp. also *Romandichtung und Mythologie*, p. 19.
5. Cp. Pabst, op. cit., p. 349.

the earth, where a life of ease is bestowed upon mortals, where there is no snow, no winter, no storms or streaming rain, but rather always the cooling breath rising from Okeanos, where the days run out in blissful leisure, trouble-free, struggle-free, dedicated only to the sun and its revels" [35].

This is the passage from the *Odyssey* (IV. 561–569)[6]—slightly revised so as to point up the theme of leisure and feasting of foremost importance in Mann's antithetical structure—in which Proteus, "the unerring old man of the sea" informs the demi-god Menelaus[7] that:

> it is not ordained that thou shouldst die . . . in horse-pasturing Argos, but to the Elysian plain and the bounds of the earth will the immortals convey thee . . . where life is easiest for men. No snow is there, nor heavy storm, nor ever rain, but ever does Oceanos send up blasts of the shrill-blowing West Wind that they may give cooling to men . . .

Here we have a supreme example of sophistication in Mann's composition, which the cultivated reader should relish. The quotation from the classical source is used to develop most effectively a deeply Romantic theme. It serves, at the same time, to furnish another link between Aschenbach and Greek mythology. The informed reader acquainted with the general context in which this passage occurs, will recognize Mann's intention to identify the hero of his *Novelle*, admittedly by way of hidden inference, with Menelaus, the demi-god and to underscore the mythical quality of Aschenbach's death by associating it with Proteus' prophecy of Menelaus' apotheosis. Though on the level of realism Aschenbach suffers an all but sordid collapse, ravaged by an unnatural passion and the onslaught of cholera, on the level of myth he does not die "in horse-pasturing Argos" but is conveyed by the "immortal" (Tadzio-Hermes-Psychopompos) "to the land of Elysium at the far ends of the earth" (178) [35], "in an immensity full of promise" (234) [63]. Thus, Aschenbach's psycho-physical disintegration is informed with the dignity and the beauty of apotheosis by being linked with the "mythical scheme," the "mythical recurrence" of a demi-god's entrance into the bliss of Elysium.[8]

In the supreme achievement of his *Meisternovelle* [master-story] Thomas Mann draws equally from both fountainheads of truly great art, from the immediate, sensible present and the endless vistas of the past, from the fleeting reality of life and the timeless reality of art. Throughout he maintains, with an unerring touch, a unique equilibrium

6. Cp. also Franz Mautner, loc. cit.
7. So regarded as the husband of Helena, the daughter of Zeus.
8. Cp. Fritz Martini, "Der Tod in Venedig," *Das Wagnis der Sprache* (Stuttgart: Klett Verlag, 1954), p. 202: "What happens to Aschenbach is, in equal measures, a factor of psychological and mythical law."

between the realism of coldly controlled observation, of self-critical analysis and that "intoxication" that inspired creative élan, that "splendid sensation of uplift" capable of infusing the specters of a mythical past with a new vibrant vitality and thus creates what must be adjudged a masterpiece of "psychology plus myth."

MANFRED DIERKS

[Nietzsche's *Birth of Tragedy* and Mann's *Death in Venice*]†

III

André von Gronicka has analyzed the two-tiered structure of *Death in Venice*—"this bifocal view of life that encompasses both the transcendent and the real"—as a principle of composition "between the poles of psychological realism and the symbolism of myth." [1] This psychophysical reality corresponds with an often cryptic symbolic, mythical reality. On this latter level the conflict is the agon between the basic Apollonian and Dionysian powers. R. A. Nichols has shown that Thomas Mann oriented himself to *The Birth of Tragedy*. [2] Aschenbach represents the Apollonian principle: as a "sculptor" [37] and conservative formalist [12], characteristics included in his "depiction," he turned away from "all sympathy with the abyss" [11]. Incidentally, this last phrase is taken from "What Do Aesthetic Ideals Mean?" [*On the Genealogy* 538f.], where it refers to "the aesthetic priest," to Wagner's inclination toward Schopenhauer's vitalistic-methaphysical original reason for will, which Nietzsche had once embraced and used to "Hellenize" *The Birth of Tragedy*, to imbue it with a Dionysian-world principle. On the mythical level Aschenbach falls victim to this principle.

Thomas Mann described the structure and the mythical antagonism of *Death in Venice* with the formula "novella-like tragedy" in his *Sketch of My Life* of 1930. As late as this qualification may have come, we do not want to disregard it as unimportant. [In segments of his working

---

† From *Studien zu Mythos und Psychologie bei Thomas Mann* [Studies of myth and psychology in Thomas Mann] (Frankfurt am Main: Vittorio Klostermann, 1972) 18–37, 232–37. Translated and edited by John M. Jeep. (Footnotes have been edited or omitted.) Reprinted by permission of Vittorio Klostermann, Frankfurt am Main. All quotations from *Death in Venice*, as well as from the letters and working notes included here, have been taken from the translations in this volume; page references to this Norton Critical Edition follow quotations in brackets.
1. André von Gronicka, " 'Myth Plus Psychology': A Style Analysis of *Death in Venice*" 191–93. [See above, pp. 115–30. Editor]
2. See R. A. Nichols, *Nietzsche in the Early Works of Thomas Mann* (Los Angeles and Berkeley, 1955). [The excerpts from Nietzsche throughout the translation of this essay are from *The Portable Nietzsche*, trans. Kaufmann (New York, 1954). Page references are to this work. Editor.]

notes, taken from an unknown source,][3] Thomas Mann included details from the Dionysus mythos, especially about the march of the Asiatic Dionysus to Greece; for example: Dionysus is said to be "one of the personifications of the 'suffering' (dying and revived) god"; he is portrayed as a "stranger invading from without by force," who could bestow madness during his mysterious rites; the god's "swarm" is said to be "joined by the inhabitants of an entire city"; the "newly arrived stranger" demands "fanatical homage and acknowledgment"; "in the myth everyone who defies this god suffers the most horrific punishment (murderous frenzy)" [see sheets 9–10, 74–75]. In a note, Thomas Mann connects this last passage in particular to Aschenbach's ecstatic dream of destruction.

Research now shows that he received the stimulus for these enquiries, not from Erwin Rohde's *Psyche*,[4] but from no other source than *The Birth of Tragedy*. So we must read them in light of that work. One should also be reminded that, whatever Nietzsche believed later, in 1871 he read Wagner's (pre-1854) revolutionary theses on art—exactly those theses Thomas Mann was working with as late as about 1911—in the light of Schopenhauer's philosophy, reinforcing them with classical models.

The first obvious agreement between [Mann's work note] excerpts and *The Birth of Tragedy* can probably be seen in the shared (false) assumption that Asia was the home of the Dionysian cult. Nietzsche found "exhortations" toward regeneration "of our weary culture" in these beliefs:

> The age of Socratic man is over; put on wreaths of ivy, take the thyrsus in your hand, and do not be surprised when tigers and panthers lie down, fawning at your feet. . . . You shall accompany the Dionysian pageant from India to Greece. [*Birth* 124]

The connection here to Aschenbach is easy to establish: he is "Socratic" in that Nietzsche sees a logical connection between the Socratic and the Apollonian, a connection that leads from tragedy to the novel [*Birth* 90f.]. The image of the "Dionysian pageant [traveling] from India to Greece" (Europe) appears psychologically motivated; in Aschenbach's Munich vision: "His desire acquired vision" [5]; he saw the "image" of an Asian jungle (draft note: Ganges delta), saw "the eyes of a lurking tiger sparkle" [5]. The season plays a role here: "It was early May and . . . a premature summer had arrived" [3]. Compare: "with

3. Manfred Dierks included portions of Thomas Mann's working notes for *Death in Venice* in an appendix to this essay. That appendix has been omitted, but the working notes themselves have been translated and are included above on pp. 70–92. Thus, Dierk's original references to Appendix I have been changed throughout this excerpt to the working notes, and relevant sheet and page numbers have been inserted in brackets. [Editor]

4. Erwin Rohde, *Psyche: Seelencult und Unsterblichkeitsglaube der Griechen*, 4th ed. (Tübingen, 1907).

the potent coming of spring that penetrates all nature with joy, these Dionysian emotions awake, and as they grow in intensity everything subjective vanishes into complete self-forgetfulness" [*Birth* 36]. (The "premature summer" characterizes the pathological, unnatural trait in Aschenbach's "Dionysian feeling," for which he, in the end, does not show himself to be ready.) That "image" can finally be explained in Nietzschean superpsychological/metaphysical terms as the Dionysian or Apollonian "artistic state of nature" with respect to which "every artist is an 'imitator' " [*Birth* 38]. When it is said of Aschenbach—balancing pathetic emotional submission against mental activity—"His desire acquired vision, and his imagination . . . created its own version" and "then the vision faded" [5], Nietzsche's analysis is evoked. By intermingling Dionysian and Apollonian "imitation"—as for example Greek tragedy does—with the artistic response stimulated by "Dionysian intoxication and mystical self-abnegation, alone and apart from the singing revelers, we may imagine how, through Apollonian dream-inspiration, his own state, i.e., his oneness with the fundamental world, is revealed to him in a *symbolic dream image*" [*Birth* 38]. The attack of "wanderlust" [5] was triggered by the offensive entrance of the mysterious wanderer, who had "the appearance of a foreigner, a traveler from afar" [4]. We will only be able to interpret this later on. In order to keep on the intended track it will suffice to recall the excerpt [in Thomas Mann's working notes] in which Dionysus was seen as a "foreigner invading from without by force," as the "one coming, or the stranger," whose preceding "swarm" of corybantes was joined by others [sheets 9–10, 74–75].

Aschenbach is on his way. "What he sought was someplace foreign, someplace isolated" [13]; a "pressure within" directs him from Brioni to Venice. On the ship he meets the false youth, an old man in inappropriate, youthful, festive garb, who "pretended to be" [15] one of the young people soon "full of excitement and Asti" [16]. Certain characteristics vaguely suggest the Munich stranger. The fact that we are dealing with a series of figures to be understood as a motif is soon made abundantly clear by the gondolier, who seemed "clearly not of Italian stock" [18], then by the "musicians . . . who waylaid the gondola" with their "exotic but mercenary tourist lyrics" [19]. The fatal discovery of the cholera epidemic follows the appearance of the street singers, whose leader— he, too, seems "strange" [50]—fits physiognomically into this series. In the last phase of his downfall and degradation, Aschenbach places himself in the series, allowing himself to be dressed up as a "false youth" like the old Polesian.

All of the figures share, among external characteristics, their "foreignness" and their offensive appearance to Aschenbach. Translated into the terminological polarity of *The Birth* and placed in relation to the excerpt cited above, they should be understood as opposing the Apollonian, as messengers of Dionysus, corybantes from his "swarm." This interpretation can only be secured by knowledge of the mythical pattern that Mann employs—not evident in the text alone; he again orients himself toward Nietzsche: *The Birth of Tragedy* describes the degradation of tragedy and its (Schopenhauerian) "mystery doctrine" [*Birth* 74]—as always loyal in its translation of Wagnerian speculations[5]—as the departure of the Dionysian from the counterplay and cooperation of the two artistic drives. It was Euripides who attempted to "base drama exclusively on the un-Dionysian," striving for the absolute Apollonian form of the "dramatized epos" [*Birth* 82]. But he was destined to fail not only because of the unavoidable "Socratic tendency"—the intellectualization of his art—but above all because of the Dionysian power itself taking revenge. In old age Euripides renounced his earlier approach: "The god Dionysus is too powerful; his most intelligent adversary—like Pentheus in *The Bacchae*—is unwittingly enchanted by him, and in this enchantment runs to meet his fate. The judgment of the two old men, Cadmus and Tiresias, seems also to be the judgment of the old poet: the reflections of the wisest individuals cannot overcome . . . the perpetually self-propagating worship of Dionysus. . . . This is what we are told by a poet who opposed Dionysus with heroic valor throughout a long life—and who finally ended his career with a glorification of his adversary and with suicide . . ." [*Birth* 81f.].

Thomas Mann believed this interpretation of Euripides' work to be exemplary. Its intellectually critical stance, its distance from the "unspeakable" of the "original reason"—these, of course, were Wagner's reasons for decrying the epos. For reasons to be explained, the attitude embodied by the epos became part of Aschenbach's character, a character for which Thomas Mann used Euripides as a metaphysical prototype. A reading of *The Bacchae*—according to Nietzsche a reflection and summation of the problem with the epos—will be useful.

The tragedy presents the fate of the Theban king, Pentheus, who—in contrast with his people—rejects the cult of Dionysus, approaching from Asia. The elders Cadmus and Tiresias, then the god ["the stranger"] himself, attempt unsuccessfully to change his mind. Finally Dionysus curses him with bacchic insanity and he, now in the costume of the maenad, proceeds toward certain destruction. When the frenzied bacchante see the eavesdropper, he pays with his life.

Parts of the tragedy can be shown to function as patterns in *Death in Venice*. The most obvious correspondence is with the *epeisodia*, which both act as motifs and offer a basic structure for scenes of the novella. Below is a concordance—with appropriate modification.

---

5. Excerpts from Wagner's writings throughout the translation of this essay are taken from Richard Wagner, *Gesammelte Schriften und Dichtungen*, 3d ed. (Leipzig: Frisch, 1897–98); references to the volume and page number of that edition follow quotations. [Editor]

[Death in Venice]	*The Bacchae*[6]

On the Polesian ship Aschenbach has an encounter that gives him a "dreamy estrangement, a bizarre distortion of the world" [15]. Among the festively dressed Polesian youths was one who was "not genuine": "He was old. . . . There were wrinkles around his eyes and mouth. The faint carmine of his cheeks was rouge; the brown hair beneath the colorfully banded hat was a wig; . . . his clipped moustache and goatee were dyed; . . . the teeth . . . dentures; . . . his hands . . . those of an old man. With a shudder Aschenbach watched him and his interaction with his friends. Did they not know, had they not noticed that he was old, that he had no right . . . to pretend to be one of their own?" [14–15]

Prior to the appearance of Pentheus. The old men, Cadmus and Tiresias, are preparing themselves to follow the call of Dionysus to the bacchanal. "*Cadmus:* . . . But here I am dressed in the costume of the god. . . . I could dance night and day, untiringly beating the earth with my thyrsus! And how sweet it is to forget my old age" (11. 179 f., 187 ff.). "*Tiresias:* . . . People may say, 'Aren't you ashamed? At your age going dancing, wreathing your head with ivy?' Well, I am not ashamed. Did the god declare that just the young should dance? No, he desires his honor from all mankind" (11. 204 ff.). Enter Pentheus. "*Pentheus:* I am also told a foreigner has come. . . ." He notices the old men. "But this is incredible! Tiresias the seer tricked out in a dappled fawnskin! And you, my own grandfather, playing at the bacchant with a wand! Sir, I shrink to see your old age so foolish" (11. 215 ff.).

Before landing in Venice, Aschenbach again notices him amidst the youths "full of excitement and Asti" [16]:

Futilely, the "swarming" elders attempted to convert Pentheus. Now they depart to place themselves in the Dionysian spring procession.

"It was disgusting, however, to see the state into which the made-up old coot's false fellowship with the young people had brought him. . . . His vision blurred, . . .

"*Tiresias:* . . . Take your staff and follow me. Support me with your hands, and I shall help you too lest we stumble and fall, a sight of shame, two old men together. But

6. Excerpts from *The Bacchae* throughout this essay are from the edition of that play in *Greek Tragedies*, ed. David Grene and Richmond Lattimore, vol. 3 (Chicago: U Chicago P, 1968). [Editor]

swaying tipsily in place, pulled to and fro by intoxication, barely able to maintain his balance. Since he would have fallen over at the first step, he dared not move from the spot." [16]

go we must, acknowledging the service that we owe to god, Bacchus, the son of Zeus" (11. 363 ff.).

The divinatory strain of Dionysian *manía* is also layered into the realistic level of the text. The departure *honneurs* of the old man foreshadow Aschenbach's experience of intoxication: " 'Keep a fond memory of us! . . . Our complements,' he babbles, . . . 'our complements to your beloved, your dearly beloved, your lovely beloved." [17]

"*Tiresias:* . . . This is a god of prophecy. His worshippers, like madmen, are endowed with divinatory powers. For when the god enters the body of a man, he fills him with the breath of prophecy. . . . Mark my words Pentheus, . . . do not mistake for wisdom the fantasies of your sick mind" (11. 298 ff., 309 ff.)

The textual passages, placed in relation to each other here, share the same compositional function: The foreshadowing effect of the "fond remembrance" requested by the false youth is fulfilled in *Death in Venice* when Aschenbach, now "a powerless victim of the demon" [57], allows himself to be made more youthful cosmetically for his beloved. In the same way the first *episodion* of *The Bacchae* corresponds to the fourth, which obtains its tragic irony from the repetition of motif. The situation of the protagonist in the novella and the tragedy is the same: defeated by hallucination, overpowered by Dionysus, he enters into the catastrophe.

Aschenbach's orgiastic dream must here again be understood in the context of Nietzsche's metapsychology.

[Death in Venice]

[The Birth of Tragedy]

" . . . the deep beckoning melody of the flute. Was it not also beckoning him, the resisting dreamer, with shameless persistence to the festival . . . ? Great was his loathing, . . . sincere his resolve to defend his own against the foreign invader, the enemy of self-controlled and dignified intellect." He sees the bacchante, "and his

". . . the dithyrambic chorus is a chorus of transformed characters whose civic past and social status have been totally forgotten: they have become timeless servants of their god. . . . In this magic transformation the Dionysian reveler sees himself as a satyr, *and as a satyr, in turn, he sees the god.*" [64].

soul longed to join in the reeling
dance of the god. . . . Now
among them, now a part of them,
the dreamer belonged to the
stranger god." [57]

A similar confrontation, with a similar meaning, precedes the fourth
Bacchae episode. Despite Pentheus's rational opposition, Dionysus per-
suades him to dress as a girl and eavesdrop on the bacchante, and, ultimately, the god imposes Bacchic madness upon the king.

[Death in Venice]	The Bacchae
Shamed "when he looked at the sweet youth with whom he was smitten," Aschenbach allows himself to be "rejuvenated" cosmetically. Thereafter he is similar in constitution and appearance to the false youth on the ship. In the barbershop:	Dionysus, "familiar with the duty of the concubine," convinces Pentheus to allow himself to be disguised as a bacchant. When the enchanted one, grotesquely made up and shaking the thyrsus, strolls through Thebes, he repeats the error of the old man reprimanded before him.
"So the glib barber washed his customer's hair with two liquids, . . . and it turned as black as it had been in youth. . . . Aschenbach . . . was . . . quite incapable of fending him off. . . . he was . . . watching . . . as . . . his eyes grew in width. . . . A little further down he could see his skin perk up with . . . delicate carmine rouge, his lips . . . swell like raspberries. . . . His heart pounded as he saw in the mirror a young man in full bloom. . . .	"*Dionysus:* I shall go inside and help you dress. . . . On your head I shall set a wig with long curls. . . . Next, robes to your feet and a net for your hair. . . . Then a thyrsus for your hand and a skin of dappled fawn" (11. 827ff.).
"The beguiled lover went out. . . . His tie was red, and his broad-brimmed straw hat was encircled by a band of many colors." [58–59]	"*Dionysus:* Pentheus, if you are still so curious to see forbidden sights, so bent on evil still, come out. Let us see you in your woman's dress, disguised in Maenad clothes" (11. 912 ff.).

The integration of the mythical pattern *The Bacchae* presents has been set forth here, in detail, as a model. As opposed to citations of Homer's or Xenophon's texts, what we have here are subtle references from actual occurrences in the novella to particular actions, basic motifs, and individual words from the play that are difficult to decode ("the stranger," "to swarm"). In adopting these things, Mann follows Nietzsche in his presentation of the metaphysical-psychological fatality inherent in Apollonian one-sidedness. In this case the paradigm was also taken from Nietzsche (unless Thomas Mann came up with it for himself): the tragic fate of Apollo's servant Pentheus, who falls victim to the foreign god advancing from Asia, reflects Euripides' artistic conflict. Therefore, not only is Aschenbach's fate tragic, but the structure of the novella also follows the tragic pattern ("novella-like tragedy"). Finally, a close connection to the excerpt [included in Mann's work notes] is also recognizable: Mann's inquiries into the Dionysus strain brought together here suggest an introduction to an edition of Euripides as the source; in any case, these inquiries were carried out for *The Bacchae* in particular.

We can now set forth fully the chain of meaning broached above. It begins with the appearance of the stranger at Munich's North Cemetery, which initiates the series of related figures. It has been noted that the role this figure plays in description and motif is semantically multilayered. Synchretism of meaning allows one to see in that figure the *Thanatos* that Lessing[7] introduced, as well as a playful reference to *Hermes psychogogos*, which may also have been intended. However, the dominant meaning can only come from the statements made above: the stranger *is* also Dionysus or a satyr from his swarm. The signal value of the words "stranger" and "come from afar" [4] can then be decoded: the reference is always to the so-called Asian Dionysus (see 11. 231, 245, 353, 452, and *passim*) in *The Bacchae* (and in the excerpts [from Mann's work notes] above). Perhaps "the look of the traveler" in the appearance of the stranger [4] also refers to *Hermes psychopompos* in the associative mixture, but the context—the stranger's appearance is said to cause Aschenbach "a sudden strange expansion of his inner space, a rambling unrest" [5]—in any case makes the reference to Dionysian *ecstasis* [74] dominant. The same goes for the "stick with an iron tip" [4], which (without the "iron tip") could be a Hermes attribute, but in the novella—through a reference in the Dionysian dream to "pointed staves" [57] is clearly more heavily weighted toward a thyrsus correspondence. The "wide and straight-brimmed straw hat" (*petasos*) may point mainly to Hermes, but that Thomas Mann may have intended a reference to the invading Dionysus does not have to be ruled out. Finally,

---

7. Lessing: Gotthold Ephraim Lessing (1729–1781), German philosopher, dramatist, and critic; *Thanatos*: the Greek God of death. Lessing emphasized the difference between the medieval depiction of death as a skeleton and the Greek representation of death as the twin brother of sleep. [Editor]

note the aggressive nature of the encounter (e.g., the word group "inquisitive survey," "belligerently," "to . . . force the other to avert")— not motivated on a realistic level—and the stereotypical description of Dionysus "as a foreigner, invading from without by force" [sheet 9, 75] (cf. *The Bacchae*, 11. 47 ff.).

All the characteristics named point again to an imitation of *The Bacchae* pattern: in the play's prologue, Dionysus, bedecked with his attributes (ivy wreath, thyrsus, mask), changed, however, into a human figure, relates the background and his intentions. The god, who has come with his swarms from "Asia's . . . shores, " visits "this city, first in Hellas"—Thebes—in order to justify again his ordination. He threatens the fallen Pentheus: "I shall prove to him and every man in Thebes that I am a god" (11. 47f.). He sends Asian maenades ahead into the city as messengers in order to announce his entrance. It is only at the end of the tragedy that the god, hitherto hidden, "disguised as a man," experiences his epiphany.

Thus, the stranger at the North Cemetery, according to the mythic pattern, reveals himself as the Dionysus of the tragedy, moving in revengefully against the Apollonian servants who have fallen away from him. The position of this passage (the prologue) in the novella betrays the fact that the strategic structure is replicated on the level of the plot.

As shown above, *The Birth of Tragedy* motivates the mythic chain of meaning from this point forward, while the similarity to *The Bacchae* remains. The encounter with the old man on the Polesian ship reaffirms the dominance of the paradigm offered by *The Bacchae* (note the dominance of the Pentheus-Cadmus scene). One can now recognize the correspondence between the young men "full of excitement and Asti" and the Dionysian swarms sent to Thebes. Now, too, an attribute can be interpreted as a motif: the straw hat of the Munich stranger, repeated in "the colorfully banded hat" of the "not genuine" youth, reveals itself to be a Dionysian symbol when Aschenbach also dons it [14]. This is the ivy wreath—like the one worn by the god in the play's prologue, by the swarms sent out by him, and by the two old Thebans—translated onto a realistic level. That attribute is passed on in its double function to the gondolier "without a license" [20] by whom, given his role as a Charon-Hades reference, the *Thanatos* motif is reactivated, but whose dominant significance lies along Dionysian lines. This also applies to the "musicians . . . who waylaid [the gondola] . . . obtrusively" [19]: "Come, and with your native Phyrgian drum, . . . pound at the palace doors of Pentheus! Let the city of Thebes behold you" (11. 58 ff.). With this, Dionysus sends his Asian corybantes off against the apostates.

After these episodes, a further, more retarding complex of references—to *The Odyssey*, Xenophon's paraphrases, the Platonic dialogues—raises the significance of the Dionysian pattern onto the mythical level. The direct, or identifiable but indirect, citation now reveals to Aschenbach, and the reader, the classical perspective. Homeric idyll and Platonic enthusiasm only cover up the pathetic Dionysian process: a multiplicity of meaningful designations reestablish the connection over and over. The "mania" [44] driving Aschenbach is intended clearly to express *manía* (Bacchic madness); the "demon" [46] that drives him is soon no longer a (Platonic-)Socratic *Daimon*—but one that puts him in a "mad position," makes him "intoxicated" [46] like a bacchant, like that old man on the ship. We recall that Nietzsche saw the Dionysian impulse ready at the foundation of every "Apollonian illusion": "The true goal is veiled by the phantasm" [*Birth* 44]. The limits of the Apollonian sphere of reference characterize the change in Tadzio's mythical designations: he who earlier appeared to Aschenbach as a (Platonic) "tool of memory" used by "the god" (Eros), he later recognizes in his true function as "an instrument of a scornful deity" [55]; one who, as an ideal, had inspired him to enthusiastic "imitation," in the Dionysian context must be translated as "idol" [44]. The psychology of love follows for long stretches exactly that of Socrates in *Phaedrus* (the palinode), who sees the fate of the lover as dependent upon which god he, by force of his character, must "imitate" (see *Phaedrus* 252c–253c). Aschenbach's Apollonian self-deception must thus give way to the Dionysian truth within.

Prior to the discovery of the fatal cholera epidemic, the Dionysian chain of signification becomes dominant once and for all. In the appearance of a "band of street singers," all the characteristics are once again gathered together; aggressiveness appears to increase in this "swarm"; the musical motif is now accentuated; just as clearly the theatrical-tragic reference shifts itself onto the realistic level: "They stood . . . next to the iron lamppost of an arc light and raised their faces, shining in the white illumination, toward the great terrace, where the guests were enjoying this traditional popular entertainment" [49]. The scornful song "in an incomprehensible dialect" [51] at the close could be placed in relation to the corresponding one by the bacchic choir (11. 1153 ff.), sung in triumph over Pentheus. The following day Aschenbach learns of the *cholera asiatica*.

And what Socrates knew would happen to the lover (see *Phaedrus* 252a), so too it happens to Aschenbach: "What value did art and virtue hold for him when he could have chaos?" [56] So now Dionysus has his epiphany in an orgiastic "physical-spiritual experience" in which—also in the semantic system of the text—the mythic-prototypical level of meaning is united with the realistic level through motifs established earlier in other settings: ". . . there was a phrase, darkly familiar that named what was coming: *'The stranger god!'* " [56]. The secondary musical motif, which was twice foreshadowed [7, 19, 28, 36] now shows its Dionysian character, taking up the basic sound of Tadzio's name when called out [27]:

. . . rattling clarion calls and muffled thunder, shrill cheering on top of it all, and a certain howl with a drawn-out *uuu* sound at the end. All this was accompanied and drowned out by the gruesomely sweet tones of a flute playing a cooing, recklessly persistent tune that penetrated to the very bowels, where it cast a shameless enchantment. [56]

Had Nietzsche not complained about the likes of Aschenbach-Wagner, that the music "is *décadence* music and no longer Dionysus's flute . . ."? Aschenbach "belonged to the stranger god" [57], for that is the fate of anyone captured by Eros, "who follows any god in the round dance: to honor and imitate this one . . . in his life (*Phaedrus* 252d). He aligns himself as a "not genuine" youth within the bacchic "swarm." The fate of Pentheus has fulfilled itself. Now the mythic gains dominance over the realistic; Aschenbach's infection by cholera occurs as if coincidentally [59].

Aschenbach again follows the example of Socrates and in "strange dream logic" offers his own palinode to Eros in which he refutes the stern decision concerning "reborn ingenuousness and . . . form" [61], for they "lead him to the abyss. Yes, they too lead to the abyss" [61]. We may remember that Nietzsche—full of modesty, like the "ascetic priest"—had attributed a tendency to the metaphysics of will—that is, to the Dionysian quality of *The Birth*—a tendency that does not suffice itself with—Apollonian—phenomenality [Nietzsche 538].

In the face of the "abyss" (of the sea) the tragedy closes: "A camera with no photographer to operate it stood on its tripod at the edge of the sea, a black cloth that covered it fluttering with a snapping noise in a wind that now blew colder" [61]. Interpreting carefully, we should limit the referential character of this image to the tripod of Apollo, now "with no photographer." The same goes for Tadzio's wrestling match with Yaschu, "which ended swiftly with the defeat of the weaker, lovely boy." It seemed "as if in the last moments before leave-taking the subservient feelings of the underling turned to vindictive cruelty as he sought to take revenge for a long period of slavery" [62]. In the economy of the text the passage also clearly has a symbolic function to which designations inappropriate to the situation point: "the sturdy boy," "victim" [62]. This play within a play repeats once again the conflict and end of the tragic plot; once more the victory of Dionysus, of that god long suppressed, is played out; here one could imagine a free analogy to Satyr drama.[8] Is it possible that Thomas Mann wanted to include the nearly homonymic association with "Yacchus" (the Latin name of Dionysus) in the Polish vocative "Yaschu"? In any event, he noted the name in Erwin Rohde's *Psyche* (cf. *The Bacchae*, 1. 725).

8. Satyr drama: short comic parodies of Greek myths presented following trios of tragedies during drama contests held to honor the Greek god Dionysus. [Editor]

Finally, in the background motif of the "diseased city," whose horrible "secret . . . fused and became one with [Aschenbach's] own innermost secret" [45], we find a final recourse to the Bacchic pattern: Thebes' fate, of course, also reflects that of the protagonist, "The whole city was possessed [by the spirit of Bacchus]" (*The Bacchae*, 1. 1296), and the populace follows the Asian swarm that brought the "strange disease and pollutes our bed" (1. 354). In Venice, "a certain demoralization" [55]' appears in the wake of the Asian cholera, and "prostitution and lasciviousness took on brazen and extravagant forms never before seen here and thought to be at home only in the southern parts of the country and in the seraglios of the orient" [55]. This passage provides us with the clearest example of the convergence of "the reality of the psychophysical world" (Gronicka) with a mythical substratum: the "increasing tendency" [53] of the Indian cholera to spread to Europe corresponds to the "Dionysian procession from India to Greece" (Nietzsche), the "tale of the coming of the 'stranger god' " (Thomas Mann, *On Myself*, 13). Thomas Mann was able to learn from Nietzsche and Erwin Rohde that it was precisely the Dionysian phenomenon that represents a union of myth and psychology (better: psychosemantics). *The Birth of Tragedy* had shown Dionysian intoxication to be mankind's ever-present metaphysical necessity [*Birth* 36f.], a necessity that has survived into the present; Greek myths merely provided a contingent, primitive form for this spiritual reality. At the same time, we must also consider Nietzsche's later pronouncement in which he diagnosed the diseased logical consequence of the ascetic movements in the Christian era [*Birth* 36f, Nietzsche 556f., 578f.]: this is also part of Aschenbach's etiology. Rohde's *Psyche* takes the myth just as seriously and analyses in it the psychophysical process of the Dionysian *ecstasis*, seen as a basic human possibility. The term "epidemic" appears explicitly here for the conjunction of the mythic cult and the physical disease [Rohdes 282ff.]. *Death in Venice* makes use of this view.

An interpretation of the melding of both levels of meaning would, to a great extent, be a linguistic-analytical task. This can be aptly demonstrated in the passage on page [53] and following. The report of the "travel agency . . . clerk" on the nature of the pestilence is not reported verbatim, so all Mann's semantic intentions can be maintained. This fusional passage, intended to be explicit, becomes effective above all in connection with earlier passages: the motifs from Aschenbach's Munich "vision" (the "tropical swamp," vaporous sky," "lurking tiger," etc.) are now repeated in reference to the cholera; the additive style makes the backwards reference clear. Already in the first sentence, the strands of meaningful reference, which before had been separated—"stranger," "from afar," "look of a traveler" [4–5]—are brought together by means of the motif now applied to the disease, an "increasing tendency to spread" [53]. Also, that which had earlier presented itself as psychologically motivated ("wanderlust," "thirst for faraway places" [5]) receives, with the migration of the disease, its physical correlate, with a tendency toward personification increasing from sentence to sentence ("had shown an increasing tendency," "roam," "raged," "following the great caravan routes" [53]). Echoes of *The Bacchae* ("having been carried in on Syrian merchant ships," "the moral decay of Venice,") are reinforced by Greco-Latin vocabulary (mephitic,[9] vibrioid bacteria, tenacity, panic, mask [54]), and finally by the cryptic parallel between Dionysus and *cholera asiatica:*

[Death in Venice]	*[The Bacchae]*

The pestilence had spread "westwards to *Afghanistan and Persia;* and . . . had brought its horrors as far as *Astrakhan* and even Moscow. . . . The specter . . . emerged simultaneously in several Mediterranean port cities. . . . It had raised its grisly head in Toulon and Malaga, *shown its grim mask* several times in Palermo and Naples. . . . in mid-May . . . the terrible vibrioid bacteria had been found [in *Venice*]." [54]

(In the prologue) *"Dionysus:* . . . those golden-rivered lands, Lydia and Phyrgia, where my journey began. Overland I went, across the steppes of Persia where the sun strikes hotly down, through Bactrian fastness and the grim waste of Media. Thence to rich Arabia I came. . . . This city, first in Hellas . . . I shall *prove* to [Pentheus] and every man in *Thebes* that I am a god indeed. And when my worship is established here, and all is well, then I *shall go my way and be revealed* to other men in other lands." (11. 14 ff., 47 ff.)

Here action verbs and personification make the emergence of the pestilence parallel the mythical plot so closely that they are almost identical. Beyond that, the multiple significance of "Venice," as far as that name can be precisely decoded, was included in the range of associations from pages [53] to [59] ("swamp," "occidental," "Thesbians," "diseased city"). The connotations of this name achieve even more, relating the various contexts in which it is placed to one another, without articulating this relation explicitly, and this leads to pure—but calculable— impressionistic effects: participation in the "plague" merges Aschenbach's mythic fate with his physical fate [63] in religious terms as well as in contextual terms: Eros-like in the midst of crisis, and both with the fate of the city of lagoons, stricken as it is by the pestilence of the

9. In the original German, Mann used a word that could also be translated as "mephitic." This translation of the novella uses the more colloquial "stagnant smelling." [Editor]

populace [55, 57]. The contextual significance of each use of the word "plague" also connects up with the others, merging the semantic levels one with the other in a preterminological fashion. Further, the text of the novella does not overtly reveal an alternative motivation for that scene: "But perhaps because the man had *the look of the traveler* about him," or perhaps because he exercised some *physical* or *mental* influence," Aschenbach realized that "it was wanderlust and nothing more, but it was an *overwhelming* wanderlust" ([5], italics mine). The relevance of the phrase the "look of the traveler" can, of course, only be recognized at the end of the novella; the word "overwhelming" loosely suggests two other possibilities. These suggestions are then made clear in retrospect, without being stated explicitly, when they can be read in terms of Aschenbach's psychophysical disposition. First, it is said about the cholera that "the evil *raged* here with extreme *ferocity*" [54]. Second, the "spread" [53] of the cholera evokes the multilayered "look of a traveler" [4]; this latter activates the chain of mythical meanings initiated by "ferocity" [54], reminding us, as it does, of the (Dionysian) "wild[ness]" [4] in the pose of the Munich stranger, which had already been even more subtly suggested by the phrase "primitive wilderness" [5]. In this way spheres of meaning created in the text become merged and extend the limits of the conceptually explicit, increasing the reader's capacity to decode and remember.

We must be content with these suggestions for reading the novella. One should not be puzzled by the fact that an interpretation, on the one hand, must often reach behind the text itself (to sources and drafts), and on the other that it should use new linguistic methods of analysis. These methods are merely the logical consequence of using a knowledge of sources and a "sensitivity to language," and this, of course, has always been practiced in scholarly research. At least since *Death in Venice*, Thomas Mann's texts have demanded that the interpreter, to the extent that he is interested in the author's intentions, reconstruct the creative process—in a constantly self-regulated way—as Thomas Mann described it for the novella:

> Here much was crystalized, in the true sense of the word "crystal-line," to produce a structure that, playing in the light of many a facet, suspended in multiple relationships, is probably capable of inducing a dreamlike state in the one who is actively guarding its realization. I love this word: "relationship." For me, the concept "relationship" coincides with the concept of "meaning," however relatively that is to be understood. That which has meaning is nothing more than that which is rich in relationships. . . . [109]

Let me draw forth here a few relationships that inhere between our observations above and three provocative Wagnerian theses:

1. Individuals in their temporo-spatial contexts are typified by primary ("mythical") motifs or a "historical" variation on these motifs. A "purely human" prototype (Pentheus's fate) and its special transformation within the historic context (Aschenbach's conflict and downfall) constitute two equally valid textual levels, a real and a symbolic, that often interact. Thus, the motif not only operates horizontally (with "literal and weighty backward reference across wide expanses" [Wagner 838]), but also operates vertically (in "symbolic elevation of the moment" [Wagner 838]). Richard Wagner's thoughts on the function of motif and symbol (thesis three) therefore apply to the text exactly.

2. Aside from this epic use of a process that Wagner thought applied only to (music) drama, there is also a second dimension of "epic" dramatic elements: the "novella-like tragedy" not only takes *The Bacchae* as a paradigm of meaning, but in important places also takes it as a structural model (see thesis one).

3. *The Birth of Tragedy* proves itself to be a guide on the psychological (realistic) level of meaning, as well as on the mythic-symbolic level. Thomas Mann found a model of thought here in that this work showed how Schopenhauer's philosophy and Wagner's theory of art were both conceived of and enacted along classical lines. Nietzsche's later criticism of Wagner acted as a corrective and allowed for the manipulation of the thought model: to be sure, the epic-Aschenbach follows Euripides' model in his failure, but he is no longer a pure type; he has grown to become the "ascetic priest" and artist of the *décadence*. Certainly the flat historico-psychological surface layer of the epic text refers back to a basic dramatic pattern, but this only forces the dramatic elements inherent in the novella genre to be absorbed by the epic. The "novella-like tragedy" therefore goes one level deeper than "tragedy" [see Wagner 28].

IV

Whatever first caused Mann to include classical mythological themes in his conception of the novella can hardly be proven. Conceivably, Mann thought that the homoerotic effect called for legitimation through Greek models—"thus he sought to offer himself support; thus he attempted to preserve his dignity" [48]. But such an attempt to legitimize would suggest an associational link, initiated in an essay by Georg Lukács, to Plato and Plutarch, and this remains secondary to the novella's conceptual structure. Or the example of the "hysterical renaissance" may have presented itself: the Duchess d'Assy lived and loved according to the classical model. As a simplification, Gerhard Hauptmann's Greek regenerative spring could have inspired a skeptical contradiction.[1] Finally, it cannot be ruled out that Thomas Mann's familiarity with Wagner (such as with his "The Future Work of Art," which offered a most important orientation to the young Nietzsche [cf. Wagner 130ff.] suggested in principle a return to the classical.

This kind of search for the exact biographical "missing link," tying theme to author, will probably have to remain somewhat unsuccessful for *Death in Venice*. But one can take solace: themes that are to become relevant in Thomas Mann's work—and this is making meaning traverse wide expanses—are always drawn from a fundamental constellation of ideas. So one must ask about this constellation. Remember: the tale Mann had planned to write about "the dishonoring of a soul that has soared by passion" [*On Myself* 19] (the Goethe-Ulrike accusation)[2] received a correction in a heavily autobiographical direction; Mann's work on Wagner, his familiarity with Nietzsche's criticism of Wagner, with *Krull*[3] in the background, would all have contributed to his choice of a "modern hero" [*On Myself* 19]. In this respect, the basic motif of the modern moralist's endangered existence, in stance and achievement, is set forth anew in one whose "fundamental artistic framework" of life is swept away with a laugh. "Little Herr Friedemann" had introduced it; it was taken up again in Thomas Buddenbrook; the friendship with Paul Ehrenberg kept it alive biographically (even Mut, the Egyptian woman from later, will in her time, whisper Thomas Mann's diary verses from this year)[4]; now it was this motif's "turn" again. From "Little Herr Friedemann" (1897) onwards it becomes clear that Thomas Mann's personality systematically orients itself toward the basic Nietzschean tension that is most clearly articulated along aesthetic-psychological lines in *The Birth of Tragedy*. Of course the conflicting positions of the artist in the novellas do not match up completely in dimension and content with the Apollonian-Dionysian dichotomy: Nietzsche is "made middle class" [Wagner, XI, 110]. But since 1897, one must reckon with *The Birth of Tragedy* as an underpinning. What is important is a critical supplement to the Apollonian stance toward the

1. Georg Lukács, *Soul and Form*. tr. Anna Bostock (London: Merlin, 1934); in *Griechischer Frühling* [Greek spring] (Berlin: Fischer, 1908) Gerhard Hauptmann (1862–1946), presents a Dionysian view of classical antiquity, opposing Goethe's famous description of the period as one of "noble simplicity, quiet grandeur." [Editor]
2. Goethe, then in his seventies, fell in love with the teenaged Ulrike von Levetzow (1804–1899) during summer stays at Marienbad 1821–1823. Mann, who on occasion drew parallels between himself and Goethe, looked down upon Goethe's scandalous behavior. [Editor]
3. Mann's novel *Confession of Felix Krull, Confidence Man*, begun 1910, published 1954. [Editor]
4. "Little Herr Friedmann": one of Mann's early stories (1898); Thomas Buddenbrook: a character in Mann's novel *Buddenbrooks* (1901); Paul Ehrenberg: a painter and close friend of Mann's (see "Why Is Tadzio a Boy? 213) Mut: A character from Mann's novel *Joseph in Egypt*; the diary verses appear in *Tagebücher* [Diaries] 1918–1943, 5 vols., ed. Peter de Mendelssohn (Frankfort/M: Fischer, 1977–82). [Editor]

world, which takes effect just as early on—that is the suspicion that the moral stance of the ascetic idealist is hostile toward life because of a weakness for life. Nietzsche explicitly connected this single-minded continuation of the Apollonian tendency with ("Socratic") science [Nietzsche 591; cf. *Birth* 22f.]. As with the Apollonian impulse, the Dionysian (life) force underlies the ascetic ideal, acting as both motivation and constant threat. The Dionysian force is able to continue existing in the ascetic precisely by means of this cunning act of self-negation. Therefore, illusory Apollonian artistic morality is supplemented by the concept of an illusory artistic mortality. On a personal level, in "What Do Ascetic Ideals Mean?" Nietzsche was aiming, above all, at Wagner, and this, in turn provides a connection to the entire complex of artistic criticism. Thomas Mann's basic orientation toward *The Birth of Tragedy* and "What Do Ascetic Ideals Mean?" comes together for the first time in the aestheticism and asceticism of little Herr Friedemann. With a psychological model shifts in accent are possible, of course: thus in Savonarola, the "ascetic monk," Nietzsche's will to power predominates, and—no different from Lorenzo—he succumbs to the Apollonian deception of worldliness.[5] The "miracle of ingenuousness reborn" [*Fiorenza* 1064], which Savonarola trusts so completely (as Aschenbach does later [11]) is ultimately life's cunning way of healing his self-destructive revulsion from knowledge (the view into the "abysses of existence" [*Fiorenza* 1060; cf. *Death in Venice* 11]). The explicit paraphrases of Schopenhauer in *Fiorenza* reveal that Mann followed the philosophical background of *The Birth of Tragedy* on his own. His orientation toward the world, which (by 1898) he took from Schopenhauer, remains constant. This will be important for *Death in Venice*.

Thus, Mann had a psychological model available in 1911 around which individual themes could cluster and be looked at objectively; it also functioned as a laboratory for considering questions that the "mind and art" complex gave rise to in terms of Nietzsche, Schopenhauer, and Wagner.

The second chapter of *Death in Venice*—in which the author of the Frederick epic, the patient artist of *Maia*, the creator of "The Wretch" who had "earned the gratitude of an entire young generation," the author, finally, of "Art and Intellect," Gustav Aschenbach is presented—recapitulates the model sketched here in almost all its essential features. The model appears here as a "development" [10] from the "embodiment" [9] and "glorification" [10] of the "ascetic ideal" to the mastery "of this new dignity and rigor," in which readers "noticed an almost excessive increase in his sense of beauty, a noble purity, simplic-

---

5. Savonarola, Lorenzo: characters from Mann's verse drama *Fiorenza* (1905). [Editor]

ity, and sense of proportion [11], a "moral determination that goes beyond knowledge" [11]. Stated as a formula, this model bespeaks the forced step back from an art of the guilty conscience to an "art, in which precisely . . . the *will to deception* has a good conscience" [Nietzsche 589]; thus it marks a step toward the Apollonian (the naïveté upon which Nietzsche has, of course, already cast doubt [*Birth* 43]). In short, these are essential elements of Nietzsche's desperate attempt to convince himself, in the epilogue to his anti-Wagner piece, to abandon Wagner and to purge himself of everything that he had taken from Wagner's work. However, during the correction of the proofs of "life's tragic play in which he summed up the European ideal [Nietzsche 675f.], he was led to catastrophe. Aschenbach's "decision . . . to disavow knowledge, to reject it, to move beyond it with head held high," his "disgust at the indecent psychologism then current," his "decisive turn away . . . from all sympathy with the abyss," his "rejection of the laxity inherent in the supposedly compassionate maxim that to understand everything is to forgive everything" [11]—all that constituted the "miracle of ingenuousness reborn"—can be found almost verbatim in Nietzsche's report on his attempt at self-purgation [Nietzsche 680–83]. There he claims to convince himself: "Out of such abysses, also out of the abyss of great suspicion, one returns newborn. . . ." For this "second dangerous innocence" again the Greeks are the model, for

> they knew how to *live!* What is required for that is to stop courageously at the surface, . . . to adore appearance, to believe in forms, tones, words, in the whole *Olympus of appearance!* Those Greeks were superficial—*out of profundity* . . . [Nietzsche 681–83]

Textual comparison confirms Thomas Mann's indebtedness to *Nietzsche contra Wagner.* However, supplementing the quote above with a contemporary aphorism is probably still valid, even if its influence can only be shown logically. It dates from *The Genealogy of Morals* and again assumes that *The Birth* offers the most cogent commentary on "Greek" antagonism and conflict, which "had to become Apollonian":

> That means to refract his will for the monstrous, multiple, unknown, horrible, on his will for the measured, the simple, regimentation in rule and idea. The immeasurable, wild, Asian is at the root: the courage of the Greek results from his struggle against his Asianness: beauty is no more a gift to him than logic; it arises not from the naturalness of custom; it is conquered, willed, fought for; it is his *victory.* [Nietzsche 792]

And was not Aschenbach's artistry based upon a "tenacity and perseverance similar to that which had conquered his home province" [9]? It

remains to be shown just how consistently the novella grasps this as a
"struggle against its Asianness."

In *Death in Venice* Thomas Mann falls back on physiological patterns
that are part of his primary system of ideas and that he has used effectively since "Little Herr Friedemann"; he falls back on the psychological
categories of *The Birth*, supplementing them with an analysis of the
"ascetic idea." For the first time, however, he follows Nietzsche's turn
to the *classical* prototype. Mann's interest in Plato's aesthetics, which he
came to independently through Lukács, may have supported this turn,
but did not cause it. Thomas Mann came to understand Nietzsche's
contention that the basic relationship for the Greeks was the conflict
between the ideal and the typical through the Euripides/*Bacchae* paradigm that Nietzsche set forth while treating another pseudoalternative
in his essay "Epos or Drama?" Of course, only a rather plausible speculation can be offered concerning the sequence of inquiries Mann undertook thereafter: one may well assume a sequential reading of *The
Bacchae*, as well as of the information that he included in [his work
notes] on the Dionysian cult. In so doing, one could reconstruct how
Thomas Mann filled Nietzsche's abstractions with illustrative material
along mythological lines. Under pressure to illustrate the basic themes,
Mann would have given Erwin Rohde's *Psyche* a first reading. Only after
he had collected sufficient material to support the complex of mythical
ideas, the Apollonian-Dionysian tragedy, at least temporarily, would
Mann have looked around for further typifying mythical themes. This
kind of a priority is further supportable through Wagner's part in the
complex as sketched: Thomas Mann could not, of course, have identified Wagnerian aesthetic and art-historical themes only in philosophical
and mythological "translation," but had to identify the entire influence
that Wagner's theory of myth had on Nietzsche; this is also true for
the central Dionysus-Apollo mythos. Thomas Mann's first approach to
mythology must also be seen in the light of this kind of examination of
Richard Wagner.

Now Thomas Mann's acquisition of mythological and other classical
themes was not very broad and was seldom intensive, especially in those
cases where Nietzsche offered no further direction. There can be no talk
of his dealing with the myths. To be sure, one should suppose that he
who had so often referred to his Romantic heritage would have had a
work by Welcker, Creuzer, Görres, Zoega, Grimm, or Bachofen[6] at

6. Friedrich Gottlieb Welcker (1784–1868), classics scholar: *Griechische Götterlehre* [Manual on
   Greek Gods], 3 vols., 1857–62; Friedrich Creuzer (1771–1858), classics scholar: *Symbolik
   und Mythlogie der ältesten Völker, besonders bei den Griechen* [Symbolism and mythology of
   the most ancient peoples, especially of the Greeks], 4 vols., 1810–12; Johann Joseph von
   Görres (1776–1848), scholar, journalist: *Mythengeschichten der asiatischen Welt* [Myths of the
   Asian world], 2 vols., 1810; Georg Zoega (1755–1809), archeologist; Jacob Grimm (1785–

hand and read it closely at least once. But this can be ruled out, just as we can completely rule out knowledge of theories of myth current around 1911, scholarly reference works, or even specific classical research. What Mann would have learned in prep school is what needs to be looked up and excerpted. This can be demonstrated by selections [in Mann's work notes] for the novella. What Thomas Mann knew about the Hermes myth in 1911 (plus whatever a nonspeculative inter-pretation can in turn extract from the text) is found in a two-line excerpt from Plutarch. In general, the selection of sources is rather casual; in addition to *Psyche*, the work of Nietzsche's friend Erwin Rohde that Mann read with very penetrating interest, he also consulted Nösselt's mythology primer "for upper-level girls' schools and the educated of the female sex,"[7] a text that his mother had used in mythology class. ("It had Pallas Athene on the cover and was one of the books the children were allowed to remove from the bookcase.")

Thomas Mann's statement to Paul Amann (September 10, 1915) that "Greek education" in *Death in Venice* is overrated, that it had merely been an "aid and spiritual refuge for the person experiencing it" [95] is accurate.

Mythological and other classical themes used in the novella can be grouped according to intensity and breadth of acquisition. This sort of differentiation by degree usually corresponds to their relative value as a textual element.

1. The group based on *The Birth of Tragedy*: Euripides' *The Bacchae*, Erwin Rohde's *Psyche*, the unidentified excerpt from [sheets 9–10 of Mann's working notes].

2. The series of readings planned around Georg von Lukács's essay "Soul and Form": Plato's *Symposium*, *Phaedrus*; Plutarch's *On Love*.

3. Secondary sources without connection to the conceptual structure: Friedrich Nösselt's *Lehrbuch der griechischen und römischen Mythologie* (Textbook of Greek and Roman mythology); Homer's *Odyssey*; Xeno-phon's *Memorabilia*; to this group also belong themes without contex-tual reference that Mann picked up from works of the other groups (as from footnotes, details from commentaries, etc.)

* * *

1863), founder of Germanic philology: *Teutonic mythology*, 1835, 4th ed., 4 vols., 1883–88, tr. James Steven Stallybrass (New York: Dover, 1966); Johann Jacob Bachofen (1815–1887), classics scholar: *Myth, religion, and mother right* (1861), tr. Ralph Manheim (Princeton: U of Princeton P, 1967).[Editor]

7. Friedrich Nösselt, *Lehrbuch der griechischen und romischen Mythologie*, 6th ed. (Leipzig, 1874). [Editor]

? T. J. REED

The Art of Ambivalence †

So ein Kunstding ist ja schwer auf eine einzige Formel zu bringen,
sondern stellt ein dichtes Gewebe von Absichten und Beziehungen
dar, das etwas Organisches und darum durchaus Vieldeutiges hat.
'An artistic object like this is of course difficult to reduce to a single
formula; it represents a dense web of intentions and relationships which
has something organic and thereby extremely ambiguous about it'. Letter to Elisabeth Zimmer, Sept. 6, 1915. [95]¹

THOMAS MANN

I

In *Der Tod in Venedig, [Death in Venice]*, Thomas Mann returns
from excursions into allegory and once more writes directly about a
literary artist. But the directness is not that of *Tonio Kröger*. There
he was expressing lyrically his immediate experience, formulating and
coming to terms with what he had gone through. In the figure of
Gustav von Aschenbach, by contrast, he experiments² with a possible
future, with 'how it would be if . . . .' Author and character have of
course a great deal in common—racially mixed ancestry, disciplined
bourgeois background, slow and tortured compositional method, con-
centration on a certain type of character, residence in Munich, Upper
Bavarian country house, and many other details: without such initial
similarities, the fictional experiment would not have been relevant to
Thomas Mann. But the most important indication of how the character is related to his author is their difference in age. Aschenbach in the
story is over fifty (fifty-three according to one of Mann's working notes)
[sheet 24, 88].³ Thomas Mann when he wrote the story was thirty-six.

Aschenbach has accomplished much that Mann had not. He has
achieved a greater eminence, he bears the *particule de noblesse*,⁴ his
works provide stylistic models for school use, he is a pillar of the cultural establishment. He has written more than Thomas Mann, in fact

---

† Reprinted from *Thomas Mann: The Uses of Tradition* by T. J. Reed (Oxford: Clarendon, 1974)
144–78, by permission of Oxford University Press. (Some footnotes have been edited or omitted.)
For the reader's convenience, page references to this Norton Critical Edition (as well as sheet
numbers for references to Mann's working notes) have been inserted in brackets. However, translations are Reed's and thus may differ from those above.
1. From Thomas Mann, *Briefe 1889–1936*, ed. Erika Mann (Frankfurt am Main: Fischer, 1961)
123 [Editor].
2. The word is Mann's own. See below p. [176].
3. Mann's "Working Notes for *Death in Venice*" are included above, pages 70–92. If you wish
to consult the originals, sheets 1–30 are housed in the Thomas Mann Archive in Zurich,
archival reference number Mp XI 13e; sheet 31 is part of the Mann collection of the Yale
University library [Editor].
4. The *von* that indicates noble rank, as in Gustav *von* Aschenbach [Editor].

he has completed all Thomas Mann's abandoned projects: 'Maja', 'Ein Elender', [A Man of Misery], the Friedrich novel, and most notably an essay 'Geist und Kunst', ["Art and Intellect"], which competent judges compare on an equal footing with Schiller's Über naive und sentimentalische Dichtung [On Naïve and Sentimental Poetry]. This last detail is important because Aschenbach has taken conscious decisions about the course of his career in which we can recognize, if we approach Aschenbach's story from the angle of Mann's own 'Geist und Kunst', solutions to the dilemmas which that project revealed.

We are given a clear picture of Aschenbach's development and its psychological background. Attention is focused particularly on the way his early analytical, 'problematic' work, his pursuit of Erkenntnis [knowledge], has yielded in mature years to the very opposite: a rejection of knowledge and of the 'improper psychologism' of the age, and an associated increase in his feeling for external beauty, a deliberate pursuit of 'classical' style. 'Psychology' was an indiscretion of youth, its supersession is the act of a grown man: '. . . gewiss ist, dass die schwermütig gewissenhafteste Gründlichkeit des Jünglings Seichtheit bedeutet im Vergleich mit dem tiefen Entschlusse des Meister gewordenen Mannes, das Wissen zu leugnen, es abzulehnen, erhobenen Hauptes darüber hinwegzugehen' (it is certain that the most gloomily conscientious thoroughness of the youth is mere shallowness in comparison with the profound decision of the matured master to deny knowledge, to reject it, to pass it over with raised head). (viii. 454) [11][5]

Wording and idea here echo the epilogue to Nietzsche contra Wagner, as does the phrase 'unanständiger Psychologismus' a few lines further on, and the description of 'Ein Elender' as 'die Abkehr . . . von jeder Sympathie mit dem Abgrund, die Absage an die Laxheit des Mitleidssatzes, dass alles verstehen alles verzeihen heisse' (the turn away . . . from all sympathy with the abyss, the renunciation of the laxity contained in the maxim of compassion, that to understand all is to forgive all). What Nietzsche expressed in one of his characteristic swings away from analytic thought has become the basis for Aschenbach's motivation. We are not told that Aschenbach has been affected by the anti-intellectual fashions of early twentieth-century Germany which that component of Nietzsche's thought had inspired, but the relevance of this central 'Geist und Kunst' problem is obvious. It hardly needs the confirmation provided by the fact that a handful of notes from 'Geist und Kunst' reappear among the work-notes for Der Tod in Venedig [sheet 29, 91].

Mann's Chapter Two, from which all the above details come, is almost an obituary of Aschenbach. In its abstract way it provides an advance explanation of his fate, for it warns expressly against the dan-

---

5. All Reed's references to Mann's essays and fiction are to the Gesammelte Werke, 12 vols. (Frankfurt am Main: S. Fischer) [Editor].

gers of Aschenbach's decision: moral resoluteness 'beyond knowledge' is an oversimplification and hence an open door to immorality. Beauty of form, to which Aschenbach is now devoted, is also potentially immoral in so far as it claims primacy over moral judgements (viii. 455) [61]. This is a remarkably clear statement of the issues which the story embodies. But how does it embody them?

Firstly by showing how Aschenbach's fatal infatuation grows out of his new aesthetic taste. He begins by admiring the boy as if he were a work of art. Tadzio on his first appearance reminds Aschenbach of Greek sculpture 'of the noblest period' (469) [21], his flowing locks recall the famous statue of a boy drawing a thorn from his foot (470) [22]. Aschenbach's sober approval is that of a connoisseur of beauty— 'fachmännisch kühl' (474) [25]. Tadzio on the beach is seen as a figure in a picture, against the horizontal of the water's edge (475) [26], with the sea behind him as 'foil and background' (489) [36]. This aesthetic pretext persists into Chapter Four, even after Aschenbach's abortive effort to escape from Venice. He has admitted to himself by now that it was really Tadzio he could not bear to leave, but the attention he devotes to the boy is still aesthetic, even religious: 'Andacht und Studium' (488) [35].

It reaches its height, and at the same time is most explicitly linked with Aschenbach's own creative aims, in the writer's meditations as he observes Tadzio on the beach. After an introduction again packed with sculptural phrases—'den zart gemeisselten Arm', 'die feine Zeichnung der Rippen', 'Achselhöhlen glatt wie bei einer Statue', etc.—we have this:

> Welch eine Zucht, welche Präzision des Gedankens war ausge-
> drückt in diesem gestreckten und jugendlich vollkommenen Leibe!
> Der strenge und reine Wille jedoch, der, dunkel tätig, dies göt-
> tliche Bildwerk ans Licht zu treiben vermocht hatte,—war er nicht
> ihm, dem Künstler, bekannt und vertraut? Wirkte er nicht auch in
> ihm, wenn er, nüchterner Leidenschaft voll, aus der Marmormasse
> der Sprache die schlanke Form befreite, die er im Geiste geschaut
> und die er als Standbild und Spiegel geistiger Schönheit den
> Menschen darstellte?
>
> (What discipline, what precision of thought was expressed in
> this outstretched and youthfully perfect body! But the pure and
> austere will, whose mysterious action had been able to thrust this
> divine creation into the light—was it not known and familiar to
> him, the artist? Was it not equally at work in him, when, filled
> with a sober passion, he freed from the marble mass of language
> the slender form which was his inner vision and which he
> presented to men as a statue and mirror of spiritual beauty?).
> (p. 490) [37]

Here the 'statuesque' language used of Tadzio is linked with the nature of Aschenbach's literary creations.[6] One could hardly have a more evident attempt to present literature as *Plastik*. It is clear what kind of ideals have dictated Aschenbach's pursuit of *Klassizität*.

But his admiration for the boy's beauty might have stayed within aesthetic bounds. It is the rejection of critical analysis—the concomitant of his mature artistic tastes—that proves fatal. This is the second way in which the story embodies the issues set out in Chapter Two. Aschenbach has no eye for his own underlying motives. Long before he has given up all pretence and admitted that he loves Tadzio (end of Chapter Four), doubt has been cast on his motives. Then, just before his admission, he fails to speak to the boy—an action which might have dispelled his intenser feelings and established a normal relationship. We are told that he did not want to, his intoxication is too dear to him. This refusal to be sobered is called immoral *(Zügellosigkeit)*, but Aschenbach has no mind for such things:

> Aschenbach war zur Selbstkritik nicht mehr aufgelegt; der Geschmack, die geistige Verfassung seiner Jahre, Selbstachtung, Reife und späte Einfachheit machten ihn nicht geneigt, Beweggründe zu zergliedern und zu entscheiden, ob er aus Gewissen, ob aus Liederlichkeit und Schwäche sein Vorhaben nicht ausgeführt habe.
>
> (Aschenbach was no longer disposed to self-criticism; the taste, the intellectual constitution of his years, self-esteem, maturity, and late simplicity made him disinclined to analyse motives and to distinguish whether he had failed to carry out his intention from conscience or from weakness and dissoluteness). (p. 494) [40]

The verdict on this late failure reflects back on Aschenbach's many preceding failures (or refusals) to suspect passionate motives beneath the aesthetic pretext.

These precise links between Aschenbach's loss of control and his artistic development settle one question critics have sometimes raised. Why did his downfall have to be brought about by a homosexual passion? Why not—since the Venice episode is only the external fulfilment of a psychological process which has begun before he ever leaves Munich— why not a passion for cards? or drink? or a woman? The answer is that these would not have followed from Aschenbach's particular state of mind. The first two would have been crude irrelevancies, the third would have served only if it could be shown to grow from an admiration initially aesthetic. But it is hardly possible for the sexual element in female beauty to be overlooked, even by one who has put aside psychol-

---

6. Luchino Visconti's film of *Der Tod in Venedig*, so faithful in atmosphere and period detail, breaks this vital link by making Aschenbach a musician, probably on the false assumption that Mann was 'really' writing about Mahler, whose external appearance he borrowed for his protagonist.

ogy. Only male beauty could so insidiously transform cool appreciation
into passion. This justifies the central encounter in *Der Tod in Venedig*
as part of the artistic whole, although it would be wrong to speak as if
Mann deliberately chose it for this reason. Like so much else in the
remarkable genesis of the work, it was something given, which fused
perfectly with other given elements.

From the point where he avows his true feelings, Aschenbach goes
from bad to worse. His reverent study of Tadzio's godlike beauty
becomes frank pursuit of an idol *(Abgott)*. Judgement is implicit in the
mere narration of his actions, and still more in the descriptions of his
state—sweating, desperate, cosmetically rejuvenated. It is made explicit
in the participle-nouns which increasingly replace Aschenbach's name:
der Betörte, der Verwirrte, etc. These establish the author's distance
from his character succinctly and unequivocally. Indeed, Mann dissociates himself from Aschenbach more obviously than from any of his
other protagonists. Towards the close he even treats him with open sarcasm, in the passage beginning 'Er sass dort, der Meister, der würdig
gewordene Künstler, der Autor des "Elenden", der in so vorbildlich
reiner Form dem Zigeunertum und der trüben Tiefe abgesagt, dem
Abgrunde die Sympathie gekündigt und das Verworfene verworfen hatte
. . .' (He sat there, the master, the artist who had achieved dignity, the
author of 'A Miserable Specimen', who in such exemplarily pure form
had declared his rejection of bohemianism and the murky depths,
renounced all sympathy with the abyss, and called depravity by its
name. . . . (p. 521) [60] The gap between Aschenbach's claims to public
respect and his present behaviour amount to an emphatic judgement.

It is a shade too emphatic for the reader accustomed to Mann's ironic
temper. Where are the reservations usually felt in every inflection of his
phrasing? The finality with which Aschenbach's case is settled is positively suspicious. Is it not very like the 'Wucht des Wortes, mit welcher
das Verworfene verworfen wurde' (p. 455) [11]—i.e. Aschenbach's own
moral decisiveness which has since proved so dubious? Is it not crudely
direct beside the informed survey of Aschenbach's development in
Chapter Two, which surely practises the maxim he rejected: 'Tout comprendre, c'est tout pardonner'? And did Mann not later write, in a letter
exhaustively analysing the genesis and attitudes of *Der Tod in Venedig*,
that the moralistic standpoint was one to be adopted only ironically? [97]
There are depths to be sounded under the polished surface of the story.

II

Der Tod in Venedig records the phases of a real experiment; it is not
a mere mental construct, manipulating an imagined character through
arbitrarily chosen adventures. To begin with, Thomas Mann's own

Venetian experiences in 1911 were close to Aschenbach's, at least in embryo. The figure in the Munich cemetery, the sordid ship from Pola to Venice, the aged dandy on board it, the unlicensed gondolier, Tadzio and his family, the attempt to leave Venice foiled by a misdirection of luggage, the cholera epidemic, the honest English clerk at the travel bureau, the street singer—everything was provided by reality, not invented for the later fiction. It all had an 'innate symbolism' (xi. 124) [109].

Equally real was the literary standstill which Mann makes the motive for Aschenbach's journey. Thomas Mann's work in the first decade of the century was in general in a transitional phase, and failure arguably outweighed success: *Fiorenza* and *Königliche Hoheit* had fallen far short of what was expected of the author of *Buddenbrooks*, the projects for 'Maja', 'Ein Elender', the Friedrich novel, and 'Geist und Kunst' had all been abandoned, and now *Felix Krull* was hardly moving. In the early months of 1911 Mann wrote very little. Reporting this to Heinrich late in March, he speaks of his present low vitality—'eine momentane Erschöpfung des Centralnervensystems';[7] the same letter announces a planned holiday in Dalmatia. In mid-May he leaves with his wife for the island of Brioni, but moves to Venice for a short stay from the 26th to 2 June. The first news of the new work comes in a letter to Philipp Witkop on 18 July 1911: he is at work on a 'recht sonderbare Sache, die ich aus Venedig mitgebracht habe, Novelle, ernst und rein in Ton, einen Fall von Knabenliebe bei einem alternden Künstler behandelnd. Sie sagen "hum, hum!" Aber es ist sehr anständig' (an exceedingly bizarre thing I brought back from Venice, a *Novelle*, serious and pure in tone, treating the case of an elderly artist's passion for a boy. 'Hm, hm!', you say. But it is all very proper) [93].

This jaunty tone is gone altogether the next time Mann reports on progress. He writes to Ernst Bertram on 16 October 1911 that he is 'von einer Arbeit gequält, die sich im Laufe der Ausführung mehr und mehr als eine unmögliche Conception herausstellt und an die ich doch schon zuviel Sorge gewandt habe, um sie aufzugeben' (tormented by a project which in the course of execution has turned out more and more to be an impossible conception and on which I have nevertheless spent too much trouble to give it up now) [93].[8] At the beginning of April he has hopes of finishing the story by the end of the month; although he thinks Heinrich may not approve of it as a whole, he is sure it has 'individual beauties', and is especially pleased with a 'classicizing' chapter (*antikisierendes Kapitel*—letter of 2 April 1912) [93]. But by the 27th, problems again dominate. Although publication arrangements are already well in hand,

---

7. Heinrich: Thomas Mann's brother, also a noted novelist. This is reported in a letter, available in Thomas Mann and Heinrich Mann, *Briefwechsel, 1900–1949*, ed. Hans Wysling (Frankfurt am Main: S. Fischer, 1968) 95. [Editor]
8. The editor of the correspondence between Mann and Ernst Bertram mistakenly refers this [93] to *Felix Krull*.

Mann writes to Heinrich that he cannot round the story off: 'ich kann den Schluss nicht finden'. And on 3 May he speaks once more of being 'schrecklich angestrengt und besorgt, einer eigenen Arbeit wegen, an die ich—vielleicht instinktloser Weise—beinahe ein Jahr gewandt habe und die nun so oder so fertig werden muss' (terribly strained and worried about a work of my own on which—perhaps I should have known better—I have now spent nearly a year and which must now be finished one way or another).

This is not a picture of issues easily mastered or of an experiment which yielded its conclusions straight away. That is hardly surprising if we remember Mann's difficulties over 'Geist und Kunst'. And if the Venice stay had provided material for working out these teasing problems in fictional form, new factors had added to their complexity. The clearest way to present the matter is to reconstruct the genesis of the story.

The clues Mann provides are suggestive and, although not precise as to time, help us to see essentially what occurred. Our knowledge of his sources and of the dates at which he came upon them also helps. The purpose of our reconstruction, which may seem at times to be suggesting 'earlier versions' of the text (there is some evidence for this) is to point up the possibilities—both literary and moral—of each contribution to the story in such a way that its final form can be grasped in all its richness of reference, and appreciated as a solution which was anything but facile.

The threads we have to follow are drawn together by Mann himself in his letter of 4 July 1920 to Carl Maria Weber. The ethos Mann discerned in Weber's poems led him to declare his own attitude to homosexuality, about which *Der Tod in Venedig* had left room for misunderstanding. Mann says that he would not wish to give the impression of rejecting a type of feeling which he honours, which almost of necessity has more spiritual value *(Geist)* than the so-called normal type, and which he is himself no stranger to. He then goes at length into the reasons why his story nevertheless appears to reject it.

First there is the nature of his artistic processes. He distinguishes between the 'Dionysiac spirit of irresponsible-individualistic lyrical effusion' and the 'Apolline spirit of epic with its moral and social responsibilities and objective limitations'. In other words, between the urge to express private and personal feeling, and the requirements of the more public genre of prose narrative. It may not be permissible to endorse in sober prose what one feels a private enthusiasm for. In fact, it may not be possible, for the execution of the literary conception has its own corrective influences, which Mann calls a 'painful process of objectivization'. He says that *Der Tod in Venedig* finally strove for a balance between sensuality and morality, analogous to Goethe's achievement in

Die Wahlverwandtschaften. But in its origin, and still at its core, the story is essentially 'hymnic'.

Mann refers Weber to his account of hymnic origin and objectivization already published in 1919, in the *Vorsatz* to *Gesang vom Kindchen*. That opens with Mann's old nagging question: 'Bin ich ein Dichter?' (viii. 1068). There follows his defence of the prose moralist as a 'poet', familiar from 'Geist und Kunst'. But what comes next is the confession of a past shame which still rankles, a secret defeat, a never-avowed failure. He means the writing of *Der Tod in Venedig*. These are the lines quoted in the letter to Weber:

Weisst du noch? Höherer Rausch, ein ausserordentlich Fühlen
Kam auch wohl über dich einmal und warf dich danieder,
Dass du lagst, die Stirn in den Händen. Hymnisch erhob sich
Da deine Seele, es drängte der ringende Geist zum Gesange
Unter Tränen sich hin. Doch leider blieb alles beim Alten.
Denn ein versachlichend Mühen begann da, ein kältend
Bemeistern,—
Siehe, es ward dir das *trunkene Lied* zur *sittlichen Fabel*.

(Remember? Intoxication, a heightened, exceptional feeling
Came over you as well on one occasion, and threw you
Down, your brow in your hands. To hymnic impulse your spirit
Rose, amid tears your struggling mind pressed urgently upward
Into song. But unhappily things stayed just as they had been:
There began a process of sobering, cooling and mastering—
Lo! there came of your *drunken song* an *ethical fable*.) [97]

Clearly Mann's Venice experience—what he calls a little further on 'ein persönlich-lyrisches Reiseerlebnis'—originally inspired an affirmative rather than critical treatment, perhaps even in verse *(Gesang)* rather than prose.[9] The hexameters in the text of *Der Tod in Venedig* could be remnants of this treatment. At all events, the failure to carry the project out in that form still rankled in 1919—even though the final form of the story had turned the shortcoming into a virtue and reaped praise (viii. 1069). The heights of *Dichtertum* were not scaled. In his letter Mann names other factors at work in the story's development: first, his Naturalist background, so alien to the younger generation Weber represents, which made him see the 'case' in a pathological as well as a symbolic light. This clearly echoes the lengthy discussion of the two literary generations and the supersession of Naturalism in [note] 103 of 'Geist und Kunst', but now from the viewpoint of one who is resigned to being what he is, who knows that he cannot deny his past and his intellectual

9. Thereby repeating the case of *Tonio Kröger*, which was preceded by a fragmentary lyrical treatment of the story's theme. See Wysling, *Studien*, p. 31.

roots. This much his experience of the 'objectivizing process' taught him, for it was rooted in the 'necessities of his nature'. Secondly, there was his personal mistrust of passion as such, a Protestant and puritanical burgher trait which he shares with Aschenbach, and which counteracted any 'Greek' view of homosexual love. The real subject of his fable, he says, was the confusion and degradation caused by passion, a theme he had previously thought of treating in a renarration of the aged Goethe's love for the seventeen-year-old Ulrike von Levetzow.

In the rest of the letter, Mann develops the idea that the erotic attraction of *Leben* for *Geist* need not correspond to the attraction between the sexes. He sums it up with a quotation from Hölderlin's poem 'Sokrates und Alkibiades': 'Wer das Tiefste gedacht, liebt das Lebendigste' (whose thought deepest has probed, most loves vitality). And he makes the judgement on homosexual love depend on the nature of the individual instance: it is morally neutral until it shows its value in its works.

This remarkably frank self-interpretation suggests why the 'bizarre thing' Mann brought back from Venice gave him such trouble in the composition, and fills in the background to the letters quoted above. By July 1911 the work was already to be a *Novelle*, though not yet necessarily a 'moral fable': the 'purity of tone' and the 'propriety' may at that stage have meant something other than adverse judgement on Aschenbach. By October of that year the difficulties have set in, Mann finds he is working with an 'impossible conception'. This surely is the point at which an affirmative treatment was abandoned. It had proved impossible 'in the course of execution'—the letter to Bertram dates the turning-point which *Gesang vom Kindchen* and the retrospective letter to Weber describe in general terms.

So we have a picture of a diametrical change in the conception of *Der Tod in Venedig*. Is it compatible with Mann's other statement, that the 'real subject' of his fable, the confusion and degradation which passion causes, was a theme he had long intended to treat?

This is certainly true. As early as 1905 a notebook jotting for a future story reads:

> Der erhöhte Respekt vor sichselbst, das gesteigerte sich Ernstnehmen [. . .] die Neigung, sich als nationaler Faktor, sich überhaupt national zu nehmen, der Blick auf die Literaturgeschichte etc. Das ist *darzustellen*, damit es nichts Gemeinsames und nur Typisches bleibe. (Ich will keine Figur sein). Das Leid und die tragische Verirrung eines Künstlers ist zu zeigen, der Phantasie und 'Ernst im Spiel' genug hat, um an den ehrgeizigen Ansprüchen, zu denen der Erfolg ihn verleitet und denen er zuletzt nicht gewachsen ist, *zu Grunde geht [sic]*.
>
> (The increased respect for oneself, the intensified taking of oneself seriously [. . .] the tendency to take oneself as a national factor,

as national in any way, the eye on literary history, etc. That is something to be *portrayed*, in such a way that it has nothing in common [viz. with TM himself] and remains merely typical. (I do not want to be a figure). The suffering and the aberration of an artist must be shown who has enough imagination and 'seriousness within artistic play' to be brought low by the ambitious claims which success leads him to make for himself and which in the end he is not up to.)[1]

The precariousness of the Artist's claim to dignity and public respect was thus a theme awaiting embodiment. But this does not mean it was from the first the keynote of the new story. Rather, it was an old theme towards which the working out of the story increasingly gravitated. Mann was in this case, it is plain from his accounts, a reluctant moralist.

Picture him as a writer at a cross-roads in his development, with the doubts and possibilities of the 'Geist und Kunst' essay in his mind, with his work seemingly much in need of a revivifying impulse. In Venice he has an intense emotional experience. It inspires him to treat it in a form which is far from his usual literary stock-in-trade and is thereby a kind of creative rebirth: in place of cold analysis and Apolline epic form, an impassioned outpouring, lyrical and Dionysiac. Tadzio is celebrated hymnically, the passion he inspires is affirmed because it is fruitful. In a milder way, *Tonio Kröger* asserted that the basis of true *Dichtertum* was emotional. Now the emotion goes deeper: it is nothing less than Nietzsche's Dionysiac spirit, described in the *Geburt der Tragödie* as indispensable for great art.

These elements are visible in the late dream orgy with the coming of the Stranger God. But long before that point, Mann has placed his clues. The phrase which describes Aschenbach's feeling when he sees the Munich stranger, the 'seltsame Ausweitung seines Innern' (strange dilation within him) (p. 446) [5] is taken from the same account of the Thracian Dionysus' orgies which yielded such graphic details for Aschenbach's dream.[2] From the very first, the process of bringing his feelings alive is Dionysiac. The encounter with Tadzio will complete this process.

The literary rebirth is a different thing from the all-too-deliberate rebirth Aschenbach had constructed for himself. It casts doubt on it, precisely, as too deliberate—'eine gewollte Klassizität' (455) [11]. Yet it also in a way supplements it (or in the case of Mann himself, who had not yet taken Aschenbach's mature decisions, replaces it). To both, as

---

1. Quoted in Lehnert, *Fiktion* [(Stuttgart, 1965)], p. 125.
2. Erwin Rohde, *Psyche*, extensively excerpted in Mann's work-notes. The idea of *Ausweitung* comes in Rohde's discussion of the spiritual aims of the Thracian Dionysus' orgies: closest possible contact with the god, state of 'mania' [sheet 8, 73]. *Manie* is Aschenbach's later condition (p. 499) [44].

　　Rohde was of course a friend of Nietzsche's, which probably stimulated Mann's interest in his mythological study.

lovers of external beauty—the one on principle, the other through chance encounter—a new poetic strength was granted. This was clearly one solution to the problems of which way to turn, raised in 'Geist und Kunst'.

Could it be carried through? Intoxication is a difficult condition to maintain, at least as a basis for creativity. Mann had always considered himself an 'Apolline' creator, mistrusting inspiration, preferring discipline. His favourite images for his art, the lyre and the bow, were Apollo's attributes. If he now tasted intoxication for once, it was almost certainly short-lived. The short prose piece he wrote on Wagner while he was actually in Venice speaks of the ideal art of the future as cooler than Wagner's and not relying on *Rausch* (x. 842).

But it also speaks of a healthier art and of a new classicism—very much the ideals which Aschenbach pursued, and the ideals of the times. For these things equally Tadzio's beauty could serve as an inspiration: a work of celebration was still possible. But if the celebration was not to be drunken and Dionysiac, what was it to be?

The answer is: Platonic. This brings us to the most important source for *Der Tod in Venedig*. The text is rich in phrases, images, and ideas from Plato's *Symposium* and *Phaedrus* and from Plutarch's *Erotikos*, a much later dialogue essentially Platonic in style and theme.[3]

The technique of weaving in quotation and allusion to famous texts was one Mann had practised skilfully before, not merely to decorate his fiction but to add a dimension of meaning to what was being narrated. The references to *Don Carlos* in *Tonio Kröger*, the retelling of the Tristan story as a burlesque,[4] in different ways place the characters' experience in a broader context than that of the immediate fiction. This is true to a yet greater extent of the Greek sources in *Der Tod in Venedig*. Even before being exploited for literary effect, they clearly helped Mann himself to a deeper, more generalized understanding of his theme. If the fate of Aschenbach embodies problems connected with the literary scene of the 1910s and Mann's place in it, the Greek dialogues placed these problems in a wider framework still. For where Mann had been concerned with a fashionable emphasis (*Zeitströmung*) on external beauty in the Germany of his day, and with a defence of intellect in art, the Platonic dialogues stated an all-embracing and timeless theory of the relationship of beauty to men's spiritual and intellectual life, ideally reconciling the two. They also discussed the kinds of love beauty provokes, its potential inspiring quality and potential dangers. And since they are mainly about homosexual love, they were precisely relevant to the subject which Mann's Venice encounter had presented him with.

---

3. There is also one quotation from Xenophon's *Memorabilia of Socrates* (p. 477) as well as a number of thematically less important ones from Homer and Virgil.

4. *Don Carlos*: a play by Schiller; the Tristan story: the basis of one of Richard Wagner's opera's [Editor].

They provided an altogether more profound explanation of Aschenbach's artistic development and his passion, and clear criteria for judging it.

Plato and Plutarch see beauty in a religious light. It is a reminder to
men of the vision which was vouchsafed to each soul before its birth
into the world: a vision of ultimate reality, Plato's realm of Forms, or
Ideas, where goodness, wisdom, truth exist unchanging in absolute perfection. Men forget this vision to varying degrees, and cannot be directly
reminded of some of the absolutes—Reason, Virtue, Justice, are not
objects of the senses. (If they were, the love they would inspire would
consume men utterly.) But Beauty is by its nature sensible, the only
absolute that is. It thus becomes the vital link between men in their
earthly existence and the higher realm. When a man whose soul is not
already too corrupted by the world sees an object of beauty, he is
reminded with a shock of that realm, his spiritual wings (in Plato's
image) grow strong. The value of beautiful forms lies not in themselves,
but in the higher reality they partake of and point to. In another image,
which Mann uses in his text, Plutarch speaks of the solid shapes to
which teachers of geometry have to resort when their pupils are not
yet capable of abstract intellectual concepts. In the same way, he says,
heavenly love has provided men with beautiful reflections of the divine,
pointers in the corrupt world of sense to a world which is beyond sense
and beyond corruption.[5]

This is why there need be no conflict between a love of external
beauty and a devotion to things intellectual and spiritual: the one stands
for the other, has its meaning from it, leads back to it. But this is the
ideal. There are problems in practice. Beauty, being sensuous, may
stimulate a purely sensuous response. The uninitiated and corrupt will
desire to possess and enjoy the particular beautiful object. This sort of
fulfilment thwarts the true purpose of beauty, which is to be a means,
not an end in itself. For Plato (though not for Plutarch) the love of men
for women seemed necessarily to come into this lower category, having
the earthly purpose of procreation. Procreation was necessary, but a relationship which had only this aim might not leave room for spiritual
development.

So it seemed obvious that the spiritual potential lay in love between
men. Since it was a relationship that could not procreate physically, it
was free to create in the spirit. It could inspire poetry or philosophy, it
could further the education of the young, it could inspire bravery in
war. All these were noble in themselves and it was thought noble to
pursue them. They were what the *Symposium* calls children of the mind
rather than the body and they promised immortality of a different order.

5. *Erotikos* 765 a. [Plutarch, *Über die Liebe* (Erotikos), trans. into German by Kaltwasser
(Munich and Liebzig, 1911). Vol. 3 of *Vermischte Schriften* (Miscellaneous Works), 3 vols.]
Cf. viii. 490 [38].

Men ambitious for fame, poets among them, would make greater sacrifices for these than for bodily children.

But the spiritual potential of homosexual love was not a guarantee of fulfilment, any more necessarily than in the case of heterosexual love. It could as easily stop short at earthly gratifications. Its advocates in the Platonic dialogues take account of this possibility, familiar enough to the Greeks, and duly speak of lovers as ignoble or noble, depending on whether their love is a mere present enjoyment or a starting-point for higher achievement. The lover's behaviour is a measure of his human quality and a condition of his right development.

We can follow Mann's assimilation of these doctrines through the markings in his copy of the *Symposium*[6] and through his extensive excerpts from all three dialogues in his work-notes. The relevance to Aschenbach's situation is obvious. Will he see in the individual boy Beauty itself, will the sight strengthen his 'spiritual wings'? Will it inspire him in his writing? Will it spur him in the pursuit of fame, through his 'spiritual children', his works? Will it point him onwards to the realm of ultimate Beauty?

The text of *Der Tod in Venedig* contains passages corresponding to each one of these questions. Mann used, very deliberately, material from Plato and Plutarch to construct the situations in which Aschenbach's love of beauty is tested. We have seen that his appreciation of Tadzio is at first markedly aesthetic, and that this was a link with the aesthetic preferences of his day, in response to which he had developed a classicizing taste. But the Platonic doctrine gave this taste a deeper grounding, and the text shows it. When Aschenbach lingers before going in to dine on the first evening in his Venice hotel, it is because Tadzio's family has not gone in yet. He is satisfied to have *das Schöne* to look at—the Beautiful itself in its chance embodiment (p. 471) [22]. During the meal he occupies his mind with philosophical reflections, which Tadzio has inspired, on the relationship between the General and the Particular inhuman beauty (*das Gesetzmässige* and *das Individuelle*) [p. 472] [23]). Although his reflections lead him nowhere, they are exactly on the central Platonic theme. For behind the theory of Forms and an absolute realm, Plato is dealing with just this question: the absolutes are related to earthly objects as the General to the Particular. (Plato speaks in the *Phaedrus* of an Idea as 'a unity gathered together by the reason from many particulars of sense' [249c].)

Even more clearly Platonic is the long reflection that follows Aschenbach's comparison of the boy's statuesque beauty with the plastic form of his own works. Once more a contemporary touch, once more taken deeper in Greek terms. In the figure at the water's edge, Aschenbach sees Beauty itself: '. . . glaubte er mit diesem Blick das Schöne selbst zu

6. Platons, *Gastmahl*, verdeutscht von [Plato's Symposium, translated into German by] Rudolf von Kassner, Jena, 1903.

begreifen, die Form als Gottesgedanken, die eine und reine Vollkommenheit, die im Geiste lebt und von der ein menschliches Gleichnis hier leicht und hold zur Anbetung aufgerichtet war' (he believed that with this glance he comprehended Beauty itself, form as a divine thought, the one and pure perfection which lives in the spirit and of which a human likeness was here set up, graceful and light, for adoration. (p. 490) [37][7] Images from Plato and Plutarch at this point come thick and fast: the 'geometry teacher' simile, then Aschenbach's mental reconstruction of the setting of the *Phaedrus* and long quotations from that dialogue, in the phrasing of the Kassner translation which Mann used. Intermingled are other literary echoes: Socrates and Phaedrus, 'der Weise beim Liebenswürdigen', recall Hölderlin's 'Und es neigen die Weisen / Oft am Ende zu Schönem sich' (Wise men often incline to / Something beautiful at the last);[38];[8] the paragraph that describes Aschenbach writing in Tadzio's presence opens appropriately with an echo from August von Platen's epigram on Venice entitled 'Rückblick'.

Aschenbach writing in view of Tadzio as the boy plays on the beach: this episode corresponds obviously to the idea that love could inspire poetry. Mann's work-notes confirm that it was meant so. The text's simple suggestion 'dass Eros im Worte sei' (that Eros is in the word [p. 492] [39]) goes back to passages in Plutarch and Plato which speak of love as the poet's teacher, and of the impossibility of shining in the arts without love's inspiration. Mann's excerpts clearly prepared this episode in the *Novelle*, for they include the words 'Arbeit am Strande' (work on the beach) [sheet 20, 83]. And in a striking reinterpretation of Aschenbach, erotic inspiration in the highest sense is read back into his whole literary career: 'Nur der glänzt in der Kunst, den Eros unterweist. Auch seine Kunst war ein nüchterner Dienst im Tempel zu Thespiä. Eros ist immer in ihm gewesen. Tadzio war immer sein König. Auch seine Liebe zum Ruhm war Eros' (A man can only shine in art if Eros instructs him. His art too was a sober service in the temple of Thespiae [a temple to Eros mentioned in Plutarch's *Erotikos*]. Eros was always in him. Tadzio was always his king. His love of fame was Eros too) [sheet 20, 83].

These notes are far from having the critical tone Mann's story finally acquired. Are they merely a preparation for constructing the awareness of classical parallels in Aschenbach himself? Taken by themselves, they do not suggest this. Rather they show how much more deeply and sympathetically it was possible to understand Aschenbach in the light of Platonic doctrine: his ascetic life a self-sacrifice to a higher form of love, his ambition one of those noble sublimations of the love of beauty, Tadzio a late embodiment of the ideal he had always served.

7. The work-note corresponding to this passage is more Platonic still in its wording: * * * "he sees the eternal Forms, Beauty itself, the eternal ground from which every beautiful form springs" [sheet 18, 82].
8. The poem 'Sokrates und Alkibiades' referred to in the letter to Weber [98].

Finally, there is the question whether Tadzio will point Aschenbach on, not just to Beauty itself and its nobler pursuits, but to an absolute realm of spiritual things. Once more, Mann constructed a passage to embody and answer this question. It is the final scene, Aschenbach's death on the beach. He is, as always, watching Tadzio, who is alone at the water's edge after the scuffle with Jascha. Cut off now even from companions, he seems an almost freely floating figure against the background of the sea—'eine höchst abgesonderte und verbindungslose Erscheinung, mit flatterndem Haar dort draussen im Meere, im Winde, vorm Nebelhaft-Grenzenlosen' (p. 524) [62]. And just as Aschenbach collapses, Tadzio has adopted a statuesque pose and seems to be beckoning: 'Ihm war, als ob der bleiche und liebliche Psychagog dort draussen ihm lächle, ihm winke; als ob er, die Hand aus der Hüfte lösend, hinausdeute, voranschwebe ins Verheissungsvoll-Ungeheure. Und wie so oft, machte er sich auf, ihm zu folgen.' (It seemed to him as if the pale and lovely conductor of souls out there were smiling to him, beckoning him; as if, taking his hand from his hip, he were pointing out, drifting on before him into the vast promising spaces. And as so often he rose to follow him.)

This crucial, because final, passage is based exactly on Plato's image for the realms into which the spiritual initiate progresses. Diotima's speech to Socrates in the *Symposium* traces a man's spiritual development from love of a single beautiful body to love of all physical beauty, then to love of spiritual qualities, of the beauty in laws and institutions, and ultimately to a vision of absolute Beauty itself. This is the final initiation and reward. Here is Kassner's translation, excerpted by Thomas Mann:

> . . . und so im Anblick dieser vielfachen Schönheit nicht mehr wie ein Sklave nach der Schönheit dieses einen Knaben verlange und dieses einen Menschen Schönheit wolle und gemein sei und kleinlich, . . . sondern, *an die Ufer des grossen Meeres der Schönheit gebracht*, hier viele edle Worte und Gedanken mit dem *unerschöpflichen Triebe nach Weisheit* zeuge, bis er dann stark und reif jenes einzige Wissen, das da das Wissen des Schönen ist, erschaue. . . . Ja, Sokrates, wer immer von dort unten, weil er den Geliebten richtig zu lieben wusste, empor zu steigen und jenes ewige Schöne zu schauen beginnt, *der ist am Ende und vollendet und geweiht.*

> (. . . and so, seeing this manifold beauty, long no more like a slave for the beauty of this one boy and desire this one human being's beauty and be common and petty . . . but, *brought to the border of the great sea of beauty*, here beget many noble words and thoughts with the *inexhaustible urge for wisdom*, until he then, strong and mature, has a vision of that unique knowledge which is the knowledge of beauty . . . Yes, Socrates, whoever has been able

to ascend through right loving of the beloved and begins to see that
eternal beauty, *he is at the end and perfected and initiated.*) [sheet
16, 80][9]

There is no better guide to higher things than Eros, Diotima continues.
Der Tod in Venedig contains elements which suggest it was constructed
to show just this. It is even possible to see Tadzio in the role of Eros—
the god Plato calls young and delicate—before his function as Aschenbach's guide to death made the analogy with Hermes, conductor of souls
to the underworld, seem more appropriate.[1]

As Mann later said (xii. 98), the death of a character is not in itself a
judgement on what he stands for. One need only think of Hanno Buddenbrook. Aschenbach's death, so exactly embodying the Platonic theory
of ascent to ever higher spiritual planes, has something of an apotheosis,
even in the critical form which Mann's story finally took on. But this
final form plays it down. No responsibility is taken by the author for the
suggestion of an apotheosis, it is only given as the record of Aschenbach's
feelings: 'Ihm war, als ob . . .' Mann never drew attention to his use of
Platonic imagery—strange, since he liked his allusions to be known—
and it has not to my knowledge been noticed before.[2] The scene stays,
but in a story whose overt intention is to pass a moral judgement.

It is conceivable that the critical intentions were already there from the
very first contact with Platonic material, but it seems on balance unlikely. Mann excerpted from Plato and Plutarch all the passages that are
positive about love: they speak of the high potential of the lover's
yearning, its fruitfulness for poetry especially, the acceptability in a lover
of behaviour that would otherwise be outrageous, the high esteem in
which love was held among respectably warlike peoples (a link here with
Aschenbach's military ancestry), the many examples of lovers who were
also heroes, the primacy of love over other obligations. One has a sense
that greater understanding of the modern incident is being drawn from
the ancient background. Moreover, if there had never been any intention to portray Aschenbach favourably in this Greek light, the collecting
of so much matter calculated to do just this is odd; it is more plausible
that a later decision turned the story in a different direction, while still
perforce retaining the structural substance which it was too late to
abandon.

When the change occurred (and it can be dated roughly as October
1911) this substance proved flexible; homosexual love, as all the Greek

9. Kassner, pp. 62–4.
1. This is Mann's first use of a mythological figure who became a favourite later. The information
   about Hermes' function was provided by a footnote to the *Erotikos*, p. 26 of the German
   translation Mann used, as is confirmed by the wording on [sheet 11, 75] of the work-notes.
   This detail was brought to light by Manfred Dierks.
2. Some attention has been given to the Greek echoes in Mann's text, but investigation of Plato
   has not gone beyond the *Phaedrus*, which is actually named there.

sources said, could be noble or debased.[3] Each episode which could yield a positive could equally yield a negative result. Nor (supposing a 'positive' interpretation which required to be changed) was it difficult to alter the stress. For instance, when Aschenbach thinks he recognizes beauty itself and the Platonic forms in Tadzio, a critical distance is created by the words: 'Das war der Rausch' (that was intoxication) and by the comment on his recollections from Plutarch: 'So dachte der Enthusiasmierte; so vermochte er zu empfinden' (thus he thought in his enthusiasm; thus was he capable of feeling). Similarly, his act of writing with Tadzio in sight, this 'seltsam zeugender Verkehr des Geistes mit einem Körper'[4] (strangely productive intercourse of the spirit with a body) can be shown in a less favourable light by the detail that Aschenbach's conscience afterwards accused him as if of a dissolute act. The increasing use of adjectival nouns as judgements—*der Verwirrte, der Starrsinnige*—are also a simple and economical way for the narrator to establish his position as a moralist. As much as anything else, the close-up view of Tadzio alters the work's whole import: not just his typically decadent bad teeth (p. 479) [29], but the knowingness he increasingly shows, his coquetry, the smile which provokes Aschenbach's indignation even as it forces his avowal of love (p. 498) [43]. Tadzio is here far from the ideal, not a mere perfect statue, nor a miraculous epiphany akin (as he had earlier seemed) to Stefan George's Maximin. His beauty is skin-deep. Significantly, this climax of Chapter 4 is preceded by the narrator's reflections on the delicate relationship between people who know each other by sight only. His conclusion removes the basis for a positive view of Aschenbach's passion, it draws its spiritual nerve, for it denies the value of yearning: 'die Sehnsucht ist ein Erzeugnis mangelhafter Erkenntnis' (yearning is a product of insufficient knowledge [p. 497] [42]). We have returned to the principle of the analytical writer, *Erkenntnis*. Mann is, after all, an analytical writer.

How and why did the change of conception occur? Mann accounted for it by the 'necessities of his nature'. These produced their own objectivizing process which was 'painful' because it conflicted with his conscious will. His wishes were refused by his deepest nature as a writer. How this operated is ultimately impenetrable, but a mixed moral and aesthetic distaste for his first conception dictated changes of detail such as we have traced. One further important factor must be added.

Georg Lukács, or von Lukács, as at that time his name officially was, published in 1911 a book of essays entitled *Die Seele und die Formen*,

---

3. Kassner also emphasized just this point with a long epigraph from Pico della Mirandola on man's freedom to choose his own way of developing * * *. One cannot of course be certain that Mann noticed this.

4. This phrase is not in itself pejorative. *Zeugen* is Kassner's word for Plato's idea of 'begetting'—physical children physically, spiritual children in the spirit. Mann's excerpts from this section of the *Symposium* (208c ff). are headed 'Ruhm und Zeugung' (fame and begetting) [Sheet 17, 80].

with a strong neo-Platonic tendency. One essay in particular, 'Sehnsucht und Form', deals at some length with Socrates as the creator of a philosophy out of the human impulse for love and yearning. He did this in two senses, firstly in that he sublimated his own and his admirers' passions into a pursuit of truth, and secondly in that he developed a general theory in which love—the commonest form of yearning—became the motive power for all spiritual progress. The matter is put clearest, Lukács says, in the *Symposium*, which asks what the lover is and what he is really pursuing, why people yearn and what the true object of their yearning is. Sexual love, which Aristophanes in Plato's dialogue explains as the urge of two halves of a once undivided being to be reunited, is merely 'die kleine Sehnsucht, die erfüllbare' (the small, fulfillable kind of yearning). Higher forms of yearning can, by their nature, find no fulfilment in life. To yearn for something is to prove thereby how deeply foreign it is to oneself, and how impossible therefore any union with it must be. 'Was einem fremd ist, wird man nie ersehnen . . . Die Sehnsucht verbindet die Ungleichen, aber vernichtet zugleich jede Hoffnung auf ihr Einswerden . . . die wahre Sehnsucht hat nie eine Heimat gehabt' (Anything that is alien to one will never be attained by longing . . . Yearning links unlikes, but simultaneously destroys all hope of their union . . . true yearning has never had a home on earth).[5]

These ideas are close to Mann's early themes, and even echo some of his formulations.[6] Lukács's bold interpretation of Plato puts in quintessential form the dilemma and mental condition of the Outsider and its ultimate grounds, and puts it in terms which were bound to catch Mann's interest. He had once called *Sehnsucht* his favourite word, a magic formula, a key to the secret of the world (to Katja Pringsheim,[7] September 1904). He had shown that the desire to bridge an unbridgeable gap was the fruitful principle in Tonio Kröger's art. He had depicted Schiller's creativity in *Schwere Stunde* as the result of a yearning for form ('Sehnsucht nach Form, Gestalt, Begrenzung, Körperlichkeit . . .') (viii. 377). Lukács's systematic account might well seem apposite to himself and also to his hero.

But the essay also gave a very definite angle on the Platonic philosophy, and struck the note of pessimism and tragedy which was finally to be dominant in *Der Tod in Venedig*. Lukács makes plain how precarious and rare was Socrates' achievement when he shaped men's longings into philosophy. In general, efforts at sublimation are almost bound to fail, because of the earthliness of the objects which first stimulate them:

---

5. Lukàcs [*Die Seele und die Formen* (Berlin, 1900)], p. 200.
6. For example in *Fiorenza*, in the closing speeches of both Savonarola and Lorenzo: * * * Do you want a sign when irreconcilability and eternal alienation are set between two worlds? Yearning is that sign (viii. 1061). * * * Wither yearning urges, is it not so? there one is not, that one is not (1062).
7. Mann's wife. [Editor]

Den Menschen und den Dichtern wird ein solcher Aufschwung immer versagt bleiben. Der Gegenstand ihrer Sehnsucht hat eine eigene Schwere und ein sich-selbst-wollendes Leben. Ihr Aufschwung ist immer die Tragödie, und Held und Schicksal müssen da zur Form werden . . . Im Leben muss die Sehnsucht Liebe bleiben: es ist ihr Glück und ihre Tragödie.

(Such spiritual flights will remain ever out of the reach of men and poets. The object of their yearning has its own gravity and a life which cares only for itself. Their aspiration is always tragedy, and hero and fate have to be turned into form . . . In life yearning must remain love: that is its happiness and its tragedy.)[8]

Formulations from this passage appear in the closing pages of the *Novelle*, in that mock-Platonic speech in which Aschenbach addresses Tadzio-Phaedrus and attains clear insight into his own downfall and its causes: '. . . Leidenschaft ist unsere Erhebung, und unsere Sehnsucht muss Liebe bleiben,—das ist unsere Lust und unsere Schande . . . wir vermögen nicht, uns aufzuschwingen, wir vermögen nur, auszuschweifen' (. . . passion is our elevation, and our yearning must remain love—that is our pleasure and our shame . . . we are not capable of spiritual flights, only of aberration) (p. 522) [60–61]. It is clear that Lukács's pessimistic view of Platonic possibilities decisively affected Thomas Mann's treatment of his theme. It provided a sterner, potentially moral view at a time when Mann was deeply dissatisfied with the story as he had begun it.

'At a time when': the timing is clearly important. The essay 'Sehnsucht und Form' first appeared in partial pre-publication form in the *Neue Rundschau* of February 1911. As a Fischer author, Mann not only contributed to the *Rundschau* but also read it. Did Lukács's suggestive title first catch his eye then? All we can be sure of is that the text he used when working on *Der Tod in Venedig* was the full text in *Die Seele und die Formen*.[9] And this volume came out, so far as can be ascertained, in the autumn of 1911.[1]

I would no longer wish to argue, as I have elsewhere, that Mann got his *positive* interest in Plato's theory of beauty and love via Lukács's essay, but then, having explored its possibilities, accepted Lukács's critical conclusions as confirmation for his own increasing resistance to the 'Greek' approach. There is a less complicated alternative.

Mann's copy of the *Symposium* bears the date of acquisition 1904.

8. Lukàcs, p. 203.
9. The passage quoted above is the conclusion of §1 and the first sentence of §2. The *Rundschau* sample consisted of sections 1 and 4. Mann's copy of *Die Seele und die Formen*, with marginal markings, is in [the Thomas Mann Archive in Zurich].
1. In the first half of October, according to Georg Lukàcs (private letter to the author of 20 July 1970). The accuracy of his recollection is not guaranteed, but is a striking independent corroboration of the time scheme sketched above. Further evidence of the publication date of *Die Seele und die Formen* was not obtainable.

There is little sign that it especially interested him in the years intervening (except that the letter singing the praises of *Sehnsucht* to Katja is also dated 1904). Nevertheless, it is quite conceivable that he turned to it when the 'hymnic' approach to his Venice subject was in full swing. Even when the very first intoxication cooled into a plan for a *Novelle* (to Witkop, July 1911) [93], its declared qualities—purity, seriousness, propriety—suggest precisely the Platonic treatment, taking homosexual passion in an elevated sense, rather than the final moralistic treatment. The Plutarch text which Mann made such intensive use of also appeared in 1911,[2] and may itself have been the initial stimulus to a 'Greek' treatment. By October Mann's growing unease and the new light Lukács threw on Platonic aspirations came together to cast the story in its final form. The critical view took over, but had to inform material which had been very differently intended. Precisely this negative reworking of what was at first a positive conception would account perfectly for the strange mixture *Der Tod in Venedig* actually is, of enthusiasm and criticism, classical beauty and penetration, elevation and sordidness.

The kinds of detailed change which resulted for the final text and the altered stress on episodes have already been illustrated. We can also see the change taking effect at its source, in the work-notes. Two consecutive notes sketch the central issue the story has now come round to treating, and the passages in which it is to be made most explicit—the *Phaedrus* pastiche and Chapter Two. The first reads:

> Aufstieg von der Problematik zur Würde. Und nun! Der Konflikt ist: von der 'Würde' aus, von der Erkenntnisfeindschaft und zweiten Unbefangenheit, aus antianalytischem Zustande gerät er in *diese* Leidenschaft. Die Form ist die Sünde. Die Oberfläche ist der Abgrund. Wie sehr wird dem würdig gewordenen Künstler die Kunst noch einmal zum Problem! Eros ist für den Künstler der Führer zum Intellektuellen, zur geistigen Schönheit, der Weg zum Höchsten geht für ihn durch die Sinne. Aber das ist ein gefährlich lieblicher Weg, ein Irr- und Sündenweg, obgleich es einen anderen nicht gibt. 'Den Dichtern wird ein solcher Aufschwung immer versagt bleiben. Ihr Aufschwung ist immer die Tragödie . . . Im *Leben* (und der Künstler ist der Mann des Lebens!) muss die Sehnsucht *Liebe* bleiben: es ist ihr Glück und ihre Tragödie.'—Einsicht, dass der Künstler nicht würdig sein *kann*, dass er notwendig in die Irre geht, Bohemien, Zigeuner, Libertiner, und ewig Abenteurer des Gefühls bleibt. Die Haltung seines Stiles erscheint ihm als Lüge und Narrentum, Orden, Ehren, Adel fast lächerlich. Die Würde rettet allein der Tod (die 'Tragödie', das 'Meer'—Rat, Ausweg und Zuflucht aller höheren Liebe[)].
> Der Ruhm des Künstlers eine Farce, das Massenzutrauen zu

2. Plutarch, *Vermischte Schriften* [Miscellaneous works], translated by Kaltwasser, Munich and Leipsig, 1911, 3 vols. Vol. 3 contains *Über die Liebe* [Erotikos].

ihm eine Dummheit. Erziehung durch die Kunst ein gewagtes,
zu verbietendes Unternehmen. Ironie, dass die Knaben ihn lesen.
Ironie der Offizialität, der Nobilitierung.

(Ascent from problematic state to dignity. And now! The conflict
is: from 'dignity', from hostility to knowledge and from second
innocence, from an anti-analytic position he gets involved in *this*
passion. Form is the sin. The surface is the abyss. How deeply art
once again becomes problematic for the artist who has attained
dignity! Eros is for the artist the guide to things intellectual, to
spiritual beauty, the path to the highest things goes, for him,
through the senses. But that is a dangerous if delightful path, a
wrong way and a sinful way, although there isn't any other. 'Such
spiritual flights will remain ever out of the reach of poets. Their
elevation is always tragedy . . . In *life* (and the artist is the man of
life!) yearning must remain *love*: that is its happiness and its tragedy.'—Realization that the artist *cannot* attain dignity, that he necessarily goes astray, remains a bohemian, a gipsy, a libertine and
eternal adventurer of the emotions. The discipline of his style
appears to him lies and foolishness, decorations, honours, noble
rank almost ludicrous. Dignity is rescued only by death (the 'tragedy', the 'sea'—solution, way out and refuge of all higher love[)].

The artist's fame a farce, popular trust in him idiotic. Education
through art a risky undertaking which should be prohibited. Ironic
that boys read him. Ironic that he is an establishment figure, with
a title.) [Sheets 4–5, 71]

In the phrase 'the conflict is:' one can sense the deliberate effort of
clarifying complex issues, making a fresh start in the light of a new
principle. Beginning at 'Eros' the Platonic material is then reinterpreted
sceptically, and the authority for this view given—a quotation from
Lukács. This is duly adjusted to fit the case—only poets, not men in
general—and key words are underlined and glossed. Then follows the
sketch for that final ironic, even sarcastic view of Aschenbach, the artist
who seemed to have attained dignity but fell. This is where the theme
which had been in Mann's mind so long, the precariousness of any
status and recognition an artist might achieve, became established as the
critical message of the Venice experiment. Only one way out was left—
death. Not now as an apotheosis, but as an emergency exit from Aschenbach's dilemma: the 'tragedy' in which Lukács said all higher flights end;
the 'sea', that borrowing of Plato's 'sea of beauty' at the close. Mann had
difficulties finding the right ending for his *Novelle* (to Heinrich Mann,
April 1912 [93]). It seems that an ending already envisaged in the 'hymnic' conception served after all the quite different 'tragic' purpose—
served it all the better because it remains profoundly ambiguous, as does
the wording of this work-note which still speaks of Aschenbach's passion
as an example of 'higher love'.

The other note starts from the *Phaedrus* sentence 'Nur die Schönheit ist zugleich sichtbar und liebenswürdig' (only beauty is at the same time visible and worthy of love)[3] and from there spells out the paradox by which Aschenbach's resolute literary development placed him at risk:

> Liebe zur Schönheit führt zum Moralischen, zur Absage an die Sympathie mit dem Abgrund, an die Psychologie, die Analyse, [added: d. h. zur Bejahung der Leidenschaft und des Lebens]; führt zur Einfachheit, Grösse und schönen Strenge, zur wiedergeborenen Unbefangenheit, zur Form. Aber eben damit auch wieder zum Abgrund.
>
> Was ist moralisch? die Analyse? (Die Vernichtung der Leidenschaft?) Sie hat keine Strenge, sie ist wissend, verstehend, ohne Haltung und Form. Sie hat Sympathie mit dem Abgrund [Added: Sie *ist* der Abgrund.) Oder die Form? Die Liebe zur Schönheit? Aber sie führt zum Rausch, zur Begierde und also ebenfalls zum Abgrund.
>
> (Love of beauty leads to what is moral, to the rejection of sympathy with the abyss, of psychology, analysis [added: i.e. to the affirming of passion and life]; leads to simplicity, grandeur, and beautiful austerity, to innocence reborn, to form. But precisely thereby to the abyss again.
>
> What is moral? analysis? (The destruction of passion?) It has no austerity, it is knowing, understanding, it lacks discipline and form. It has sympathy with the abyss. [Added: It *is* the abyss.] Or form? Love of beauty? But that leads to intoxication, to desire, and thus equally to the abyss. [Sheet 6, 72])

The directness with which the crux of the story is given in this passage is the directness of Chapter Two, which was referred to above as an obituary and advance explanation of Aschenbach's fate. But if it is 'advance' in the order of the completed text, it seems likely that it was actually written later on in the experiment. The first of the two passages just quoted is preceded in the work-notes, on the same sheet, by a list of 'Beziehungen von Kap. II zu V' (links from Chapter II to V). The points listed are: Aschenbach's forebears and their courageous service; love of fame and ability to carry it; the motto *Durchhalten*, discipline, soldierly service; the production of great works in a state of tension; the principle of working against the grain *(das Trotzdem)*. [Sheet 4, 71] This, coming as it does on the same sheet which works out the story's crucial issue as finally treated, suggests that Chapter Two is chronologically as well as essentially the conclusion of the experiment. For narrative purposes, to set the points for a reading of the work as a 'moral fable', it rightly stands near the beginning. But it was surely a simple matter to interpose it

---

3. Platons *Phaidros* ins Deutsche übertragen von [Plato's *Phaedrus* in German translation by] Rudolf Kassner, Jena, 1910, p. 44.

there, breaking the otherwise uninterrupted flow of the narrative from Chapter One to Chapter Three.

Yet by a further twist the presence of a synoptic view of Aschenbach's development in Chapter Two again alters the story's moral impact. It may warn against the dangers of beauty and thus prepare us for a cautionary tale; but it also understands Aschenbach's behaviour as the product of his period and of his years.[4] In so doing, it surely goes beyond those all too obvious condemnations which the narrator intersperses in the later part of the action, and rises instead to the plane of 'tout comprendre, c'est tout pardonner'. In this respect too, Thomas Mann remains the writer he was.

III

We are still not at the end of the complexities in Mann's story; but those that remain are beneficial to the text as finally completed, not problems in the path of its completion. Indeed, even the tortuous genesis so far discussed left enriching elements behind it. For, when the intricate development is over, what remains is a single text, which creates effects. Understanding these fully may depend on some knowledge of the story's genesis—our reading loses a dimension if we know nothing of the specifically Platonic symbolism, or if we cannot connect the details of Aschenbach's behaviour with Plutarch's description of lovers who 'pursue by day and haunt the door by night'.[5] But a proper standard for judging the text is the degree of unity it finally has for the reader. The extent to which genetic difficulties and a variety of sources are reconciled in *Der Tod in Venedig* into such a unified statement is remarkable.

Mann's actual experience, his latent preoccupations, philosophical theory, psychological analysis, mythology, and literary parallels all came together and without any intervention on the author's part offered suggestive connections, those *Beziehungen* whose fascination Mann speaks of in the *Lebensabriss* apropos of precisely this story (xi. 123 f.) [109].

Der Tod in Venedig is about psychological decay finding in the outside world pretext and occasion for its fulfilment. Aschenbach's creative discipline is essentially broken at the very outset. The long years of too deliberate application and self-control have begun to take their revenge. This is the psychological premiss of the whole story. It is coloured specifically by Nietzsche's theory of the components in artistic creation, the Apolline and the Dionysiac: this second element is Aschenbach's 'geknechtete Empfindung' (p. 449) [6]. Nietzsche's terms already led over into Greek mythology. On investigation, Dionysus proved to be a

---

4. The letter to Weber [97] refers to the 'Klimakterium'.
5. Cf. *Erotikos* 759b: 'He loves when present and longs when absent, pursues by day and haunts the door by night."

foreign god originating in India and superimposed on an older Greek deity. But the cholera epidemic, which in Naturalistic terms is what kills Aschenbach, also came from India. This coincidence between the external cause and a mythologically understood inner cause was sugges- tive, especially to a writer on the look-out for ways to elevate prose narra- tive above the literal Naturalistic level. If the epidemic was in Aschenbach's eyes a secret accomplice in disorder, for Thomas Mann the epidemic which broke out in Italy during his Venice stay was cer- tainly an ideal accomplice in the creation of a symbolic pattern. Myth, psychology, and real events coincided in such a way that to state the one was simultaneously to allude to the others. Reality took on a new reso- nance.

The coincidental encounter with Tadzio takes its place in this com- plex as the stimulus to an insidious enthusiasm, which is related pre- cisely to the aesthetic fashions of Mann-Aschenbach's time. The inspirer of Aschenbach's heightened condition is also a perfect embodi- ment of the coincidentally encountered, or re-encountered, Platonic theory of beauty. This gives ideal criteria against which Aschenbach can eventually be found wanting. His failure and degradation exactly illus- trate the long-latent theme that the Artist's life is precariously based and should not lay claim to dignity too soon. Phrasing, images, and motifs are appropriately introduced from the Platonic dialogues and from the Plutarch dialogue coincidentally just to hand. Aschenbach's initially Platonic passion can be condemned as itself a form of *Rausch*: the gen- eral psychological theme of a Dionysiac reawakening subsumes the Pla- tonic theme. Plutarch too spoke of a heightened condition— *enthousiasmos*[6]—which could take the form of literary inspiration; this, like Platonic love, fits into the scheme of Aschenbach's decline and can be finally rejected. But all these contributions, including the psychologi- cal framework itself, in turn fitted exactly the investigation of the artistic and intellectual problems which become clear in Chapter Two—the nature of artistic development, the problem of ageing for the artist, the problem of maintaining enough self-awareness to preserve himself from danger in his vulnerable existence. And these in turn are a generalized version of the problems of 'Geist und Kunst'.

The experiences of the Venice visit—apart from the coincidence of the cholera epidemic, with its Indian source, which aided the construc- tion of a symbolic story—appear in the text in ideal integration with all these guiding themes and concepts. As Mann wrote in retrospect, they all had an innate symbolism, and only needed placing. So rich were they in symbolic potential, in fact, that they could have served the hym- nic purpose just as well: the old disgusting dandy on the boat to Venice could have been an ignoble contrasting figure to set off Aschenbach's

6. *Erotikos* 758e, excerpted in work-notes [sheet 11, 76]. Hence the reference to Aschenbach as *der Enthusiasmierte* (p. 491) [37].

pure and serious passion; but in the critical history of a psychological break-up he becomes an omen. Omens of death itself, and figures whose features allude to the death's head or to the hat and staff of Hermes are numerous and by now common knowledge. The psychological process is converted into an apparently fated course, it is *realized* in symbolic figures and motifs. This is not to say that fate in any other sense than the psychological is being seriously put forward as the reality of Aschenbach's death: the end must be distinguished from the means. But they are brilliantly matched to each other. Despite the compositional difficulties his letters record, it is clear why Mann spoke of a feeling that, in writing *Der Tod in Venedig*, he was at times being borne along by it ('das Gefühl eines gewissen absoluten Wandels, einer gewissen souveränen Getragenheit') (xi. 124). The meanings interlocked so remarkably. Mann's preoccupations and the varied materials which chance placed in his hands together created a wholly new suggestiveness, an art of rich ambivalence.

At the thematic level then, all ends well. At the symbolic level too, if one is prepared to accept the mingling of myths, the interplay of Eros and Hermes and Dionysus: for the writer in a sober age, myth is an exciting material which invites intensive exploitation. Criticism would have to start from the style, because here one can speak of ambiguity in the word's more dubious sense: not richness of meaning, but uncertainty of meaning, disunity.

Whose is the style? It has proved possible to detach Mann from the emphatic condemnations of the later pages. These formulations, despite the more critical view the author is by now taking of his character, are Mann's concession to more confident moralists than himself. But there are other features of the style, more firmly rooted in the text as a whole. There is its *gewollte Klassizität*, its deliberate classicism. In his response to early reviews which assumed the straight equation Aschenbach-Thomas Mann, and criticized it as presumptuous, Mann stressed the element of parody in the writing, and this view has become popular among scholars. The extreme formality, the wording which contrives to be both elaborate and lapidary, the set-piece descriptions and evocations of Venetian setting and sea-shore, the symbolic externals which stand in place of analysis, all these are attributed to Aschenbach himself. They are part of his mode of experiencing which the author recreates from within, by a process he himself labelled 'mimicry'.[7]

But then is there not much else in this story which began by being part of Mann's own experiment and ended by being passed on to Aschenbach? May this not also be true of the style? Was Thomas Mann not concerned with the idea of a future classicism? His Venice article on Wagner shows he was. Was there not, among the temptations which

---

7. To Paul Amann [95].

Mann-Aschenbach underwent, a pressure to move away from the analytical to the beauties of the surface, to plastic re-creation and richness
of external detail? We know there was. Was there not also a tendency to
associate such ambitions with things Greek? Hauptmann's *Griechischer
Frühling* shows it; and although Mann commented on this work ironically, his irony may have been open to revision, as were so many of the
attitudes of 'Geist und Kunst'. It seems distinctly possible that the style
of *Der Tod in Venedig* originally partook of ambitions which were discarded as part of the complex genesis, only coming to be a means to
characterize Aschenbach at the last. After all, the critical placing of
Aschenbach's style as a *gewollte Klassizität* occurs in Chapter Two,
where the experiment's final conclusions are made clear. It questions
the value of Aschenbach's literary manner when everything else about
him has become questionable. The problem is, how conclusively has
responsibility for that manner been transferred from Mann to
Aschenbach?

The way the story affected contemporaries is relevant. Wilhelm
Alberts, whose book on Mann [8] appeared the year after *Der Tod in Venedig* and dealt with the new work in a postscript, felt that the pursuit of
beauty had now taken over from satire as the main aim of Mann's art.
This seemed to Alberts clearly due to the influence of Greek art and
outlook: Mann too, he says, seems to have experienced a 'Greek spring'.
The allusion is significant. Had Hauptmann's example, his method of
sich arrangieren with the changing tastes of the times, been in Mann's
mind when he began to work with Greek motifs? Common ground
seemed obvious to a perceptive contemporary. And did not Mann write
to Heinrich of an *antikisierendes Kapitel* as one of the story's undeniable
beauties? At that point in time, not long before publication, classical
motifs and the highly wrought language in which they were introduced
could still claim attention as special effects, although the heightened
conception to which they originally corresponded had long been abandoned.

But if there was too much 'beauty' left in the text to be stylistically
quite compatible with the changed conception, there was also too much
'criticism' for the earnest devotee of the Beautiful. At the opposite
extreme from Alberts was Stefan George, who totally rejected Mann's
Novelle because it had compromised the most elevated things with decadence ('das Höchste in die Sphäre des Verfalls hinabgezogen'). [9] The
classicizing externals were not enough to reconcile George to the Naturalistic pathological treatment of an emotion towards which he was aus-
terely sympathetic.

Mann had sought to work out a changed conception in materials and

8. William Alberts, *Thomas Mann und sein Beruf* [Thomas Mann and his profession] (Leipzig,
   1913).
9. Quoted in Mann's letter to Weber [98].

language ideally suited to an earlier one. In the style of the resulting story, it can be argued, he managed to have his cake and eat it, arrive at critical conclusions about a certain kind of beauty while at the same time creating a literary equivalent of that beauty; just as it can be argued that he managed to construct from the sequence of hymnic and moral conceptions a single tragic vision of impulse and failure. Mann argued so himself, writing to Weber that he had striven for a synthesis of sensual and moral. But equally it could be said that his story falls stylistically between two stools, that the classicizing element which went with the still perceptible hymnic origin remains at odds with the story's moral purport, leaving a disharmony between style and substance. When Mann represented the style as being a parody of Aschenbach's own, he made the one adjustment that could restore unity. But his suggestion is hard to bear out from the text. As a sweeping explanation applied to a whole story, parody is almost impossible to verify. *Der Tod in Venedig* remains to this extent ambiguous. It is perhaps revealing that Mann wrote to Bertram soon after the story was published that he did not know what to think of it: 'Ich bin noch heute völlig ohne eigenes Urteil'.[1]

Mann's later retrospects offer other angles. In the *Betrachtungen* of 1918 he speaks of himself as one of those European writers who grew up in the age of decadence but are now at least experimenting with ways to overcome it ('mit der Überwindung von Dekadenz und Nihilismus wenigstens *experimentieren*' [xii. 201, Mann's italics]) and goes on to talk of *Der Tod in Venedig*. Their search is for new absolute values, some 'inner tyrant' controlling attitude and form: a need which, Mann says, he treated long before others were aware of it, not as a propagandist, but 'novellistisch, das heisst: experimentell und ohne letzte Verbindlichkeit' (in a *Novelle*, i.e.: experimentally and without final commitment [xii. 517]). This comes closer to the uncertainties at the core of the work. And that the experiment was essentially with Thomas Mann himself he makes explicit later, telling Graf Kessler that the hero of *Der Tod in Venedig* was 'more or less' himself,[2] and writing in his Princeton lecture that the story is not only a criticism of the artist in general:

> zugleich werden die pädagogischen Ansprüche gegeisselt, die sich etwa ins Künstler-Selbstgefühl einschleichen sollten: Ansprüche, Neigungen, Ideen, die doch in meinem eigenen Leben, seitdem es aus seiner jugendlichen Einsamkeits- und Boheme-Epoche herausgetreten war, eine Rolle zu spielen begonnen hatte[n].
>
> (at the same time the pedagogical pretensions are flayed which might perhaps infiltrate an artist's feeling about himself: pretensions, inclinations, ideas, which had in fact begun to take on a

1. *Thomas Mann an Ernst Bertram. Briefe aus den Jahren 1910–1955*, ed. Inge Jens (Pfullinger, 1960), 12 [Editor].
2. Harry Graf Kessler, *Tagebücher* [Diaries], Frankfurt, 1961, p. 173.

significance in my own life since it had emerged from its youthful period of isolation and bohemianism.)[3]

In other words, it was an experiment with the condition and the risks of being a 'Master'.

Despite the ambiguities which are rooted in the genesis of *Der Tod in Venedig*, at least the direction of development is clear: in what it implies about the Artist, the story constitutes a moral victory which is nothing to do with the morality of homosexual love. Through Aschenbach Mann had experimented with a change in his literary ways, a decision to reject the values by which he had so far lived and worked. The forces influencing him in that direction were stated in 'Geist und Kunst'—a work which Aschenbach, significantly, had brought to completion, we can easily infer in what sense. Subjected to the temptation of swimming with the stream, and even for a time actively wishing to do so, Mann nevertheless remained true to himself. The nature of his talent asserted itself against his more superficial motives. In place of the new kind of form he yearned to achieve, it drew him back towards a soberer, more critical, still 'intellectual' work. This is surely what he meant when he spoke in the *Lebensabriss* of the surprises the work had in store for its author (xi. 123). The failure to achieve undeniable *Dichtertum*, which he still speaks bitterly of in *Gesang vom Kindchen*, was thus only a failure in a limited sense.

The ambivalent art which was first brought to maturity in *Der Tod in Venedig* was a permanent acquisition. It is the basis for many later ambiguities and for an adroit manipulation of levels of meaning. For example, the teasing description of Hans Castorp's heightened state in his early days on the mountain: is it caused by love? or by disease? or does love create disease? or vice versa? And are both these things mere external pointers to his intellectual destiny? The play with *Beziehungen* is akin to that in the Venice story: *Der Zauberberg* was conceived just before *Der Tod in Venedig* was completed, and was originally planned as a short pendant piece to it.

Or again there is the Naturalistic surface of the Joseph novel, showing how all that 'really' happened, but with underlying suggestions of mythical re-enactment. And a yet more radical doubt and suggestiveness surround *Doktor Faustus*. Are Adrian Leverkühn's inspirations the product of syphilis or of a pact with the devil? The dubiousness itself parallels the two interpretations of Germany's descent into Nazism: pathological and mythical.

The creation of ambivalence was the breakthrough in Mann's long-standing programme to 'elevate' the novel. It rescued the novel of ideas from the mechanical methods of simple allegory. 'Allegory' still fairly

---

3. 'On Myself', *Blätter [der Thomas Mann Gesellschaft]* 6, p. 20.

describes some aspects of *Der Zauberberg* or *Doktor Faustus;* but the door has been opened to intellectual complexities of a quite different order from the encoded self-concern of *Königliche Hoheit.* From *Der Tod in Venedig* on, ambivalence is the central technique of Mann's art, suggesting, but not affirming, layers of meaning which lie beneath the surface of immediate experience.

Less permanent than the acquisition of this technique was Mann's commitment to critical intellect as the watchdog over human aberration. This had been reaffirmed after a testing experiment. It was soon to be swept aside by an enthusiasm less private and out of all proportion more powerful than the one provoked by a chance encounter in Venice.

✯ DORRIT COHN

The Second Author of *Death in Venice* †

I

In his review of a now forgotten contemporary novel Thomas Mann draws the following distinction between the author and the narrator of a fictional work: "Narrating is something totally different from writing, and what distinguishes them is an indirection in the former. . . ." This indirectness, he goes on to explain, is most slyly effective when it veils itself in directness: when the author interpolates between himself and his reader a second voice, "the voice of a second, interposed author," "as when . . . a gentleman announces himself and makes speeches who, however, is in no way identical with the epic author but rather an invented and shadowy observer".[1] Clearly Mann does not have in mind here a simple "first-person narrator" who tells his own life in the manner of Felix Krull, or even the peripheral type of first-person narrator who tells the life of a friend in the manner of Serenus Zeitblom. The reader needs hardly be told that a narrator so spectacularly equipped with a name, a civic identity and a body of his own should not be confused with the author of the work in which he appears. It is primarily when a narrator remains a truly "shadowy observer," a disincarnated voice without name or face, that the reader will be inclined to attribute to him the mind, if not the body, of the author whose name appears on the title page. This is especially likely to happen with a teller who intrudes loudly

† From *Probleme der Moderne: Studien zer deutschen Literatur von Nietzsche bis Brecht* (Tübingen: Niemeyer, 1983). (Some footnotes have been edited or omitted.) Reprinted by permission of the publisher. For the reader's convenience, page references to this Norton Critical Edition have been inserted in brackets following Dorritt Cohn's original references. However, translations are Cohn's and thus may differ from those above.

1. *Gesammelte Werke in zwölf Bänden* [Complete works in twelve volumes] (Frankfurt, a. M. 1960), X, pp. 631 f. The novel under review is Adolf von Hatzfeld's *Die Lemminge* (1923).

and volubly into his tale, as the narrators of Mann's own third-person novels almost invariably do. Like so many of his comments concerning the works of other writers, the distinction Mann draws in the passage quoted above looks suspiciously as though it were meant primarily *pro domo*.

In recent times, with our consciousness raised by modern literary theory, we have learned to resist the tendency to equate that authorial narrator—as we now generally call Mann's "second author"—with the author himself. At least in theory. In critical practice the distinction has been slow to sink in, perhaps because it has never been freighted sufficiently with demonstrations and qualifications. The author-narrator equation has been peculiarly tenacious in cases where a narrator takes earnest moralistic stands on weighty problems of morality; the reader then is given to extending the narrator's authority in matters of fictional fact onto his normative commentary. When his tone is more jocular, and especially when he plays self-conscious games with the narrative genre, it seems easier to grant him a personality of his own. This may well be why Mann's narrators in *Der Zauberberg* [*The Magic Mountain*] and the Joseph novels have long since been recognized as "second authors," whereas the seriously perorating monsieur who narrates *Der Tod in Venedig* [*Death in Venice*] has almost invariably been identified with Thomas Mann himself.

Nor can we automatically assume that this identification is incorrect. But since it has decisively affected interpretation of Mann's most enigmatic novella, my contention is that it needs to be questioned once and for all. In taking up this problem I follow a general directive provided by Franz Stanzel in his *Theorie des Erzählens* [*Theory of Narrative*]. Having reminded us that the separation of the authorial narrator from the personality of the author is a fairly recent narratological acquisition, he states: "One must start with the assumption that the authorial narrator is, within certain limits, an autonomous figure . . . which thus is accessible to the interpreter in his own personality. It is only when this kind of an interpretative attempt has proved conclusively negative that we can assume the identity of the authorial narrator with the author".[2] I assume from the wider context of his *Theorie* that Stanzel would insist that such interpretive assays be carried out intra-textually, without regard to evidence that might be gathered about the author from outside the text. My own intention, at any rate, is to perform my experiment with *Tod in Venedig* as far as possible *en vase clos*.

My principal focus will be the relationship of the narrator to his protagonist, such as it emerges from the language he employs in telling the story of Aschenbach's Venetian love and death. This story itself must of course be attributed to the invention of its author; the narrator, for his

2. Franz Stanzel, *Theorie des Ezrählens* (Göttingen, 1979), p. 27 f.

part, recounts it as though it were historically real. We can therefore
hold him accountable only for his narrative *manner*, not his narrative
matter (or, as the Russian Formalists would say, only for the *sujet*, not
for the *fabula*). It follows that his personality—his "Eigenpersönlich-
keit"—will stand out most clearly at those textual moments when he
departs furthest from straightforward narration, when he moves from the
mimetic, story-telling level to the non-mimetic level of ideology and
evaluation. In this respect, as we will see, the narrator of *Tod in Venedig*
provides a profusion of data for drawing his mental portrait: generalizations, exclamations, homilies, aphorisms and other expressions of normative subjectivity. These will ultimately allow us to assess his
objectivity, to decide whether he is, ideologically speaking, a reliable
narrator, and thus a spokesman for the norms of the author who has
invented both him and his story.[3]

II

In briefest summary the relationship of the narrator to his protagonist
in *Tod in Venedig* may be described as one of increasing distance. In
the early phases of the story it is essentially sympathetic, respectful, even
reverent; in the later phases a deepening rift develops, building an
increasingly ironic narratorial stance. In this regard Mann's novella
evolves in a manner diametrically opposed to the typical Bildungsroman, where we usually witness a gradual approach of the mind of the
protagonist to that of the narrator. Here the protagonist does not rise to
his narrator's ethical and cultural standards but falls away from them.
The events of Aschenbach's final dream, we are told "left behind the
cultivation of life annihilated, destroyed" (516) [56],[4] and subsequently,
as he shamelessly pursues Tadzio through the streets of Venice, "the
monstrous appeared promising to him, and the moral law appeared
invalid" (518) [58]. The narrator meanwhile—as the words he uses here
to describe Aschenbach's moral debacle indicate—remains poised on
the cultural pinnacle that has brought forth his protagonist's own artistic achievement.

It should be noted from the outset, however, that this bifurcating
narrative schema unfolds solely on the ideological or evaluative level of
the story, without in the least affecting the point of view (in the technical
sense of the word) from which the story is presented. On the perceptual
level the narrator steadfastly adheres to his protagonist's perspective on

---

3. I here use the term "reliable narrator" in the sense defined by Wayne Booth: "I have called a
narrator *reliable* when he speaks for . . . the norms of the work (which is to say, the implied
author's norms), *unreliable* when he does not" (*The Rhetoric of Fiction* [Chicago: U of Chicago
P, 1961], p. 158 f.).
4. Page numbers in parentheses refer to *Gesammelte Werke in zwölf Bänden* (Frankfurt, a. M.
1960), VIII.

the outside world; from the initial moment when he observes the strange wanderer standing on the steps of the funeral chapel to the final moment when he watches Tadzio standing on the sandbar we see the events and figures of the outside world through Aschenbach's eyes. The narrator also upholds from start to finish his free access to his protagonist's inner life (whereas he never so much as mentions what goes on in the mind of Tadzio). In sum, the narrator maintains his intimacy with Aschenbach's sensations, thoughts, and feelings, even as he distances himself from him more and more on the ideological level.

Now to follow this relationship through the text in greater detail. The most obtrusive indicator of the narrator's personality—and of the fact that he *has* a clearly defined personality—is the series of statements of "eternal truths" he formulates. There are in all some twenty glosses of this kind scattered through the text, and they express a consistent system of values. This narrator is for discipline, dignity, decorum, achievement and sobriety, against disorder, intoxication, passion and passivity. In short, he volubly upholds within the story a heavily rationalistic and moralistic cultural code, most strikingly in the maxims that culminate many of his statements *ex cathedra*:

> For it is dissolute not to be able to want a wholesome disen-chantment. For human beings love and honor each other as long as they are not capable of judging each other, and longing is the product of a lack of understanding. (496) [42]
> . . . for passion paralyzes the sense of fastidiousness and lets itself be drawn into dealing with charms that sobriety would take humorously or reject with indignation. (506) [49]
> He who is beyond himself detests nothing more than to have to return into himself. (515) [55]

With their causal inceptions *(denn)* these *sententiae* profess full accountability for the case under discussion. They embed Aschenbach's story in a predictable world, a system of stable psychological concepts and moral precepts.

That the narrator's code of values in fact closely matches the protagonist's own before his fall can be seen from the flashback on Aschenbach's career as a writer provided in chapter 2. As others have noted, this summary biography sounds rather like a eulogy penned in advance by the deceased himself. The narrator clearly takes the role of apologist, and his gnomic generalizations—more extensive here than elsewhere in the text, and all concerned, as the subject demands, with the psychology and sociology of artistic achievement—serve only to heighten the representative import of Aschenbach's existence. With one notable exception—to which I will return below—they unreservedly enhance the *laudatio* (see e.g. the passages starting with the words "For an important intellectual production"; "A living, intellectually uncommitted concreteness;" "But it seems that there is nothing against which a noble and diligent spirit" (452–55) [9–10].

The ideological concord between the narrator and Aschenbach continues into the narrated time of the story itself: in the starting episode, the voyage South, the early phases of the Venice adventure authorial generalizations are barely differentiated from figural thoughts. During Aschenbach's introspection while he awaits his Munich tramway: "he had reined in and cooled off his feelings because he knew that he had an inclination to be content with a gay approximation and a half perfection. Was it now the enslaved emotion that was avenging itself by abandoning him, in refusing to bear and give wings to his art . . . ?" (449) [6]. Note that tensual sequence in the first sentence: Aschenbach *knew* what the narrator *knows to be* true. Note also that the second sentence may quite as validly be read as a question Aschenbach puts to himself (in narrated monologue form) and as a question posed by the analytic narrator. Or take the scene where Aschenbach first perceives Tadzio in the hall of the hotel and wonders why he is allowed to escape the monastic dress code of his sisters: "Was he ill? . . . Or was he simply an indulged favorite child, elevated by a partial and capricious love? Aschenbach tended to believe the latter. *Almost every artist has a voluptuous and treacherous tendency to approve the injustice that brings about beauty and to greet aristocratic favoritism with understanding and respect*" (470; my italics) [22]. The narrator's speculation about artists flows from Aschenbach's speculations about Tadzio as smoothly as if the latter had self-indulgently accounted for his own reactions. Again, during Aschenbach's first contemplation of the ocean, narratorial comment dovetails with figural emotions:

> I will stay then, thought Aschenbach. Where could it be better? . . . He loved the sea for deep reasons; out of the need for peace of the hard working artist who wants to rest from the demanding multiplicity of appearances at the breast of the simple, the immense; "out of a forbidden penchant for the unstructured, immeasurable, eternal, for nothingness, a tendency that was directly opposed to his calling and for that very reason seductive. *He who labors at the production of the excellent longs to repose in the perfect; and is nothingness not a form of perfection?* But, as he was dreaming away into the emptiness. . . . (475; my italics)[26]

Fused almost seamlessly at both ends with Aschenbach's oceanic feelings, the narrator's intervention creates not a trace of distancing irony. This is true despite the ominous notes he sounds: "at the breast of . . . the immense, out of a forbidden . . . seductive tendency to nothingness" [26]. Aschenbach is still "the hard working artist who struggles to produce the excellent" [26] and who may be allowed—by way of vacation—a temporary indulgence in thanatos.

This *entente cordiale* between authorial and figural minds is disrupted at just about the mid-point of the Venetian adventure in a scene to be considered in detail below. From this point on the authorial commentary becomes emphatically distanced and judgmental. A clear example is the scene where Aschenbach, having followed Tadzio with the "salutary" intention of striking up a casual conversation with him finds himself too strongly moved to speak:

> Too late! he thought at this moment. Too late! But was it really too late? The step that he neglected to take could very possibly have lead to something wholesome, light, and serene, to a healthy sobriety. But it must have been a matter of the aging man not wanting sobriety because the intoxication was too precious for him. *Who is to unravel the essence and character of the artist! Who can comprehend the deeply instinctual fusion of discipline and licentiousness on which it rests. For it is licentious not to be able to want a wholesome disenchantment.* [39–40]

The narrator distances himself from Aschenbach explicitly and immediately when he questions the directly quoted "too late!". He now provides his interpretation for the failed action, which he attributes to a weakening of willpower, a falling away from the unquestioned values of health and sobriety. The exclamatory authorial rhetoric subsequently reinforces the critical analysis, grounds it in generalizations concerning the moral lability of artists, and caps it with the sententious final judgment. Then, returning to the individual case at hand, the narrator explicitly excludes Aschenbach from this authorial wisdom: "Aschenbach was not in the mood for self-criticism any more".

There are numerous instances in the later parts of the story that follow this same general pattern: an inside view of Aschenbach's mind, followed by a judgmental intervention cast in gnomic present tense, followed by a return to Aschenbach's now properly adjudged reactions. To quote one further example: when Aschenbach reads about the Venetian plague in the German newspapers,

> "One should be silent," Aschenbach thought excitedly. . . . But at the same time his heart was filled with satisfaction about the adventure that wanted to descend upon the world outside. *For passion, like crime, does not thrive in the secure order and comfort of the commonplace. Instead, it must welcome any relaxation of civil order, any confusion and affliction in the world for it can vaguely hope to gain some advantage for itself from it.* So Aschenbach felt a dark satisfaction about the officially concealed events in the dirty alleys of Venice (500; my italics). [45]

Again Aschenbach's response (this time plainly immoral) is instantly denounced and explained by the narrator, and in the severest terms.

Even a shade too severe, perhaps. The unwonted analogy between passion and crime makes it appear as though the narrator were bent on imposing his moral standards with the utmost rigidity. At the same time the syllogistic "So . . ." with which he reverts to Aschenbach's sinful thoughts maintains the sense that he is a perfectly dispassionate analyst.

A further device that underscores the narrator's progressive disengagement is his increasingly estranging and negative way of referring to Aschenbach. In the early sections distancing appellations appear sparingly and remain neutral and descriptive: "the traveler," "the waiting one," "the resting one." After the narrator parts company with his character, ideologically speaking, we find on a regular basis the more condescending epithets "the aging man," "the lonely one." And at crucial stations of his descent Aschenbach becomes "the afflicted," "the stubborn one," "the crazed one," "the besotted," "the confused one," "the one who has gone astray," and on, in a more and more degrading name-calling series that leads down to the final "degraded one."

So far the schismatic trend I have been tracing has, to all appearances, its objective motivation in the story's mimetic stratum. Faced with a character who manifests such progressively deviant behavior this severely judgmental narrator can hardly be expected to react differently. Even so, the smugness and narrowness of his evaluative code in the passages already cited may cause some irritation in the reader, akin to that nauseated intolerance Roland Barthes attributes to the reader of Balzac at moments when he laces his novels with cultural adages.[5] Perennial reactions of this type aside, however, there are at least two of the narrator's interventions in *Tod in Venedig* that give one pause on more substantial grounds. In these two instances the narrator indulges in a kind of ideological overkill that produces an effect contrary to the one he is ostensibly trying to achieve. It is to these two moments in their episodic context that I will now turn for close inspection.

III

As previously mentioned, the turning point in the relationship between narrator and character on the ideological level roughly coincides with the midpoint of Aschenbach's Venetian adventure: the pivotal scene when the enamored writer for the first and last time practices his art. Before this point is reached however, a long section (480–492) [29–38] intervenes where authorial generalizations have disappeared from the text altogether; this section comprises mainly Aschenbach's abortive attempt to leave Venice (end of chapter 3) and the first quiescently

5. Roland Barthes, S/Z (Paris, 1970), p. 104.

serene phase of his love (beginning of chapter 4). In these pages the narrator goes beyond adopting merely Aschenbach's visual perspective, he also emulates the hymnic diction (complete with Homeric hexameters), the Hellenic allusions and the mythical imagery that properly belong to Aschenbach's consciousness. This stylistic contagion—technically a form of free indirect style—has often been mistaken for stylistic parody, an interpretation for which I find no evidence in the text. The employment of free indirect style, in the absence of other distancing devices, points rather to a momentary "sharing" of Aschenbach's inner experience by the narrator—as though he were himself temporarily on vacation from his post as moral preceptor.

This consonance reaches its apogee in the moments of high intensity that immediately precede the writing scene, when the Platonic theory of beauty surfaces in Aschenbach's mind as he watches Tadzio cavorting on the beach: "Statue and mirror! His eyes took in the noble figure over there at the edge of the blue, and, with rising ecstasy, he felt he was encompassing with this same glance beauty itself, form as divine thought, the one and pure perfection that lives in the spirit . . ." (490) [37]. Both the initial exclamation in this quote, and the final present tense *(lebt)* indicate the extent of the narratorial identification with the figural thoughts. The Platonic montage that now follows (combining passages from the *Phaedrus* and the *Symposium*) is largely cast in narrated monologue form, fusing the narrator *verbatim* with Aschenbach's mental language. An intensely emotive tone thus pervades the text as the narrator, in concert with Aschenbach, approaches the climactic writing scene. His sudden *change* of tone in the course of narrating this episode is therefore all the more discordant.

The scene opens with a strikingly balanced gnomic statement: "The happiness of the writer consists in the thought that can fully become feeling, in the feeling that can fully become thought" (492) [38]. No other narratorial generalization in the entire text is as harmoniously attuned to the mood of the protagonist. Its syntactical symmetry reflects with utmost precision the creative equipoise Aschenbach himself seeks between thought and feeling. But already in the next sentence, even as the narrator grants Aschenbach this supreme "happiness," he begins to withdraw from the miraculous moment: "It was such a pulsing thought, such a precise feeling that belonged to and obeyed *the lonely man then.* . . . Suddenly, he wanted to write" (492; my italics) [38]. Both the estranging epithet and the distancing adverb underline the narrator's disengagement from the creative act that will ensue. Other even more strongly alienating phrases follow presently: the writer is called "the afflicted one," the moment of writing "at this moment of crisis," the object of his emotion "the idol," and so forth.

When we consider the radical nature of Aschenbach's creative performance in this scene, it is hardly surprising that the narrator refuses to follow him in silent consonance: "And it was his desire to work in the presence of Tadzio, to use the figure of the boy as a model in his writing, to let his style follow the lines of this body . . . and to transport his beauty into the spiritual" (492) [39]. As T. J. Reed has pointed out, Aschenbach here tries to enact (literally and literarily) the truth Diotima imparts to Socrates that Eros alone can serve as guide to absolute beauty. [163] In this light his act of "writing Tadzio" can be interpreted as his attempt at gaining direct access to the realm of Platonic ideas. But this mystic creative urge is of course in flagrant violation of Aschenbach's own past aesthetic credo, a credo that the narrator had explicitly endorsed. Its dominant principle, as we recall, had precisely been that the artist can *not* create in the heat of emotion: "he had reined in and cooled off his feelings because he knew that he tended to be content with a gay approximation and a half perfection" (449) [6]. Aschenbach's scriptural intercourse with Tadzio thus clearly contradicts the ethos to which he has dedicated his creative life. And beyond that it also counter- mands the entire process of mimetic art, the patient art of the novelist who had woven "Maja"—"the novellistic tapestry rich in figures that brought together such a multiplicity of fates in the shadow of an idea" (450) [7], as the narrator had admiringly described it. These horizontal images of shadow and carpet point up the radical contrast between the reflected phenomenal world Aschenbach had formerly created, and the direct vertical ascension of the Platonic writing act he presently per- forms.

But if all this helps to explain why the writing scene brings about the sudden change in the level-headed narrator's attitude toward Aschen- bach, it also draws attention to his limitations. These come to be clearly in evidence in the drastic distancing move he undertakes in the immedi- ate aftermath of Aschenbach's scriptural act, when he momentarily, but quite literally, steps out of and away from his story. Not the least shock- ing aspect of his breakaway is that it breaks all the unities—of time, place, and action—to which the novella so classically adheres from the moment of Aschenbach's arrival in Venice. Flashing forward to the public reception the writer's creative offspring will receive, the narrator at first describes it with unrestrained admiration as "that page and a half of consummate prose . . . whose purity, nobility, and soaring emotional tension was soon to arouse the admiration of many" (493) [39]. The comment that now follows, however, deflates both the writer and the writing in almost brutally sobering terms: "Surely it is good that the world knows only the beautiful work but not its origins or the conditions for its creation; for knowledge of the sources from which the artist's inspiration flowed would often cause confusion and repulsion and thus cancel out the impression of excellence" (493) [39]. This is in every respect the least motivated, most jarring and disconcerting of the narra- tor's interventions. It almost seems as though he were taking headlong

flight onto familiar ground—the psychology of the reading public—
from the mysteries of a creative process that is beyond his comprehen-
sion. The substance of his comment itself raises several questions. Is it
not, within its context, plainly contradictory? Having just revealed the
sources of Aschenbach's newly created piece, what is the sense of now
declaring that these sources had better remain hidden? Finally, is not
the attribution of "confusing" and even "repulsive" effects to Aschenbach's sublimated "Platonic" procreation excessively moralistic and
unnecessarily aggressive?

These questions will, in my view, inevitably arise in the mind of a
reader who dissociates the narrator from the author of *Tod in Venedig*.
And since this, the narrator's most questionable intervention, is located
precisely at the point of origin of the ideological schism in the story, it
tends to reduce the trustworthiness of his distancing comments from this
point forward. At the very least the reader's allegiance will henceforth
be divided between the narrator and his protagonist. I would even suggest that Mann may have designedly made his narrator jump the gun:
his overreaction within an episode that still clearly belongs to, and
indeed climaxes the Apollonian phase of Aschenbach's erotic adventure
welds the reader's sympathy more firmly to the protagonist than if the
narrator had waited with his distancing move until after Aschenbach
had begun his Dionysian descent.

IV

A second, even clearer, instance of evaluative overstatement occurs
in the scene where Aschenbach reaches his nadir: the paragraph-long
sentence that introduces his second Socratic monologue (in the scene
that immediately precedes the death scene). I cannot demonstrate its
rhetorical impact without quoting it in full:

> There he sat, the master, the artist who had achieved dignity, the
> author of "The Wretch" who had renounced gypsy instincts and
> turbid depths in such exemplary and pure fashion, who had broken
> relations with the abyss and rejected depravity, the high-climber
> who had overcome his own knowledge and left all irony behind
> and grown accustomed to the amenities of popularity, he whose
> fame was officially endorsed, whose name had been titled and
> whose style boys were encouraged to emulate—there he sat, lids
> closed, with only an occasional, quickly suppressed mocking and
> perplexed glance flitting forth sideways, and his drooping lips, cos-
> metically enhanced, formed a few words from the strange dream
> logic of his half slumbering brain. (521) [60]

The most obviously "destructive" aspect of this passage is of course the
grotesque "falling distance" it builds between the before and after, the

former self-image and the present reality. The elevation itself is constructed by sardonically piling up phrases we have heard before in a different context: they are the very phrases the narrator had employed in the laudatory curriculum vitae of the summary interchapter. What is perhaps less obvious is that this sentence parodistically echoes that earlier chapter's opening sentence. The syntactical analogy becomes clear from a skeletal alignment of constituent parts:

(A)	(B)
The author of . . . the prose epic about the life of Frederick of Prussia;	There he sat, *the master, the artist* who had achieved dignity,
the patient artist who . . . wove the novellistic tapestry "Maja"	
the creator of that powerful tale titled "The Wretch"	*the author* of "The Wretch" . . .
the writer finally . . . of the impassioned	*the high-climber* who had overcome his own knowledge and left all irony . . .
essay about "Intellect and Art"	
Gustav Aschenbach, then (405) [7]	he, whose . . . whose . . . he sat there. . . . (521) [60]

As Oskar Seidlin has pointed out, the four nominal clauses of the earlier sentence (A) mark the steps of Aschenbach's artistic achievement—"The four stages . . . of creative life."[6] In the later sentence (B) we again have four nominal clauses, with the first three very nearly corresponding (but in reverse order) to those in (A). But with the fourth—"the high-climber"—(B) begins to climb hectically, finally culminating in three elaborate genitive constructions. Note also that the nominal series of (A) no longer stands up independently in (B) but is framed by the verbal phrase "he sat there," so that the inflated "master" is now subordinated to the disreputable state in which he "sits there."

Another, even more striking modification is that while (A) pairs each of the four epithets with one of Aschenbach's major works, (B) reduces him to the authorship of a single work, the story "Ein Elender." The reason for singling out this work is immediately apparent: unlike Aschenbach's other heroes, the protagonist of "Ein Elender" is an anti-

6. Von *Goethe zu Thomas Mann* [From Goethe to Thomas Mann] (Göttingen, 1963), p. 151.

hero, the anti-type of his creator's mature self who represents everything Aschenbach has wanted to reject. This despised figure, so the narrator's verbal irony implies, is precisely what the Aschenbach who "sits there" has now become. But the language employed to evoke this identity in turn associates the narrator with the writer who has created this repulsive character. For he applies to the degraded Aschenbach the same unequivocally negative rhetoric that—according to the narrator's own earlier description—Aschenbach had applied to his degraded creature: "The force of words with which depravity was rejected here spoke for the renunciation of all moral doubt, of any sympathy for the abyss, the refusal of the easily compassionate expression that to understand all meant to forgive all" (455) [11]. The fact that the narrator now applies these same phrases to the author of "Der Elende"—"who . . . had refused the turbid depths, renounced sympathy with the abyss, and rejected the depraved" (521) [60]—confirms that he continues to emulate the values for which Aschenbach had opted at the pivotal moment of his career when he had created his story.

The entire weighty sentence finally leads up to the inquit phrase signaling the quotation of Aschenbach's monologue: "his drooping lips, cosmetically enhanced, formed a few words from the strange dream logic of his half slumbering brain" (521) [60]. The fact that the narrator quotes his character's thoughts directly on this occasion is in itself significant: no other mode of presentation could have disengaged him as effectively from the ensuing discourse. But the terms he uses to introduce it—"slumbering brain," "dream logic"—are of course even more alienating; they disqualify its meaning in advance, as much as to warn us that the words we are about to hear will be errant nonsense. When one examines the actual content of Aschenbach's slumberous mind, however, one is forced to conclude that his dream-logic produces nothing less than the moment of truth toward which the entire story has been moving: a lucidly hopeless diagnosis of the artist's fate.

Aschenbach's Socratic address takes us back again to the Platonic doctrine of beauty as found in the *Phaedrus* and the *Symposium*. But he now turns this doctrine to profoundly pessimistic account—at least so far as the poet is concerned; "we poets", he tells Phaedrus "cannot follow the path of beauty . . . without having Eros join us and set himself up as the leader, . . . for passion is our exaltation, and our longing must remain love—that is our happiness and our shame" (521 f.) [60]. Having acknowledged the poet's defeat on the Platonic path to the higher realm, Aschenbach now denounces with particular bitterness his own erstwhile pedagogic pretensions, with words that clearly echo Plato-Socrates' ultimate decision (in Book X of *The Republic*) to exile the poet from the ideal state: "The masterly posing of our style is a lie and a foolishness, our fame and standing a farce, the trust the public has in us is highly ridiculous, and the notion of educating the people and the youth through art is a risky undertaking that ought to be prohibited" (522) [61]. Isn't Aschenbach saying here exactly the same thing the narrator has just finished saying in his introduction, and in almost identical terms? His self-criticism is, if anything, even more biting than the narrator's sarcasm—which now appears as gratuitous aggression, merely intended to add insult to injury.

When we come to consider Aschenbach's despairing statement concerning the constitutional immorality of the poet at the conclusion of his monologue, the narrator's prefatory venom takes on an even more dubious air. To understand this we must briefly turn back to an earlier moment of his rhetoric. In the interchapter the narrator explains—in entirely approving terms—why Aschenbach had, at a decisive point of his artistic development, renounced his youthful indulgence in immoral "psychologism"—"the indecent psychologism of the times" (455) [11]— and had opted for a disciplined and dignified pursuit of beauty. At this point the narrator queries—in the form of three elaborately phrased rhetorical questions—whether this "moral decisiveness" of the mature master might not in turn lead him back to immoral behavior. The exact terms of his predictive speculation (see the quotation in note)[7] are less important for our purposes than the fact that he dismisses it indecisively with a decisive shrug of the shoulder—"Be that as it may"—and then immediately calls on a philosophical adage—"A development is a fate"—to lead him back to and on with his admiring account of Aschenbach's development as an artist.

Now it is precisely to this crossroads in his career—the point when he made his decisive choice against "psychologism" and in favor of purely aesthetic values—that Aschenbach returns at the conclusion of his monologue. And as he does so, he repeats almost verbatim the account the narrator had previously given of this crucial moment. Except that now, far from shrugging off the question of the artist's immorality, as the narrator had done in the interchapter, Aschenbach provides it with an unequivocally affirmative answer: "Form and detachment, Phaidros, lead to intoxication and desire, . . . to horrifying emotional outrage, . . . they lead to the abyss, they too lead to the abyss. They lead us poets there, I tell you, because we cannot manage to elevate ourselves but only to dissipate" (522) [61]. For all its dream-logic, this conclusion to Aschenbach's monologue is tragically clear (as well as clearly tragic): the poet at the crossroads is forced to choose between two paths that both equally lead to the "abyss." In evading one form of immoral behavior

7. "But is moral decisiveness on the other side of knowledge, of disintegrating and hampering realization—is this not again a simplification, a moral reduction of world and soul, and thus also a strengthening in the direction of evil, of the forbidden, the morally impossible? And does form not have two faces? Is it not at the same time moral and immoral—moral as the result and expression of discipline, immoral, or even amoral, insofar as it by its very nature includes a moral indifference, yes in that it even strives to subdue the moral faculty under its proud and unrestricted scepter? Be that as it may! A development is a fate" (455) [11].

he inevitably falls into another. In short, Aschenbach's retrospective cognition exactly confirms the narrator's prospective suspicion. How, in view of this, are we to understand the destructive rhetoric with which the narrator introduces Aschenbach's articulation of the dark truth?

Inevitably, if one equates the narrator with Thomas Mann, one is forced to find reasons to denigrate Aschenbach's famous last words. Critics have generally done so. They have understood his monologue as an inauthentic self-justification: instead of facing up to his individual guilt—his false choice at the crossroads—Aschenbach attributes his abysmal end to the fate of poets generally, the generic "us poets." One critic puts it this way: "The tendency to the abyss is not an essential part of the determination of beauty, as Aschenbach would have it, but the result of a false life."[8] In my opinion this interpretation cannot be substantiated on the basis of the text itself. Within its boundaries only two paths are open to the artist, and both lead to the same abyss. To open an alternate, "moral" path for Aschenbach one has to look outside the text: to Mann's other, more optimistic works (*Tonio Kröger*, the Joseph novels), or to certain of his autobiographical pronouncements.

On the other hand, if one dissociates the narrator from Thomas Mann, one is free to denigrate his introduction to the monologue and to understand Aschenbach's last words for what they are: his (and the story's) moment of truth, which the narrator is unwilling or unable to share to the bitter end. It is surely significant that only Aschenbach can sound this truth, that he can sound it only with lips drooping under his make-up, and only after these lips have taken in the fatal germs of the plague. In this light his monologue takes on the meaning of an anagnorisis, the expression of that lethal knowledge the hero of Greek tragedy reaches when he stands on the verge of death. The irony the narrator directs at Aschenbach in this moment can then be turned back on its speaker—by a reader who, for his part, is willing and able to share the tragic truth *the author* imparts to him with this story.

V

To this point my argument for the "second author" of *Tod in Venedig* has rested solely on what the narrator says and how he says it. But what he leaves unsaid is equally important for my case. To this other, tacit half of his story I now turn to complement and complete the tell-tale evidence.

It is tell-tale in the literal sense: for with *Tod in Venedig* Mann (though not his narrator) gives us—among other things—a *fantastic* tale. His vehicle is of course the population of uncanny figures Aschen-

8. [Hans W.] Nicklas, [*Thomas Manns Novelle Der Tod in Venedig*, (Marburg, 1968], p. 14; see also p. 81. Similarly [Inge] Diersen, [*Untersuchungen zu* (Investigations regarding) *Thomas Mann*, 2nd ed. (Berlin, 1965)], pp. 113, 121.

bach encounters on his lethal journey. These figures acquire their ominous meaning less by way of their individual appearances—though their death- and/or devil-like features have often been noted—than by way of their serial reappearances. The unlikeliness (on realistic grounds) of their uncanny likeness suggests cumulatively that they all represent the *same* sinister power, a power relentlessly bent on driving Aschenbach to his ruinous end. Now these hints of supernatural doings, which even a first reader finds too strong to miss and dismiss, are never picked up by the narrator himself. Though he meticulously describes each individual stranger, he passes silently over their obtrusive sameness, to all appearances studiously closing his eyes to it. This willful blindness is the natural counterpart to the moralistic, realistic, and rationalistic world view he voices throughout.

Yet for all the narrator's closely woven cover-up on the non-mimetic level of the text, the underlying mystery on the mimetic level keeps shining through the causal fabric. And these abysmal glimpses into a covert realm make the reader feel increasingly uneasy with the overt explanations he is offered. The narrator's silence, in short, speaks louder than his words; it perhaps undercuts his trustworthiness even more effectively than his normative excesses. For nowhere else does it become quite as evident that the author *behind* the work is communicating a message that escapes the narrator he placed *within* the work. The exact content of this message—whether it signifies otherworldly, cosmic powers or the powers of the individual unconscious, myth or (depth-) psychology or, as is most likely, both at once—is less important in the present context than the fact that it refers to a realm that escapes the narrator, escapes him precisely because he is bent on ignoring all questions that point above or below his plane conception of the world and of the psyche. In this respect his disregard of the demonic figures corresponds exactly to his rhetorical stand-off from Aschenbach's mental experience at both its zenith (the writing scene) and its nadir (the final monologue). By the same token, the demonic figures themselves reinforce the truth value of Aschenbach's anagnorisis in the latter instance; for what can their dark presence in the story intimate, if not that a fateful force is at work in the universe, a force that irresistibly draws those who strive for beauty down into the abyss—"down to the abyss, they too down to the abyss" [61].

But the fantastic undercurrent in the *fabula* of *Tod in Venedig* also has an essential aesthetic function. As Christine Brooke-Rose has recently suggested, every good story needs to keep back something: "whatever overdetermination may occur in any one work, . . . some underdetermination is necessary for it to retain its hold over us, its peculiar mixture of recognition-pleasure and mystery."[9] In Mann's novella

9. "The Readerhood of Man," in *The Reader in the Text*, eds. Susan R. Suleiman and Inge Crosman (Princeton, 1980), p. 131.

it is clearly the series of mysterious strangers that creates underdetermination, counterbalancing the narrator's *over*determination on the ideological level. In terms of Roland Barthes codes, to which Brooke-Rose refers in the same essay, these strangers would have to be assigned to the story's hermeneutic code, the enigma-creating code that the narrator disregards and that the text leaves unresolved. The *fact* that it remains unresolved tacitly ironizes—behind the narrator's back—the univocal interpretation he tries to impose on Aschenbach's story.

VI

At this point I call my intratextual "experiment" to a halt. Not, needless to say, because I have arrived at a complete or completely new interpretation of Mann's novella but because I feel that I have provided sufficient evidence to confirm my starting hypothesis: that the narrator of *Tod in Venedig* is not identical with its author. But before closing I want to turn back on my experiment to face a crucial methodological question: granted that the positing of a "second author" may explain in a plausible manner certain discrepancies between the narrator's commentary on Aschenbach's story and this story itself, is this the *only* plausible way to account for these discrepancies? Is it even the *most* plausible way?

My answer is yes, but with one very important provision: if, and only if, we grant (or assume, or believe) that *Tod in Venedig* is a flawless work—flawless in the sense that it perfectly achieves its author's intentions. As soon as we abandon that assumption an alternate way becomes available to us: namely to attribute the narrator's shortcomings to Thomas Mann himself, more precisely, to the peculiar circumstances—personal, historical, etc.—that attended the composition of this work and that made him fall short of his creative goal.

Now this is precisely the way taken by T. J. Reed in his book *Thomas Mann: The Uses of Tradition*. To my knowledge Reed is the only scholar to have squarely faced the problems raised by the narrator's ideological excesses toward the end of *Tod in Venedig*. Referring specifically to the sentence that introduces Aschenbach's final monologue (discussed in section IV above), Reed points up the narrator's "emphatic judgement," and adds: "It is a shade too emphatic for the reader accustomed to Mann's ironic temper. Where are the reservations usually felt in every inflection of his phrasing? The finality with which Aschenbach's case is settled is positively suspicious. . . . Is it not crudely direct beside the informed survey of Aschenbach's development in Chapter Two . . . ? There are depths to be sounded under the polished surface of the story" [154]. These words serve as the opening gambit for a probing investigation into the genesis of Mann's novella. They clearly indicate that Reed's admirable study is a specific attempt to account for the "posi-

tively suspicious" nature of the narrator's judgmental rhetoric. Significantly Reed pursues his genetic interpretation without ever questioning
the reliability of this narrator, whom he seems to identify automatically
with the author. What he questions instead is the coherence and aesthetic integrity of the work itself: by following through the stages of
Mann's creative process he reveals what he finds concealed beneath the
"polished surface" of the final product—that Mann has superimposed
"a moral tale" on a text he had originally conceived "hymnically" (pp.
151–54) [156–58]. This "diametrical change" explains for Reed what
he describes as the novella's ambiguity in the word's more dubious sense:
. . . uncertainty of meaning, disunity" (p. 173) [174]. Mann has
"sought to work out a changed conception in materials and language
ideally suited to an earlier one" (p. 175) [176]. And although Reed has
by this point shifted the ground of his critique from the narrator's narrow
moralism to what he calls the story's "disharmony between style and
substance" (p. 176) [176], the fact remains that it was the vexing narrator
who sent him on his way in the first place—sent him, that is, outside
the text to probe the vagaries of its composition.

On the face of it Reed's extratextual approach to the textual ambiguities in *Tod in Venedig* would appear to differ radically from the intratextual approach I have followed in this paper. Yet from a certain
theoretical perspective these two approaches can be related, if not reconciled, with each other. We owe this perspective to a recent article by
Tamar Yacobi where the problem of fictional reliability is discussed on
the basis of a reader-oriented theory of literary texts.[1] According to
Yacobi, a reader who attributes unreliability to the narrator of a work
of fiction is merely choosing one of several "principles of resolution"
potentially available to him when he is faced with the "tensions, incon-
gruities, contradictions and other infelicities" of a literary work (p. 119).
A rival principle, equally available to him, is what Yacobi calls the
"genetic principle," which places the blame on the biographical-histori-
cal background of the work. These two principles of resolution have in
common that they "both resolve referential problems by attributing their
occurrence to some source of report." The difference between them
"lies in the answer to the question: who is responsible . . . ?" (p. 121).
The reader who calls on the genetic principle will answer: the author.
The reader who calls on the unreliability principle will answer: the narrator—which signifies, in the case of an authorial third-person text like
Tod in Venedig, that he refuses to regard the narrator as the mouthpiece
of the author.

From this theoretical vantage point, then, Reed's genetic explanation
appears—even to myself—no less (and no more) valid and plausible
than my "second author" explanation. But my equanimity gives way

1. "Fictional Reliability as a Communicative Problem," *Poetics Today*, 2 (1981), 113–126.

when I return from the plane of abstract generality to the concrete singularity of Mann's novella. For within the interpretive arena of an individual text these two explanations are mutually exclusive, and the reader is forced to choose between them. Which brings me—at the risk of stating the obvious—to mention some of my reasons for preferring my perspectival over Reed's genetic resolution.

I have already alluded to what is no doubt my primary reason: the severance of the narrator from the author seems to me a necessary interpretive move for a reader bent on affirming the aesthetic integrity of Mann's novella. Obviously one's willingness to make this move will depend to some degree on one's estimation of Mann's œuvre as a whole. And it is no doubt because my own high esteem is due in large part to the complexity of vision I find incarnated in his other major narrative works—though not always in his extraliterary pronouncements—that I am unwilling to ascribe to Mann the ideological simplicities voiced in *Tod in Venedig*. The fact, moreover, that these pronouncements address the subject of Mann's deepest concerns and most differentiated views— art and the artist—reinforces my reluctance. In his other novels and novellas Mann always approaches this subject obliquely, most obliquely of all in his only other full-fledged tragedy of a creative artist, *Doktor Faustus*. I take it to be no mere coincidence that Mann here reverts— three decades later—to the same basic narrative indirection I attribute to him in *Tod in Venedig*.

Admittedly the ironic interval that separates Mann from Zeitblom is far more blatant than the interval that separates him from the teller of the earlier work. Yet the proximity of the narrative situations in these two works offers a kind of proof by the absurd of my "second author" hypothesis: for is it not equally difficult to imagine the narrator of *Tod in Venedig* to be the creator of Aschenbach as it is to imagine Zeitblom to be the creator of Adrian Leverkühn? Only a mind capable of Mann's famous "irony in both directions" could have conceived both members of these pairs in dialectical unison.

DAVID LUKE

[Thomas Mann's "Iridescent Interweaving"] †

During the eight years or so between the completion of *Tonio Kröger* and the writing of *Death in Venice*—a period which also included the

† From *Death in Venice and Other Stories* by Thomas Mann, trans. and intro. David Luke (New York: Bantam, 1988), xxxii–xlv. Translation copyright © 1988 by David Luke. Used by permission of Bantam Books, a division of Bantam Doubleday Dell Publishing Group, Inc. For the reader's convenience, page references to this Norton Critical Edition have been inserted in brackets. However, translations are Luke's and thus may differ from those above.

first six years of his marriage—Mann produced no major work. *Fiorenza* is generally accounted a failure, and the short novel *Royal Highness* (1909), though it has interest and charm, cannot begin to compare in significance with *Buddenbrooks* or *The Magic Mountain*, any more than the few *Novellen* written during those years can stand comparison with those of the breakthrough period at the turn of the century, 1897–1902, which must count as Mann's first mature creative phase. On the other hand, these relatively unproductive intermediate years saw a number of important beginnings and reorientations. Mann's reflections were now being influenced by his own increasing fame and by new ideas about art current in the generation that was following him. What were the special problems and vulnerabilities of being the kind of writer he was, in the years of maturity that lay ahead? Could he perhaps become a different kind of writer? Could not some intoxicating impulse be found, some *Rausch*, even if it were of diabolic origin, that would give his flagging creativity a new direction? It is no accident that in 1904 one of Mann's notebooks briefly records for future use the motif of an artist of genius who bargains with the Devil for special inspiration by deliberately contracting syphilis. It is the germ of *Doctor Faustus*, to be used forty years later; and one of the at first inconspicuous links between *Doctor Faustus* and *Death in Venice* is that the latter opens with Aschenbach, a mature but tired writer, unconsciously desiring just such a new and mysterious stimulus.

At the *Tonio Kröger* stage, the problem of *Geist*, of the critical intellect, had been that it combined with artistic creativity to threaten the writer with personal dehumanization. But *Geist* is now threatening his creativity itself, by binding it to a mode now outmoded. The coming generation seemed tired of analysis and introspection, of pathological themes, of naturalism and psychology. The appeal was increasingly to the other pole of the Nietzschean dialectic: *Leben*, regeneration, vitality, irrationalism, the Renaissance cult. The world of passion and beauty was now again intellectually fashionable. But Mann, although he had already taken sides with Savonarola against Lorenzo,[1] had not yet resolved the personal Lorenzo-Savonarola conflict in himself, the conflict between passion and puritanism. It seems also to underlie his continuing interest in the Friedemann motif,[2] that of the erotic visitation, the emotional invasion that changes a whole existence. He perceived the same conflict in Nietzsche and was fascinated by a perhaps apocryphal anecdote which he had read in the memoirs of one of Nietzsche's friends: the young Nietzsche, it reported, had as a shy and austere stu-

---

1. Savonarola: Girolamo Savonarola (1452–98), Italian reformer and ascetic; Lorenzo: Lorenzo de' Medici (1449–92), Italian merchant prince and Savonarola's enemy. Both were character's in Mann's verse drama *Fiorenza*. [Editor]
2. From Mann's early story "Little Herr Friedemann" [Editor]

dent unwittingly strayed into a brothel, fled from it in embarrassment, but returned later to seek out the beautiful prostitute he had encountered. Mann was to transfer this story to the Nietzsche-like hero of *Doctor Faustus*, combining it with the 1904 germ idea for his Devil's-bargain novel. It was a variant of the Friedemann theme, and a variant also of the theme of the creative artist's tragedy. A further modulation of the latter also appears in a 1905 notebook, as the tragedy of an *older* writer who destroys himself by ambitiously pursuing achievements that exceed his capacities. This version (also eventually reflected in the Aschenbach story) clearly had dramatic possibilities if combined with the Friedemann motif as well.

At some stage in these pre-*Death in Venice* years (we do not know the exact chronology) Mann came to consider a specific historical instance of an elderly and renowned writer who loses his dignity by falling in love: that of the seventy-four-year-old Goethe and his infatuation, while on holiday in Marienbad in 1823, with the seventeen-year-old Ulrike von Levetzow. (Goethe, in fact, came quickly to his senses, though not before going so far, almost incredibly, as to initiate a proposal of marriage with the girl.) It seems from Mann's own account that his plan to write a story on this subject which might be called *Goethe in Marienbad* dated from before 1911; in any case, it was not dropped until some years after the publication of *Death in Venice*, to which the proposed Goethe-*Novelle* would have been a tragi-comic parallel piece. The story in both cases was that of a highly disciplined but emotionally isolated and perhaps instinctually deprived man of mature years whose 'Olympian' existence is invaded by the dark inner forces of disorder. The *Novelle* Mann actually wrote, as we know, was this story with a difference. It was still a story about an artist's *loss of dignity* (*Entwürdigung*), and Mann afterwards frequently insisted that the essential theme was this, the capacity of 'passion' as such—any infatuation or obsessive love—to destroy dignity. In Mann's personal variant the passion becomes a homosexual one, although by his account this was not of the essence of the original conception. The reason for the change, we are not surprised to learn, was the final precipitating personal factor in the genesis of *Death in Venice*: a journey involving an emotional experience. The same had happened in the genesis of *Tonio Kröger*, but with the journey taking place at the beginning of the work's incubation period: in 1911 it came at the end.

In May of that year Mann travelled to the Adriatic for a short holiday with his wife and his brother Heinrich; they stayed first on the island of Brioni near Pola, where they read in the Austrian papers the news of the death of Gustav Mahler (whom Mann had recently met and whom he deeply admired). After about a week they crossed to Venice. Mann tells us in *A Sketch of My Life* that on this journey everything played into his hands, as indeed it had done in *Tonio Kröger*:

Nothing is invented: the wanderer at the Northern Cemetery in
Munich, the gloomy ship from Pola, the foppish old man, the
suspect gondolier, Tadzio and his family, the departure prevented
by a muddle with the luggage, the cholera, the honest clerk at the
travel agency, the sinister singer . . . [109]

He did in fact modify certain details (the cholera outbreak was in Palermo, not in Venice, the lost luggage was Heinrich's, etc.), but the
essential point which he of course does not underline in the autobiographical essay, the inner event round which the rest of the story crystallized, was the 'passion' itself, his sudden intense, if brief, infatuation
with the real 'Tadzio'. The Polish boy was identified in 1964 as Władysław, the future Baron Moes, born on 17 November 1900, who was on
holiday at the Lido in May 1911 with his mother and three sisters.
Mann heard this attractive child addressed by diminutives of his name
such as 'Władzio' or 'Adzio' and, after taking advice, decided to stylize
this as Tadzio (from Tadeusz). Baroness Moes's friend Mme Fudakow-
ska was also there with her own son, Jan, the Jasio (vocative 'Jasiu') of
the story who fights with Tadzio. Władysław Moes learned twelve
years later that a story had been written 'about him' and read it, but
never identified himself to Mann; only some years after the latter's death
did he give Mann's Polish translator an impeccable account, supported
by photographs, of the details of that particular Venetian holiday
(including 'an old man' looking at him on the beach and his quarrel
with Fudakowski). Curiously, too, while Luchino Visconti was making
his film of *Death in Venice* in the late 1960s, Jan Fudakowski also
turned up, bearing a photograph of himself and Władysław taken on
the Lido in May 1911.

Mann no doubt somewhat dramatizes his feelings about this preado-
lescent boy, whose age he amended from ten and a half to fourteen.
Katia in her later recollections confirmed that her husband was 'fascinated' by him, though not to the point of following him all over Venice.
But in this extrapolated self 'Aschenbach' (his age too is fictionalized to
fifty-three, seventeen years older than Mann was in 1911) the experiment is clearly, on the personal level, an exploration of the possibilities
of homosexual emotion, while on the intellectual and creative level it
tries out in earnest those of a certain kind of post-naturalistic, post-deca-
dent aesthetic theory and practice. Mann was here specifically influenced by the short-lived 'Neo-classical' reaction against naturalism, a
movement represented by some of his minor contemporaries (Paul
Ernst, Samuel Lublinski) to which for a time he felt drawn. We have
to distinguish here (though the distinction is very fine) between what
Aschenbach is represented as doing in writing his own works and what
Mann himself does in writing *Death in Venice*. In the former, the
emphasis falls strongly on the creation and exaltation of beauty, though
this is not the neo-romantic, musical and decadent, introverted and life-

negating aesthetic cult represented by Spinell[3] (which Aschenbach has 'overcome') but a 'neo-classical' principle, with a strongly ethical, educative and humanistic colouring; Aschenbach stresses the 'moral' value of disciplined artistic form, as well as resolutely repudiating all introspective *Erkenntnisekel* [disgust with knowledge] and cynicism. Mann, too, in telling the story of Aschenbach, seeks to create and evoke a kind of visible, concrete, external but symbolic beauty, such as he has not aimed at before in his fiction; the basis, nevertheless, is still one of 'naturalism' in the sense of literary realism, and there is a continuing 'naturalistic' implication of compassionate psychological understanding. He thus seems both to encapsulate the contemporary neo-classical tendency and to distance himself from it. The *Death in Venice* 'experiment' with the noble aesthetic moralist Aschenbach ends unsuccessfully, that is to say tragically, in Aschenbach's destruction; nevertheless, the story itself, transcending the traditional and prosaic modes in what was probably Mann's most important technical breakthrough, creates a noble stylistic synthesis worthy of its regretfully repudiated hero.

In achieving this striking fusion of realism and concrete symbolism, Mann was decisively assisted by the nature of the subject-matter and by the strange complex of real-life experiences on his Venetian journey, this uncanny coming-together of seemingly significant and interconnected events as if by some unwitting and magical authorial command. A nexus of coincidences and chance impressions, none inexplicable but many indefinably disturbing, is heightened in its meaningfulness by the use of leitmotif: recurring phrases hint at the identity of recurring figures, noticeable to the reader but apparently never to Aschenbach, who thus moves ironically to his doom like a Greek hero only half aware of what is happening. Strangers he 'happens' to meet or observe are on another level messengers of death, incarnations of the wild god Dionysus to whom his excessive Apolline discipline betrays him. Lingering too long in the breakfast-room at the behest of his still half-conscious passion (and one of the most remarkable features of the story is the subtlety with which it portrays the *process* of falling in love), he himself unwittingly causes the 'fateful' loss of his luggage. Sinister, half-apprehended forces intrude into the naturalist-realist world as externalizations of half-understood psychological developments. Aschenbach's 'case' could have been presented merely as a medical-psychological study (reaction against libidinal over-deprivation, a 'climacteric' episode at the age of fifty-three, as Mann himself pointed out): instead, it is given a mythological dimension as well, as the drama of a foredoomed initiate and the revenge of an insulted god. Venice, too, as a setting both shabbily real and mythically mysterious, lent itself to this double purpose. Even the cholera epidemic, invading Europe from India, is on its other

3. A character in Mann's story "Tristan." [Editor]

level the irruption of Dionysus, whose cult swept into Greece from the east.

But the chief visible yet enigmatic, real yet symbolic element is of course Tadzio himself. He is the meeting-point of the Apolline cult of disciplined sculptured beauty and the dark destructive longing of Eros-Dionysus. He is presented with extraordinary subtlety, mysteriously yet very realistically poised somewhere between innocence and a certain half-conscious sensuous coquetry. The remarkable descriptions of him in the last three chapters rise above Mann's normal ironic tone to an ecstatic seriousness, lyrically exalted yet saturated with sensuality and emotion, in which the narrating author and the fictional contemplative lover are unmistakably identified. Tadzio's 'sublime background', the sun and the sea, are evoked in similar celebratory language, which breaks from time to time into the rhythm of Homer's hexameters. These central 'hymnic' passages (as Mann was to call them) resemble in some ways the unironic evocations of Wagner's music in the central scene of *Tristan*, but with a decisive difference. Ten years after *Tristan*, Mann is seeking to break both the Wagnerian spell and the naturalistic counter-spell. His post–*Tonio Kröger* aesthetic programme has been a struggle to move from *Geist* [intellect] to *Kunst* [art], from moralizing or demor-alizing analysis to a more resolute and extroverted cult of beautiful form. But he now seems more clearly than before to be engaged in a corres-ponding personal struggle to achieve the kind of neo-pagan sensibility in which his sensuous impulses could be affirmed. The model for such a breakthrough was evidently the culture of ancient Greece, as Mann came to understand it at the time of writing *Death in Venice*.

The classical Greek element in the story is essential and central, and one of the ways in which Visconti seriously damaged his film version was by totally omitting it, preferring to identify his Aschenbach with the post-Wagnerian, neo-romantic atmosphere of Mahler's music (although, in fact, Mahler has virtually nothing to do with *Death in Venice* except that Mann had been moved by the news of his death and decided to give Aschenbach the composer's first name and physical appearance). But in treating a homosexual theme, it was natural that Mann should seek to associate it strongly with a pre-Christian world which looked upon homosexuality as normal; and his notebooks attest that while working on *Death in Venice* he not only refreshed his memo-ries of Homer but, above all, immersed himself in the study of the Pla-tonic theory of love. He read especially the *Symposium* and the *Phaedrus* and Plutarch's *Erotikos*—all of which he interestingly and per-haps knowingly misquotes in the text of the story. His understanding of the theory (for purposes of the Aschenbach project and as transmitted through Aschenbach) has a strongly monistic and paganizing, aesthetic and sensuous tendency; in fact it has been shown that Mann's use of the material seems to aim at a synthesis of Platonic doctrine with pagan mythological elements. He evidently understood Plato's perception of the profound continuity between 'Eros' and the 'higher' intellectual or spiritual faculties—a perception which of course amounts to a transfiguration of sexual love rather than a devaluation of it. Mann was familiar with Nietzsche's observation that human sexuality (*Geschlechtlichkeit*) branches upwards into the highest reaches of our intellectuality (*Geistigkeit*); and this observation may be said to reach back to Plato as well as forwards to Freud, if we understand Freud as integrative rather than reductive, and Plato as integrative rather than 'puritanical'. Mann's excerpts from Plato and Plutarch in his *Death in Venice* work notes, as well as the Platonizing passages in the story itself, suggest that he was aware of this. The Platonic Eros theory, with its 'positive' aspects thus emphasized, offered him the most appropriate cultural framework for an experience of love which was both sexual and visionary: it could become the classical philosophic endorsement for Aschenbach's passionate vision of Tadzio. Why then, we may ask, is Mann's view of this passion polarized rather than integrated? In other words, why does *Death in Venice* end tragically, rather than as a story of inner liberation? The answer seems to lie both in Mann's psychology and in his artistry, his instinct as a dramatic storyteller.

In Mann's presentation of Aschenbach's experience, the reader is constantly invited to take two opposite views simultaneously: one of them positive (because aesthetic, neo-pagan, imaginative and mythologizing) and the other negative (because naturalistic-moralistic). This *ambiguity* in the best sense of the word is of course an artistic enrichment, but it also seems to reflect a profound *ambivalence* (in the sense of emotional conflict) in Mann himself, such as we have already noticed in other contexts. *Death in Venice* is even plainer evidence than *Friedemann* or *Gladius Dei*[4] that Mann's 'puritan' temperament conflicted at a deep psychological level with the passionate and sensuous elements in his nature, whether homosexual or otherwise. The inner drama of the story is sustained by this struggle, this schizoid cerebral dread of instinctual disorder, which we encounter again and again in Mann's works. In Aschenbach's case we have a man committed to order, who in his maturity has turned even beautiful form into moral affirmation and art itself into discipline and service, into respectability and dignity. But the compromise solution cannot hold, the element of sensuality in the vision of beauty cannot be accepted and integrated. Instead, it is rejected (in a quite un-Platonic way), and the opposites thus remain dramatically polarized. Mann projects into Aschenbach not only his homosexuality but also his puritan repudiation of it: Aschenbach's declaration of love to the absent Tadzio at the end of Chapter 4 is described as 'impossible, absurd, depraved and ludicrous' as well as 'sacred nevertheless, still wor-

---

4. "Gladius Dei" [The Sword of God]—an early story by Mann. [Editor]

thy of honour' [43–44], and in his last interior monologue of Chapter 5 he condemns it as 'horrifying criminal emotion *(grauenhafter Gefühls-frevel)*' [61]. The absurdity of imagining such strictures in the mouth of Plato or even of Socrates at once reveals their modern, quite un-Greek and indeed idiosyncratic character.

Mann's own most far-reaching and interesting published statement about *Death in Venice* is his letter of 4 July 1920 to Carl Maria Weber. Weber was a young poet who had understandably formed the impression that the story was an exercise in anti-homosexual propaganda (that the opposite impression was formed by some of its other indignant readers is also understandable). He wrote anxiously to Mann for clarification. Mann replies diplomatically that he respects homosexual feeling, that it is far from alien to his own experience, and that he had no intention of negating or repudiating it in the story. He goes on to analyse the conflicting underlying tendencies of *Death in Venice* as he sees them:

> The *artistic* reason [for the misunderstanding] lies in the difference between the Dionysian spirit of lyric poetry as it individualistically and irresponsibly pours itself out, and the Apolline spirit of epic narrative with its objective commitment and its moral responsibilities to society. What I was trying to achieve was an equilibrium of sensuality and morality, such as I found ideally realized in [Goethe's novel] *The Elective Affinities*, which, if I remember rightly, I read five times while I was writing *Death in Venice*. But you cannot have failed to notice that the story in its innermost nucleus has a hymnic character, indeed that it is hymnic in origin. The painful process of objectivization which the necessities of my nature obliged me to carry out is described in the prologue to my otherwise quite unsuccessful poem *The Lay of the Little Child*:
>
> > 'Do you remember? A higher intoxication, amazing
> > Passionate feelings once visited you as well, and they cast you
> > Down, your brow in your hands. To hymnic impulse your spirit
> > Rose, amid tears your struggling mind pressed urgently upwards
> > Into song. But unhappily things stayed just as they had been:
> > For there began a process of sobering, cooling, and mastering—
> > See, what came of your *drunken song?* An *ethical fable!*'[5]

But the artistic occasion for misunderstanding is in fact only one among others, the purely intellectual reasons are even more

---

5. Translation (which I have slightly altered) by T. J. Reed, in *Thomas Mann: The Uses of Tradition* (1974), p. 152 [157]. As Mr Reed points out, these lines taken in conjunction with Mann's remarks to Weber may mean that his original impulse was to write about the Venice experience in verse, probably in hexameters, rather than to turn it into a *Novelle*.

important: for example, the *naturalistic* attitude of my generation, which is so alien to you younger writers: it forced me to see the 'case' as *also* pathological and to allow this motif (climacteric) to interweave iridescently with the symbolic theme (Tadzio as Hermes Psychopompos). An additional factor was something even more intellectual, because more personal: a fundamentally *not at all 'Greek'* but Protestant and puritanical ('bourgeois') nature, my own nature as well as that of the hero who undergoes the experience; in other words our *fundamentally mistrustful, fundamentally pessimistic view of passion as such and in general* . . . [italics here mine]. Passion that drives to distraction and destroys dignity—that was really the subject-matter of my tale. [96–97]

Mann goes on to explain that he had not originally intended a homosexual theme but that of Goethe and Ulrike, and that what had changed his mind was 'a personal lyrical travel-experience which moved me to make it all still more pointed by introducing the motif of "forbidden love" '. The letter then continues at some length, but these extracts contain the essential points. Mann was evidently aware that neither he nor 'Aschenbach' had been 'Greek' enough for a real breakthrough into an integrated neo-pagan sensibility, much as he perhaps desired to achieve this. Nor, indeed, were they moralists enough either; certainly no whole-hearted moralist speaks in the letter to Weber, in one passage of which Mann also remarks that 'the moralist's standpoint [is] *of course one that can only be adopted ironically*' (italics mine) [97]. In *Death in Venice*, it seems, he had been nearly successful in achieving an affirmative view of the 'Aschenbach' experience, only to be defeated by the old self-punitive puritan tendency which comes so strongly to the fore in the last chapter of the story. How, under its pressure, was he to devise a more positive, balanced ending?

We should bear in mind that this whole last chapter belongs to the purely fictional stage of the 'experiment', when Aschenbach has been acting as Mann himself never did in reality. It is here that Aschenbach embarks on his final self-destructive course and (to use Mann's terms) 'loses his dignity', both in a quite ordinary sense (by following Tadzio about, resorting to cosmetics, letting his passion become noticeable to the boy's family) and more importantly in the deeper sense of losing that rational freedom of the will which moralists in the Kantian tradition would call the specific dignity *(Würde)* of man. Aschenbach becomes unable to do the rational, self-preservative and 'decent' thing, which is to warn the Polish family of the epidemic and leave Venice himself immediately. This failure (and not of course the homosexual infatuation as such) is his real 'fall', his *Entwürdigung* as Mann calls it—meaning 'degradation' in the strict sense of demotion from a higher rank to a lower, from dignity to indignity. In terms of Mann's psychology, we may interpret this self-damaging, 'degraded' behaviour of the experimental ego as a fictional development or extrapolation which Mann's own self-disapproval needed in order to corroborate and rationalize itself. There are, however, artistic as well as psychological reasons why the last chapter of *Death in Venice* should take this negative turn. Whatever may have been the degree of Mann's or Aschenbach's intolerance or tolerance of the emotional and behavioural extravagance portrayed by the story, *Death in Venice* was clearly intended as a *dramatization* of the Venice events in *Novelle* form, a dramatic *Novelle* which required a dramatic conclusion. It is structurally necessary that 'Ashenbach's' experience should be brought full cycle; rather as Goethe remarked of the tragic ending of his *Elective Affinities* that it was needed to restore the balance after 'sensuality' had triumphed. Mann knew that tragic implications were inherent from the start in such a love, as in any serious realistic treatment of an erotic theme, and they demanded to be represented in the story's structure.

This temperamentally and artistically necessary combination of contrasting elements in *Death in Venice* was seen by Mann himself, in the letter to Weber, not as a discrepancy or inconsistency but as an 'iridescent interweaving' (*changieren*; I have slightly expanded the translation of this word to bring out the clearly implied metaphor of *changierende Seide*, i.e. alternating or 'shot' silk, in which threads of contrasting colour are interwoven). This striking image is in fact the key to the structure of *Death in Venice*. It is not really necessary to postulate (as T. J. Reed did in the book already referred to and in his earlier annotated edition of the story[6]) any radical change of plan by Mann in the course of writing it, if by this is meant a simple linear development from an originally celebratory conception of the homosexual theme (possibly in verse) to a later more prosaic, critical and, at least ostensibly, moralizing treatment. It is more likely that a complexity of conflicting elements was fully present from the beginning. There may have been some shift of emphasis (as seems to be suggested by the last two lines of the passage from *The Lay of the Little Child* that Mann quotes to Weber), but we know too little about the process of the story's composition to be able to reconstruct it with certainty. The finished version is the only one extant and the only one we need. To detect an author's exact attitude to his fictional hero is always problematic, not least with an author of so ironic a disposition as Mann. The remarkable thing is that, notwithstanding any complexity of conception or underlying dramatic conflict in his sensibility, Mann has achieved in *Death in Venice* (as Mr Reed also points out) so near-perfect an artistic synthesis. The finished *Novelle* is, in fact, remarkably lucid and formally integrated; its *opposita* are paradoxically and realistically embraced in a convincing organic whole. Mann himself, after its completion, remarked that for once he seemed to have

6. Thomas Mann, *Der Tod in Venedig* (with introduction and notes), Oxford University Press, 1971 (Clarendon German Series).

written something 'completely successful', something entirely self-con-
sistent ('es stimmt einmal alles'), which he compared to a many-faceted
and 'pure' crystal (letter to Philip Witkop, 12 March 1913) [94]. In his
letters to his friends during the year it took him to write the story there
are, not surprisingly, occasional complaints that he is finding it a difficult task, but the correspondence also, no less naturally, contains
expressions of confidence in the progress of his work. Indeed the *Sketch
of My Life*, looking back, recalls how the happy coincidences of the
'given' material filled him during the process of composition with a
sense of being 'borne up with sovereign ease'. If he felt some indecision
about how to end the story (as a letter of April 1912 to his brother suggests), we may guess that this may have been due to a sense that if
Aschenbach's drama was to be brought to a not wholly negative, aesthet-
ically satisfying (because balanced) full close, he would have to reach an
accommodation with his past and take a step back from Homer and
Plato towards naturalism—and perhaps also towards the kind of con-
summation he had celebrated ten years earlier in *Tristan*.

He did both these things in the two climaxes of the last chapter: the
scene of Aschenbach's concluding reflections by the fountain in the
depths of Venice, and the closing scene of his death on the beach. In
the inner monologue by the fountain, both Mann and Aschenbach
finally spell out their negative, disillusioned view not only of Aschenbach but of artistic creativity and 'classical' beauty in general, as well as
of the neo-pagan, integrative interpretation of the Eros theory that
Mann had tried and failed to embrace. Yet, even at this point, as the
defeated and degraded hero collapses despairingly in the shabby,
haunted little square, his dramatically necessary 'tragic fall' is mitigated
for the sake of a more complex truth. His bitter recital of the ironies of
his own situation ('There he sat, the master . . .' [60]) itself ironically
recalls the 'forthright' moralism of his earlier stance, and this too-much-
protesting moralism is thereby implicitly relativized. And Aschenbach's
speech of final self-*Erkenntnis* [knowledge] has a sad, paradoxical dignity, the dignity of man's awareness and acceptance of his own destruction ('And now I shall go, Phaedrus . . .' [61]). Contemplating the
failure of his *alter ego* to achieve regeneration, Mann must himself
revert to the psychological method of his own unregenerate days and to
the all-embracing principle that 'understanding is forgiving'. Aschenbach, refusing unlike Mann to mix irony with morality, had repudiated
this principle, which now is his only absolution. The 'moral' of Mann's
unintended 'ethical fable' seems to be his sobering insight into the difficulty of radically changing, by sheer 'resolution', the kind of person and
the kind of artist one is; his conclusion—that a writer born into a 'decadent' generation is and remains a vulnerable type, since even the 'overcoming' of decadence may reveal itself as decadence in yet another
form.

In the last short section of Chapter 5 that follows, the naturalistic and symbolic threads are again 'iridescently interwoven', and a double view is demanded. Aschenbach sits on the beach watching Tadzio for the last time as he wanders out to sea. Prosaically and factually, Aschenbach is now dying of cholera (in its milder form of rapid collapse into coma) and is in a state of 'menopausal' infatuation verging on delusion. Mythically and poetically, Tadzio's allurement has now become that of the death-god Hermes Psychopompos, the 'guide of souls' to the underworld. And whether or not Aschenbach merely imagines the boy's final gesture as it beckons him out to sea into 'an immensity rich with unutterable expectation' [63], this last pursuit of his vision—of the finite god silhouetted against infinity—raises him paradoxically into a mysterious apotheosis, into that region of indefinable reconciliation in which true tragedy has always ended. In Plato's *Symposium*, the 'wise woman' Diotima explains to Socrates how the initiate of Eros, in the end, 'turns to the open sea of Beauty'; and it may be significant that Mann copied and underlined these words (in Kassner's rather neo-romantically elaborated translation) in his *Death in Venice* notebook. Equally it may be relevant here to notice the subject-matter of Mann's short essay written in May 1911 on the paper of the Hotel des Bains, which became the 'page and a half of exquisite prose' written by Aschenbach, at an earlier and central scene of the story, on the beach in Tadzio's presence. Mann's essay, in reality, was about Wagner; but we are not told that this was Aschenbach's topic, merely that he had been asked in a circular letter to contribute his views on 'a certain important cultural problem, a burning question of taste'. Transmuting the biographical reality, the text seems here to hint ('the theme was familiar to him, it was close to his experience' [39]) that the topic proposed to Aschenbach was the role of homosexuality in literature and the arts. In reality, again, Mann in this essay (originally published in 1911 as *A Critical View of Richard Wagner*) was anti-Wagnerian as so often, calling for a post-Wagnerian 'neo-classical' culture. But there was perhaps a further transmutation when, about a year later, he wrote the carefully balanced scene of Aschenbach's death, the scene that has been called the '*Liebestod* [love-death] ending' to this classical and classic tale of romantic passion. The city in which Aschenbach dies was profoundly associated with Wagner, the arch-romantic, who had composed much of *Tristan and Isolde* there and had died there; Aschenbach himself seemed to allude to him in his thoughts as he drifted along the canals in pursuit of Tadzio ('Venice . . . where composers have been inspired to lulling tones of somniferous eroticism' [47]). If in the fictional death-scene's nexus of associations Diotima's words implicitly accompany the hero's last journey, so too perhaps does the final climax of what to Mann, even in 1912, was still music's ultimate statement: the mystic trance of Isolde as she contemplates the dead Tristan and breathes the murmur of waves, listens and drowns as the odour of music, 'the world-soul's vast breath', engulfs her consciousness.

So movingly retrogressive a 'full close' is of course immediately followed by the few lines prosaically narrating Aschenbach's physical collapse and death, rather as Goethe's *Werther* ends with chilling details of what happens after the hero has in final ecstasy shot himself. They are the necessary naturalistic postscript, by which the preceding passage is not so much contradicted as completed.

A double view also suggests itself when we consider the prose style of the story and Mann's comments on this aspect of it. In the lecture *On Myself* delivered in Princeton in 1940, he described *Death in Venice* as

> a strange sort of moral self-castigation by means of a book which itself, with intentional irony, displays in its manner and style that very stance of dignity and mastery which is denounced in it as spurious and foolish. [110]

And quite soon after the story's publication, irritated by critics who read into the elevated prose a pompously implied authorial claim to magisterial status, he insisted that it was not his own style but Aschenbach's, that it was parody and mimicry, yet another way of exposing Aschenbach's pretensions (10 September 1915, to Paul Amann [95]; 6 June 1919, to Joseph Ponten [96]). But this self-interpretation, like some of Mann's remarks on Spinell, is again too one-sidedly negative: if it were the whole truth, the language of the story, as a deliberate *reductio ad absurdum*, would carry a faint aura of ridicule throughout. Instead, it remains a serious, heightened and noble language, 'parodistic' only if parody can also be filled with sadness, the sadness of leave-taking from a noble impossibility.

ROBERT TOBIN

Why Is Tadzio a Boy? Perspectives on Homoeroticism in *Death in Venice* †

"Was he in poor health?" (22) Although, in *Death in Venice* (1911), this particular question appears with reference to Tadzio, it could just as easily apply to the novella's protagonist, Gustav von Aschenbach, who dies of cholera while suffering from lovesickness, as well as to its author, Thomas Mann, who in 1896 wrote to Otto Grautoff, a childhood friend and confidant, about a health "problem" of his own, a "suffering" that happened to have to do with "sexuality": "will it destroy me? . . . How

---

† Reprinted by permission of the author. For the reader's convenience, page references are to this Norton Critical Edition unless otherwise noted.

do I escape sexuality? Through a diet of rice?"[1] Tadzio's "poor health" (in the German he is "leidend") and Mann's "suffering" (in the German "Leiden") are both related to "sexuality," perhaps not surprisingly, given the etymological relationship between "Leiden," suffering or passion in the religious sense, and "Leidenschaft," passion, in a general emotional sense. Interestingly, however, in the same letter to Grautoff, Mann admits his fear that sexuality "is the *poison* that lurks in all beauty" (*Briefe an Otto Grautoff* 80). This connection between suffering, sexuality, and beauty or art receives further attention in a letter Mann wrote to his brother Heinrich in 1903, where he distinguishes between "sexualism," "the naked, the unspiritualized, the simply named by name" and "erotica," which "is poetry, is that which speaks out of the depths, is the unnamed that gives everything its eeriness, its sweet attraction and its mystery."[2] How to connect one's suffering and one's literature—the move from the sexual, prosaic, poisonous, "named by name" to the erotic, poetic, beautiful, "unnamed"—is the central issue of *Death in Venice*. How various discourses affect Aschenbach's desire and how Aschenbach's homosexual passion in turn becomes art sheds light both on how Mann names and unnames his own homosexuality in his writing and on the general interrelationship of sexuality and textuality.

The relationship between an author's life, including sexuality and suffering, and his or her work is of central concern for literary theory. Many modern approaches to literature, from New Criticism to deconstruction, stress the importance of interpreting a text on its own merits, without regard to historical context or biography of the author. Other approaches—examining gender, class, and racial or ethnic issues—have found, however, that the realia of the author's life and times frequently are textualized and thus play a significant role in the understanding of any written work. Precisely these issues come to the fore in *Death in Venice*. In order to ascertain whether the authorial passion has any effect on literature or, on the other hand, whether textual constructs inform sexuality, it is necessary to place passion and sexuality in a historical and biographical context.

Discourses of Homosexuality

Galvanized by the hard work of classicists analyzing the specifics of ancient Greek and Roman sexual behavior, historians have, at least since Michel Foucault's *History of Sexuality* (1976), come to view sexuality as a constantly changing construct, rather than an essential and

1. *Thomas Mann. Briefe an Otto Grautoff 1894–1901 und Ida Boy-Ed 1903–1928*, [Thomas Mann. Letters to Otto Grautoff 1894–1901 and Ida-Boy-Ed 1903–1928], ed. Peter de Mendelssohn (Frankfurt/M: Fischer, 1975) 80.
2. *Thomas Mann—Heinrich Mann. Briefwechsel 1900–1949* [Thomas Mann—Heinrich Mann. Correspondence 1900–1949] (Frankfurt/M: Fischer, 1984) 36.

eternal truth. While the title of one book on the subject, *One Hundred Years of Homosexuality* (1990), based on the appearance in the English language of the word "homosexuality" in 1892, is perhaps hyperbolic, the first people who identified themselves as having a specifically same-sex orientation, as opposed to occasionally engaging in sexual acts with members of the same sex, appear fairly recently, in the late eighteenth century. In philosophy, medicine, religion, and law, varied discourses—all of which play a role in *Death in Venice*—gave birth to the sexuality of the eighteenth and nineteenth centuries.

Thomas Mann was certainly aware of the homosexual proclivities of late eighteenth- and early nineteenth-century literary and cultural figures like Winckelmann, Müller, and Platen. Johann Joachim Winckelmann (1717–1768), the first modern art historian, was, according to one recent scholar, also the first modern German homosexual.[3] He moved to Rome to work at the Vatican, surrounded himself with male youths, set a bias in art history toward classical male nudes that lasted over a century, and eventually ended up murdered under suspicious circumstance by a young man whom he had met while traveling. A generation after Winckelmann, the famous Swiss historian Johannes Müller (1752–1809) also had well-known homosexual inclinations. Müller's homosexual desires became scandalously public when he fell in love with and corresponded extensively with a fictive Count Batthiany, invented by one of his students for the purpose of extorting money from Müller (Derks 314 ff.). After Müller, August von Platen (1796–1835) similarly spent much of his life torturously in love with young men. Heinrich Heine (1797–1856) brutally and publicly satirized Platen's same-sex desires in a series of poems called "The Baths of Lucca" (Derks 479–613). In 1930, Thomas Mann devoted an essay entitled "On Platen" to the positive impulses emanating from this poet's homosexuality.

Starting with Winckelmann, German classicists began to establish a discourse about ancient Greek sexuality that constantly circled around the theme of "Greek love."[4] Soon, a philosophical discourse emerged out of this philological discourse, with German philosophers using references to Plato and Sappho in order to speculate on the nature and place of same-sex desire. Johann Wolfgang von Goethe (1749–1832) described homosexuality as both in and against nature, since its existence was as old as humanity.[5] In the third edition of *The World as Will and Representation* (1859), Arthur Schopenhauer (1788–1860) attached

3. Paul Derks, *Die Schande der heiligen Päderastie. Homosexualität und Öffentlichkeit in der deutschen Literatur 1750–1850* [The shame of holy pederasty. Homosexuality and the public in German literature 1750–1850], (Berlin: Verlag Rosa Winkel, 1990) 183.

4. Joan DeJean, "Sex and Philology: Sappho and the Rise of German Nationalism," *Representations* 27 (1989): 148–71.

5. Friedrich Müller, *Goethes Unterhaltungen mit Kanzler Müller*, [Goethe's conversations with Chancellor Müller], ed. Albrecht Knaus (Munich: 1950) 71.

a long explanation of pederasty as a technique of nature to redirect the erotic energy of weak and old men, whom he assumed produced feeble offspring, away from women to male youths, where they could have a favorable impact on the race. In the second half of the century Friedrich Nietzsche (1844–1900) used a language redolent with homoerotic praise of "fraternal union" and the "union of man and man."[6] In "On the German Republic," Mann cites both Goethe and Schopenhauer in defense of homosexuality,[7] while in his Platen essay he backs up his claim that sexuality deeply affects intellect with an aphorism attributed to Nietzsche.

The appearance of people who defined themselves by their same-sex orientation and the emergence of philosophical discourse about the place of such people in the universe was interconnected with a new medical discourse about sexuality as well. In 1869, Carl Friedrich Westphal, published the first psychiatric article devoted to homosexuality or, to use his vocabulary, "contrary sexuality." For Westphal, the reversal of sexual desire was an innate quality that became a basic part of human identity, expressing itself in the "entire inner being" of the subject.[8] In his *Psychopathia Sexualis* (1886), Richard von Krafft-Ebing carried Westphal's work further, declaring: "Every case of real homosexuality has its etiology, its accompanying bodily and psychic characteristics, its effects on the entire psychic being" (Cited in Müller 127). *Psychopathia Sexualis* was crucial for the twentieth-century understanding of all sexual perversions, including sadism and masochism, as well as male and female homosexuality. In the English-speaking world, it inspired a corollary, *Studies in the Psychology of Sex: Sexual Inversion* (1897) by Havelock Ellis. In the German-speaking world, it prompted the publication of over a thousand articles on homosexuality between 1898 and 1908 (Faderman 248).

One of the most prominent sexologists, Albert Moll, who wrote an important monograph on sexual inversion, is the subject of an epistolary exchange between Mann and Grautoff, because the latter was seeing Moll regularly, presumably for some kind of sexual inversion.[9] Mann is

6. Cited by Isadore Traschen, "The Uses of Myth in 'Death in Venice,' " *Modern Critical Views: Thomas Mann*, ed. Harold Bloom (New York: Chelsea, 1986) 98.
7. Thomas Mann, *Von Deutscher Republik. Politische Schriften und Reden in Deutschland*, [Of the German republic. Political writings and speeches in Germany], ed. Peter de Mendelssohn (Frankfurt/M: Fischer, 1984) 154. This paragraph is omitted in H. T. Lowe-Porter's translation, "The German Republic," *Order of the Day: Political Essays and Speeches of Two Decades*, (Freeport, NY: Books for Libraries Press, 1937), 42.
8. Cited in Klaus Müller, *Aber in meinem Herzen sprach eine Stimme so laut. Homosexuelle Autobiographien und medizinische Pathographien im neunzehnten Jahrhundert* [But in my heart spoke a voice so loud. Homosexual autobiographies and medical pathographies in the nineteenth century] (Berlin: Verlag Rosa Winkel, 1991) 120. See also Lillian Faderman, *Surpassing the Love of Men: Romantic Friendship and Love between Women from the Renaissance to the Present* (New York: Morrow, 1981) 239–53.
9. Klaus Werner Böhm, *Zwischen Selbstzucht und Verlangen. Thomas Mann und das Stigma Homosexualität* [Between self-discipline and desire. Thomas Mann and the stigma of homosexuality] (Würzburg: Königshaus und Neumann, 1991) 119.

skeptical of Moll's work, at one point saying flat out that he has little sympathy for science, "least of all for that of Mr. Moll." In the same letter, Mann insists that he views the world "neither with moral, nor with medical, but with artistic eyes" (*Briefe an Otto Grautoff* 88). In a letter to Carl Maria Weber, written in 1920, Mann refers to the "naturalistic" attitude of his generation, which "forced" him to see Aschenbach's " 'case' *also* in a pathological light" (Letters 103).[1] Although these passages directly attack medical approaches to sexuality as incidental to his primary objective, they indicate a familiarity with medical discourse, which will prove to have a bearing on *Death in Venice*.

The next wave of medical thinking on homosexuality came from psychoanalysis. If the sexologists had modified traditional views by admitting the possibility of congenital sexual inversion, Sigmund Freud (1865–1939) radically reshaped the debate by positing a basic human bisexuality:

> Psychoanalytic research very strongly opposes the attempt to separate homosexuals from other persons as a group of a special nature. . . . All men are capable of homosexual object selection and actually accomplish this in the unconscious.[2]

While Freud's theories attacked traditional moralistic beliefs in the sanctity of heterosexuality, they also undercut the notion of a homosexual identity. Despite Freud's radical early thoughts on the inherent bisexuality of the human condition, however, psychoanalysis quickly reverted to the pattern set by the sexologists, who saw homosexuality as a treatable disease. In 1925, Mann speculated that he would never have treated homosexuality in *Death in Venice* without Freud.[3] Freud's original assumption that everyone can love homosexually allows for a universalizing interpretation of Aschenbach's passion, which is certainly appropriate for the story, but the novella's association of Aschenbach's love with cholera indicates that it also mirrors the later turn by psychoanalysis toward a view of homosexuality as pathological.

As medical discourses about sexuality were changing, so were religious and legal ones. Enlightened thinkers like Cesare Beccaria had attempted to reform the legal system by separating morality from legality, church from state, and removing consensual sexual acts among adults from the penal system. Many of these reforms were taken up in the Napoleonic Code, which, after Napoleon's victorious campaign through Germany in 1806, was adopted by a number of German states. By 1811, sodomy

---

1. This letter is excerpted above on pages 96–98. The complete text of the letter is available in *Letters of Thomas Mann 1889–1955*, trans. Richard and Clara Winston (New York: Knopf, 1971).
2. Sigmund Freud, "Three Contributions to the Theory of Sex," *The Basic Writing of Sigmund Freud*, trans. and ed. A. A. Brill (New York: Modern Library, 1938) 560. The quote is in a 1915 footnote to the essay originally written 1904–1905.
3. Cited in James W. Jones, *"We of the Third Sex": Literary Representations of Homosexuality in Wilhelmine Germany* (New York: Lang, 1990) 280.

laws had been abolished and homosexuality between consenting adults
legalized in many parts of Germany, for instance, in Bavaria and much
German territory west of the Rhine (Derks 161, 163). Soon however,
opposition to the Napoleonic Code and its alleged sanctioning of homosexual behavior became part of German patriotism. Throughout the
nineteenth century, the individual principalities of Germany gradually
recriminalized sodomy (Derks 163). Once Germany was unified, the
new basic law of the land made sodomy a criminal offence:

> For even if one could justify the cessation of legal penalties from
> the standpoint of medicine . . . the legal convictions of the people
> regard this act not merely as a *vice* but also a crime. (Cited in
> Derks 168)

Tellingly, as it goes about criminalizing homosexuality, the new basic
law of the land acknowledges both the new medical discourses of the
day and the old Enlightenment distinction between vice and crime,
without, in the final analysis, granting them credence.

The tensions between the discourses arising about sexuality—the
medical notion of innate "inversion" versus the legal insistence on crim-
inality—produced, at the end of the nineteenth century, a series of sensational court cases about homosexuality. The most famous was the trial
of Oscar Wilde (1856–1900) in England in 1895, which resulted in his
conviction and from which he never recovered. German trials analogous to Wilde's took place in 1907 and 1908, after a newspaper publisher accused Philipp Prince zu Eulenburg-Hertefeld, a member of the
Kaiser's entourage and cabinet, and General Kuno Count von Moltke,
military commandant from Berlin, of homosexuality. The ensuing
court cases, which Mann followed closely (Böhm 302–5), caused an
enormous sensation, splashing revelations about homosexual behavior
in all segments of German society across the headlines of all the European newspapers, seriously embarrassing the Hohenzollern court and
the German government.[4]

No wonder the young Thomas Mann wrote to Grautoff that he was
suffering from his sexuality! By the second half of the nineteenth century, philosophy, medicine, and law were all struggling with sexuality,
specifically homosexuality. Nor was homosexuality an issue solely for
the big cities—in 1882, Mann's hometown of Lübeck, a port commu-
nity of 25,000 residents, uncovered a major scandal involving male
prostitutes. A German news agency reported:

> The Lübeck morals scandal, in which almost one hundred men
> and around thirty youths between the ages of ten and seventeen

---

4. James Steakley, "Iconography of a Scandal: Political Cartoons and the Eulenburg Affair in
Wilhelmine Germany," *Hidden from History: Reclaiming the Gay and Lesbian Past*, ed. Martin Duberman, Martha Vicinus, and George Chauncey, Jr. (New York: Meridian, 1990)
233–65.

are involved, is apparently growing. . . . The possibility of making money quickly in the grounds of the city wall between Holstentor [5] and the main rail station has apparently spread by word of mouth. (Cited in Böhm 92)

A scandal of this proportion in Mann's relatively small hometown points to the prominence of homosexuality in late nineteenth-century Germany. The controversial nature of homosexuality in this era results from the contradictory discourses constructing sexuality at this time: a philological and philosophical discourse in which the classics of ancient and modern society endorse or explain homosexuality, a medical discourse that promotes the idea of innate homosexuality, and a battle between religious and legal discourses as to who gets to penalize homosexuality. It is important to read Thomas Mann and his literary creations against these contradictory discourses.

Mann's Homosexuality

Homosexual desire surfaced quite early in Mann's own life. At the age of fourteen, in 1890, he entered a new school, where he met Armin Martens, who appears in idealized form in the novella *Tonio Kröger* as Hans Hansen, the beautiful blond, blue-eyed bourgeois, with whom the fourteen-year-old protagonist falls in love (Böhm 108–11). After the schoolboy crush on Armin Martens, Mann fell in love, sometime between 1890 and 1892, with another school friend, Willri Timpe, son of a high-school teacher. Mann's intimate friendship with Grautoff seems to date from this relationship, as he indicated when he wrote in his diary about "O. Grautoff, my schoolboy friend, and the confidant of my passion for W. T., later elevated to Pribislav Hippe" (1935–36, 143).[6] In *The Magic Mountain*, Pribislav Hippe is the object of Hans Castorp's schoolboy love; this becomes his love of Claudia Chauchat, which is mystically related to his "disease," and thus becomes central to the intellectual plot of this novel.

In a long diary entry of May 6, 1934, in which he summarizes his homosexual loves, however, Mann writes that both "the A. M. and the W. T. experiences recede far into childishness" when compared to the relationship with Paul Ehrenberg, a painter from an artistic and academic family from Dresden. About this passion, which developed between 1899 and 1903, Mann wrote on September 13, 1919: "I loved

---

5. The "Holstenwall," (Holsten rampart), if not the "Holstentor" (Holsten gate) is where Tonio Kröger and Hans Hansen take their walks in *Tonio Kröger* (1914).
6. References to Thomas Mann's diary entries (in *Tagebücher* [Diaries] *1918–1943*, 5 vols., ed. Peter de Mendelssohn [Frankfurt/M: Fischer, 1977–82] and *Tagebücher* [Diaries] *1944–1950*, 3 vols., ed. Inge Jens [Frankfurt/M: Fischer, 1986, 1989]) will be indicated parenthetically in the text by the page number and the years covered by the volume (where necessary). An abridged translation of the earlier diary entries is also available in Thomas Mann, *Diaries 1918–1939*, trans. Richard and Clara Winston (New York: Abrams, 1982).

him and [it] was something like a happy love" (301). Later, in the 1940s,
he wrote: "One cannot experience love more strongly" (1940–43, 551).
Calling it "that central experience of the heart in my twenty-five years,"
he declares in the May 1934 entry: "Yes, I have lived and loved, I have
in my own way 'paid' for being human" (411). This same diary entry
refers to "the Faust novella" (411), the original idea behind the text in
which this beloved has been immortalized: *Doktor Faustus*. In that novel
of 1947, Paul Ehrenberg appears as Rudi Schwerdtfeger, the handsome,
flirtatious, talented musician who seduces Adrian Leverkühn and
thereby draws upon himself the jealousy and love of the narrator, Serenus Zeitblom. Once again, <u>Mann enshrouds the most important figures
of one of his most influential novels in homoeroticism.</u>

Not surprisingly, this homosexual desire in Mann's biography is
behind *Death in Venice*, as well. Mann frequently maintained that his
original intent had been to write a story about the ridiculous and foolish
love of the elderly Goethe for a young girl at Marienbad, Ulrike von Lev-
entzow. This seemingly heterosexual explanation of the story actually
points to the homoerotic origins of the text, for, in his letter to Weber
(96–98) Mann explains that the change from the heterosexual story of
the planned novella about Goethe to the homosexual one of *Death in
Venice* would never have taken place "without a personal emotional
adventure."[7] This personal emotional adventure was a trip in 1911 to
Venice where Thomas Mann, traveling with his new wife Katia and his
brother Heinrich, took a fancy to a young Polish boy of noble family
named Wladislav Moes. Katia Mann describes her husband's fascination
with the boy:

> He immediately had a weakness for this youth, he liked him inordi-
> nately, and he always watched him on the beach with his friends.
> He did not follow him through all of Venice, but the youth did
> fascinate him, and he thought about him often.[8]

Katia Mann then describes her husband's textualization of his desire:
"My husband transferred the pleasure, which he indeed had from this
very charming youth, to Aschenbach and stylized it to most extreme
passion" (Katia Mann 72). Wladislav Moes thus shares with the other
young men who caught Thomas Mann's eye the privilege of having
been textualized, transformed into one of Mann's literary characters.

Although the affair with Paul Ehrenberg ended when Thomas Mann
married Katia, with whom he had six children, it is worthwhile looking
at some of the homosexual desire that Mann exhibited over the next

---

7. In the very interesting diary entry of September 14, 1935, Mann moves from a discussion his
children (!) had about whether a certain Albert R. or Klaus Heuser (a subsequent love of
Mann's) was more beautiful to reflections on Goethe's long lasting love-life, with the final,
perhaps somewhat rueful comment: " 'always girls' " (173–74).

8. Katia Mann *Meine ungeschrieben Memoiren*, [My unwritten memoirs], ed. Elisabeth Plessen
and Michael Mann (Frankfurt/M: Fischer, 1974), 71.

decades, because Mann's thoughts about them help clarify the meaning of the homosexuality in *Death in Venice*.

References to attractive young men abound in the diaries that survive. A particularly troubling aspect of Mann's homosexual desire from May to October of 1920 was his increasing attraction to his thirteen-year-old son, Klaus, nicknamed "Eissi." "In love with Klaus these days," he writes on July 5, 1920, typically attempting to turn his desire into a text: "Germ of a father-son novella" (451). Shortly thereafter, he mentions again that Eissi "enchants" him (452). In October of that year, he surprises the young Klaus "fully naked" and reports a "strong impression from his radiant, adolescent body" (470). On July 25, 1920, he writes about a pleasing conversation with "a sympathetic young man" and wonders: "It seems that I'm finally done with the feminine?" This general question relating to Mann's troubled sexuality is entangled in a number of expressions of desire for his son, mentioned in the same diary entry: he is "confused" when Klaus lies "with naked brown torso in bed." On the same day, he notes "delight in Eissi, who is frighteningly cute in the bath. Find it very natural that I'm falling in love with my son" (454). Mann's self-assurance that his desire is "natural" seems a bit too bland, given that around the same time, August 1, 1920, Mann spends midday with Katia discussing " 'incest,' that is, sensual love of the father for a daughter youthfully repeating the mother," a case that he considers, once again, "very natural" (457). The repetition of the phrase "very natural" within a few pages of the diary entry discussing sensual parent-child relationships suggests that Mann's real interest was not in father-daughter but father-son incest.[9]

Following his usual pattern Thomas Mann attempted to move even this, doubly taboo object of desire into his literary works. Klaus Mann found himself caricatured as the son Bert in the short story, "Disorder and Early Sorrow." One of the many links between the fictional Bert and the real Klaus Mann is the implication that Bert is homosexual, for Klaus Mann eventually turned out to be homosexual himself, a fact that gave his father a way of discussing homosexuality from a distance.

Despite this distance, Thomas Mann certainly continued to have homosexual desires. He fell deeply in love with Klaus Heuser, the seventeen-year-old son of a professor at the Düsseldorf art academy, in the summer of 1927.[1] He reports on it in the January 1, 1934, entry:

> Yesterday evening it got late while reading the old diary 1927/28, written in the time of K. H.'s stay in our house and my visits to

---

9. In this respect, it is suspicious that the October 17, 1920, entry (470), "strong impression of his radiant, adolescent body. Shock," is followed by an editorial cut, presumably of something that the editor of the diaries, Peter de Mendelssohn, found particularly shocking. Böhm, however, finds nothing more in Mann's interest in incest than a fascination with "forbidden loves" (70, 238–40).

1. Hans Mayer, *Thomas Mann* (Frankfurt/M: Fischer, 1980) 466–68.

Düsseldorf. I was deeply agitated, moved and stirred by the reflection on this experience, which seems to me today to belong to
another, stronger, life-epoch and which I protect with pride and
gratitude, because it was the unhoped-for fulfillment of a life-
yearning, happiness, as it is stands in the book of humanity,
although not of normalcy, and because the memory of it means:
"Me too." (296)

Elsewhere, Mann describes this relationship with Heuser positively,
calling it on September 22, 1933, "my last passion—and it was my happiest" (185). A number of times Mann uses vocabulary to describe his
relationship with Heuser similar to the vocabulary he used to describe
his love of Ehrenberg.

The Heuser relationship may be the last high point in Mann's homosexual relationships, although Mann continued to make note of attractive men throughout the 1930s, 1940s, and 1950s. Of these late
passions, the most important was the twenty-five-year-old waiter Franz
Westermayer, about whom Mann wrote in the summer of 1950. Thinking about Westermayer on August 6, 1950, Mann is racked by regret as
he watches another young man play tennis:

On the tennis courts below, during a certain morning hour, young
Argentinean. . . . Deep erotic interest. Stand up from work to
watch. Pain, Desire, Sorrow, Undirected yearning. The knees. He
strokes his leg—which everyone would like to do. (238)

These experiences reminded the seventy-five-year-old Mann once again
of his "insane and passionately maintained enthusiasm for the attraction
of male youth, unsurpassed by anything in the world, which lies at the
basis of everything" (239). This passion, "at the basis of everything," had
an effect on Mann's writing. Some of Mann's statements about homosexuality from the latter part of his life help clarify what that effect was.

In his reflections on homosexuality that appear scattered in the letters,
diaries, speeches, and essays of the later part of his life, he is generally
positive about his own experiences. His passion for Martens was "innocent." His loves of both Ehrenberg and Heuser allowed him to say he
had experienced human emotion. Mann associates this love with
strength, pride, gratitude, fulfillment, happiness, and humanity. At the
same time he chooses to renounce homosexuality, insists in his letter to
Weber that he is a "family man," and tells friends that he has never had
a homosexual experience. The letter to Weber provides some clues concerning the origins of this ambivalence. On the one hand, he assures
Weber that "in both [heterosexual and homosexual love], everything
depends on the individual case, both produce commonness and kitsch
and both are capable of the highest" (*Letters* 104). Nonetheless, there are
certain discourses—medical, religious, sociological, aesthetic—mentioned in this letter and other documents by Mann that show that, above

and beyond the individual case, homosexuality has been constructed to have certain meanings, about which Mann has doubts.

In his letters to both Grautoff and Weber, Mann emphasizes that the most important discourse for him in which homosexuality has meaning is the artistic. [2] In Mann's own life, the homosexual relationships after the marriage to Katia seem to have been nonphysical and specifically visual. Mann claims that he kissed Heuser, but Heuser, who eventually resided as an openly gay man in Hong Kong, denies that there were ever any physical intimacies (see interview in Böhm 371–81). In other cases, Mann himself writes that his desire cannot be satisfied physically. Indeed, near the end of his life, contemplating Westermeyer, Mann attributes to his love of men "only a renunciation, specifically a not-to-be determined, wishful-impossible one" (239). At other, less profoundly depressed moments, Mann sees his desire as expressing itself primarily in terms of viewing: On May 25, 1934, for instance, he sees "with great pleasure and emotion in the garden a young man, dark-haired, a small cap on his head, very pretty, naked above the belt." He reflects that the "enthusiasm" that he feels "at the sight of this so cheap, pedestrian, and natural 'beauty,' the chest, the swelling biceps" leads him to contemplate "the unreal, illusionary . . . aesthetic of such an inclination, whose goal, it would seem, remains in looking and 'admiring' and, although erotic, does not know of any realization" (397–98). For this reason Mann sees homosexual desire as an aesthetic and nonphysical phenomenon. As far as Mann is concerned, homosexual desire is primarily satisfied through visual observation.

The aestheticism of homosexuality explains for Mann its connection to form. An attractive young man he saw on the California coast in 1943 was "extraordinarily pure of form" (565). In his 1930 essay on Platen, Mann attributes the beauty of that poet's works to his homosexual desire, which Mann claims expresses itself, not physically, but formally:

> I am convinced that his choice of the poetic forms in which he so wonderfully shone was conditioned by the source of all his ardors and anguishes. Yet not alone out of caution, not out of fearfulness as Heine thought, but above all because the strictly formal and form-plastic character of the verse forms had an aesthetic and psychological affinity with his Eros. [3]

Platen's "Eros," "the source of all his ardors and anguishes," was of course his homosexuality. According to Mann, a Platonic homosexual desire produced a Platenic attendance to form.

Mann links the desire for men with "formality" in realms other than

2. In the letter to Weber, Mann distinguishes between "pathological," "medicinal," and "humanitarian" spheres on the one hand and "symbolic," "spiritual," and "cultural" spheres on the other (*Letters* 103–4).
3. Thomas Mann, *Essays of Three Generations*, trans. H. T. Lowe-Porter (New York: Knopf, 1947) 265.

the aesthetic as well. In the letter to Weber, he reveals and discusses his
fascination with and debt to Hans Blüher, the early twentieth-century
psychoanalytically trained intellectual, who divided society into the categories of family and the "Männerbund," the male society. Blüher
shocked Germany by arguing in a two-volume work, just before World
War I, that male-bonding organizations, such as the freemasons, military units, and society and state in general, were cemented by eroticism.[4] Following Blüher, Mann, in the letter to Weber, contrasts his
life as a family man, who loves wife and children, and his other interest
in male society (*Letters* 103). Since Mann opposes heterosexuality to
Blüher's homosocial male bonding, rather than to homosexuality, he
has relatively little to say about female homosexuality. Biologically fruitful heterosexuality is what stands in contrast with societally structuring
male homosociality for Mann.

The military in particular is a site for the homosexuality about which
Mann writes. In his essay, "On the German Republic," Mann suggests
that many of the believers in "this Eros" are militarists (*Von deutscher
Republik* 154–55).[5] Once the Nazis took over Germany, Mann linked
them with homosexuality as well, making fun of the moralistic campaign surrounding the persecution of the cadre of high level homosexual
officers around Ernst Röhm (1887–1933), head of the Nazi private mili-
tia known as the SA (for "Sturmabtoilung"—"storm troopers") or the
Brown shirts, because homosexuality "belonged essentially to the movement, to warfare, yes, to Germanness" (1933–34, 470). He objects to
the Nazi "denial of another of its essential features, homosexuality" on
August 5, 1934 (497). And in some published memoirs of the time,
Mann asserts again that homosexuality is an essential part of Nazism,
because it consists of "supermanliness," is "militaristic-heroic," and is
at home in militaristic nations like Germany. The Germans he calls
a "homoerotic folk."[6] When his son wrote an essay denouncing the
identification of homosexuality and fascism,[7] Mann's response in his
diaries was "problematic" (1933–34, 592).

All of Mann's thoughts on homosexuality, both its good and its bad
sides, show up in a complaint he entered in his diary while in exile on
February 2, 1934. He had noted, essentially, that non-German films
did not show enough unclothed men:

---

4. Julius H. Schoeps, *Leiden an Deutschland: Vom antisemitischen Wahn und der Last der
    Erinnerung* [Suffering from Germany: On anti-Semitic madness and the burden of the past]
    (Munich: Piper, 1990) 139–58.
5. Omitted from *Order of the Day* 42.
6. Thomas Mann, "Leiden an Deutschland. Tagebuchblätter aus den Jahren 1933 und 1934"
    [Suffering from Germany. Diaries from the years 1933 and 1934], *An die gesittete Welt: Poli-
    tische Schriften und Reden im Exil*, [To the civilized world: Political Writings and lectures in
    exile], ed. Peter de Mendelssohn and Hanno Helbling (Frankfurt/M: Fischer, 1986), 57–58.
7. Klaus Mann, "Homosexualität und Faschismus" [Homosexulity and fascism], *Die Neue Welt-
    bühne* [The new world stage] (Prague, 1934), pp. 130–7. Reprinted in Klaus Mann and Kurt
    Tucholsky, *Homosexualität und Faschismus* [Homosexulity and fascism], (Hamburg: Frühlin-
    gserwachen, 1981).

German films give me something that those of other nationalities scarcely offer: pleasure in youthful bodies, particularly male ones, in their nakedness. This is connected with German "homosexuality" and is lacking in the attractions of French and also American products: the showing of young male nudity in flattering, indeed loving photographic lighting whenever the opportunity presents itself. . . . The Germans, or the German Jews, that do this are certainly right: there is basically nothing "more beautiful." (309)

On the one hand, by putting German "homosexuality" in quotation marks, Mann is pointing to his construct of male-male desire as a bond for the military and the state. This "homosexuality" then accords well with the Germany that made films and the military portrayed in those films. At the same time, the visual aspect of this homosexuality, rather than any physical nature, points to its "beauty"—the quotation marks here referring specifically to the formal aesthetic quality that Mann associates with homosexuality in a number of passages. These thoughts, linking homosexuality with form in aesthetics and politics, shed light on *Death in Venice*. In fact, given that *Death in Venice* was written much earlier than much of his writing about homosexuality, it could well be that the novella contains the seeds of the thoughts that Mann articulated more clearly later.

Homosexuality in Death in Venice

For Mann, the theme of homosexuality clearly has a host of resonances, which makes it doubly important to study the male-male erotics of *Death in Venice*. Aschenbach's infatuation with the youth Tadzio allowed the story to move into the canon of homosexual literature immediately. Early homosexual critics generally reacted positively to the novella (see Böhm 21–23). Other critics have been forced to deal with the male-male desire of the novella, however cursorily and abstractly. While the critics, gay or straight, often affect a surprised tone, actually homosexuality, rather than heterosexuality, should be assumed in Mann's works, given its increasing importance both in late nineteenth-century Germany and in his personal life. Although a fleeting reference in *Death in Venice* appears to Aschenbach's wife, "a girl from a learned family," she plays no role in the story (12). Homosexual desire, on the other hand, obviously plays a crucial role at the end of the narration. An experimental reading, assuming homosexuality and pursuing homosexual connotations from the very beginning, however, draws many more of the details, besides those of Aschenbach's infatuation with Tadzio, into a richly coherent pattern. The first three chapters of the novella can each be read as referring to Aschenbach's homosexuality as it relates to his life in Munich, his work, and his trip to Italy.

how?

specific places - map

With a subtext about a botched homosexual encounter in a park, the first chapter of the novella sets the scene for an experimental gay reading. Geography provides the first clues. One critic remarks on the realism of the "specificity of address," unprecedented for Mann, provided by the reference in the first paragraph to Aschenbach's apartment on "Prinzreg-entenstrasse."[8] Perhaps, however, Mann's mentioning the specific Munich address plays a more significant role than simply indicating the presence of the "real world"—perhaps it and the other geographical ref-erences to Aschenbach's life in Munich carry homosexual connotations as well. In the late nineteenth century Munich had a reputation as one of the most sexually liberal cities in Germany; it was the capital of Bavaria, one of the last German states to recriminalize homosexuality, and was ruled by King Ludwig II (1845–86), who was known to have fallen in love with a series of young men.[9] Aschenbach's walk through the English Garden, the large park stretching from downtown Munich to the outskirts of town, points to homosexuality, for the park has been a meeting place for homosexuals from shortly after its construction in the late eighteenth century to the present day. The direction of Aschenbach's walk gives an indication of what that "productive machinery within him" is, helps define that " 'motus animi continuus' which Cicero claims is the essence of eloquence" (4): it is lust or sexual energy.

Aschenbach's restless drive to the parks achieves a kind of satisfaction, for he meets someone else wandering through the public spaces of Munich. In the North Cemetery, abutting the English Garden, he meets the first "stranger," a man whose milky, freckled skin, slight (if tall) build, and lack of a beard suggest to at least one critic "youthful innocence, yet with homosexual implications" (Traschen 90). Certainly the man is odd, queer—his appearance has the character of the foreign and exotic. Throughout the novella, "strangers" appear, culminating in the appearance of "the stranger God" in Aschenbach's final dream (56–57). While Mann obviously did not have in mind the connotations that the word "queer" has in American slang, the "strangers" and the "strangeness" that recur throughout the novella represent an otherness that is at the root of the modern usage of the word "queer."

An indication that the man's otherness has to do with sexuality is the aggressive eye contact with which the two strangers in the cemetery silently proposition each other. Recognizing that it was "entirely possi-ble" that he "had been somewhat indiscreet in his half-distracted, half-inquisitive survey of the stranger," Aschenbach

> suddenly realized that his gaze was being returned, and indeed returned so belligerently, so directly eye to eye, with such a clear intent to bring matters to a head. . . . (4)

8. Esther Lesér, *Thomas Mann's Short Fiction: An Intellectual Biography*, ed. Mitzi Brunsdale (Rutherford, NJ: Farleigh Dickenson UP, 1989) 163.
9. Mann refers to Ludwig II as a "type" of homosexual in his letter to Weber (*Letters* 104).

It is important in this context to bring out all the connotations of the phrase "die Sache aufs Äußereste zu treiben" (to bring matters to a head). The word "treiben," related to English "drive," can have sexual connotations in German ("es mit jemandem treiben" means "to have sex with someone"). The German word used at the beginning of the novella for the "machinery" that keeps Aschenbach going is "Triebwerk," a mechanism that may well have to do with his sexual energies. In the Michelangelo essay, Mann uses the same root to describe that artist's erotics as the glowing driving force ("die glühende Triebkraft") behind his "hypermanly" art.[1] In the context of Mann's life and Aschenbach's story, the visual challenge issued and the extreme to which the stranger pushes the connection are both highly likely to be sexual.

[margin note: speculation + assumption..]

Further evidence for the erotic nature of this encounter between two men in the cemetery comes in the description of Aschenbach's reaction. The stranger disappears, but he affects Aschenbach's imagination or has "some physical or spiritual influence" on him (4). Vaguely and surprisingly, Aschenbach becomes aware of an "expansion of his inner space," "a rambling unrest, a youthful thirst," "a feeling so intense, so new—or rather so long unused and forgotten" (5), all of which refer to a long-repressed, perhaps homosexual, desire. The narrator, acting as a guarantor of propriety, interrupts by calling this desire "wanderlust and nothing more," albeit an "overwhelming" example (5). The sexual nature of travel or "Weltverkehr," however, becomes clear in the following paragraph. In this context "Weltverkehr" (literally "world traffic") means travel, but with the added connotation of "Verkehr" as (sexual) intercourse.[2] Aschenbach views this erotically tinged travel as a "measure one had to take for one's health," placing it in the same medical discourse that was engulfing sexual intercourse in the late nineteenth century. The physical and emotional desire associated with Aschenbach's "wanderlust" becomes apparent in the vision provoked by the stranger, a vision of a tropical swamp with "rank" ferns and hairy and misshapen trunks of palms and mangroves. The German word translated as "rank" is "geil," which also means "lewd" when referring to people. In Aschenbach's last vision the word appears in its other meaning, when the satyrs drive each other on "with lewd gestures," "mit geilen Gebärden" (57). The fact that the vision in the cemetery makes Aschenbach's heart pound with "horror and mysterious desire" further points to its erotic origins. *[margin note: why not just fear?]*

1. Thomas Mann, "Die Erotik Michelangelo's" [The erotics of Michelangelo], *Leiden und Größe der Meister*, [Suffering and greatness of the masters], ed. Peter de Mendelssohn (Frankfurt/M-Fischer, 1982), 1018.

2. Several crucial sentences from later on in the novella reinforce the sexual nature of "Verkehr": "Strangely fertile intercourse ("Verkehr") between a mind and a body!" [39]. "A horrifyingly brisk traffic" ("Verkehr") between the hospital and the cemetery is mentioned in the same paragraph that concludes with the reference to wild prostitution: "Prostitution and lasciviousness took on brazen and extravagant forms never before seen here and thought to be at home only in the southern parts of the country and in the seraglios of the orient" (55).

The phallic nature of the hairy and misshapen tree trunks suggests that this sexual desire is concentrated on men (Jofen 240). The strange "exotic birds" possibly refer to homosexual men, who were often seen in this era as eccentric unmarried bachelors. The curious bills of these birds could then be read as phallic. The final evidence of the homosexual nature of the desire triggered by the sight of the stranger in the cemetery is the connection between desire and sight. When Aschenbach sees the stranger, the narrator reports: "His desire acquired vision" (5). The German is somewhat different: "Seine Begierde ward sehend" ("his desire became seeing"). Its unusual, untranslatable, construction, with an archaic preterit of the verb "werden" (to become) and unconventional use for German of the present participle "sehend" (seeing) makes the sentence stand out, sound almost biblical. Since it is clear from Mann's statements about homosexuality in his diary that he regards same-sex desire as something for the visual realm, the prominence of this sentence underscores it as an important clue, pointing to the visual, aesthetic, and thus for Mann homosexual nature of this desire.

Having intimated Aschenbach's deeply rooted homosexual desire, the novella moves on to Aschenbach's literary works. Just as Mann renounced his homosexual desire in order to become the married writer he wanted to be, Aschenbach lives, loves, yokes his feelings, and renounces happiness for his writings (8–10). Strongly corroborating the thesis that Aschenbach has repressed homosexual desire for the sake of his writing, all of his works contain a kind of return of the repressed in powerful allusions to homosexuality. His protagonists are all St. Sebastian figures, representing "intellectual and youthful manliness, which grits its teeth in proud modesty and calmly endures the swords and spears as they pass through its body" (9). The erotically charged reference to St. Sebastian has a homosexual subtext, for aestheticized and eroticized images of the penetrated saint, said to have been a beloved of Diocletian before turning to Christianity, have been popular with homosexuals for generations.[3] In addition, this passage itself represents a kind of homosexual penetration of one man's text by another man's words, as it is an actual citation of the literary historian and critic Samuel Lublinski's analysis of Mann's character Thomas Buddenbrooks.[4]

The specifics of Aschenbach's works overflow with homosexual implications. The novel *Maia* is named for a concept taken from Schopenhauer, the misogynistic old bachelor who provided an early formulation of the role of pederasty in nature. The next narrative mentioned is "The

---

3. Gerd Schäfer, "Pasolinis Auge. Über die Wahrnehmung im Werk Hubert Fichtes" [Pasolini's eye. On perception in the work of Hubert Fiche], *Forum Homosexualität und Literatur* 1 [Forum homosexuality and literature] (1987): 31. Oscar Wilde, for instance, adopted the name Sebastian Melmoth after his trial and move to Paris. See also Böhm 339–341.
4. Samuel Lublinski, *Bilanz der Moderne* [Balance of the modern] (Berlin: 1904; Tübingen, 1974) 226. Discussed in Böhm 339.

Man of Misery," a rendering of "Ein Elender," an ancient German word originally meaning "in a strange land" or "banned,"[5] linking that work's main character to all the strangers in this novella, like the man in the cemetery and the gondolier, who are foreigners and homosexually tinged. "Elender" comes up in Mann's letter to Grautoff of April 6, 1897, as a possible (although not desirable) reaction to homosexuality. The "Man of Misery" treats "moral resolution" reached despite "the deepest knowledge" (7). Regarding this story as "an outbreak of disgust at the indecent psychologism then current" (11), the narrator may well be referring to the era's increasingly medical and psychiatric approach to the human condition, which it "indecently" reduced to sexuality. Although the narrator's comment attacks the sexologists and psychoanalysts, it points nonetheless to their growing power. Indeed, the narrator concentrates as much on "indecent" psychology as anyone else in describing the plot of "A Man of Misery"—it is about a man, who, out of "weakness, viciousness, and moral impotence" sends his wife to a "beardless boy" (11). The language of the "beardless boy" comes directly from ancient Greek pederastic relationships, tipping the reader off to a homosexual subtext, while the language of "weakness" and "viciousness" emerges from a more modern discourse, aimed at describing sexuality in terms of physical stature and psychological constitution. Finally, the language of "moral impotence" suggests that this weak, depraved man of psychologically indecent modernity, who sends his wife to the beardless youth of antiquity, may well have secretly and ineffectively desired that youth. In this context, the narrator's repeated emphasis on the message of moral resolution in Aschenbach's works make sense: he refers to a steadfast resistance to homosexual temptation.

The text written by Aschenbach referred to first, last, and most frequently in the second section of *Death in Venice*, however, is his prose epic on the life of Frederick the Great, an epic that concerns "selflessly active virtue" and the command to "endure" (8). That which has to be endured and the reason virtue must be selfless—both these qualities have to do with homosexuality, for Mann knew the rumors of homosexuality surrounding Frederick the Great. These rumors originated in part in the "scintillating repartee between Voltaire and King Frederick" (12), when the French philosopher accused the Prussian King of sodomy. Because the first reference to these stories only appears on the forty-fifth page of fifty pages of notes Mann made around 1906 in preparation for his own novel, Böhm assumes that Mann learned of the king's alleged homosexuality relatively late and perhaps even gave up the project on account of his own difficulties with that subject (Böhm

---

5. Friedrich Kluge and Alfred Götze, *Etymologisches Wörterbuch der deutschen Sprache* [Etymological dictionary of the German Language], 15th ed. (Berlin: de Gruyter, 1951) 168.

278–87).[6] In any case, it is clear that by the time he wrote *Death in Venice*, Mann already knew that Frederick II was said to have been a sodomite. Mann's awareness of this homosexuality reverberates well with his decision to hand this project off to his character Aschenbach.

All of Aschenbach's protagonists thus exhibit the "heroism . . . of weakness" (10), a weakness circling around sexuality. "Passivity," not heterosexual activity, describes his heroes (9). Like Oscar Wilde's Dorian Gray, another figure quickly recognized by homosexual readers as one of their own, Aschenbach's characters demonstrate "elegant self-discipline that managed right up to the last moment to hide from the eyes of the world the undermining process, the biological decline, taking place within" (9). The biological decay clearly points to a bodily disorder made specific in that "yellow,[7] physically handicapped ugliness," a disorder that, like homosexuality for Thomas Mann, cannot express itself physically. Unable thus to express itself, this ugliness must hide itself always, producing "the false, dangerous life of the born deceiver" (10), similar to the closeted secrecy of the homosexual at the turn of the century. This secrecy, however, simultaneously produces the self-control that results in the "lovable charm that survives even the empty and rigorous service of pure form" (10), a charm clearly related to the formalism that Mann believes Platen's poetry derives from that author's homosexuality. The narrator assures his readers that there are many such heroes and that they "recognized themselves in his work; they saw themselves justified, exalted, their praises sung. And they were grateful; they heralded his name" (10). Certainly many homosexuals of the early twentieth century recognized themselves and the "hymnic" nature of the depiction of homosexuality in Mann's novella (96), indicating that Aschenbach is a man (or Mann) willing to write the Frederick novel, depicting a homosexuality with which his readers identify.

Having established the presence of homosexuality in his literary works, the narrator returns to Aschenbach's "wanderlust" in the third section of the novella. Continuing to read experimentally, with an eye especially sensitive to gay themes, one could argue that, in wanting the "incomparable," Aschenbach wants the strange, i.e., the "queer" (13); in any case, he wants the "fabulously deviant,"[8] and he wants it "in a single night," stressing the nocturnal realm in which sexuality is at home (13). For Germans of Mann's era, the place to find such queerness was Italy, at least since Goethe made his erotic discoveries

6. Some of the notebooks on *Friedrich* have been published by Peter Richner in *Thomas Manns Projekt eines Friedrich-Romans* [Thomas Mann's Project of a Frederick Novel] (Zürich: Juris-Verlag, 1975).
7. "Yellowish" is the color of the head of "Eros" (25), but also of the fingers of the ticket salesman (14) and the dentures of the old fop (14).
8. In the original German—"Das märchenhaft Abweichende," taking "abweichend" in the sense of "abweichendes Verhalten," social deviancy. In this volume, the phrase is rendered more idiomatically with "as out of the ordinary as a fairytale," but for the purposes of a "queer" reading, it is necessary to emphasize the German connotations of "abweichend."

[margin handwritten note:] "Despair" heroes (ch. 2)

there and Winckelmann moved there to lead his life more freely. In particular, Venice had become by the late nineteenth century a vacation center for homosexuals with means. Mann himself had played on this topos in an early story, "Disappointment," which describes a conversation between two solitary men in the Piazza San Marco of Venice; this can easily be read as a kind of attempted pick-up in which the cynicism and depression resulting from the clandestine lives of upper-class homosexuals in the late nineteenth century is discussed (Härle 168 ff.). Given this background, Aschenbach's desire to visit Venice is a logical extension of both his writing and his encounter with the stranger in the park.

In accordance with the homosexual aura surrounding Venice, a series of "queer" men accompany Aschenbach's arrival by sea to the fabled city. The first man, a "scruffy sailor" (13), leads Aschenbach to the salesman who sells him his ticket to Venice. This salesman speaks with "empty chatter" (14), echoing unflatteringly Aschenbach's protagonists, who, like Platen, rely on a highly formal textual style to confront their homosexuality. The next man on the way to Venice who suggests homosexuality is the fop who wears make-up in pretence of youth. His unpleasant behavior has explicit sexual overtones: "he . . . ran the tip of his tongue around the corners of his mouth in an obscenely suggestive manner" (16). Upon disembarking from the ship, he sends his compliments to "the beloved," using a suspiciously neuter noun in the German original, "Liebchen." The fourth character whose homosexuality sets the stage for events in Venice is the gondolier who, roughly but pleasantly, takes control of Aschenbach's life: "The smartest thing to do was to let matters take their course; more important, it was also the most pleasant" (19). The physical pleasure that Aschenbach takes in the actions of the strong man behind him has been seen by psychoanalysis as a wish for "a homosexual union" (Jofen 242). The disregarded anxiety that he may have fallen into the hands of a criminal reflects both the "dangerous life" of Aschenbach's heroes, the "born deceivers," and the actual life of homosexuals in the late nineteenth century, confined to dark corners and constantly endangered by blackmail. All of these "events of the journey that brought him here" cause Aschenbach to dwell on "the perverse . . . the forbidden" (21). Specifically, this perversity is "das Verkehrte," "wrong," but literally "backwards," "turned-around," referring to a tradition of seeing sodomy as sex on the wrong side, especially in this story, with its emphasis on "Verkehr," traffic and intercourse.

Throughout the novella, the weather is hot and humid. Although it is May, the English Gardens in Munich are "as muggy as in August" (3). On the Adriatic, the air is "oppressive" (13), while Venice suffers from "the brooding heat of this exceptionally warm weather" (48). These oppressive atmospheric conditions suggest a general heavy sultriness that can be sexual. But as Aschenbach's passion develops, the air becomes

"odiously oppressive," (29) in German "eine widerliche Schwüle." The
word "Schwül," very close to "schwul," which at least since the time of
King Ludwig II of Bavaria has meant "gay," appears with increasing
frequency in the novella, for the last time describing the piazza where
Aschenbach buys strawberries, before his final speech to Phaedrus/Tad-
zio (60). Although, in English, the connection between the weather and
Aschenbach's passion depends on the general sensuality of sultriness, in
German, this sultriness, "schwül," is only an umlaut away from a the
specifically homosexual desire indicated in the word "schwul."

After such extensive preparation, no reader of the novella should be
particularly surprised that Aschenbach develops a homosexual passion
upon reaching Venice. Although Aschenbach's relationship with Tadzio is obviously homosexual, it is worth examining how its depiction
corresponds with Mann's opinion concerning homosexuality in his
other writings. To begin with, it is specifically a visual phenomenon.
Falling under the spell of the Polish youth, Aschenbach becomes "the
onlooker" (21). This visual relationship becomes mutual quickly, as
Tadzio meets Aschenbach's eyes in a move reminiscent of the encounter
with the stranger in the cemetery:

> For some reason he turned around before crossing the threshold.
> Since there was no one else left in the lobby, his strangely misty
> gray eyes met those of Aschenbach, who was sunk deep in contem-
> plation of the departing group, his newspaper on his knees. (23)

The remainder of the text has so many references to the eye as the
main organ uniting Tadzio and Aschenbach that the narrator is forced
to remark on this visual relationship:

> There is nothing stranger or more precarious than the relationship
> between people who know each other only by sight, who meet and
> watch each other every day, even every hour, yet are compelled
> by convention or their own whim to maintain the appearance of
> indifference and unfamiliarity. . . . (42)

That force of convention ("Sittenzwang"), which forces the "visually
related" to act like strangers, could be seen as the force that makes
homoerotic desire (always visual in Mann's world) queer, like the strangers in this novella. The narrator uses medical and psychoanalytical
terms—"the hysteria of an unsatisfied, unnaturally suppressed urge"
(42)—to describe the effect of this visual relationship on people linking
this text up with pathological understandings of homosexuality. The
mysterious camera standing alone on the beach "with no photographer"
(61) at the end of the novella represents the visual nature of desire, a
desire that Mann is attempting to free from a human agent, who might
really engage in sexual acts, and that Mann wants to use exclusively as
an aesthetic tool.

Tadzio's visual quality also emerges in the comparisons made between him and the "Greek statues from the noblest period of antiquity" (21), specifically the beautiful "Boy Pulling a Thorn from his Foot" (22). The references to "the Trojan shepherd," Ganymede, enraptured by Zeus in an eagle's form (39) and Hyacinthos, beloved of the two gods Apollo and Zephyr (42), link Tadzio to Cellini's two famous sculptures of scenes from the Greek tradition of homosexuality (Traschen 94). Observing Tadzio, Aschenbach compares him to a statue and glides effortlessly into thoughts of his own writing as sculpture (37). The form of the boy's body is compared to the "slender form" of Aschenbach's writing. Soon he decides "to let his style follow the lines of that body" (39). Aschenbach's physical homoerotic desire thus quickly becomes aesthetic and specifically formal.

This writing style is connected to the schooling system, in a way supporting the thesis that Blücher would later develop and that Mann would find so intriguing: that homosexual desire cemented the bonds of society's institutions. Early in the novella, the narrator mentions that "educational authorities began using selected passages from his works in their prescribed textbooks" (12). At the end of the novella, the narrator reminds the readers that the made-up, lovesick protagonist eating strawberries in a small squalid square of Venice is the great writer "whose style children were encouraged to emulate" (60). Although the sarcasm shows how far the mighty master has fallen, the narrator is in no way ahead of Aschenbach, who, following Plato, calls "the education of the populace and of the young by means of art a risky enterprise that ought not to be allowed" (61). Despite Aschenbach's Platonic critique of art as educator, the presence of his works in school textbooks provides further evidence that Mann saw homosexuality as central to societal structures such as education.

Sedgwick sees this link between Phaedrus and Tadzio, Aschenbach and Socrates, as indicating that "the history of Western thought is importantly constituted and motivated by a priceless history of male-male pedagogic or pederastic relations."[9] Her analysis points to the exclusion of women from the societal (for instance, pedagogical) institutions held together by bonds between men. Indeed misogyny, a part of Mann's understanding of homosexuality, plays a role in this novella as well. "Widely differing views on child-rearing," it is said when the Polish family first appears, "had evidently directed the dress and general treatment of the siblings" (22). While Tadzio merits comparison with masterpieces of Greek and Renaissance sculpture, his sisters seem "almost disfiguringly chaste and austere," wearing clothes "tailored as if to be deliberately unflattering," with hairstyles that make them seem "nunnishly vacant and expressionless" (22). Clearly, the narrator is

9. Eve Sedgwick, *Epistemology of the Closet* (Berkeley: U California P, 1990) 55.

relating Aschenbach's opinions here. Aschenbach's own writing, all about men, is characterized as a kind of "manliness" (9). Concerned about what his ancestors, with their "manly respectability," would have thought about his "exotic emotional aberrations" (47), he defensively reflects that his whole project has been "manly" (48). In his final speech, Aschenbach recants, telling Phaedrus/Tadzio that "we are as women, for passion is our exultation, and our longing must ever be for love. That is our bliss and our shame" (60). This recantation reveals the short-circuit of misogynistic male homosexuality, for, in loving a male, Aschenbach behaves like a heterosexual woman, thus putting himself into a position he despises.

Defending his masculinity against the imaginary reproaches of his forefathers, Aschenbach links "the love-god [i.e., homoerotic desire] who had taken possession of him" both with his previous life of letters and the military, just as Mann had:

> Had not that very god enjoyed the highest respect among the brav-est nations of the earth? Did they not say that it was because of their courage that he had flourished in their cities? Numerous war heroes of ages past had willingly borne the yoke imposed by the god. . . . (48)

Aschenbach's attempts to link up his specific desire for a boy to the warrior traditions of ancient Greece presages Mann's statement in "On the German Republic" that followers of "this eros" were militarists. When Aschenbach subsequently puts his own masculinity into doubt, he still insists that his kind made "disciplined warriors" (60). One of the "queer" men who leads him to Venice wears a sailor's uniform, rein-forcing the military and specifically naval image of homosexuality. The playful pendant to the linkage of homosexuality with the military is the sailor suit that Tadzio wears when he first appears (22) and the sailor's coat and hat that he wears when he smiles at Aschenbach (43).

Like homosexuality in Mann's diaries, letters, and essays, then, Aschenbach's desire appears as an aesthetic, formalistic, visual phenom-enon. Its formalism connects it with basic structures of society, for instance, the educational system and the military, all of which have a misogynistic bias. Mann locates homosexuality—which, in the letter to Weber, he contends can on an individual level achieve great highs or sink to miserable lows—in Aschenbach's case in the general societal discourses that give it meaning.

Homosexuality's Meaning

If this reading of *Death in Venice* has required something of a stretch, it has certainly not violated the text. While readers may disagree with some of the homosexual interpretations above, it is impossible to dispute the importance of homosexuality to this text. Clearly Mann not only laced his novella with indications of Aschenbach's homosexual desires, but also connected those desires with a series of concepts—aesthetics, formalism, societal structures, misogyny, militarism—that Mann suggests have links to homosexuality. These connections can help determine the meaning of homosexuality in *Death in Venice*, a meaning that is as ambivalent as Mann's assessment of homosexual desire in his personal papers.

Readers have always seen the link between the discourses of sexuality and pathology in *Death in Venice* (Bohm 29ff., 34ff., 48ff.). The course of Aschenbach's love for Tadzio follows a similar trajectory to that of the cholera, with the author's desire for the youth growing in intensity as the plague increases in virulence. At one point, the narrator identifies "the heinous secret belonging to the city," i.e., the epidemic, with Aschenbach's "innermost secret," i.e., his love of Tadzio (45). While nineteenth-century medical discourses on sexuality enable Mann to construct this comparison in a way that is still quite compelling today, Mann—true to the rejection of pathological views of homosexuality expressed in his letter to Weber—does not allow the equation of homosexuality and pathology to go entirely unchallenged. Aschenbach contracts the cholera late in the story, long after his infatuation with Tadzio has set in, long after the story makes his homosexual desires clear. The relationship between disease and sexuality remains an uneasy one for Mann, perhaps because Mann sees homosexuality as so crucially involved in his own life and in so many elements of modern society that he is unwilling to relinquish it entirely to medicine.

Besides associating Aschenbach's passion with Venice's pestilence, many critics are also willing to discuss the homosexuality in the text in terms of ancient Greek philosophy, particularly Plato's *Phaedrus*. Aschenbach's two speeches addressed to Tadzio as Phaedrus—consisting of excerpts from the *Phaedrus*, the *Symposium*, the *Republic*, and other texts of Greek antiquity—seem to reverse the arguments that Plato presents on Platonic love: in Plato's *Phaedrus*, Socrates first argues against and then for love (secs. 239–41, 244–57), whereas Aschenbach first speaks in favor of desire for beauty as a means of reaching the divine and the spiritual (38), but then condemns in his second speech the poetic attraction to beauty as inherently unable to transcend the corporeal (60–61).[1] Even Aschenbach's first speech, which praises beauty, reveals at the end a powerful critique of the Platonic model, when it points out how self-serving its arguments are:

> And then he said the subtlest thing of all, crafty wooer that he was: he said that the lover was more divine than the beloved,

---

1. Jeffrey Meyers, *Homosexuality and Literature 1890–1930* (Atlantic Highlands, NJ: Athelone, 1977) 50.

because the god was in the former and not in the latter—perhaps the tenderest, most mocking thought that ever was thought, a thought alive with all the guile and the most secret bliss of love's longing. (38)

In his first speech, Socrates had described a certain unmannered kind of lover who strives to keep his beloved inferior to him. Although he then recants and describes true love as a phenomenon in which the lover strives to improve his beloved, to remake him in the image of his god, this belief that the lover is closer to the divine than the beloved actually suggests that this second kind of love is closer to the first than those who believe in an entirely innocent Platonic eros can admit. By the end of Aschenbach's first speech, the notion of a Platonic love that moves from the carnal to the spiritual begins to unravel in a way that prepares for Aschenbach's subsequent self-identification with Zephyr, the lover who kills Hyacinthos out of jealous possessiveness (42). When Aschenbach refuses to tell Tadzio's family about the cholera epidemic, he strengthens the argument that he is a destructive lover, like one of the figures from the first speeches of *Phaedrus*, who destroys his beloved and is therefore rejected by Socrates. Aschenbach's reversal of Plato's hopes for a desire that leads to art, rather than to an art stuck in lust, explains why Stefan George was upset with the way in which *Death in Venice* dragged "the highest" down into the mud (Böhm 21).

Just as a study of homosexual allusions in the novella shows that Aschenbach's homosexuality precedes his contraction of cholera, any understanding of Aschenbach's desire as a retraction of Plato's teachings must keep in mind that the author is not falling from a previously held moral position into an immoral one, for he was always in love with the body. At most, one can speak of Aschenbach as becoming aware of a desire that is constitutive of him. In his working notes to *Death in Venice*, Mann writes "Eros has always resided within him. Tadzio was always his king" (83). Like Hans Castorp, who, because he always loved Pribislav Hippe, developed tuberculosis, Aschenbach's eternal love for boyish youth gives him cholera and refuses Platonic transcendence. Both of the most frequent interpretations of homosexuality in *Death in Venice*—its pathology and its anti-Platonism—while textually justified are too frequently read as "falls" from states of grace that never existed in the novella.

The implicit notion of Aschenbach's "fall" into sickness and carnality is inadequate not only because it inaccurately suggests that Aschenbach was once healthy and spiritual, but also because it portrays Aschenbach's homosexual passion as too unambiguously negative. While the narrator clearly portrays Aschenbach's love as ridiculous and worthy of censure, Mann, the ironic German, has never used narrators whose words could be taken at face value.[2] Thus the careful reader must assume that a

2. See Dorrit Cohn, "The Second Author of 'Der Tod in Venedig,' " pages 178–95 above.

fallible narrator provides the negative descriptions of Aschenbach's passions, particularly the attempt to cover up the relationship between "that page-and-a-half of choice prose that soon would amaze many a reader with its purity, nobility, and surging depth of feeling" and Aschenbach's homosexual desire:

> It is surely for the best that the world knows only the lovely work and not also its origins, not the conditions under which it came into being; for knowledge of the origins from which flowed the artist's inspiration would surely often confuse the world, repel it, and thus vitiate the effects of excellence. (39) — *secret love*

In his final speech, Aschenbach sees through this dichotomy of dirty origin and lofty result, which perhaps explains why the narrator has to break his habit of working strictly sequentially and mention the positive reception of Aschenbach's short essay before it happens: if he were to discuss the essay after Aschenbach's second speech, which is when, chronologically, its reception takes place, he would not be able to argue that it was the clean product of an unclean imagination. Whereas the Platonic model offered in Aschenbach's first speech had seen the artist moving from the flesh to the mind, the second speech sees the artist remaining in the flesh the whole time.

And yet the little essay written after the first speech merits great admiration. Aschenbach does not deny in his second speech the origins of art in desire, merely the desirability, necessity, or even possibility of separating the two categories. His new explanation for the connection between beauty and the poet's desire is the (male) poet's yearning for discipline and form (61), masculine categories in Mann's world. Earlier, Aschenbach makes the link between male homosexuality and poetry clear when claiming that his own life of writing corresponds well with the military careers of his ancestors and the particular homosexual eros that is appropriate to both writers and warriors. Aschenbach thus relates artistic beauty to the strict formalistic desire that Mann had always viewed in his personal writings as masculine and homosexual. In *Death in Venice*, Aschenbach therefore suggests that the male author has to be "womanly" or homosexual because of his desire for form, which is masculine in Mann's thinking.

Aschenbach not only implies that male homosexuality produces the desire for form that leads to art, but he also indicates indirectly the specific effect on form that this homosexuality has as well. When he identifies the cholera epidemic, the city's evil secret, with pederastic desire, his own secret, he develops a rhetorical strategy: " 'Best to keep quiet,' thought Aschenbach anxiously. . . . 'Best to keep it under wraps' " (45). The male author's homosexual desire for form thus has the formal effect of encouraging secrecy, covering tracks, closeting sexuality. The form that results from the artist's desire is the basic narrative of secrets hidden and disclosed.

Aschenbach's remarks clearly reflect on the story in which he is a character as well, for Mann's homosexuality has insinuated itself, not only quite obviously into the thematics of man-boy love, but also metaphorically into Venice's closeting of the cholera. This closeting makes the novella a story of secrets. The emphasis on closeting then brings the sexuality behind *Death in Venice* into the realm of the erotic that Mann described in his letter to his brother, the realm, that is, of the "unnamed," which can truly produce poetry. In this sense, the narrator is (probably unwittingly) correct when he argues that the public should not know of the origins of Aschenbach's brilliant short final essay—not because poetry should be Platonically divorced from the sexuality that begets it, but because poetry consists of a sexuality that is erotic because it is not named by name. This "unnaming" is the effect on form that the desire for form produces.

Formalism and aestheticism, being without morals in *Death in Venice*, lead astray and do not produce role models for youth. The narrator criticizes Aschenbach as strongly as Mann at times felt compelled to renounce and deny his own homosexuality. Yet homosexuality, with all its ambiguities, is clearly portrayed as central in *Death in Venice*. Constitutive of Aschenbach's character, it informs his writings from the first pieces mentioned to the last brilliant essay. Although Aschenbach is of course not identical with Mann, the novella comments on the ways in which Mann's own sexuality moved into his writing. In so doing, it provides insights into the more general relationship between sexuality and textuality. About Platen, Mann wrote that "literary history, out of lack of knowledge, and with a reserve today out of date, has spoken with foolish circumlocution about the decisive fact in Platen's life, his exclusively homosexual constitution" (*Essays of Three Decades* 263). Quite clearly, the homosexual constitution of both Aschenbach and Mann merits attention because it affects both of their writings. Just as clearly, the nineteenth-century textual discourses emanating from philosophy, medicine, religion, and law, and surrounding and defining homosexuality, merit attention because they inform that "constitution" which seemed to be so firmly rooted in the author's life. The presence of these discourses in *Death in Venice* show Mann's awareness, not only of the influences of sexuality on textuality, but also of the effect of textuality on sexuality.

Chronology of Thomas Mann's Life

1875 Paul Thomas Mann born June 6 in Lübeck, Germany, the second son of Johann Heinrich Mann, merchant and senator of
Lübeck, and of his wife, Julia Da Silva-Bruhns Mann.

1890 Johann Heinrich Mann dies.

1893 Mann follows his family to Munich and works briefly at an
insurance company as an apprentice clerk.

1894 "Gefallen," Mann's first published story, appears in the monthly
Die Gesellschaft.
Mann leaves his position as clerk and registers at the University
of Munich.

1898 The volume of stories *"Little Herr Friedemann" and Other Stories* appears.

1901 The novel *Buddenbrooks* is published.

1903 Publication of *Tristan: Six Stories*.

1905 Marries Katharina (Katja) Pringsheim.

1907 In late winter agrees to write an essay on the theater. "I decided
to interrupt work on my novel *[Royal Highness]* 'for a few days.'
* * * But instead of days, I spent weeks in my struggle and was
more than once sick to the point of despair with the whole thing
* * * but I had agreed to write it, and so I obeyed my categorli-
cal imperative 'Endure!' "
In May travels to Venice and the Lido.

1909 *Royal Highness* appears.

1910 In January begins work on *Felix Krull*.
Meets Gustav Mahler on September 12.

1911 Writes to Korfitz Holm, March 20: "I am so worn out in mind
and body that I am on the point of retiring to a trustworthy
naturopathic sanatorium for several weeks."
Writes to his brother Heinrich in late March that he is planning
a holiday in Dalmatia.
In mid-May breaks off work on *Felix Krull* and travels with his
family to Brioni, an island off the coast of Istria.
On May 18 learns of Gustav Mahler's death.

Vacations with his family May 26–June 2 at the Hotel des Bains on the Lido at Venice, where he writes "On Richard Wagner's Art."

Returns to his country house in Bad Tölz in early June, where he begins work on *Death in Venice*.

1912   In June finishes *Death in Venice*, which is published later that summer.

1918   *Reflections of an Unpolitical Man* appears.

1921   Delivers the lecture "Goethe and Tolstoy."

1924   Publication of *The Magic Mountain*.

1929   Receives the Nobel Prize for literature.

1933   On January 30 Hitler becomes chancellor. That winter Mann leaves Germany on a lecture tour.

On February 27 Reichstag burns. Mann is warned that it would not be safe for him to return to Germany. Takes up residence in Switzerland in early fall.

The Tales of Jacob, the first volume of the tetralogy *Joseph and His Brothers*, appears.

1934   Publication of the second volume of the Joseph tetralogy, *Young Joseph*.

1936   The third volume, *Joseph in Egypt*, appears.

On December 2 Mann's German citizenship is revoked.

1938   Offered a position at Princeton University in May and moves to Princeton that September.

1939   Publication of the novel *The Beloved Returns*.

1941   Moves to California.

1943   The last of the Joseph books, *Joseph the Provider*, appears.

1947   Publication of *Doctor Faustus*.

1952   Returns to Europe, residing once again in Switzerland.

1954   *Confessions of Felix Krull, Confidence Man* appears.

1955   On August 12 Mann dies in his sleep in a hospital in Zürich.

A Selected Bibliography

Amory, Frederic. "The Classical Style of 'Der Tod in Venedig.' " *Modern Language Review* 59 (1964): 399–409.

Apter, T. E. *Thomas Mann: The Devil's Advocate*. London: Macmillan, 1978.

Bance, A. F. " 'Der Tod in Venedig' and the Triadic Structure." *Forum for Modern Language Studies* 8 (1972): 148–61.

Baron, Frank. "Sensuality and Morality in Thomas Mann's 'Tod in Venedig.' " *Germanic Review* 45 (1970): 115–25.

Bernhard, Frank. "Mann's 'Death in Venice.' " *Explicator* 45.1 (1987): 31–32.

Braverman, Albert, and Larry Nachman. "The Dialectic of Decadence: An Analysis of Thomas Mann's 'Death in Venice.' " *Germanic Review* 45 (1970): 289–98.

Bridges, George. "The Problem of Pederastic Love in Thomas Mann's 'Death in Venice' and Plato's 'Phaedrus.' " *Selecta* 7 (1986): 39–46.

Bronsen, David. "The Artist against Himself: Henrik Ibsen's 'Master Builder' and Thomas Mann's 'Death in Venice.' " *Neohelicon* 11.1 (1984): 323–44.

Butler, Christopher. "Joyce and the Displaced Author." *James Joyce and Modern Literature*. Eds. W. J. McCormack and Alistair Stead. London: Routledge, 1982.

Cadieux, Andre. "The Jungle of Dionysus: The Self in Mann and Nietzsche." *Philosophy and Literature* 3.1 (1978): 53–63.

Carnegy, Patrick. "The Novella Transformed: Thomas Mann as Opera." *Benjamin Britten: Death in Venice*. Ed. Donald Mitchell. New York: Cambridge UP, 1987.

Cerf, Steven R. "Benjamin Britten's 'Death in Venice': Operatic Stream of Consciousness." *Bucknell Review* 31.1 (1988): 124–38.

Conley, John. "Thomas Mann on the Sources of Two Passages in 'Death in Venice.' " *German Quarterly* 40 (1967): 152–55.

Cox, Catherine. "Pater's 'Apollo in Picardy' and Mann's 'Death in Venice.' " *Anglia* (Munich) 86 (1963): 143–54.

Daemmrich, Horst S. "The Infernal Fairy Tale: Inversion of Archetypal Motifs in Modern European Literature." *Mosaic* 5.3 (1971): 85–95.

Dassanowsky-Harris, Robert von. "Thomas Mann's 'Der Tod in Venedig': Unfulfilled 'Aufbruch' from the Wilhelminian World." *Germanic Notes* 18.1–2 (1987): 16–17.

Davidson, Leah. "Mid-Life Crisis in Thomas Mann's 'Death in Venice.' " *Journal of the American Academy of Psychoanalysis* 4 (1976): 203–14.

Dyson, A. E. "The Stranger God: 'Death in Venice.' " *Critical Quarterly* 13 (1971): 5–20.

Eggenschwiller, David. "The Very Glance of Art: Ironic Narrative in Thomas Mann's Novellen." *Modern Language Quarterly* 48 (1987): 59–85.

Egri, Peter. "The Functions of Dreams and Visions in 'A Portrait' and 'Death in Venice.' " *James Joyce Quarterly* 5 (1967): 85–102.

Farrelly, D. J. "Apollo and Dionysus Interpreted in Thomas Mann's 'Der Tod in Venedig.' " *New German Studies* 3 (1975): 1–15.

Feder, Lilian. "The Return of the Dionysiac." *Madness in Literature*. Princeton: Princeton UP, 1980. 204–247.

Fletcher, Agnus. "Music, Visconti, Mann, Nietzsche: 'Death in Venice.' " *Stanford Italian Review* 6.1–2 (1984): 301–12.

Frank, Yakira H., et al. "The Telltale Teeth," *PMLA* 91 (1976): 460–64.

Galerstein, Carolyn. "Images of Decadence in Visconti's 'Death in Venice.' " *Literature/Film Quarterly* 13.1 (1985): 29–34.

Glassco, David. "Films Out of Books: Bergman, Visconti and Mann." *Mosaic* 16.1–2 (1982): 165–73.

Glebe, William V. "The Artist's 'Disease' in Some of Thomas Mann's Earliest Tales." *Books Abroad* 39.3 (1965): 261–68.

Golden, Kenneth L. "Archetypes and Immoralists in Andre Gide and Thomas Mann." *College Literature* 15.2 (1988): 189–98.

Good, Graham. "The Death of Language in 'Death in Venice.' " *Mosaic* 5.3 (1971): 43–52.

Grossvogel, David I. "Visconti and the Too, Too Solid Flesh." *Diacritics* 1.2 (1971): 52–55.

Gullette, Margaret Morganroth. "The Exile of Adulthood: Pedophilia in the Midlife Novel." *Novel* 17.3 (1983): 215–32.

Hanson, W. P. "The Achievement of Chandos and Aschenbach." *New German Studies* 7 (1979): 41–57.

Heller, Peter. "Spheres of Ambiguity." *Dialectics and Nihilism: Essays on Lessing, Nietzsche, Mann, and Kafka.* Amherst: U of Massachusetts P, 1966. 149–226.

Hepworth, James B. "Tadzio-Sabazios: Notes on 'Death in Venice.' " *Western Humanities Review* 17 (1963): 172–75.

Hijiya-Kirschnereit, Irmela. "Thomas Mann's Short Novel 'Der Tod in Venedig' and Mishima Yukio's 'Kinjiki': A Comparison." *European Studies on Japan.* Eds. Ian Nish and Charles Dunn. Tenterden, Eng.: Norbury, 1979.

Jofen, Jean. "A Freudian Commentary on Thomas Mann's 'Death in Venice.' " *Journal of Evolutionary Psychology* 6.3–4 (1984): 238–47.

Kelley, Alice van Buren. "Von Aschenbach's *Phaedrus*: Platonic Allusion in 'Der Tod in Venedig.' " *Journal of English and Germanic Philology* 75 (1973): 228–40.

Kirchberger, Lida. " 'Death in Venice' and the Eighteenth Century." *Monatshefte* 58.5 (1966): 321–34.

Klawiter, Randolph J. "The Artist-Intellectual: In or Versus Society? A Dilemma." *Studies in German Literature of the Nineteenth and Twentieth Centuries: Festschrift for Frederic E. Coenen.* Ed. Siegfried Mews. Chapel Hill, NC: U North Carolina P 236–50.

Kraft, Quentin G. "Life Against 'Death in Venice.' " *Criticism* 7 (1965): 217–23.

Lehnert, Herbert. "Another Note on 'Motus Animi Continuus' and the Clenched-Fist Image in 'Der Tod in Venedig.' " *German Quarterly* 40 (1967): 452–53.

———. "Note on Mann's 'Der Tod in Venedig' and the 'Odyssey.' " *PMLA* 80 (1965): 306–7.

———. "Thomas Mann's Early Interest in Myth and Erwin Rohde's *Psyche.*" *PMLA* 79 (1964): 297–304.

———. "Thomas Mann's Interpretations of 'Der Tod in Venedig' and Their Reliability." *Rice University Studies* 50.4 (1964): 41–60.

Leppmann, Wolfgang. "Time and Place in 'Death in Venice.' " *German Quarterly* 48 (1975): 66–75.

Marson, E. L. *The Ascetic Artist: Prefigurations in Thomas Mann's 'Der Tod in Venedig.'* Bern: Lang, 1979.

Martin, John S. "Circean Seduction in Three Works by Thomas Mann." *Modern Language Notes* 78.4 (1963): 346–52.

Mazzela, Anthony J. " 'Death in Venice': Fiction and Film." *College Literature* 5 (1978): 183–94.

McClain, William H. "Wagnerian Overtones in 'Der Tod in Venedig.' " *Modern Language Notes* 79 (1964): 481–95.

McIntyre, Allan J. "Psychology and Symbol: Correspondences Between 'Heart of Darkness' and 'Death in Venice.' " *University of Hartford Studies in Literature* 7 (1975): 216–35.

McWilliams, J. R. "The Failure of a Repression: Thomas Mann's 'Tod in Venedig.' " *German Life & Letters* 20.3 (1966): 233–41.

Meyers, Jeffrey. "Mann and Musil: 'Death in Venice' and 'Young Törless.' " *Homosexuality and Literature, 1890–1930.* London: Athlone, U of London, 1977. 42–57.

Miller, R. D. *Beyond Anarchy: Studies in Modern Literature.* Harrogate, Eng.: Duchy, 1976.

Mitchell, Donald. " 'Death in Venice': The Dark Side of Perfection." *The Britten Companion.* Ed. Christopher Palmer. Cambridge: Cambridge UP, 1984.

Nicholls, R. A. "Death in Venice." *Nietzsche in the Early Work of Thomas Mann.* Ed. A. H. Rowbotham, et al. Berkeley: U of California P, 1955. 77–91.

Northcote-Bade, James. "The Background to the 'Liebestod' Plot Pattern in the Works of Thomas Mann." *The Germanic Review* 59 (1984): 11–18.

———. " 'Der Tod in Venedig' and 'Felix Krull': The Effect of the Interruption in the Composition of Thomas Mann's 'Felix Krull' Caused by 'Der Tod in Venedig.' " *Deutsche Vierteljahrsschaft für Literaturwissenschaft und Geistesgeschichte (DVLG)* 52 (19): 271–78.

Palmer, Christopher. "Towards a Genealogy of 'Death in Venice.' " *The Britten Companion.* Ed. Christopher Palmer. Cambridge: Cambridge UP, 1984.

Parkes, Ford B. "The Image of the Tiger in Thomas Mann's 'Tod in Venedig.' " *Studies in Twentieth Century Literature* 3 (1978): 73–83.

Phillips, Kathy J. "Conversion to Text, Initiation to Symbolism, in Mann's 'Der Tod in Venedig' and James' 'The Ambassadors.' " *Canadian Review of Comparative Literature* 6 (1979): 376–88.

Pike, Burton. "Thomas Mann and the Problematic Self." *Publications of the English Goethe Society* 37 (1967): 120–41.

Piper, Myfanwy. "Writing for Britten." *The Operas of Benjamin Britten.* Ed. David Herbert. New York: Columbia UP, 1979.

Plank, Robert. " 'Death in Venice': Tragedy or Mishap?" *University of Hartford Studies in Literature* 4 (1972): 95–103.

Porter, Andrew. "The Last Opera: 'Death in Venice.' " *The Operas of Benjamin Britten*. Ed. David Herbert. New York: Columbia UP, 1979.

Radcliff-Umstead, Douglas. "The Journey of Fatal Longing: Mann and Visconti." *Annali d'Italianistica* 6 (1988): 199–219.

Reed, Philip. "Aschenbach Becomes Mahler: Thomas Mann as Film," in *Benjamin Britten: Death in Venice*. Ed. Donald Mitchell. New York: Cambridge UP, 1987.

Rey, William. "Tragic Aspects of the Artist in Thomas Mann's Work." *Modern Language Quarterly* 19 (1958): 195–203.

Rockwood, Heidi. "Mann's 'Death in Venice.' " *Explicator* 39.4 (1981): 34.

Rockwood, Heidi M., and Robert J. R. Rockwood. "The Psychological Reality of Myth in 'Der Tod in Venedig.' " *Germanic Review* 59.4 (1984): 137–41.

Rohde, Erwin. *Psyche: The Cult of Souls and Belief in Immortality among the Greeks*. New York: Books for Libraries, 1972.

Rotkin, Charlotte. "Form and Function: The Art and Architecture of 'Death in Venice.' " *Midwest Quarterly* 29.4 (1988): 497–505.

———. "Oceanic Animals: Allegory in 'Death in Venice.' " *Papers on Language and Literature* 23.1 (1987): 84–88.

Singer, Irving. " 'Death in Venice': Visconti and Mann." *Modern Language Notes* 91 (1976): 1348–59.

Slochower, Harry. "Thomas Mann's 'Death in Venice.' " *American Imago* 26 (1969): 99–122.

Smith, Duncan. "The Education to Despair: Some Thoughts on 'Death in Venice.' " *Praxis* 1.1 (1975): 73–80.

Springer, Mary Doyle. "Degenerative 'Tragedy' in the Novella." *Forms of the Modern Novella*. Chicago: U of Chicago P, 1975. 102–5.

Stewart, Walter K. " 'Der Tod in Venedig': The Path to Insight." *Germanic Review* 53 (1978): 50–55.

Stelzmann, Rainulf A. "Thomas Mann's 'Death in Venice': Res et Imago." *Xavier Review* 3 (1982): 160–67.

Tarbox, Raymond. " 'Death in Venice': The Aesthetic Object as Dream Guide." *American Imago* 26 (1969): 123–44.

Traschen, Isadore. "The Uses of Myth in 'Death in Venice.' " *Modern Fiction Studies* 11 (1965): 165–79.

Vaget, Hans Rudolf. "Film and Literature: The Case of 'Death in Venice': Luchino Visconti and Thomas Mann." *German Quarterly* 53 (1980): 159–75.

Watts, Cedric. "The Protean Dionysus in Euripides' 'The Bacchae' and Mann's 'Death in Venice.' " *Studi dell'Istituto Linguistico* 3: 151–63.

Weiner, Marc A. "Silence, Sound, and Song in 'Der Tod in Venedig': A Study in Psycho-Social Repression." *Seminar* 23.2 (1987): 137–55.

Wiehe, Roger E. "Of Art and Death: Film and Fiction Versions of 'Death in Venice.' " *Literature/Film Quarterly* 16.3 (1988): 210–15.

Winkler, Michael. "Tadzio-Anastasios: A Note on 'Der Tod in Venedig.' " *Modern Language Notes* 92 (1977): 607–9.

Woodward, Anthony. "The Figure of the Artist in Thomas Mann's 'Tonio Kroger' and 'Death in Venice.' " *English Studies in Africa* 9 (1966): 158–67.

Woodward, Kathleen. "Youthfulness as a Masquerade." *Discourse* 11.1 (1988): 119–42.

Wootton, Carol. "The Lure of the Basilisk: Chopin's Music in Writings of Thomas Mann, John Galsworthy and Hermann Hesse." *Arcadia* 9 (1974): 23–38.

Wyatt, Frederick. "The Choice of Topic in Fiction: Risks and Rewards (A Comparison of Andre Gide's 'The Immoralist' and Thomas Mann's 'Death in Venice')." *Janus: Essays in Ancient and Modern Studies*. Ed. Louis L. Orlin. Ann Arbor: Center for Coordination of Ancient and Modern Studies, U of Michigan, 1975. 213–41.

Ziolkowski, Theodore. "The Telltale Teeth: Psychodontia to Sociodontia." *PMLA* 91 (1976): 9–22.

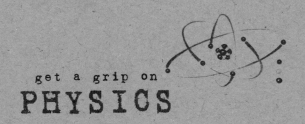

get a grip on
PHYSICS

Get a Grip on PHYSICS

JOHN GRIBBIN

BARNES
& NOBLE
BOOKS
NEW YORK

This edition published by Barnes & Noble, Inc.,
by arrangement with The Ivy Press Limited

2002 Barnes & Noble Books

M 10 9 8 7 6 5 4

ISBN: 0-7607-3748-7

This book was conceived, designed, and produced by The Ivy Press Limited,
The Old Candlemakers, West Street, Lewes, East Sussex BN7 2NZ, England

Creative Director	Peter Bridgewater
Publisher	Sophie Collins
Designer	Angela English
Editor	Peter Leek
Picture Research	Vanessa Fletcher
Illustrations	Andrew Kulman

Reproduction and printing in China by
Hong Kong Graphics and Printing Ltd.

CONTENTS

INTRODUCTION

THE OLD PHYSICS

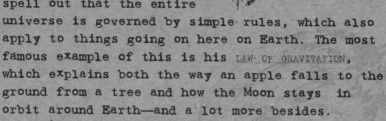

Isaac Newton

there's a rule for everything, and everything has its rule

* Modern physics—or, at least, the first phase of modern physics —began with Isaac Newton, in the second half of the 17th century. The most important thing Newton did was to spell out that the entire universe is governed by simple rules, which also apply to things going on here on Earth. The most famous example of this is his LAW OF GRAVITATION, which explains both the way an apple falls to the ground from a tree and how the Moon stays in orbit around Earth—and a lot more besides.

OLD AND NEW PHYSICS

Old physics is the stuff we learn in school, the kind of laws that apply to objects we can see and touch, like billiard balls or cars. New physics deals with things that are inaccessible to our senses, like atoms and black holes.

Newton's telescope

NEWTON AND GRAVITY

* *This law of nature is what is known as an* <u>INVERSE-SQUARE LAW</u>—*the force of attraction between two objects depends on their two masses multiplied together, divided by the square of the distance between them.* So if the same two objects are twice as far apart the force is reduced to a quarter, while if they're three times as far apart it is reduced to a ninth. And so on.

* But, for the moment, the law itself is less important than the fact that there is a unique law that describes the force of GRAVITATIONAL ATTRACTION operating between any two objects in the universe—

between a pencil on my desk and the cat in the next room, between the Moon and the Earth, or between two galaxies on opposite sides of the Universe, or even between my cat and a distant galaxy.

BEFORE NEWTON

✱ Before Newton came along, even scientifically minded people commonly believed the universe was governed by rules devised by the gods, or God. When, in 1609, **Johannes Kepler** realized that something made the planets stay in orbit around the Sun, he called it the "Holy Spirit Force," and nobody laughed at him for doing so. *The universe was seemingly at the mercy of mysterious and incomprehensible forces, which might change from day to day or from place to place.*

Newton's cradle

KEY WORDS

GRAVITY:
the force of attraction between two masses
GRAVITATION:
the influence any object exerts on other objects in the universe simply by having mass

Johannes Kepler (1571–1630)
German astronomer who discovered the laws of planetary motion, which helped Newton develop his theory of gravity. Kepler used observations of the planets compiled by **Tycho Brahe** (1546–1601). Before joining Brahe in Prague, he trained for a career in the Church, then worked as a teacher of mathematics at a Protestant seminary in Graz.

7

Isaac Newton (1642–1727)

Newton was active in many fields. He studied alchemy (still almost respectable at that time) and theology, and served as a member of parliament (his knighthood was for political work, not science) and as master of the Royal Mint and president of the Royal Society. Newton was very secretive about his work, and often got involved in huge arguments with other scientists about who had thought of an idea first (usually he had thought of it, but hadn't bothered to tell anyone!). His great work in physics was completed before he was 30, but only published in 1687, at the urging of Edmond Halley. In the 1690s Newton suffered a mental breakdown, and although he recovered sufficiently to lead a normal life, he did no more scientific work.

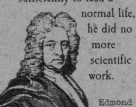

Edmond Halley

A CLOCKWORK UNIVERSE

* After Newton, the universe was perceived in a very different way—as a kind of cosmic clockwork mechanism, running predictably in accordance with laws of physics that could be determined from experiments here on Earth. The laws might be God-given (Newton thought they were), but they were now seen as being the same everywhere and at all times.

tick
tick
tick

these laws are God-given

God

Man

Newton identified the laws of the Universe

I'm just so stressed!

Newton suffered a breakdown from overwork

FUNDAMENTAL LAWS

✱ *The predictability of the Newtonian universe was based on three other fundamental laws discovered by Newton.* Known as Newton's LAWS OF MECHANICS (or laws of motion), they are spelled out in his great book *Philosophiae Naturalis Principia Mathematica (The Mathematical Principles of Natural Philosophy)*, usually referred to simply as the Principia.

✱ *These three laws formed the basis of physics for the next 200 years—and still suffice to explain the way things behave in the everyday world, even though some of the things explained by them (such*

as the flight of a jet aircraft, or the journey of a space probe to the planet Jupiter) were undreamed of by Newton himself.

Newton's first law of mechanics

The first of Newton's three laws of mechanics immediately shows how physicists often have to discount "common sense" in order to get a grip on the way the world works. *It insists that any object—by implication, any object in the entire universe—either stays still or keeps moving in a straight line unless some force is applied to the object.* The standing still part is no problem, as far as common sense is concerned. Here on the surface of Earth most things do stay still, unless they are given a push. But if given a push, they certainly don't keep moving in a straight line for ever. They slow down and come to a halt.

> ### KEY WORDS
>
> **MECHANICS:**
> the branch of physics that deals with the way things move and the forces that make them do so

ON AND ON AND ON...

this could go on forever

* The first step in Newton's insight was to realize that things only come to a halt because they are being influenced by an outside force - the force of friction. Things stop moving because they are rubbing against other things, even if the other things are only molecules of air brushing past.

Galileo realized the balls would keep on rolling unless something stopped them

UNSTOPPABLE

Imagine something sitting in empty space then given a quick push (a fairly obvious thing to imagine today, in the age of space flight, but a huge leap of the imagination in the 17th century). It will keep moving in a straight line forever unless some other force acts on it.

...FOR EVER

* This business about friction bringing things to a halt was, in fact, already partly understood before Newton came onto the scene. In particular, **Galileo Galilei** had realized that things would keep moving forever if no external force acted on them. He came to this conclusion after carrying out a series of experiments in which balls were rolled down inclined planes. *The balls rolled off toward the horizon, and Galileo realized that without friction they would keep rolling forever.*

who knows where this ball will end up

...OR ROUND AND ROUND

* At this point Galileo made a daring but erroneous extrapolation. Like all educated people of his day, he knew that Earth is round. So an object that keeps moving toward the horizon forever must be following a circular path around the surface of Earth, and will eventually end up back where it started from. A least it would do if there were no mountains or other obstructions in its way. *This led Galileo to believe there was a fundamental law of nature which said that, left to their own devices, things move in circles.*

Galileo was tried for proclaiming that Earth went round the Sun

Galileo Galilei

Galileo Galilei (1564–1642)

Galileo was the first person to use a telescope to observe the stars and planets scientifically. He studied medicine at the University of Pisa, but dropped out to become a scientist. His astronomical observations made him famous, and he was one of the first scientists to publicly support the idea that Earth goes around the Sun. As a result, when 69 years old and in frail health, he was tried for heresy, forced to recant under threat of torture, and confined to house arrest for the rest of his life. The publicity of his trial in Roman Catholic Rome helped to ensure that his ideas were taken up in Protestant northern Europe.

CIRCULAR THINKING

WOW!
it's going around
in circles

orbiting spaceships
follow a circular path

* Don't believe everything you see on TV. Those spaceships that appear to be steering a straight course are actually in orbit around Earth, moving along more or less circular paths. And the things moving "in straight lines" inside the spaceships—that is, in straight lines relative to the walls of the spaceship—are also circling Earth.

Heretical thinking

Nicolaus Copernicus (1473–1543) was a Polish astronomer who was the first scientist to promote the idea that the Earth goes around the Sun.

Nicolaus
Copernicus

NEW, EXCITING, AND HERETICAL

* Galileo would have quite happily accepted those TV pictures as evidence in favor of his argument. In fact, the idea that circular motion was the natural order of things would have seemed particularly convincing to Galileo and the better educated of his contemporaries because of a relatively new, exciting, and (literally) heretical idea, proposed by **Nicolaus Copernicus**, that the planets—including Earth—move in circles around the Sun.

ALL BECAUSE OF GRAVITY

* *When Newton said that the natural order of things in the universe is for objects to move in straight lines, he had to explain why the planets stay in orbit around the Sun and don't fly off into space.* This is where his law of gravity came into the picture, not only explaining how the Sun maintains a grip on its family of planets, but also why the orbits of the planets around the Sun are—as Johannes Kepler had discovered, in 1609, to the embarrassment of Galileo—actually elliptical, not circular.

* *It is all thanks to Newton's inverse-square law of gravity. Stated more fully, this law says that the force of* <u>ATTRACTION</u> *operating between two masses is equal to the two masses multiplied together, all divided by the square of the distance between them (hence "inverse square") and then multiplied by a constant, known as the constant of gravity, which is the same everywhere in the universe and at all times.*

* The only way to find out the constant of gravity, which tells you the strength of the force of gravity, is by experiments—but once you know this constant everything else is easy to calculate.

Saturn

GRAVITY SIMPLIFIED

The simplest way to picture the effect of gravity is to imagine a stone, tied to a string, being whirled around and around in a circle. The analogy isn't exact, because the stone is moving in a circle, not an ellipse. But the force acting along the string is just like the force of gravity: it pulls the stone inward and keeps it "in orbit." If the string breaks, the stone will fly off in a straight line, at a tangent to its "orbit."

NEWTON'S SECOND LAW

* Newton's second law of mechanics also comes into the picture. The second law tells you how much the motion of an object is affected by a force applied to it. It says that a force applied to a mass causes an acceleration.

ACCELERATION AND VELOCITY

* ACCELERATION *means a change in the* VELOCITY *of an object.* And velocity—which is speed measured in a certain direction—has two properties. When the velocity changes, it may mean that the speed changes, as when you put the brakes on and bring a car to a halt in a straight line. Or it may mean that the direction of motion changes, as when you turn the wheel and take the car around a bend (or when a stone tied to a string whizzes around in a circle).

* *So a change in velocity may involve a change in speed without any change in direction, or it may involve a change in direction without any change in speed, or it may involve a bit of both. They are all accelerations.*

FIRE!

if a cannonball is fired powerfully enough, it will travel right around the planet...

14

CURVING CANNONBALLS

* *Newton himself made an analogy with a superpowerful cannon fired from the top of a tall mountain. Ignoring the effects of friction, imagine firing cannonballs off horizontally with increasingly powerful blasts from the cannon.*

* The first ball flies a little way toward the horizon and falls to the ground, tugged toward the center of Earth by gravity (it actually follows a curving, parabolic, path from the mouth of the cannon to the ground). The next ball travels a little farther before gravity is able to pull it to the ground, and so on.

* *But remember that the Earth is not flat – it curves away under the flying cannonball, which is, of course, always being accelerated toward the center of Earth. Because the surface of Earth is curved, the cannonballs fly farther over it than they would if Earth was flat.* (In fact, firing cannonballs off like this and measuring how far they travel would be a way of proving that Earth is not flat!)

Good shot!

If the cannon is capable of producing a powerful enough blast, the flying cannonball will travel right around the planet and hit the rear of the cannon. It will have gone into orbit. *Because it moves forward and falls sideways all the time, the sideways fall is exactly enough to keep it in orbit—in a state that is sometimes described as "free fall".*

DUCK!

...and hit the rear of the cannon

Moon

CANNONBALLS AND THE MOON

✱ Like the cannonball, the Moon is always falling and always accelerating, even though its speed in its orbit does not vary significantly.

The tug of gravity

The orbit of the Moon around Earth is a good example of acceleration at constant speed. The Moon would "like" to keep moving in a straight line, but every time it moves forward, even a tiny bit, the force of Earth's gravity tugs it sideways, deflecting it from a straight course. This constant sideways tugging keeps the Moon in its orbit.

THAT APPLE AND THE MOON

✱ Newton's second law says that when a force (F) is applied to a mass (m) it causes an acceleration that can be expressed as
$a = F/m$. *The bigger the force applied to the mass, or the smaller the mass subjected to the same force, the bigger the acceleration produced.*

✱ This second law of motion combined with the inverse-square law of gravity explains both the acceleration produced in an apple falling from a tree at the surface of Earth and the acceleration of the Moon falling sideways in its orbit around Earth. *In both cases, the cause is the same—the Earth's gravity.*

NEWTON'S THIRD LAW

✱ Newton's third (and last) law of motion can also be understood by thinking about what happens when a cannon is fired. The cannonball goes out of the mouth of the cannon and off into

come here... you're not getting away...

Earth's gravity keeps
the Moon in orbit

the distance, while the cannon itself rolls backward in the opposite direction. Similarly, when you fire a rifle you feel a kick as the rifle recoils.

✱ *Using the word "action" where we would probably say "force," Newton pointed out that for every* <u>ACTION</u> *there is an equal and opposite* <u>REACTION</u>. A masterpiece of brevity, this law contains a large amount of information.

First, it states that if you hit something, it hits back. This is quite easy to test. If you thump your fist on the table you can feel the reaction, quite unambiguously. The law also says that the action and the reaction are simultaneous.

FOR EVERY ACTION THERE IS AN EQUAL AND OPPOSITE REACTION.

Newton's third law
of motion

Newton's third law also points out that the reaction is equal and opposite to the initial force. In spite of this, the cannon only recoils a little bit, while the cannonball goes off into the distance—because the same force is being applied to a more massive object, and the acceleration produced is, remember, inversely proportional to the mass it is applied to. But the forces themselves (the action and reaction) always cancel out exactly.

17

ACTION AND REACTION

* There's more to action and reaction than you might think. The equality of action and reaction applies all the time: to yourself and everything around you. You are being pulled downward by Earth's gravity, which gives you your weight—but you are also pulling Earth upward by the same amount.

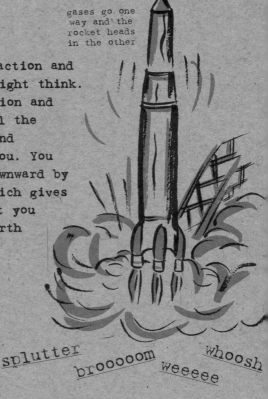

gases go one way and the rocket heads in the other

How a rocket works

Newton's law of action and reaction also explains how a rocket works. The rocket motor fires exhaust gases out in one direction, and this produces a reaction that pushes the rocket in the other direction. There is no need for the exhaust gases to have anything to push against, which is why rockets work in the vacuum of space. **All that matters is that hot gases are fired one way, and the rocket heads the other.**

splutter brooooom weeeee whoosh

THE EARTH MOVES?

* If you were falling toward the ground from the top of a tall building, *the Earth would also be moving up to meet you* (but only by a tiny amount, since the acceleration depends inversely on the mass).

* *When you stand still on the ground, your weight is a force pressing downward on the ground, which responds by pushing upward with an equal and opposite force, keeping you in place.*

Albert Einstein

THE FUNDAMENTAL THINGS APPLY...

✱ As the foregoing examples show, Newton's laws are still the fundamental principles on which physics operates for everyday purposes—on the scale of human beings, or even planets and stars.

✱ But on a much larger scale—when we are talking about very massive objects, or the whole universe—Newton's law of gravity is not quite good enough and we have to use the ideas developed by Albert Einstein in the 20th century, in his general theory of relativity. On a much smaller scale (smaller than atoms), Newton's laws of mechanics are not quite good enough either and we have to use another theory developed in the 20th century, quantum mechanics.

FROM STARS TO ATOMS

These two great ideas, relativity and quantum mechanics, form the basis of the new physics. But it is a sign of just how powerful Newtonian physics is that it applies very accurately to the behavior of everything from stars to atoms, even though hardly anything was known about atoms when Newton was alive. *Indeed, one of the greatest achievements of Newtonian mechanics is the way in which it has been used to explain the behavior of gases, liquids, and solids in terms of atoms and molecules, which move around and collide with one another in perfect obedience to Newton's laws.* This second flowering of Newtonian theory happened in the second half of the 19th century—two centuries after he wrote the *Principia*.

it looks like the ground is moving toward me

CHAPTER 1

here is a model
of an atom, or is
it the jawbreaker
I bought
yesterday?

ATOMS AND MOLECULES

* An atom is the smallest unit
of an element that can exist.
The most appropriate image of
it is a tiny hard sphere, like
a minute bowling ball. Some
substances in the everyday world
(such as pure gold) are made of
only one kind of atom. A pure-
gold ring, for example, simply
contains billions and billions
of gold atoms.

H_2O

LINKING UP

* In some elements, identical ATOMS join
together to form MOLECULES. This happens
in the case of hydrogen, where each
molecule is made up of two hydrogen
atoms and is written as H_2. Other
substances, such as water, are made of two
or more different types of atom combined
with one another to form molecules. The
symbol for a hydrogen atom is H and the
symbol for an oxygen atom is O—so, since
two hydrogen atoms combine with one
oxygen atom to form a molecule of water,
the symbol for a molecule of water is H_2O.

* When they are on
their own, oxygen atoms
also like to link up with
one another—so that
the most common form
of oxygen, including the

H_2O

Tragic genius

Austrian physicist **Ludwig
Boltzmann** (1844–1906)
played a key role in
developing the kinetic
theory of gases, thereby
helping to establish,
albeit indirectly, that
atoms are real. He
became clinically
depressed, partly because
the atomic theory came
under attack in his native
Austria, and killed
himself in 1906—just a
year after Einstein's work
had, unknown to
Boltzmann, proved the
existence of atoms.

stuff we all breathe, is O_2. *For the moment, though, all that matters is that these atoms and molecules can all be pictured as tiny balls, constantly in motion, bouncing off one another.*

he's so kinetic...

the word kinetic comes from the Greek for motion

HOW GASES BEHAVE

★ The people who worked out the details of this image of a gas as molecules in motion were **James Clerk Maxwell**, in Britain, and **Ludwig Boltzmann**, in Germany, in the mid-19th century. They didn't just speculate about this image of little balls bouncing off one another, but instead they developed a fully worked-out kinetic theory of gases founded upon Newton's laws.

★ *The word "kinetic" comes from the Greek for motion, and according to Maxwell and Boltzmann's theory the pressure that a gas applies to the walls of its container is explained in terms of action and reaction (Newton's third law again)—each atom or molecule collides with the wall and bounces off, giving a push to the wall as it does so. This happens time and again, as the atoms rebound off each other and bounce back to hit the walls again.*

KEY WORDS

ATOM:
the smallest unit of a chemical element that can take part in a chemical reaction

MOLECULE:
two or more atoms of the same element or different elements held together by their chemical attraction

KINETIC THEORY:
theory describing the behavior of matter in terms of the movement of its component atoms and molecules

21

MOLECULES IN MOTION

✱ A key feature of the kinetic theory is that it explains heat simply in terms of the motion of the molecules involved. If you heat up a container full of gas, the molecules move faster—so they give a bigger kick to the walls of the container each time they hit them, and the pressure increases. All of this was described mathematically, using equations (based on Newton's laws) that made it possible to calculate, for example, how much the temperature of a container full of gas would go up if it was heated by a particular amount.

mom, all the molecules are jiggling around again!

heating a solid breaks the bonds holding the molecules together

SOLID TO LIQUID

✱ The kinetic theory also explains the differences between solids, liquids, and gases. In a solid, the atoms and molecules are held together—we now know, by electric forces—but jiggle around slightly as if they were running on the spot. This is a bit like a restless theater audience shifting in their seats during a dull play.
✱ When the solid is heated, the molecules jiggle around more and more

steam engine

(which is why the solid expands), until they have generated enough kinetic energy (energy arising from motion) to break the bonds that hold them in place and are able to slide past one another relatively freely. **The solid has now become a liquid.**

LIQUID TO GAS

✳ In a liquid, the molecules are still more or less in contact with one another, but constantly brush past each other. You might make an analogy with the jostling crowd of theater-goers streaming out of the auditorium after the show.

it's going to explode!

gas molecules have enough energy to move freely past each other

✳ Carry on heating the liquid, and at a critical temperature the molecules will have so much energy that they fly freely past one another and can bounce off each other, ricocheting wildly, like balls in a crazy pinball machine. **The liquid has now become a gas.**

Piston power

If you imagine not a fixed container of gas but a cylinder fitted with a piston, you can see how the flying molecules in the gas will push the piston outward. If the piston is held in place by a force pushing inward, the hotter the gas inside, the more force you will have to apply to the piston. This classic example of Newton's laws at work relates directly to the branch of science known as THERMODYNAMICS (the study of heat and motion). Thermodynamics was hugely important in the 19th century, because at the heart of the Industrial Revolution were steam engines, which were driven by pistons.

steam

heat

piston

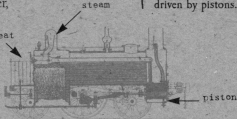

I hope I don't hit anything

THE ARROW OF TIME

There's something curious about many of the experiments described so far. *Newton's laws of motion do not take any account of the direction of the flow of time.* It may *seem* as if there's an "arrow of time" involved in Newtonian mechanics, because we can talk about some events occurring "before" or "after" others. But think about the simplest Newtonian interaction, when two billiard balls (or two atoms) move toward one another, collide, and move apart. If you reversed the whole process, the backwards-in-time collision would still conform to Newton's laws of physics. *In fact, if you made a movie of such a collision and ran it backward through a cine projector, the audience wouldn't suspect there was anything wrong.*

SEQUENCE AND CONSEQUENCE

✳ Something peculiar happens when you deal with large numbers of atoms and molecules. Although every collision between those individual molecules happens in accordance with Newton's laws, the interactions of all the molecules, taken as a whole, follow what we recognize as chronological time. It doesn't look peculiar, because it is what we are used to in everyday life—but in terms of Newtonian physics it really is very strange indeed.

...now boys, heat flows naturally from a hot object to a cool one...

the flow of energy from hot objects to cool ones is a fundamental principle of the universe

HALFWAY IN OR HALFWAY OUT?

★ Think about that piston with the cylinder full of hot gas. As the gas pushes the piston, it moves it farther and farther out of the cylinder. This takes energy away from the molecules of the gas, so they move more slowly—they cool down. This is a fundamental feature of the universe: heat flows naturally from a hot object to a cool one. To restore heat to the gas in the cylinder you would have to push the piston in, using energy to do so.

★ If you saw a photograph of the piston pushed deep into the cylinder and another showing it much farther out, you would know immediately which photo was taken first. When there are lots of molecules and atoms involved, nature has a built-in arrow of time.

Half full or half empty?

Instead of a smoothly sliding piston, imagine a box divided into two halves by a wall, with gas in one side and a vacuum in the other. If you open a trapdoor in the dividing wall, the gas will spread so that it fills both halves of the box evenly (and it will cool down as it does so). No matter how long you wait, the gas will never, of its own accord, all move back into one half of the box. Again, if you saw a photograph of the box with all the gas in one half, and another photo showing the gas evenly spread through both halves of the box, you would know which photo was taken first. *Nobody fully understands how the arrow of time emerges when interactions that individually take no notice of it are put together, but it is a fundamental feature of the physical world.*

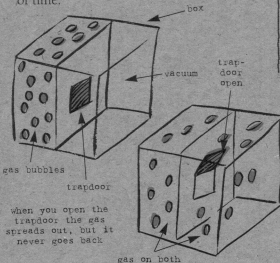

box

vacuum

trap-door open

gas bubbles

trapdoor

when you open the trapdoor the gas spreads out, but it never goes back

gas on both sides

DISORDER:
In thermodynamics, disorder doesn't just mean a mess, but a lack of pattern. A black-and-white chessboard has order. The same quantity of paint making the board a uniform gray is disordered.

ENTROPY:
A measure of the amount of disorder in a system being studied, or in the entire universe. The entropy of the universe always increases.

THE FIRST
LAW OF
THERMODYNAMICS

This is in effect a preamble to the second law. It states that heat and work are two facets of the same thing, energy, and that the total amount of energy in a closed system stays the same.

THERMODYNAMICS

* This business about the arrow of time and about heat always flowing from a hotter object to a cooler one is part of a law that is regarded as the most fundamental law in the whole of physics—the second law of thermodynamics.

THE SECOND LAW OF THERMODYNAMICS

* The second law was established by the work of **William Thompson, 1st Baron Kelvin** (1824–1907), in England, and **Rudolf Clausius** (1822–88), in Germany, early in the 1850s. *It can be summarized in three words: "things wear out." Or, to put it in slightly more technical language, the amount of* <u>DISORDER</u> *in the universe always increases.*

Lord Kelvin

And if you want to get more technical still, the scientific term for disorder is <u>ENTROPY</u>—*so you can simply say "entropy increases." Just these two words sum up the most fundamental law of science.*

INCREASING DISORDER

★ The classic example of disorder (or entropy) increasing in this way is when you put an ice cube in a glass of water and watch it melt. The water with the ice floating in it has a kind of structure, a pattern. But when the ice cube melts (an example of heat flowing from the hotter object into the cooler object), there is just a featureless, amorphous, uniform blob of water. *And again, the arrow of time appears—you often see ice cubes melting in glasses of water, but you never see a glass of water in which ice cubes appear spontaneously while the rest of the water warms up, even though that would not require any input of energy and so would not violate the first law of thermodynamics.*

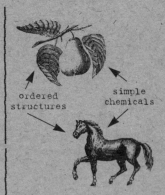

ordered structures

simple chemicals

More or less entropy?

One thing that seems to violate the second law of thermodynamics is life itself. Plants and animals are very complicated ordered structures, built out of simple chemicals, that create order (thereby decreasing entropy) on a local scale. They are only able to do this with the aid of a large input of energy, which comes, ultimately, from sunlight. But the amount of order created by life on Earth in this way is more than compensated for by the amount of disorder (entropy) being created inside the Sun—by the processes that release energy in the form of sunlight. *In the universe at large, entropy always increases.*

this is better than watching paint dry

as the ice melts, order is replaced by disorder

Thomas Young

THOMAS YOUNG (1773-1829)

A child prodigy, Young could read at the age of two, absorbed Latin and Greek as a child, and mastered several Middle Eastern languages before his teens. He had read and understood all Newton's work before he was 17. After qualifying as a doctor (in 1796), he became interested in optics through work on the human eye. As a result, Young carried out a series of experiments involving sound and light, and in 1800 published a book proposing (among other things) that light travels as a wave. He was also fascinated by Egyptology, and was instrumental in deciphering the Rosetta Stone.

NEW LIGHT ON LIGHT

* As we shall see, the new physics offers at least one way of explaining problems such as entropy and where the arrow of time comes from. But before we get to grips with them, there's an important piece of old physics to consider—the physics of light.

Young spent his childhood reading clever books

A KEY CONCEPT

* The behavior of light proved to be the key to the two great revolutions that swept through physics in the first decades of the 20th century—the quantum revolution and the relativity revolution. Ironically, though, these two breakthroughs occurred just after the theory of light had been put on what seemed to be a secure footing by the physicists of the 19th century—and by two of them in particular, **Michael Faraday** and **James Clerk Maxwell**.

WAVES, NOT CANNONBALLS

* Isaac Newton had had the idea that light is like a stream of tiny cannonballs, flying through space and bouncing off things. This tied in with his laws of motion, so it was a natural model for him to adopt.

* Then at the beginning of the 19th century experiments by Thomas Young in England and Augustin Fresnel in France showed that light actually moves through space (or any transparent medium) in the form of a wave. The clearest proof of this is a famous experiment used by Young, known as "Young's double-slit experiment" or "the experiment with two holes." *It will be very important when we come to the new physics, so it is worth spelling out in detail what Young discovered.*

Augustin Fresnel invented a special lens for lighthouses

hmmm.. I wonder what light really is

Politics and optics

A civil engineer, Augustin Fresnel (1788–1827) became head of the public works department in Paris under Napoleon. He was also interested in optics and invented a special lens for lighthouses. When Napoleon was exiled to Elba, Fresnel supported the restoration of the monarchy, thus showing a good eye for the main chance. Alas for Fresnel, Napoleon came back, and he was placed under house arrest in Normandy, where he developed his wave theory of light. However, Waterloo brought Fresnel back into the open and he went back to engineering.

THE EXPERIMENT WITH TWO HOLES

* If you take a bright
light and shine it on a
piece of cardboard
with a tiny hole in
it, the light passes
through the hole and
spreads out on the
other side. Now, you
put a second piece of
cardboard with two holes (tiny
pinholes) in it in the path of the
light spreading out from the first
hole. The light spreads out from
both of the holes in the second card. Finally, you
put a third piece of cardboard in the path of the
light spreading out from the two holes, and look at
the pattern of light and shade that is made on this
final screen (of course, you have to do this in a
darkened room, in order to see the pattern at all).
You get a pattern of alternating bright and dark
bands (light and shade). This can be explained
if the light is traveling in the form of a wave,
very much like ripples on a pond.

all you need
is some
cardboard and
a flashlight

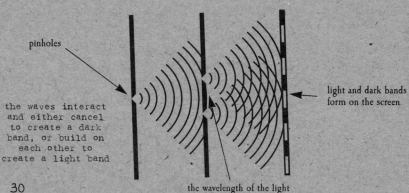

pinholes

the waves interact
and either cancel
to create a dark
band, or build on
each other to
create a light band

light and dark bands
form on the screen

the wavelength of the light
from each hole is the same

MAKING RIPPLES

✳ The waves from each of the two holes in the intermediate piece of cardboard start out in step with one another, because they come from the same single hole in the first piece of cardboard. They spread out like ripples on a pond produced by dropping two stones in at the same time, and they interfere with one another to make a more complicated ripple pattern.

light waves interfere with each other like ripples on a pond

PEAKS AND TROUGHS

✳ Where the waves overlap, in some places the peaks in the waves from each set of ripples coincide, so you get an extra high peak—a bright stripe on the far screen. In some places, the peak of one wave coincides with the trough of the other wave, so they cancel each other out and there is no light on the far screen—a dark stripe. And if two troughs coincide, that also produces a bright stripe, because the waves are adding together, even though they are adding in the opposite direction.

stop making it ripple it's making me sick

electricity and magnetism are a single force

Faraday identified electromagnetism

FARADAY AND ELECTROMAGNETISM

* We all have some idea of the nature of electricity and magnetism from practical experience. The experiments carried out by Michael Faraday, beginning in the 1820s, however, demonstrated that electricity and magnetism are actually a single force (electromagnetism) that shows two different facets to the world, depending on which way you look at it.

magnetic force

MOTORS AND MAGNETS

The field of force

Faraday was not content with discovering the links between electricity and magnetism and showing how they could be put to practical use. He tried to explain how the effects worked, and in doing so invented the scientific concept of THE FIELD OF FORCE (often referred to simply as "the field").

* *A moving electric charge (an electric current) produces a magnetic field, which is the reason why when electricity flows along a wire, the needle of an ordinary magnetic compass placed near the wire is deflected.* In fact, this is the principle of the electric motor, in which varying electric currents moving along wires make magnets with drive shafts attached to them spin around in circles.

MAGNETS AND DYNAMOS

* *A moving magnet, on the other hand, makes an electric current flow in a nearby conductor.* So if you wave a magnet around near a piece of wire, electricity flows in the wire. This is the principle behind the electric generator, or dynamo, in which magnets being whirled around mechanically on the end of a drive shaft make electric currents flow along wires. *A dynamo is, in effect, an electric motor in reverse.*

Michael Faraday

waving a magnet near a wire creates an electric current

MICHAEL
FARADAY
(1791-1867)

A self-taught genius, Faraday was the son of a blacksmith and received only a rudimentary education. While apprenticed to a bookbinder, he became fascinated by science, thanks to reading entries in a copy of the *Encyclopaedia Britannica* that he was working on. Through night school and wider reading he became more and more knowledgeable. Then got a job as assistant to Humphry Davy at the Royal Institution, where he eventually succeeded Davy as Director. In addition to his work on electromagnetism and field theory, Faraday made important contributions to chemistry and served as a scientific adviser to the government. A member of a strict religious sect, he was extremely modest, declining a knighthood and the chance to be president of the Royal Society.

33

THE FORCE AND THE FIELD

* The best way to get to grips with what is meant by a field of force is the same way that Faraday himself got hold of the idea—by means of the following experiment.

AN INTRIGUING WEB

* Take an ordinary bar magnet and place a piece of paper on top of the magnet, then sprinkle iron filings on top of the paper. If you tap the paper gently, the filings arrange themselves in a series of curving lines, or arcs, linking the north and south magnetic poles of the magnet. *These lines represent the field of force of the magnet, a kind of (usually) invisible spider's web stretching out all around the magnet. Faraday deduced that electric charges, as well as magnets, have their own field of force.*

* Dynamo and electric motor effects result when the LINES OF FORCE cut across each other, making a complex web of interactions in the FIELD.

MAY THE FORCE BE WITH YOU!

34

you can see the lines of force if
you hold a magnet underneath a
piece of paper with some iron
filings sprinkled on it

For example, it is because magnetic lines of force are moving through the wire that the electricity is forced to flow in a dynamo, even though the moving magnet itself never touches the wire.

FARADAY'S FIELD THEORY

✳ Having worked out the nature of electromagnetism, Faraday took his thinking a step further. He suggested that the field idea ought to apply to the only other force known to 19th-century science, gravity. *He pictured the Sun, for example, sitting in a web of force lines stretching out across space, and holding the planets—including Earth— in its grip.*

Responding to the field

Let's see how Faraday's field theory applies to Earth. *All that matters is the nature of the field of force at the point in space where Earth happens to be.* Suppose you could remove Earth from its orbit around the Sun. If, once the field had settled down, you were able to drop Earth back into its orbit (at the correct speed and so on), it would immediately feel the force and follow its orbit again. It wouldn't fly off into space before the Sun noticed it was there. Nor would it have to wait for a signal from the Sun instructing it how to move. The field is already there, in space, providing information about the existence of the Sun. All Earth has to do is to respond to the field at the point in space where Earth happens to be.

Earth is held
in its orbit
by the Sun's
field of
force

AHEAD OF HIS TIME

* Faraday's ultimate extension of his field theory was heady stuff, which his Victorian contemporaries didn't really understand. In fact, with these speculations he was nearly 100 years ahead of his time. In contrast, his ideas about electric and magnetic fields spreading out from their sources were taken up almost immediately.

THE FIELD ITSELF

In the 1840s Faraday took his thinking further still. *He suggested that—instead of thinking of magnets as the source of the magnetic field, electric charges as the source of the electric field, and massive objects like the Sun (or an apple, or Earth) as the source of the gravitational field—the field itself was what really mattered.* The Universe, he concluded, is full of fields of one kind or another. And things like magnets, electric charges, and lumps of matter are simply places where the appropriate fields get tangled up in certain ways.

this is simply a place where fields get tangled up

Faraday was nearly 100 years ahead of his time

FARADAY AND MAXWELL

* The person who took up these ideas was James Clerk Maxwell, who turned them into a complete, worked out mathematical theory of electromagnetism (published in 1864), and along the way, almost accidentally, explained the nature of light—or so it seemed at the time.

* It was Faraday who first suggested that light might be produced by some sort of vibration in the lines of force associated with charged particles and

Maxwell developed a
color theory of light
still used in TV design

James Clerk Maxwell (1831–79)

When, at the age of 10, Maxwell went to school in Edinburgh, his country-bumpkin ways earned him the nickname "Dafty." Nevertheless, he became a professor in Aberdeen, then in 1860 moved to King's College, London. Following his father's death, in 1865, Maxwell retired to look after the family land. In 1871 he was persuaded to head the new Cavendish Laboratory in Cambridge. He had just established it as a scientific center of excellence when he died, at the age of 48. In addition to his work on electromagnetism, he proved that the rings of Saturn had to be made up of myriads of tiny moons, developed a color theory of light still used in TV design, and made major contributions to thermodynamics and statistical mechanics.

magnets—with the lines vibrating or twanging, rather like plucked violin strings, and with light being transmitted by waves running along the lines of force, outward from the source. But, despite all his success as a practical physicist and experimenter, and his remarkable insight into the nature of fields, Faraday was no good at mathematics and he was never able to convert this vague suggestion about the nature of light into a comprehensive theory.

Viol

James Clerk Maxwell

Maxwell's equations
tell you
all you
need to know

MAXWELL'S EQUATIONS

* For all practical purposes, the set of equations that Maxwell came up with is valid for every electric or magnetic phenomenon that you are likely to come into direct contact with in everyday life at the beginning of the 21st century, except perhaps for the occasional laser beam. They describe all of the aspects of electromagnetism that are covered by the description "classical" physics—meaning everything that does not involve quantum effects.

Measuring the speed of light

The speed of light was first measured by Danish astronomer **Olaus Roemer** (1644–1710) from an analysis of the eclipses of the moons of Jupiter in 1675. Ground-based measurements became accurate in the 1860s, when French physicist **Léon Foucault** (1819–68) developed a technique in which a beam of light was bounced between mirrors, giving a long enough path for its "flight time" to be measured.

FOUR FUNDAMENTAL FORMULAS

* There are just four of these equations. Known simply as Maxwell's equations, together they describe all classical electric and magnetic phenomena—the dynamo effect, how electric motors work, why compass needles point north (as long as they are not close to a wire carrying an electric current, or to a permanent magnet), how big the force between two electric charges of a certain size a certain distance apart is, and a whole lot more.

* *Every problem involving electricity and*

compass

magnetism known at the time could be explained using Maxwell's equations.

ANSWERS TO EVERYTHING

✱ This was a huge and wonderful leap forward for science, which put Maxwell almost on a par with Newton. After all, Newton's laws described the workings of everything in the known world of physics of the mid-19th century except electromagnetism—and Maxwell's

together we can explain everything about physics

Newton

Maxwell

equations explained everything there was to explain (at that time) about electromagnetism. Together, Newton and Maxwell explained everything known to physical science.

AN UNEXPECTED BY-PRODUCT

The greatest and most wonderful thing about Maxwell's equations was the way that a description of light fell out of them without being asked for. Among the many things that the equations describe are the properties of electromagnetic waves— ripples in the electromagnetic fields. And the most important property of these waves is the speed with which they travel. A couple of numbers, specifying the strength of the electric and magnetic parts of the interaction, had to be put into the equations from experimental observations and measurements. **But once those numbers were fed into them, the equations specified, uniquely and precisely, the speed with which electromagnetic waves must move. That speed turned out to be exactly the same as the speed of light, which by the 1860s had been measured very accurately.**

WAVES AND WAVELENGTHS

✳ What distinguishes the different varieties of electromagnetic wave from one another is the wavelength of the radiation—just as different musical notes (which are all sound waves) are distinguishable by their different wavelengths.

all this jiggling is making me feel real weird

as you move the rope up and down, waves travel along it

Electromagnetic Waves

Visible light, radio waves, the infrared heat you feel as the warmth radiating from a radiator, the microwaves that cook the food in your microwave oven, Xrays, and even bursts of gamma radiation from distant galaxies are all varieties of electromagnetic radiation. All of them are described by Maxwell's equations.

LIKE A JIGGLING ROPE

✳ *The best way to get a mental image of how electromagnetic waves travel through space is to picture waves rippling along a tightly stretched rope.* If you tie one end of a rope to a fence post and hold the other end in your hand, you can make ripples run along the rope by jiggling the end you are holding up and down. The energy that makes the ripples move along the rope comes from the work you are doing by moving the end you are holding. For

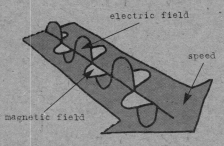

electric field

speed

magnetic field

an electromagnetic wave is really two
waves at right angles to each other—
one is the electric field and one is
the magnetic field

variety, as a change from making the ripples
move vertically (up and down), you can
make them move horizontally (side to side).

DOUBLE ACT

* The energy that makes electromagnetic
waves move through space is provided by
electric charges (or magnets) being jiggled
side to side, in much the same way that
the energy to make the ripples in the rope
comes from jiggling it horizontally.

* *But electromagnetic waves are more
complicated, because they are composed
of two waves running along together
and sustaining
each other. In
fact, as long as
the waves are at right
angles to each other,
the whole pattern can
be twisted and oriented
in any direction—but it
is easier to think of
them as vertical and
horizontal waves.*

thank goodness
for electromagnetic
radiation

microwave ovens use
electromagnetic radiation

ETERNAL
TWOSOME

Suppose the vertical
wave is an electric wave,
produced by jiggling an
electric charge up and
down. It is a changing
electric field, moving
through space. But as
Faraday discovered, a
changing *electric field*
produces a *magnetic
field*, at right angles to
the electric field. So
the vertical electric
wave is accompanied by
a horizontal *magnetic
wave*, moving through
space. And as Faraday
also discovered, a
changing *magnetic field*
produces an *electric
field*, at right angles to
the magnetic field. So
the horizontal *magnetic
wave* is accompanied by
a vertical *electric wave*,
moving through space.
And so on. *It doesn't
matter whether you
start with a jiggling
magnet or a jiggling
electric charge. The
two changing fields
sustain each other,
and you can't have
one without the other.*

PARTICLES IN A BOX

* If you have a box of a certain size, filled with gas at a certain temperature and pressure, no matter what kind of gas it is there will always be the same number of particles (that is, atoms or molecules) bouncing around in the box. How do we know? Because they produce the same pressure on the walls of their container.

JUST THE RIGHT SIZE

* For a gas at 32°F (0°C) and 1 standard atmosphere of pressure (the usual example used), you can make the box just the right size to hold a mass of gas equal to the molecular weight of that gas expressed in grams. The volume of the box would be 22.4 liters, or 5.91 gallons. Atomic and molecular weights are measured in units based on the mass of a hydrogen atom, which counts as 1. There are two hydrogen atoms in each molecule of hydrogen, so the molecular weight of hydrogen is 2, and the box would hold 2 grams of hydrogen. Similarly, each oxygen atom has an atomic weight of 16 (16 times the atomic weight of hydrogen) and there are two atoms in each molecule of oxygen, so the filled box would hold 32 grams of oxygen.

Amadeo Avogadro

Making waves

The energy that makes electromagnetic waves has to be generated in the first place, by moving electric charges or magnets side to side. The most common way we do this is by means of electric currents—which are just electric charges, consisting of huge numbers of ELECTRONS—flowing along wires. Discovered in the 1890s, electrons play an important role in the new physics, though they seemed to fit neatly into the world of Newtonian mechanics and Maxwell's equations.

the Greeks and Chinese had a
form of atomic theory

AVOGADRO'S NUMBER

✳ Whatever the gas used, the number
of molecules in the box will always be the
same—a number known as Avogadro's
number, which is 6×10^{23} (a 6 followed
by 23 zeros, or a hundred thousand
billion billion).

✳ *This huge number, which was worked
out by the Italian physicist* Amadeo
Avogadro (1776–1856) *in 1811, gives you
some idea of just how small atoms and
molecules are. Yet by the end of
the 19th century
physicists were
beginning to divide
atoms into their
component parts.
Atoms were not
indestructible,
after all.*

John Dalton splitting water
into its component parts by
means of electrolysis

In ancient times both
the Greeks and the
Chinese had thought
of the world as
being composed of
"essential" particles,
but the modern idea of
atoms developed in the
17th century and later,
from the work of
scientists like **Robert
Boyle (1627–91)** and
Christiaan Huygens
(1629–93). In 1738
Daniel Bernoulli
(1700–82) suggested
that a gas might be
made up of tiny
particles that bounced
around within their
container. But it was
only at the start of the
19th century that **John
Dalton (1766–1844)**
proposed that an atom
was the smallest unit of
an element that could
take part in a chemical
reaction.

43

NOVEL EXPERIMENTS

* In the middle of the 19th century physicists began to study the effect of electric currents on traces of gas left in glass tubes from which air had been almost completely evacuated—now possible thanks to the invention of the vacuum pump.

WOW! It's glowing

physicists were interested in the effect of electricity on gases

J.J. THOMSON (1856—1940)

In 1897 Thomson demonstrated that electric currents consisted of streams of electrically charged particles (electrons). Although he devised and supervised the experiments, he never did them himself—he was so clumsy that his colleagues claimed the apparatus would break if he even looked at it. Head of the Cavendish Laboratory during its "glory years" around the start of the 20th century, he received the Nobel prize in 1905 and was knighted in 1908.

J.J. Thomson

ILLUMINATING DISCOVERIES

* For these experiments, the current was made to flow between a positively charged plate at one end of the tube (the anode) and a negatively charged plate at the other end (the cathode). This resulted in a stream of negatively charged rays streaming away from the cathode. Logically enough, these were dubbed CATHODE RAYS.

In 1895 German physicist **Wilhelm Röntgen** (1845–1923) discovered XRAYS— a previously unknown form of radiation, produced when cathode rays hit the glass wall of the tube. *Xrays proved to be a very energetic (short-wavelength) form of electromagnetic wave.*

✱ Two years later, in 1897, a British physicist, **J. J. Thomson** (1856–1940), showed that cathode rays were quite different from Xrays—*being a stream of tiny particles, much smaller than atoms, that carry a negative electric charge.* These were soon given the name "electrons," by the Dutch physicist **Hendrik Lorentz** (1853–1928).

TWO NAGGING QUESTIONS

✱ So, at the end of the 19th century, the scene was set for the new physics. Physicists had Newton's laws to describe the behavior of matter, and Maxwell's equations to describe radiation. They had an emerging picture of the atom as a not-quite-indivisible particle, which could be described in terms of Newtonian mechanics to explain such things as the behavior of a gas in a container, but which could be subdivided (somehow) by having negatively charged electrons (which themselves seemed to be Newtonian particles) chipped away from them, leaving a positively charged remnant (an ion), which also obeyed Newton's laws and Maxwell's equations. Everything in the garden looked rosy—except for two nagging questions about the behavior of light.

Glowing achievement

Wilhelm Röntgen discovered Xrays while studying the way an electric current flowing through an evacuated glass tube makes the tube glow. He noticed that radiation given off by the tube was causing a nearby fluorescent screen to glow, too. He received the first Nobel prize in physics, in 1901.

we have Röntgen to thank for Xray spex!

CHAPTER 2

this physics is really new territory

Postprandial physics

Because he was believed to be erratic, Einstein found it impossible to obtain a university job, even as a junior assistant. But he kept on thinking about physics in his spare time—or rather, he thought about physics full time and only did enough other work to make ends meet. The story is that in the patent office he was so good at understanding the technicalities of the patent applications he was judging that he would zip through a day's work before lunch, then devote the afternoon to thinking about scientific problems— including the ones he resolved in his special theory of relativity.

BEYOND NEWTON

* By a neat coincidence, the new physics begins at the beginning of the 20th century, so it is now 100 years old. But it is still thought of as "new" because it uses ideas and concepts that go beyond those of Newtonian physics. Even Maxwell's wave theory of light would have been entirely intelligible to Newton (although he might have been disappointed to find that his own "corpuscular" theory of light had not been proved valid), but with the new physics he would have been entering unfamiliar territory.

new physics is nearly 100 years old

"LAZY DOG" –OR QUICK FOX?

* Albert Einstein (1879–1955) *worked out his first innovative theory—the special theory of relativity—in the first years of the 20th century, and published it in 1905.*

Einstein wouldn't work at anything unless it interested him

At the time he had no university appointment, but was working as a technical expert (second-class!) at the Swiss patent office, in Bern.

✱ Although he had graduated, in 1900, with reasonably good marks in his final examinations, as an undergraduate Einstein had gained a reputation for being —in the words of one of his tutors, Hermann Minkowski (see page 66)—"a lazy dog" who wouldn't work at anything unless it interested him. In fact, having skipped most of the lectures, he only got his degree by cramming frantically for a few weeks, using lecture notes taken by one of his friends, Marcel Grossman.

I'm no lazy dog

KEY WORDS

RELATIVITY:
According to Einstein's theory, any "observer" is entitled to consider that he or she is "at rest." All motion is therefore relative to the observer.

Albert Einstein

Enter Einstein

The first part of the new physics to be completed as a fully worked-out theory—and tested by experiments which proved that it was "better" (that is, more complete) than Newtonian mechanics— was Einstein's theory of relativity. Or rather, his two theories of relativity.

47

A PUZZLING PARADOX

* The thing that set Einstein thinking about relativity was a conflict between Newtonian physics and Maxwell's equations. Remember that one of the greatest triumphs of Maxwell's equations is that they automatically give the speed with which electromagnetic waves travel through space—a value identical to the speed of light, which never varies.

"But officer I was only doing 30"

the speed with which anything passes you depends on how fast you are moving

THE NEWTONIAN VIEW

* In Newtonian mechanics, on the other hand, the speed with which anything passes you depends on how fast you are moving. If I stand by the side of a road and a car drives past me at 37 mph, the car is regarded as moving at 37 mph relative to the road. And relative to the road, I am stationary. Similarly, if I am in a car moving at 18mph relative to the road and am

Trains and

Boats

and Planes

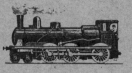

48

overtaken by a car moving at 37mph relative to the road, then the second car is traveling at 18mph relative to me, not at 37mph.

THE MAXWELLIAN VIEW

★ *But for light, Maxwell's equations make no allowance for any effect of this kind.* If I stand by the side of the road and measure the speed of light coming from the headlights of a car moving toward me at 37mph, according to Newtonian mechanics the speed I measure ought to be $c + 60$. But according to Maxwell's equations, the speed of light is c, pure and simple.

★ It doesn't matter if the source of the light is moving toward you, or away from you, or around in circles, or standing still. In fact, it doesn't matter if you are in a spaceship traveling at half the speed of light relative to the Sun and measure the speed of the light coming from the Sun. *Maxwell's equations insist that the speed of light is always c.*

★ And if there are two spaceships, one hurtling toward the Sun at half the speed of light and the other hurtling away from the Sun at half the speed of light, they will still each measure the speed of light from the Sun as c—as will anybody on any of the planets, although they orbit around the Sun at different speeds.

Trains, not spaceships

Einstein did not, of course, talk about spaceships. In fact, he liked to use examples involving railroad trains hurtling along the tracks. But the underlying point was the same: Maxwell's equations do not allow for the possibility that velocities involving light add up in the way described by Newtonian mechanics—the "common-sense" way, in which $2 + 2 = 4$.

the speed of light
is the same
however the source
is moving

Maxwell versus Newton

At the end of the 19th century the Newtonian view of the world, by then established for more than 200 years, was endowed with almost the authority of Holy Writ. In contrast, Maxwell's theory of light was a newcomer, only a few decades old. Maxwell himself had died as recently as 1879 and had not achieved the almost mythical status of Isaac Newton.

CONFLICTING VIEWS

* The few people who were bothered by the apparent conflict between Newtonian and Maxwellian theory tended to assume that there was something wrong with Maxwell's equations. But Einstein's great quality was his refusal to take anything for granted.

people began to be bothered by the conflict between Maxwell and Newton

THINKING THE UNTHINKABLE

I've been stuck here for hours

Newton was seen almost as God in the 19th century

* The very things that made Einstein such a poor student—his independence, his questioning of received ideas, and ability to work stubbornly at problems that interested him—made him start to think the unthinkable.

* What if Maxwell were right and Newton were wrong? What would the world be like if the laws of mechanics really were set up in such a way that the speed of light is exactly the same for all observers, everywhere in the Universe, no matter how they are moving relative to each other, or relative to the source of the light?

EINSTEIN'S SPECIAL THEORY OF RELATIVITY

things moving in circles

* *At first, Einstein restricted himself to thinking about things moving at constant velocities relative to one another—at constant speeds in straight lines.* He did not try to deal with accelerations, either straight-line accelerations or things moving in circles and other curved paths. *This is the sense in which the theory he came up with in 1905 is "special": the term means "restricted," as in something being a special case of a more general phenomenon.* But although his theory was restricted in this sense, it was nothing like anything that had been seen before.

* Einstein found that in order for the speed of light to be the same for all observers, velocities could not add up in the way Newton thought they did (2 + 2 = 4). *So he formulated a new law to describe the way velocities add up, which is described by a simple mathematical expression.*

$$V = \frac{(v_1 + v_2)}{(1 + (v_1 v_2)/c^2)}$$

important equation

NEWTON'S MATHS AND MAXWELL'S

If v_1 and v_2 are the velocities of two objects moving toward one another through space, in Newtonian terms they would be approaching at a combined speed V, with $V = v_1 + v_2$. But if we go by Maxwell's equations, then we have to use the expression

$$V = \frac{(v_1 + v_2)}{(1 + (v_1 v_2)/c^2)}$$

In other words, the Newtonian way of adding up the velocities has to be divided by a number equal to 1 plus the result of multiplying the two velocities together and dividing them by the square of the speed of light.

51

NEWTON DIVIDED BY ONE

* There are two important things about Einstein's equation. The first is that if the velocities involved are a lot smaller than the speed of light, by the time you do the dividing by the speed of light squared, that bit of the expression is tiny. So, in effect, you get the Newtonian "answer" divided by 1.

Einstein's maths are hard to follow

Do-It-Yourself relativity

It's easy to use a calculator to work out exactly how two velocities less than *c* add up according to Einsteinian mechanics. Try calculating the relative velocity for two spaceships flying straight at each other, each moving at three-quarters of the speed of light relative to an observer on Earth. You should find that the people on board each of the spaceships will measure the velocity of the other spaceship as 0.96*c*.

AN IMPERCEPTIBLE DIFFERENCE

* This means that at slow speeds (slow compared with the speed of light) the combined velocities are so nearly in line with Newtonian mechanics that you cannot measure the difference. *In other words, for everyday things like cars driving down roads, or trains hurtling along railroad tracks, Einstein's way of adding up velocities gives exactly the same answers as Newton's.*

how fast are they going relative to us?

THE SPEED OF LIGHT PLUS THE SPEED OF LIGHT

I'm going as fast as I can

* The other important feature of the Einsteinian way of adding up velocities is that if you look carefully at the new equation you will see that you can never add up two velocities that are smaller than the speed of light (less than c) to give a relative velocity larger than the speed of light.

special case

I can't tell the difference

for speeds less than the speed of light, Newton and Einstein give the same answer

A SPECIAL CASE

Newtonian mechanics isn't "wrong." It is in effect the version of Einsteinian mechanics that applies for velocities much smaller than the speed of light—a "special case" of the special theory of relativity. *To put it another way, Newtonian mechanics, in all its glory, is entirely contained within Einstein's description of the world.*

* If the two objects we are interested in—spaceships, trains, or whatever—are moving toward one another at the speed of light, then both v_1 and v_2 are equal to c. So the top of the fraction becomes $2c$. But $v_1 v_2$ (which simply means $v_1 \times v_2$) becomes $c \times c$, which is c^2, so the bottom of the fraction becomes $(1 + c^2/c^2)$, which is $1 + 1$, which any child knows makes 2. So the 2s cancel out, and the relative velocity V is equal to c. In Einsteinian mechanics, $c + c = c$.

it's child's play

C + C = C

* But does the new way of adding
up velocities really always give
the same speed for light itself?
Yes, subject to the following
provisos. If either v_1 or v_2 is
equal to c, then whatever the
other velocity you put into the
calculation, the answer you get
is always c—provided that the
other speed you put in is less
than c.

TWO PROVISOS

* If you try this on your calculator,
though, you'll probably need to put a lot
of digits in after the decimal point to make
it work, because calculators are only
approximate guides to reality, while nature
has as many decimal
places as it needs to
do the trick.

** The speed of
light through
space really is
exactly the
same for all
observers.*

*However, it is true
that light moves slightly
more slowly when
passing through
something like glass, or*

STANDING STILL IN SPACE

Because relative motion
is so important, we
have to be clear exactly
what we are talking
about. *In all this
discussion, we imagine
an observer standing
still in space, while
various objects whiz
past at high speeds
relative to the observer.*
To illustrate this point,
Einstein wrote about an
observer standing on
the platform of a
station, with high-
speed trains
whistling along
the tracks.

various objects
whiz past at
high speeds
relative to
the observer

water, or even air. So, strictly speaking, this discussion applies <u>only</u> to the speed of light traveling <u>through empty space</u>— through a vacuum.

it's all about light traveling through a vacuum

IN THE FAST LANE

* On its own, Einstein's version of the rule for adding up velocities wouldn't be very sensational. *But it is just one part of a comprehensive theory that describes what happens to objects traveling at close to the speed of light.*

speed really does matter you know

but what about relativity

Relativistic effects

Einstein's equations tell us that the mass of a moving object (as measured by the observer) increases, while its length (again, as measured by the observer) contracts. Strangest of all, they also tell us that time measured on a moving clock runs more slowly than time measured by a clock stationary relative to the observer's clock (see page 58).

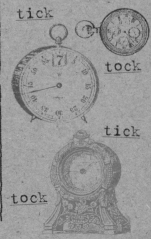

tick

tock

tick

tock

* Of course, it also describes what happens to slow-moving objects—but for them, as we have seen, Einstein's equations give exactly the same answers as Newton's. *In the context of the special theory of relativity, the fast-moving objects are the ones that are interesting.*

it must be reaching the speed of light

SIMPLY AND ELEGANTLY EXPRESSED

* As with the addition of velocities, Einstein's relativistic effects are described by surprisingly simple mathematical expressions. Indeed, they are all described by the same conversion factor.

THE CONVERSION FACTOR

* If v is the velocity of the object relative to the observer, then the appropriate expression that comes into the calculation is the square root of $(1-v^2/c^2)$, which is written as $\sqrt{(1-v^2/c^2)}$. The mass of an object moving at velocity v is equal to the mass of the same object when stationary (relative to the observer) divided by this factor, while the length of the moving object is equal to its length when stationary (always referred to as the "rest length") multiplied by this same factor.

* The bigger v is (up to the speed of light), the smaller the factor (which is always less than 1). Anything it multiplies is therefore smaller, while anything

Relativity in the lab

Ideas about the effects of relativity are difficult to accept, but they have all been tested by experiments. Physicists play with things that move at speeds close to the speed of light when they fire charged particles such as electrons and protons along evacuated tubes at places like Fermilab (the American particle-physics laboratory) or CERN (the European counterpart).

"the maths is very simple"

as things approach the
speed of light they
become shorter

divided by it is bigger. And the time
between ticks of a moving clock is equal to
the time between ticks of the same clock
when at rest, again divided by the factor
$\sqrt{(1-v^2/c^2)}$.

TAKEN TO EXTREMES

★ For low velocities, v is much less than c.
So v^2/c^2 is very small, and the factor
reduces to the square root of 1, which is
itself 1. *There is therefore no noticeable
difference from the Newtonian world.*

★ At the other extreme, if v is equal to c,
the factor becomes zero (1 minus 1).
Anything multiplied by zero is zero, and
anything divided by zero is infinitely big.
*Consequently, as things approach the
speed of light they become heavier and
heavier, without any limit, and at the same
time become shorter and shorter, shrinking
away to nothing. With a moving clock, the
ticks stretch out more and more as its
speed approaches the speed of light.
Anything moving at the speed of light—
such as light itself—does not notice the
passage of time at all.*

TESTING
RELATIVITY

It is possible, by
monitoring how
beams of particles
respond to magnetic
fields, to measure the
extent to which the
masses of the
particles are changed
by the effects of
relativity. Even the
strangest effect of all,
the so-called TIME-
DILATION EFFECT, has
been measured (see
page 58).

a fast
moving
flame

TIME DILATION

* It's worth explaining how time dilation can be monitored in the laboratory. I'll describe a slightly idealized hypothetical version of the experiment. Although no one has conducted an experiment quite this way, equivalent tests have been carried out in a slightly more complicated experimental set-up and have confirmed the accuracy of Einstein's equations.

PUFF!

nature provides us with a variety of different "clocks."

TIMED DECAY

* Nature provides us with a variety of different "clocks." *For example, when particles are produced in nuclear interactions they live for a certain length of time before they are spontaneously converted into other forms (in physicists' jargon, they "decay"). Measurements in the lab tell us how long, when it is stationary relative to the observer, each kind of particle lives before it decays.*

* Imagine such a particle being shot along a perfectly straight tube, exactly 100 meters (10^4cm) long. For the sake of this example, let's choose a variety of particle that is known to live for exactly one-millionth (10^{-7}) of a second, which is typical of the kind of LIFETIME these unstable particles have. Even if it were travelling at the speed of light (which is 3×10^{10} centimeters per second in the same notation), without time dilation such a particle could only travel a distance of 30 meters before expiring, because $(3 \times 10^{10}) \times 10^{-7} = 3 \times 10^{3}\text{cm} = 30\text{m}$. In this particular experiment, it couldn't even get halfway to the other end.

WHIZZING DOWN THE TUBE

* Now think about an identical particle traveling at twelve-thirteenths of the speed of light (again, an entirely realistic speed in this kind of experiment), and make allowance for time dilation.

* Without time dilation, the particle would get 30 x ($^{12}/_{13}$) meters down the tube—a distance of 27.7 meters. But (as you can easily verify, using the relativistic correction factor and your calculator) at twelve-thirteenths of c, the lifetime of the particle is stretched by a factor of 2.6. Since it lives 2.6 times as long (according to stationary clocks in the laboratory), it can get 2.6 times as far down the tube—a distance of 72 meters.

* *By measuring how far such particles travel in experiments of this kind, physicists have observed time dilation at work and have confirmed on very many occasions that it really does obey Einstein's equations.*

how slow is this moving clock running?

SO WHAT'S THE PARTICLE'S VIEW?

well my point of view is...

* But how do things look from the particle's point of view? It is a key tenet of Einstein's theory that (as long as we are dealing with constant velocities) the moving object is entitled to consider itself at rest. There's no reason for it to feel any of the effects we are talking about;

a tiny particle

it doesn't feel any heavier, or notice that it has shrunk, or detect anything wrong with its clocks. So how can it get farther down the tube than it "should"?

I'm sure this test tube has shrunk

IT'S THE LAB THAT MOVES

* *According to Einstein, because the particle is entitled to regard itself as being at rest, it follows that the laboratory (and everything else on Earth) is hurtling past it at twelve-thirteenths of the speed of light.*

* Now, as already mentioned, the particle only lives for a millionth of a second. But the tube that is flying past it is "shrunk" by its high velocity—and it is shrunk by exactly the same factor as we used in the time-dilation calculation, 2.6. So the

> ### KEY WORDS
>
> **FRAME OF REFERENCE:**
> the place measurements are made from—the "point of view" of an observer

particle still gets 2.6 times farther toward the end of the tube than it would if there were no relativistic effects at work. Everything fits together and it all works perfectly, no matter how you are moving, ___provided you are moving at a constant velocity.___

if I stand still you can hurtle past, OK?

FRAMES OF REFERENCE

* *Things that are moving at a certain (constant) velocity are said to be in a certain* FRAME OF REFERENCE, *and any frame of reference can be chosen as the one you make measurements from.* The observers in each frame of reference think their own clocks, rulers, and so on are perfectly normal, and it is everyone else's clocks and rulers that are affected by relativistic effects. But when you compare notes with observers in other frames of reference, *you always get consistent answers about how the universe works— not necessarily the same answers, but consistent ones.*

the answer depends on where you are looking from

DIFFERENT POINTS OF VIEW

Because observers moving at different velocities are in different frames of reference, they each have their own picture of the universe and their own ideas about, for example, whose clocks are running slow. Observers in two different frames of reference won't even agree on the mass of an object moving past both of them in a third frame of reference. But they can agree to differ, because they can each calculate what mass the object would have if it were brought to rest in their own frame of reference and will each get the same answer to this calculation.

THAT MOVING CLOCK AGAIN

* There's one more example worth looking at in detail that helps us understand how and why a moving clock can run slow. People often argue about which kind of clock is most reliable, and you might perhaps be worried about how the change in mass of the moving clock would affect its timekeeping properties. But there is an ultimate clock that cannot be argued with, and that is light itself.

$$V = \frac{(v_1 + v_2)}{(1 + (v_1 v_2)/c^2)}$$

$E = Mc^2$

Einstein's famous equations

EINSTEIN'S FAMOUS EQUATION

This business about moving objects gaining mass explains where the most famous equation in all of science, $E = mc^2$, comes from. According to Newtonian physics, if you push an object you put energy in to make it move faster—it gains kinetic energy of motion simply by increasing its velocity (acceleration equals force divided by mass). *But in Einsteinian physics, some of the energy you put in when you push an object goes into making it move faster—and some of the energy goes into making it heavier.* This tells you that *mass and energy are equivalent and interchangeable,* and leads to the relation expressed in Einstein's famous equation by way of a calculation just a little too complicated to bother with right now.

Push!!

the faster
you push,
the heavier
it gets

LIGHT TIME

★ Since light always travels at the same speed, for all observers, it provides the ultimate measure of time. We can define one second as the time it takes for light to travel a certain distance (and this is, in fact, the way time is defined today, in terms of the properties of a particular wavelength of light emitted by cesium atoms).

★ There is no argument about this. In any frame of reference, you can choose light from any source in the universe, measure how long it takes to cover a chosen distance, and work out how much time has passed.

Guaranteed accurate

The ultimate clock would be a kind of light clock in which light bounces up and down between two perfectly shiny mirrors, situated a set distance (perhaps a yard) apart. Each tick of the clock would correspond to the time it took for a pulse of light to go from the top mirror down to the bottom mirror and back to the top mirror again, giving a steady beat for anyone in the same frame of reference as the clock.

**RIGHT THIS WAY
FOR THE
ULTIMATE
CLOCK**

63

ZIGZAG LIGHT

the light is moving sideways

* How do things look to an observer in another frame of reference, watching the light clock just described move past at a constant velocity? We have to bear in mind that the light pulse is moving sideways as well as up and down. In the time it takes for the pulse to travel from the top mirror to the bottom mirror, the whole clock has moved sideways.

Pythagoras' theorem

The square of the hypotenuse of a right-angled triangle equals the sum of the squares of the other two sides.

$$a^2 + b^2 = c^2$$

right-angled triangle

ENTER PYTHAGORAS

* To the observer in the second frame of reference, the light pulse flies along a diagonal path to the other mirror, and along an equivalent diagonal path back up to the top mirror. As this process repeats, the light zigzags up and down between the two mirrors.

* *Anyone who remembers learning at school about right-angled triangles and Pythagoras' theorem, will be aware that the diagonal path taken by the light beam is the hypotenuse of a right-angled triangle, and so*

Pythagoras

is longer than the vertical path between the mirrors. Since it is a longer path, the light must take longer to complete its journey. The moving clock must therefore run slow.

* The geometry of right-angled triangles tells us how much longer the path is, and therefore how much slower the moving clock is. The correction factor is, of course, Einstein's relativistic factor that we met before: $\sqrt{(1-v^2/c^2)}$.

* The faster the moving clock moves, the more the bouncing light pulse is forced into a stretched-out zigzag—until at the speed of light it is moving sideways as fast as it is moving up and down, and can never complete even a single bounce between the mirrors. *Time stands still for anything moving at the speed of light.*

this will help you understand relativity...

The concept of spacetime

It has become a cliché — almost as familiar as $E = mc^2$ itself—that Einstein's special theory is all about the four-dimensional geometry of SPACETIME (see page 70), a merging together of space and time. So it may come as a surprise to learn that this geometrical merging of space and time was not Einstein's idea. In fact, at first he was not impressed by it at all.

EXTENSION:
(in spacetime) the
four-dimensional
equivalent of length

Hermann Minkowski

Hermann Minkowski (1864–1909)

Born in Lithuania (then
under Russian rule),
Minkowski was
Professor of
Mathematics at the
Zurich Federal Institute
of Technology when
Einstein was a student
there. He claimed that
as a student Einstein
"never bothered about
mathematics at all."
Minkowski died of
appendicitis before his
lecture putting the
geometry into relativity
appeared in print.

PICTURING RELATIVITY

* In 1905, and for years
afterwards, Einstein presented
his special theory in terms of
algebra (equations), not in
terms of geometry (pictures).
The equations work perfectly
well, of course—but they don't
give you a physical feel for
what is going on when things
move at velocities that are a
sizeable fraction of the speed
of light.

it's my view of relativity

REENTER MINKOWSKI

* It was only in 1908 that Einstein's old
teacher **Hermann Minkowski**—who had
described Einstein as a "lazy dog"—came up
with a geometrical version of the special
theory, which made it much more accessible
and intelligible to nonmathematicians.

Minkowski introduced the idea of time as the "fourth dimension," in some sense at right angles to the familiar three dimensions of space (up/down, left/right, forward/back). This led to the idea that things possess a property called EXTENSION, *which is the four-dimensional equivalent of length.*

you can make the shadow bigger or smaller than the length of the ruler

THE FOURTH DIMENSION

* A ruler, for example, has a definite length in three dimensions. But if you hold it so that it casts a shadow on the ground, you can make the shadow bigger or smaller than the length of the ruler.

* In the same way, a ruler (or anything else) has an extension in four dimensions (in spacetime) that stays the same. But relative motion changes your perspective of the extension—as if the ruler was being twisted in spacetime. As the ruler moves faster, *the shadow in space* gets shorter and the *shadow in time* gets longer. And when it moves more slowly, the reverse occurs (the shadow in space increases and the shadow in time decreases).

In his lecture Minkowski made a portentous prediction: "The views of space and time which I wish to lay before you have sprung from the soil of experimental physics, and therein lies their strength. They are radical. Henceforth space by itself, and time by itself, are doomed to fade into mere shadows, and only a kind of union of the two will preserve an independent reality."

67

EINSTEIN'S GENERAL THEORY

* The general theory gets its name because it deals with motion in general, including acceleration, not just motion in a straight line at a constant speed. But it does much more than that. It explains gravity, as well. As Einstein put it, a man falling from a roof would not feel the force of gravity—he might be well aware that he was accelerating toward the ground, but he would be weightless.

Toward the general theory

From the moment when Minkowski presented his own version of the special theory of relativity, Einstein's reputation took off and in 1909 he at last left the patent office and took up his first academic post. At first, Einstein was reluctant to accept that one of his old teachers had come up with a good idea. But when, at last, he did take to the idea of the geometrization of spacetime, it helped him to develop his masterwork—the general theory of relativity.

this is one way to lose weight

ACCELERATION AND GRAVITY

* There are many familiar examples of what Einstein meant. The simplest is a high-speed elevator. When the elevator starts accelerating, as it begins to move upward, you feel heavier and are pressed

come this way for a demonstration
of Einstein's general theory

CONVENIENT SHORT-CUT

Einstein struggled for years to find a route to a general theory, including acceleration, and later said that the happiest insight of his entire career came when he realized that gravity and acceleration are the same thing. There's no need to try to follow the mathematical complexities of Einstein's reasoning that led from this insight to a complete theory of gravity. We can jump to its finished form, using the geometrization of spacetime devised by Minkowski.

to the floor; when it slows down (decelerates), you feel light and rise upward on your toes. The acceleration of the lift acts just like gravity. Not merely *like* gravity (we are all aware of that) but *just like it*, because acceleration is exactly the same as gravity—which was Einstein's momentous insight.

★ So far as any scientific experiments to test the theory are concerned, if you were in a steadily accelerating windowless elevator, accelerating at the same rate forever, you would not be able to tell whether you were accelerating or standing still on the surface of a planet.

they are the same!

Einstein realized that gravity and acceleration are the same

69

SPACETIME MADE INTELLIGIBLE

but I can only see three

* Most people have trouble visualizing four dimensions, so relativists use a neat trick to make spacetime more intelligible. Imagine all three dimensions of space as being represented by just one dimension. Time is now the second dimension, at right angles to this minispace.

Unequal parts

There is an inequality between the time part of spacetime and the space part. Since the speed of light is 186,390 miles (300,000km) per second, one second of time is, in a sense, equivalent to 186,390 miles (300,000km) of space. If you had a gadget that interchanged the dimensions of space and time so you could travel in time just by walking along a road, you would have to walk 186,390 miles (300,000km) (three-quarters of the way to the Moon) in order to go back in time just one second.

WHEN MATTER IS ABSENT

* Imagine spacetime as a tautly stretched rubber sheet, very much like the surface of a trampoline. The presence of matter in spacetime is represented by a dent in the trampoline. Without any matter, spacetime is flat. If you roll a marble across the undented sheet, the marble proceeds in a straight line.

that's not fair you'll make a dent

spacetime is like a taut sheet with objects resting on it

* *The mechanics of flat spacetime is, in fact, none other than the special theory of relativity. And since the general theory includes the special theory within itself, everything we have learned about moving clocks and rulers is relevant to the general theory too.*

DENTS IN SPACETIME

* Now imagine what happens if you place a heavy bowling ball on the stretched rubber sheet to represent the Sun. With the Sun in place, spacetime is curved. If you roll a marble near the dent in spacetime made by the presence of matter, then it follows a curved path and is deflected.

this will show them!

a solar eclipse in 1919 gave evidence for Einstein's theory

* *Because it is spacetime itself that is bent, this deflection happens for anything moving through spacetime—any particle, obviously, but also for light. Matter tells spacetime how to bend; and spacetime tells both matter and light how to move.*

Einstein's general theory was published in 1916. Among other things, it suggested that any light from distant stars that happened to pass near the Sun would be deflected, very slightly, sideways by the bending of spacetime near the Sun. Usually, you cannot see stars that lie in the direction of (but far beyond) the Sun, because it is so bright. But in 1919 there was a total eclipse of the Sun, with the stars visible in daytime. Photographs taken during the course of the eclipse showed that the apparent positions of the stars had shifted slightly. The amount of the shift turned out to be exactly the amount Einstein's theory had predicted.

BOTTOMLESS PITS IN SPACE

* Continuing our trampoline analogy, imagine placing a weight on the sheet so heavy that it stretches it to breaking point, making a hole right through. If you had enough mass concentrated in a small enough region of space, you would be able to bend spacetime so much that it closed itself off from the rest of the Universe, creating a bottomless pit in the middle of flat space. This is what astronomers and physicists call a black hole.

black holes are messy eaters

ENERGETIC OBJECTS...

* The mathematics of black holes was worked out by the German astronomer **Karl Schwarzschild** (1873–1916) just before the publication of the general theory of relativity (Schwarzschild having received advance information about the theory from Einstein). Nevertheless, his work was regarded as no more than a mathematical curiosity until the 1960s, when the discovery of ENERGETIC OBJECTS in space (X-RAY STARS and QUASARS) led astronomers to think that black holes

objects around black holes radiate lots
of energy and are very bright

might really exist. *Today, they are firmly established as part of the Universe we live in.*

...AND MESSY EATERS

* High-energy objects such as X-ray stars and quasars are believed to be associated with black holes because the intense gravitational pull of a black hole attracts matter, which forms a swirling disk (called an accretion disk) around the hole. *Material drains inward from the inner edge of this disk and is swallowed up by the hole, from which nothing—not even light—can escape.*

* But in the swirling disk, just outside the hole, particles bash together vigorously and get very hot, so they radiate Xrays, radio waves, and visible light. *Consequently, although black holes themselves are invisible, the activity surrounding them produces some of the brightest objects in the Universe.* Black holes are messy eaters, and it shows.

Black holes

Black holes were given their name by the American physicist **John Wheeler** in 1967, but their existence had been posited decades earlier by the Indian astronomer **Subrahmanyan Chandrasekhar** (1910–95). A black hole, he suggested, would have about as much mass as our Sun, packed into a ball about 2 miles (3km) across, which seemed nonsensical to most scientists in the 1930s. Then in the 1960s astronomers discovered neutron stars about 6 miles (10km) across containing as much mass as our Sun. This is so close to being a black hole that it made the idea respectable. *Actual black holes, in the form of X-ray stars, were first*

John Wheeler

73

black hole

MAKING BLACK HOLES

* A black hole is simply a region of spacetime where gravity is strong enough to bend spacetime around, so that it's pinched off from the rest of the Universe. There are two ways you can make a black hole.

Karl Schwarzschild

Karl Schwarzschild (1873–1916)

Schwarzschild kept in touch with scientific developments even while serving as a technical expert on the Eastern Front during the First World War. After contracting an incurable disease, he was invalided out of the army to Potsdam. There, on his deathbed, he worked out the mathematics of what later became known as the theory of black holes.

METHOD NUMBER ONE

* *The first (the way Schwarzschild envisaged) is to take any mass and squeeze it into a small enough volume.* Assuming the mass is the same, the smaller the object is then the stronger the tug of gravity is at its surface—and the more curved spacetime is. The Sun, for example, would become a black hole if it could be squeezed into a sphere just 1.8 miles (2.9km) in radius. But it is harder to do the trick for smaller masses. In

black holes swallow up matter from all around them

order to turn the Earth into a black hole, you would need to squeeze it down to just .35 inches (0.88cm) in radius.

METHOD NUMBER TWO

★ The other way to make a black hole is to add more mass, thus increasing the strength of the gravitational field associated with the object without increasing its density.

For example, imagine that you could pile stars like the Sun side by side without them merging into a single blob and shrinking under their own weight. Once you had made an object about 500 times the radius of the Sun—but with the same density as the Sun—then spacetime would once again be bent round the outside of the object so that nothing could escape. It would have become a black hole.

★ It would only have the density of water, but it would be as big across as our Solar System. In fact, you could make a black hole out of water, if you had enough of it—though you would need the equivalent of a few million times the mass of our Sun.

the Earth would have to be squeezed very small to make a black hole

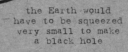

a large mass in a small volume would create a black hole

OUR LOCAL BLACK HOLE

Black holes about as big across as our entire solar system and containing as much mass as a few million Suns are thought to exist at the hearts of some galaxies and in quasars. There may even be a slightly smaller black hole at the center of our own Milky Way galaxy, although no longer active— probably because it has swallowed up all the matter nearby.

hello, can anybody hear me?

CAN GET IN, CAN'T GET OUT

* A key feature of a black hole is that anything can get into it, tugged by its gravitational attraction (according to the old picture) or falling down its steep gradient in spacetime (according to Einsteinian physics), but nothing can get out—not even light.

SINGULARLY DOOMED

* The equations that describe black holes describe matter plunging inexorably to its doom at a mathematical point called a SINGULARITY, at the center of the hole. Nobody knows what happens then. At the singularity, the known laws of physics break down.

* There has been speculation that stuff falling into a singularity may get shunted through HYPERSPACE to emerge in other universes, or in another part of our own universe. But these ideas are nothing more than speculation.

so what happens at singularity?

FROM BLACK HOLES TO THE UNIVERSE

At the end of the 1920s two American astronomers discovered that the galaxies beyond the Milky Way are receding from each other, which implied that the universe is expanding. *Einstein's general theory had, in a sense, predicted this discovery, which has remained the cornerstone of cosmology ever since. The contracting version of his equations describes what goes on in black holes. The expanding version of them describes what goes on in the Universe at large.*

EQUALLY APPLICABLE

✱ As with the other fundamental equations of physics, Einstein's equations work just as well whichever direction time is running in. The same equations that describe matter and radiation plunging to their doom in a singularity can be turned around to describe matter and radiation bursting out from a singularity and spreading through a burgeoning spacetime.

✱ It is these equations that describe the expanding universe of the BIG BANG and also give what appears to be a very good description of the universe we live in.

BANG

the Big Bang was the outburst in which the universe was born

SINGULARITY:
a mathematical point with zero volume

HYPERSPACE:
extension of the idea of four-dimensional spacetime to more dimensions (four-dimensional spacetime may be embedded in hyperspace, just as a two-dimensional sheet of paper is embedded in three-dimensional space)

THE BIG BANG:
the outburst in which the universe was born—in a superhot, superdense state, possibly from a singularity

The expanding universe

Einstein first encountered the idea of an expanding universe in 1917. At that time, nobody knew that the universe was expanding, so Einstein was completely baffled when his cosmological solutions to the equations of the general theory told him that spacetime could only be expanding or contracting, and could not stand still.

Edwin Hubble
observing with the
100-inch Hooker

HUBBLE AND HUMASON

The two American astronomers who discovered that the Universe is expanding were **Edwin Hubble** (1889–1953) and **Milton Humason** (1891–1972). Hubble usually gets most credit, although Humason obtained the all-important data that Hubble interpreted. Humason was the best astronomical observer of his generation and used the best telescope on Earth at the time, the huge new reflector at Mount Wilson in California. His measurements of the spectra of light from distant galaxies revealed a RED-SHIFT EFFECT, which Hubble interpreted as evidence that all the galaxies are receding.

I want the last word on this!

BEYOND EINSTEIN

* Even Einstein's general theory of relativity is not the last word on the subject of gravity. It can't be, because it can't describe what happens at singularities. Physicists don't know what the ultimate theory of the Universe will be. But they do have a good idea of the kind of theory that will be needed to explain such phenomena.

Hubble and Humason
established that
the Universe was
expanding

FRAGMENTS OF SPACE AND TIME

* The trouble with Einstein's general theory is that it is still, to a certain extent, a "classical" theory. *Like Newtonian mechanics or Maxwell's description of light, it deals with things that change smoothly and continuously from place to place and from time to time.*

★ Indeed, it takes no account of the other great revolution in physics that occurred during the first decades of the 20th century, the theory of QUANTUM MECHANICS —*which describes the world of the very small (atoms and smaller) and, in a complete break from everything that went before, asserts that the world is not smooth and continuous, but is broken up into tiny pieces called* QUANTA. And not just tiny pieces of matter, but also tiny pieces of radiation, and even tiny pieces of space and tiny pieces of time.

A WEIRD IDEA

★ What we need to complete our description of the world is a quantum theory of gravity – and later we will see where people are looking for such a theory. But first, what are quanta, and how did physicists come up with such a weird idea?

★ *Once again, a revolution in scientific thinking came about because of a puzzle regarding the nature of light.* Toward the end of the 19th century, physicists realized that if light waves really did behave like classical waves (like waves on a plucked guitar string or ripples on a pond) then they could not explain how it is radiated from a hot object, such as a candle flame, or a red-hot lump of iron, or the Sun.

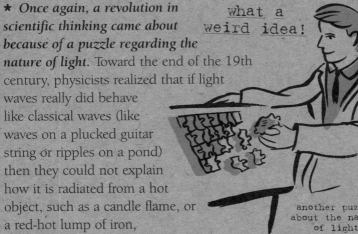

what a weird idea!

another puzzle about the nature of light

79

you can see the visible spectrum of
light in a rainbow

THE PUZZLE
ABOUT LIGHT

* A hot object
radiates light
(electromagnetic
energy) because charged
particles (electrons) are
jiggling around inside it.
Red light has the longest
wavelength (lowest
frequency) in the visible
spectrum of light, which
runs from red through
orange, yellow, green, blue,
and indigo to violet. And
just beyond the violet end of the
visible spectrum, there is a form of electromagnetic
radiation not quite visible to our eyes, called
ultraviolet light.

THE NATURE OF
THE PUZZLE

The puzzle concerning
the nature of light can
be expressed very
simply, without any
mathematics. Classical
physics tells you, and
experiments confirm,
that if you put energy
into making ripples,
more energy goes into
making ripples with
higher frequency
(shorter wavelengths)
than ones with lower
frequency (longer
wavelengths).

THE ULTRAVIOLET
CATASTROPHE

* According to classical theory,
preferentially any hot object ought to
radiate energy at shorter wavelengths
(higher frequencies)—that is, at
the violet and ultraviolet end
of the spectrum. *So, when
possible, any hot object would
radiate all its energy away in
a burst of ultraviolet
radiation* (or at even shorter
wavelengths, though Xrays

blacksmith

and gamma rays were unknown at the time the puzzle was formulated). *This became known as the ultraviolet catastrophe—a catastrophe for classical physics, because clearly nature did not behave like that.*

any hot object would radiate all its energy away in a burst of ultraviolet radiation

Peak energy

The black-body relationship was worked out from experiments involving hot objects, before there was a theory to explain it. *Puzzlingly, those experiments showed that although a little energy is radiated at longer and shorter wavelengths, the peak emission from a black body is centred on a particular narrow band of wavelength that depends only on its temperature.*

VISIBLY GLOWING

★ What really happens when an object like a lump of iron is heated to successively higher temperatures is that at first most of the energy is radiated as infrared heat, at wavelengths just too long to be seen by our eyes. Then, it begins to glow. First it becomes red hot—then, at successively higher temperatures, orange, and blue-white. The hotter the object is, the shorter the wavelengths at which most of its energy is radiated.

★ The way the radiation from a hot object depends on its temperature is known as the BLACK-BODY RELATIONSHIP, because the equations that describe how energy is absorbed by a perfectly black object also describe how energy is radiated by the same object when it is heated up. *This is another example of the way the equations of physics take no notice of the direction of time—emission of radiation is the time-reversed counterpart to absorption of radiation.*

it's a trick of the light

CHAPTER 3

THE QUANTUM WORLD

* The answer to the puzzle about the nature of light came from Max Planck, in 1900. Planck realized that the problem could be solved if the radiating objects (which we would now identify as atoms) could only emit (or, indeed, absorb) electromagnetic energy in certain fixed amounts, which he called quanta.

QUANTIFYING QUANTA

* *The quanta for a particular frequency of light had to carry a certain amount of energy, with the energy proportional to the frequency (and therefore inversely proportional to the wavelength) of the light involved.* The constant of proportionality needed to make the theory fit the observations could be worked out from experiment —and is now known as Planck's constant, h. Planck stated that the energy of each quantum was given by the simple expression $E = hf$, where f is the frequency of the light being radiated.

QUANTITIES OF QUANTA

Planck thought of atoms as being able to dispense light only in certain quanta—rather like a drinks machine that is designed to dispense fruit juice in fixed quantities, to match the sizes of the cups. The machine will only give you a small cup of juice, or a medium cup, or a large one. But because you can only get drinks from the machine in three sizes, that doesn't mean fruit juice never exists in other quantities. *It's just that the machine is set up to dispense it in these "quanta" only.*

I'd like a cup a little bit bigger than medium please

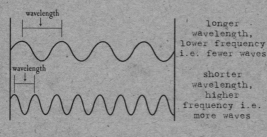

longer wavelength, lower frequency i.e. fewer waves

shorter wavelength, higher frequency i.e. more waves

PROBLEM SOLVED

* Planck's theory solved the puzzle, because cool objects do not have enough energy to make very many high-frequency quanta. They can only radiate energy at the range of frequencies where the energy available from each atom is comparable to the energy of the quanta involved in the radiation. *The more energy you put into the object (and the hotter it gets), the easier it is for individual atoms to radiate high-energy quanta.* So the peak of the energy radiated (indicated by the color of the object) shifts through the spectrum in the way previously described (see page 81).

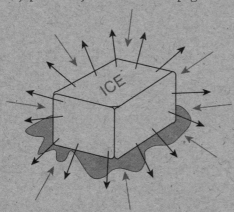

ice radiates energy, but it receives more than it gives out

Max Planck (1858–1947)

Most scientists do their best work in their twenties or thirties, but Planck was already in his forties when he made his great contribution to physics and was then still less than halfway through a full and active life. He was professor of physics at the University of Berlin until 1926 (when he was succeeded by Erwin Schrödinger); then in 1930, at 72, became president of the Kaiser Wilhelm Institute of Physics in Berlin. He resigned in 1937 as a protest against the Nazi regime's treatment of the Jews, but in 1945 became head of the institute again, when it moved to Göttingen and was renamed the Max Planck Institute.

Max Planck

STREAMS OF PARTICLES

* The person who suggested that light might be quantized was Einstein, in a paper published in 1905 (the same year he published the special theory of relativity). In an attempt to solve a puzzle about the behavior of light, he harked back to Isaac Newton's idea (see page 29) that light behaves like a stream of tiny cannonballs or, in less picturesque terms, consists of particles. Although these particles were not given the name photons until the 1920s, the term can appropriately be used here.

dim light produces few electrons

particles

Einstein suggested that light was a stream of particles

Planck and light

Although Planck introduced the idea of quanta into physics, he did not suggest that light *only* existed in little packets of energy. *He thought that the quantization was a property of the particles that were radiating the light— that they were physically incapable of radiating all wavelengths at once.* By 1900, when Planck formulated his quantum theory, the power of Maxwell's equations had convinced just about everybody that light travels in the form of a wave, like ripples on a pond.

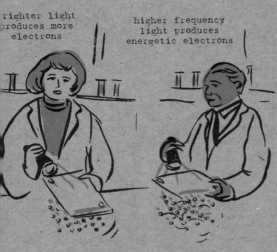

brighter light produces more electrons

higher frequency light produces energetic electrons

the energy of the electrons produced by shining light on metal depends on the frequency of the light not on its brightness

ILLOGICAL BUT TRUE

* The puzzle Einstein solved with the aid of <u>PHOTONS</u> has to do with the so-called <u>PHOTOELECTRIC EFFECT</u>, which occurs when light shining on a metal surface knocks electrons out of the metal. The energy of the electromagnetic radiation in the light is transferred to the electrons, enabling them to escape from the grip of their parent atoms in the metal.

* *Since a bright light has more energy than a dim light, it seems logical to expect that if you shine a bright light onto the metal you will get electrons with more energy coming off. That is certainly what the pioneering experimenters expected— but that is not what happens.*

KEY WORDS

PHOTON:
a particle of light

THE PHOTOELECTRIC EFFECT

The photoelectric effect is seen most clearly by using light of a particular color. **Philipp Lenard** had been conducting experiments of this kind since 1899; and by 1905, when Einstein published his paper, they were well known. For a particular colour of light, each electron that is produced by the photoelectric effect has the same energy. For a dim light, only a few electrons are produced. For a brighter light, more are produced —but each electron has exactly the same energy as when the light is dim. *The only way to get electrons with more energy is to use light with a higher frequency (that is, a shorter wavelength).* Blue light stimulates the release of electrons with more energy than those released by red.

little
packets
of
energy

EINSTEIN'S VIEW OF LIGHT

* Einstein's explanation of the photoelectric effect was characteristically unexpected. He suggested that light arrives at the surface of the metal in the form of quanta—what are now called photons.

PACKETS OF ENERGY

* Light with a particular color is made up of photons that each have the same particular energy—little packets of energy determined by Planck's equation $E = hf$. So when each single photon gives up its energy to a single electron, each electron has the same energy. *Bright light does carry more energy, but only because it is made up of a larger number of photons. Each of its photons still gives the same kick to the metal surface.*

* But because blue light has a higher frequency than red light, each photon of blue light gives a bigger kick to the metal surface than each photon of red light. *The electrons liberated by blue light therefore carry more energy than electrons liberated by red— even if you use a dim blue light and a bright red light in the experiment.*

Philipp Lenard (1862–1947)

As well as his work on the photoelectric effect, Lenard studied the nature of cathode rays at the end of the 1890s and, independently of J. J. Thomson, showed that they are streams of charged particles. He also came close to discovering Xrays. In the 20th century he became very bitter that all the credit for these discoveries went to Thomson and Röntgen, turned against his colleagues, and was the only leading scientist to actively support the Nazis.

Philipp Lenard

DOUBTS AND ACCOLADES

Robert Millikan

* *Einstein's claim that light exists in the form of a stream of particles was so startling in 1905 that at first nobody took it seriously.* Indeed, the American physicist **Robert Millikan** (1868–1953) spent 10 years carrying out subtle experiments designed to prove Einstein was wrong. In the end, he succeeded only in convincing himself (and everyone else) that Einstein was right—and that there was no other explanation of the photoelectric effect.

* As a result, Einstein received the Nobel Prize (for his work on the photoelectric effect, not for either of his theories of relativity) in 1922, and Millikan got the Nobel Prize in 1923. (No need to feel sorry for Lenard—he'd already been awarded a Nobel Prize, back in 1905, for his studies of electrons.)

EINSTEIN'S QUEST FOR TRUTH

Einstein's work on the photoelectric effect is a splendid example of how he questioned everything in his search for solutions. He had arrived at his special theory of relativity partly by rejecting Newton's view of the world and accepting the truth of Maxwell's equations— yet in the very same year, his exploration of photons and quantum theory led him to reject Maxwell's description of light and accept Newton's view of the world as correct!

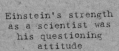

Einstein's strength as a scientist was his questioning attitude

why don't electrons get attracted by the nucleus?

THE BEHAVIOR OF ATOMS

* By the 1920s physicists had clear proof, from the experiment with two holes, that light is a wave— and also, thanks to Lenard, Einstein, and Millikan, that it consists of particles. This blurring of the distinction between waves and particles paved the way for a full theory of quantum mechanics in the 1920s. But even with only a half-baked quantum theory to work with, Niels Bohr managed to come up with a description of how individual atoms work and how they get together to form molecules.

FOILED BY GOLD

* Bohr's description of the atom built on the experimental work of **Ernest Rutherford** and the theoretical ideas of Max Planck. In 1909 Rutherford and his colleagues at Manchester University discovered that when a beam of alpha particles was fired at a thin sheet of gold foil, although most of the particles went straight through the sheet, a few of them bounced back again.

ALPHA PARTICLES

We now know that alpha particles are the nuclei of helium atoms. Each alpha particle consists of two protons and two neutrons, held together by the strong nuclear force (see page 120). This makes a very stable unit, which behaves like a single particle in many interactions.

* *Rutherford explained this by saying that most of the mass of an atom is concentrated in a tiny central nucleus which, like alpha particles, is positively charged— while the electrons associated with the atom, which carry negative charge (so each atom is electrically neutral overall), are somehow distributed in a cloud around the nucleus.*

* Consequently when an alpha particle hits the electron cloud, it brushes through it without noticing. But if it happens to head straight for the nucleus, then the electric repulsion of the two sets of positive charge pushes it back the way it came or off at a sharp angle.

WHY NO ATTRACTION?

* From the statistics of the experiment, Rutherford was able to work out that the nucleus is 100,000 times smaller than the electron cloud around an atom. But this left a big puzzle. *Why didn't the electrons (which have negative charge) get attracted by the nucleus (which has positive charge) and fall into it?*

Three kinds of radiation

At the beginning of the 20th century, Ernest Rutherford gave the names "alpha rays" and "beta rays" to the two kinds of radiation produced by radioactivity. A little later, when a third kind of radiation was discovered, it was called "gamma rays." Beta rays turned out to be fast-moving electrons. Gamma rays are electromagnetic radiation, like Xrays but even more energetic. Alpha rays are also particles (see opposite).

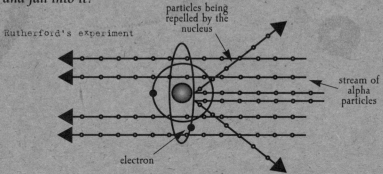

Rutherford's experiment

particles being repelled by the nucleus

stream of alpha particles

electron

89

at the center of each atom
there is a nucleus of
neutrons and protons

ELECTRONS IN ORBIT

* Bohr's idea was that the electrons must, in some sense, be "in orbit" around the nucleus, rather like the planets orbiting around the Sun. However, this wasn't enough to stabilize the atom—because an accelerated electric charge radiates energy, and circular motion constitutes an acceleration. According to classical physics (including Maxwell's equations), the electrons orbiting in an atom would radiate energy away and spiral into the nucleus.

THE QUANTUM LEAP

* Max Planck had shown that electromagnetic radiation could only be radiated in quanta. Bohr now suggested that the electrons in the atom could only radiate whole quanta of light, not smaller bits. So they couldn't spiral inward. *They could only jump from one orbit to the next —exactly one quantum of energy closer to the nucleus.*

* This is the famous "QUANTUM LEAP." It is rather as if Earth disappeared from its own orbit and instantly appeared in the orbit of Venus, without having crossed the space in between.

Niels Bohr (1885–1962)

After completing his Ph.D., Bohr worked with Rutherford's group at Manchester University, where he came up with his model of the atom. By 1918, he was so highly regarded that he was invited to head a new institute of physics in Copenhagen (now called the Niels Bohr Institute). Most of the great theoretical physicists of the day visited his institute at various times, and in the 1920s it was a catalyst for the development of the theory of quantum mechanics —which is how the Copenhagen Interpretation got its name.

the famous Quantum Leap

WHY THE LEAP?

* But why don't the electrons simply jump down step by step, as if bouncing down a staircase, until they all pile up on the bottom step?

there's only room for two

* *Bohr's answer was to say that there must be a rule of quantum physics that only allows a certain number of electrons in each orbit. There is only room for two electrons in the orbit closest to the nucleus. An atom of lithium, for example, which has three electrons would therefore have to put the third one in the next orbit out from the nucleus, a quantum of energy further away.*

Rutherford and his laboratory

KEY WORDS

QUANTUM LEAP: so called because quanta (such as atoms) "leap" abruptly from one state to another

Ernest Rutherford (1871–1937)

Born in New Zealand, Rutherford worked in England, then Canada, then back in England, where he eventually became the head of the Cavendish Laboratory. Together with **Frederick Soddy**, he showed that radioactivity involves atoms of one element being transformed into atoms of another. In 1909 he devised the experiment, carried out by **Hans Geiger** and **Ernest Marsden**, that led to the discovery of the atomic nucleus. When Rutherford received the Nobel Prize, in 1908, it was for chemistry (for his work on elements), although he considered chemistry an inferior discipline and once said that "all of science is either physics or stamp collecting."

BOHR'S MODEL OF THE ATOM

* The reason why Bohr's model was greeted as a significant step forward was that by spacing the electron orbits out in the way demanded by Planck's equation, he could explain the spectrum of light from a simple atom.

let's get into orbit

jump

the electron orbits are like a flight of stairs

Niels Bohr

JUMPING UP AND DOWN

* *All atoms radiate or absorb light at specific wavelengths, making sharply defined lines in the spectrum.* The pattern made by these lines (sometimes known as the spectral signature) is unique for each element—as unique as a fingerprint.

* *Bohr showed that each line corresponds to an electron jumping from one orbit (or one "energy level") to another—or rather, many identical electrons making the* identical jump in many atoms of the same element. A jump down releases energy and produces a bright line, while if the atom absorbs energy it makes a dark line in the spectrum as the electron jumps upward.

* The important point is that the jumps always involve emission or absorption of a whole number of quanta—an amount of energy equivalent to *hf*, or some multiple of *hf*, but never any amount in between.

the molecules themselves are
made up of atoms

BONDS AND SHELLS

* By the early 1920s Bohr had developed his model of the structure of the atom to explain the basics of chemistry – how and why atoms join together to make molecules.

* *A link that holds atoms together to make molecules is called a* BOND. *The electrons in different orbits are said to occupy* "SHELLS"*—with different energy levels —around the central nucleus of an atom. The shells are like layered onion skins, each containing a certain number of electrons.*

oxygen molecule O_2

carbon dioxide
molecule CO_2

FILLING THE SHELLS

The most stable arrangement for each shell occurs when it contains the maximum number of electrons allowed by the quantum rules, which is two for the innermost shell and eight for most others. The simplest atom, hydrogen, has one PROTON in its nucleus and one electron in orbit around it. The next element, helium, has two protons and also a couple of NEUTRONS, orbited by two electrons in the same shell. But, as we have seen, lithium has to put its third electron in the next shell, and so on.

one carbon and four hydrogen should do it

ATOMIC BONDS

* Bonding results from the atoms' attempts to reach the desirable state of having a full outer shell. One way the optimum distribution of electrons between shells can be achieved is by sharing electrons between two atoms.

we could agree to share...

Electronic illusion

Water is another example of a covalent bond. Two hydrogen atoms, each possessing a single electron, link up with one oxygen atom, which has six electrons in its outermost occupied shell. Again, each atom has the illusion of a filled shell.

COVALENT BOND

* Each hydrogen atom has one electron, and would "like" to have two to fill its only occupied shell. Each carbon atom has six electrons, two in its (full) innermost shell and four in its (half-empty) outer shell. If four hydrogen atoms surround a carbon atom in the right way, the four hydrogen atoms each get a share of one of the outer four electrons of the carbon atom; and the carbon atom gets a share of each of the four electrons associated with the hydrogen atoms. Consequently, all of the atoms in the resulting molecule—CH_4 (methane)—have the illusion of a full outer shell. *This is called a covalent bond.*

hydrogen atom

2 4

carbon atom

IONIC BOND

⁕ Another type of bond keeps sodium and chlorine bound together in common salt. Each sodium atom has 11 electrons: two in a full innermost shell, eight in another full shell, and one on its own outside. If it could lose the outermost electron; it would be left with a full shell as its visible face. Chlorine atoms, on the other hand, each have 17 electrons: two in a full innermost shell, eight in the next (full) shell, and seven in the outermost occupied shell. They need one additional electron to fill the outermost shell.

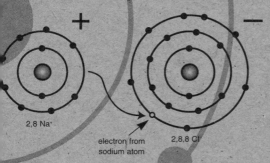

the sodium atom loses one electron, the chlorine atom gains one electron

2,8 Na⁺

electron from sodium atom

2,8,8 Cl⁻

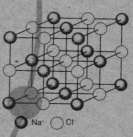

◉ Na⁺ ◯ Cl⁻

sodium chloride lattice

⁕ When sodium and chlorine combine, each sodium atom in effect gives up one electron to a chlorine atom, so both have obtained a full outermost occupied shell. But this leaves each sodium atom with one unit of positive charge; and each chlorine atom with one unit of negative charge. *The charged particles are held together by electric forces, arranged in a* CRYSTAL LATTICE. *This is called an* IONIC BOND.

DE BROGLIE'S INSIGHT

* Bohr had used a mixture of classical and quantum ideas, plus ad hoc rules about the behavior of electrons based on spectroscopy and other experiments. It was a mishmash, but worked in its own way. Then in the mid-1920s Louis de Broglie pointed out that if things like light that had been thought of as waves also behaved like particles (photons), maybe things regarded as particles (electrons and the like) should also be thought of as waves.

Louis de Broglie

The Braggs

The Braggs were the only team consisting of father (William, 1862–1942) and son (Lawrence, 1890–1971) to receive the Nobel Prize for physics for work they carried out together. The work involved the diffraction of X-rays by crystal lattices, which revealed details of the structure of crystals. When the prize was awarded to them, in 1915, Lawrence was only 25 and was serving in the army in France.

THE IMPLICATION OF MOMENTUM

* *One of the things that had convinced Einstein himself that photons must be real is that the equations show that they must carry momentum, just like other particles.*
* The momentum of a particle of light is a prediction of the special theory of relativity, and is found by dividing its energy by its speed. Planck had shown that the energy of a light quantum is equal to hf. And the speed of light is just c. So the momentum of a photon is hf/c. Momentum is usually denoted by the letter p (because m is used for mass) and

wavelength by the Greek letter *l* (lambda). The frequency of a wave divided by its speed is equal to one over its wavelength, so we can write $p = h/l$ or $pl = h$.

* This was true for light. But electrons also have momentum—*so de Broglie realized that they must obey the same equation*, and that an electron with momentum *p* must have a wavelength given by the equation $l = h/p$.

A MOMENTOUS IMPLICATION

* De Broglie's hypothesis was soon confirmed by experiments in which beams of electrons were fired at crystal lattices—just as Xrays had been fired at crystal lattices by **William** and **Lawrence Bragg**, the pioneers of Xray crystallography.

* Like the Xrays, or like light in the experiment with two holes, the electrons interfered with one another and produced a <u>DIFFRACTION PATTERN</u>, proving that they were waves. *All quantum entities, it was realized, not just light, have this dual wave-particle nature.*
What did it mean?

crystal

Louis de Broglie (1892–1987)

De Broglie was a French aristocrat, whose family intended for him to join the diplomatic corps. But, encouraged by his older brother Maurice, he turned to physics. His studies were interrupted by army service during the First World War. He worked on radio communications and was based at the Eiffel Tower for a time. As a result, he did not complete his Ph.D., presenting his wave theory of electrons, until 1924, when he was already in his thirties. Louis and Maurice both served on the French High Commission of Atomic Energy, and were involved in the peaceful applications of atomic energy after the Second World War.

KEY WORDS

DIFFRACTION PATTERN: pattern made when waves (of any kind) bend around an obstruction or spread out from a small hole

THE EXPERIMENT WITH TWO HOLES REVISITED

* The experiment with two holes has now been refined to such an extent that it is possible to fire individual photons one at a time, so each of them arrives at the detector screen on the other side and makes a pinpoint of light. It is also possible to do the same kind of thing with electrons, using a detector screen like a TV screen where each electron makes a single point of light as it arrives.

there must be something better on tv than these two points of light

CENTRAL PARADOX

The experiment with two holes incorporates what Richard Feynman (see page 145) used to call 'the central mystery' of quantum mechanics: **all particles are waves, and all waves are particles.**

SPONTANEOUS INTERFERENCE...

* Both versions of the experiment have actually been done. In both cases, the single quantum entities (photons and electrons) start out on one side of the experiment as particles and arrive at the other side as particles.

* *But if you run the experiment many times, either with photons or with electrons, then the spots of light on the detector screen add up to produce an interference pattern. The implication is that both the photons and the electrons* pass through the two holes as waves, and somehow interfere with themselves to make the interference pattern.

...AND TELEPATHIC PARTICLES?

* Stranger still, each individual particle travels through the experiment on its own. And makes the spot of light on the screen on its own. *But if you send hundreds or thousands of particles through the experiment, not even all together but one after the other, they conspire to produce an interference pattern.* Each quantum entity seems to be aware of the whole experimental set-up—including the presence of the two holes in the middle of the experiment, and the presence of the preceding and following particles.

* *Quantum entities somehow seem to take no notice of space and time—or rather to take account of all of space and all of time at once.*

It's the three of clubs

PARTICLE 1

PARTICLE 2

Revolutionary physics

The development of the theory of quantum physics in the 1920s has been described by Nobel Laureate Steven Weinberg as "the most profound revolution in physical theory since the birth of modern physics in the 17th century." It "changed our idea of the questions we are allowed to ask."

KEY WORDS

INTERFERENCE PATTERN: pattern made when two sets of waves overlap one another

RIVAL THEORIES

* In 1925 two different teams of physicists came up with two different ways to describe all this mathematically. The one approach, which was pioneered by Werner Heisenberg, discarded the idea of waves and offered a solution based on quantum jumping. The other, pioneered by Erwin Schrödinger, deliberately tried to get rid of what he called "this damned quantum jumping" and used the idea of waves.

Werner Heisenberg

I don't agree with waves

Erwin Schrödin...

Paul Dirac (1902–84)

Probably the greatest English scientist since Newton, Dirac was so self-effacing that his name is almost unknown outside scientific circles. He came up with the most complete early version of quantum mechanics, and showed that both Heisenberg's and Schrödinger's theories were special cases of his own theory. The idea of antimatter, a kind of mirror-image matter in which properties like electric charge are reversed, was also originated by him.

THAT DAMNED JUMPING!

* *Strangely, both approaches to the quantum world gave exactly the same answers when used to calculate things like the behavior of electrons in atoms—and both, of course, agreed with the findings of the experimenters.*

* Within a year, **Paul Dirac** had shown why. Both of the approaches were mathematically equivalent to one another—*because each of them was a special case of a more abstract kind of mathematical formalism that didn't involve the*

Paul Dirac

Werner Heisenberg

image of quantum entities as either waves or particles (or as anything we are at all familiar with).

* This discovery—with its implication that even his wave equation could not get rid of that "damned quantum jumping"—led Schrödinger to express his disgust with the theory he had helped to develop, saying, "I don't like it, and I'm sorry I ever had anything to do with it."

QUANTUM REALITY?

* But Niels Bohr, Max Born, and others seized on the new mathematical equations of quantum mechanics and produced a picture of what seemed to be going on in the quantum world. The picture didn't make sense—at least not in terms of everyday common sense—but it did have its own internal logic and it did seem to describe quantum reality.

FEVERISH EFFORT

Werner Heisenberg (1901–76) was able to work out his version of quantum mechanics, in the spring of 1925, thanks to a vicious attack of hay fever. Recuperating on the island of Heligoland, without distractions, he had the opportunity to develop his radically new vision of the way the world worked. Since Heisenberg was the only prominent physicist of his generation to stay at his post in Germany during the Second World War, the Allies feared he might be leading a Nazi program to develop an atomic bomb. However, he always maintained that he steered the Nazis away from atomic weapons. The truth will never be known.

the Allies were concerned that Heisenberg might make an atomic bomb for the Nazis

One of the most famous aspects of the quantum world is Heisenberg's uncertainty principle. Heisenberg used the wave-particle duality to show that you can never measure both the exact position of an entity such as an electron and its exact momentum at the same time. *In other words, you cannot simultaneously know where the electron is and where it is going. Worse still, the electron itself can't know both where it is and where it is going (at least not exactly).* Quantum uncertainty isn't anything to do with the imperfection of our experiments or the deficiencies of our measuring equipment —it is built into the very fabric of the quantum world.

WHAT IS MEANT BY UNCERTAINTY

* To understand what Heisenberg meant by uncertainty, think about the properties of waves (also, remember that all quantum entities have a wave nature). A wave cannot possibly be located at a single point in space, because by its very nature a wave is a spread-out thing. A pure wave (with a single wavelength) stretches out forever and carries momentum, but has no location and no resemblance to a particle. In contrast, a particle has a definite position but it has no wave properties.

WAVE PACKETS

* However, if you mix different waves together, you can make what is called a WAVE PACKET, *where the waves cancel each other out everywhere except in a small region.* The wave packet is a bit like a particle—but with a rather fuzzy boundary and no exact location. It can be made as small as you like, up to a point (or rather, not quite literally up to a point).

wave packet →

what a wave!

a wave has momentum but it has
no definite location, because it
is spread out

Momentum and position

Heisenberg showed that there is a very precise trade-off between momentum and position. If you multiply the amount by which the position of an electron (or anything else) is uncertain by the amount by which its momentum is uncertain, the number you get is always bigger than Planck's constant, h.

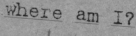

where am I?

ELECTRON

* Now think about momentum. A single pure wave has a definite momentum, which can be determined by the equation Einstein worked out from his special theory of relativity. *But in a wave packet there is a mixture of waves and a mixture of momenta. In order to make the wave packet smaller, you need more waves in the packet, to do the crucial canceling out, and that creates more uncertainty about the momentum of the wave packet.*

Heisenberg said you cannot
simultaneously know where
the electron is and where
it is going

103

THE STRANGENESS OF THE QUANTUM WORLD

it's all so strange

* Now you can see why the strange features of the quantum world don't show up in everyday life, and are not common sense. But the reason why we don't have any doubt about the position of a bag of sugar on a shelf, or the momentum of a billiard ball rolling across a table, is that they are so big—compared with things like electrons.

Talking about quanta

When we talk about a quantum entity being *like* a wave or *like* a particle, we mean just that—and nothing more. All we are doing is using our everyday experience, and everyday language, to provide us with an image of what is going on.

TINY DIFFERENCES

* Planck's constant (h) is absolutely tiny. Using the system of units where energy is measured in ergs and mass in grams, $h = 6.6 \times 10^{-27}$ (that is, a decimal point followed by 26 zeros before the 66). Quantum effects only become important for entities that have masses (measured in grams) in this sort of range, or smaller. The mass of an electron, for example, is 9×10^{-28} grams.

* An uncertainty of h in the momentum or position of an electron is a big deal—while a

$h = 6.6 \times 10^{-27}$ (that is, a decimal point followed by 26 zeros before the 66)

similar uncertainty in the position or momentum of a bag of sugar or a billiard ball, or a human being, is far too small to be noticed at all.

WOW! Just look at that wave

waves are an everyday way of thinking about quantum physics, but in reality quantum particles are not like anything we can see

MARCHING TO THE QUANTUM RULES

★ Uncertainty and wave-particle duality are intimately linked—but the important thing to remember about all the strangeness of the quantum world is that nobody is saying that a thing like an electron "really is" a particle, or that it "really is" a wave. Its very nature is different from anything we are used to in everyday life. It obeys a different set of rules—the quantum rules—and marches to the beat of a different drum.

I do hate uncertainty

105

QUANTUM THEORY IN ACTION

* A nice example of the way in which quantum entities differ from everyday entities, and how the wave picture helps as an analogy, is a phenomenon known as the HYDROGEN BOND.

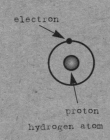

electron

proton

hydrogen atom

ALTERNATIVE PERCEPTIONS

* A hydrogen atom consists of a single proton (the nucleus), surrounded by a single electron. The words "surrounded by" are completely appropriate. One way of looking at things is to say that the position of the electron is uncertain—it could be anywhere in a cloud surrounding the proton. Alternatively, instead of talking about a tiny particle in orbit around the proton, you could say that there is a wave that winds right around the atom. Either way, the hydrogen atom behaves as if the electric charge carried by the electron is spread out uniformly around the proton.

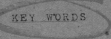

KEY WORDS

HYDROGEN BOND:
a weak form of chemical bonding that sometimes occurs between two molecules when one of them is made up partly of hydrogen atoms

The ratio of hydrogen to oxygen in water. There are two atoms of hydrogen for every atom of oxygen

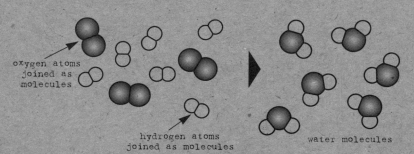

oxygen atoms joined as molecules

hydrogen atoms joined as molecules

water molecules

THE NICETIES OF THE HYDROGEN BOND

* When a hydrogen atom links up with something else to form a molecule—for example, when two hydrogen atoms join onto a single atom of oxygen to make water (H_2O)—the electron cloud is gripped both by the hydrogen atom's nucleus and by the nucleus of the other atom. It forms a bridge between the two atoms. *But because the electron is now concentrated at one end of the hydrogen atom, the other end is partly uncovered.*

* If electrons really were little particles, and chemical bonds formed in exactly the way Bohr described, the other end of the hydrogen atom would be completely bare, exposing its proton's positive charge. So water molecules would interact strongly with almost anything they came into contact with. But because even a single electron is spread out around the hydrogen nucleus, there is still a little shielding of the positive charge on the hydrogen nucleus. *This means that the end of the hydrogen atom opposite the chemical bond acts as if it has a fraction of a positive electric charge.*

* Although the quantum theory of hydrogen bonds was worked out by **Linus Pauling** (1901–94) in the 1930s, it was only in the late 1990s that experiments became subtle enough to measure all the details of the effect he predicted and confirm that he was right.

PREDICTABLE BEHAVIOR

This difference between how particles behave and how quantum entities behave produces a measurable effect, in terms of the strength with which the partly exposed proton interacts with other atoms and molecules. *The strength of this interaction can be measured in chemical experiments—and matches the predictions of quantum theory, not classical ideas.*

your behavior is so predictable

107

THE COPENHAGEN INTERPRETATION

* The "explanation" of the quantum world that Bohr and others developed is called the Copenhagen Interpretation, because a lot of it was worked out at Niels Bohr's institute in that city. We have already encountered two of the main planks of the Copenhagen Interpretation, uncertainty and wave-particle duality. Another key idea, the role of PROBABILITY in quantum processes, was introduced by Max Born.

Max Born

you are looking lovely tonight

Complementarity

Wave-particle duality is sometimes known as COMPLEMENTARITY, because the two aspects of quantum reality complement each other. You can't have one without the other.

THOSE TWO HOLES AGAIN

* In a quantum system, you can never be sure of the outcome of an experiment. If there are several possible outcomes, *all you can do is work out the probability of each one*—exactly like working out the odds of a particular hand being dealt at cards. In the simplest example, when an electron confronts the two holes in the experiment with two holes, *provided nobody looks*, it seems to go both ways at once and interfere with itself. *But if you set up a detector at each of the holes to monitor the electrons*

working out the odds

108

passing by, you
find that half of them go
one way and half go the other
way—with no interference.

DISTURBING OBSERVATION

* *This is also an example
of the fourth
plank of the Copenhagen
Interpretation—which
asserts that the system is
disturbed by the very act of
observing or measuring it.*

if you look you
will spoil the
experiment

* This idea can be seen at work in the
COLLAPSE OF THE WAVE FUNCTION. An
electron wave function is quite happy
going through both holes at once if
nobody looks at it. *But if you look, it
collapses into a particle and goes one way
or the other—with, in this particular
case, equal probability.* There's a 50:50
chance that any individual electron will be
seen going through one hole or the other
one, but you can never predict from the
laws of physics which hole it will choose.

ONE OR OTHER

* The collapse of the wave function
doesn't matter if you are designing
something practical like the picture tube
of a TV set, because billions of electrons
are involved. *Provided half go one way
and half go the other way, you don't care
what each individual electron does.*

KEY WORDS

WAVE FUNCTION:
mathematical
representation of the
wave nature of a
quantum system

Max Born (1882–1970)

Max Born, who
introduced the concept
of quantum probability,
was professor of physics
at Göttingen University
from 1921 to 1933. A
warm and friendly man,
he made Göttingen a
leading center of quantum
physics and was greatly
irritated when the
standard theory (to
which he made major
contributions) became
known as the Copenhagen
Interpretation. Forced to
leave Germany when
Hitler came to power,
during the 1930s he
lectured at Cambridge
then became Professor
of Natural Philosophy
at Edinburgh University.

the universe is like
a huge casino

QUANTUM PROBABILITY

* This business of quantum probability shows up very clearly in RADIOACTIVE DECAY— which occurs when an unstable atom (strictly speaking, an unstable nucleus) spits out particles and transforms itself into something else.

"I cannot believe that God plays dice."

ALBERT EINSTEIN

A DICEY BUSINESS

* *Each kind of* RADIOACTIVE ATOM *has a characteristic lifetime, known as its* HALF-LIFE. *In any pile of radioactive atoms of the same kind, exactly half will transform themselves in this way in one half-life.* Half the rest (a quarter of the original) will decay in the next half-life, and so on. Yet any individual atom in the pile might decay at once, or it could stick around for very many half-lives before decaying—exactly as if each atom flips a coin, repeatedly, and decides to decay only if the coin comes up heads.

* It was the role of probability in quantum mechanics, and in the Copenhagen Interpretation in particular, that led Einstein to make the famous remark, "I cannot believe that God plays dice." *But all the evidence suggests that Einstein was wrong: nature (what Einstein, an atheist, always meant by "God") operates on the same principles as a casino.*

THE VALUE OF QUANTUM PHYSICS

* *It is important to appreciate that the package of ideas enshrined in the Copenhagen Interpretation really does work.* It is the toolkit most practical physicists use when they are dealing with quantum entities—which, for practical physicists, usually means electrons and/or light.

* Far from being some abstract byway of science, quantum physics underpins all of the modern understanding of chemistry. To take the most profound example, the famous double-helix structure of DNA— the molecule of life—is held together by hydrogen bonds, which are a quintessentially quantum phenomenon.

DNA double helix

thanks to quantum physics..

* More obviously, quantum physics also describes the behavior of electrons moving through circuits and semiconductors, including the microchips at the heart of modern computers. And it describes the behavior of lasers, those intense pulses of light now used prosaically in everyday items such as CD players.

111

SCHRÖDINGER'S CAT

don't think I'm going to like this

* Erwin Schrödinger's dislike of the Copenhagen Interpretation led him to devise a "thought experiment" to demonstrate its absurdity, known as his "Cat Paradox."

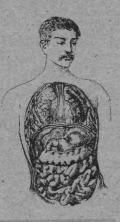

INDIGESTIBLE PHYSICS

Quantum physics is weird, but it works. Which doesn't make the Copenhagen Interpretation any easier to digest. The person who found it most difficult to stomach was Erwin Schrödinger. That was why he came up with his 'Cat Paradox' in 1935. But his experiment is not so much a paradox as a graphic illustration of the weirdness of the quantum world.

DIABOLICAL SCENARIO

* Schrödinger asks us to imagine a sealed chamber in which there is a cat, supplied with food and drink and all the other things it needs for a comfortable and healthy life. But in the chamber there is also a "diabolical device," which is hooked up to a sample of radioactive material (perhaps just a single atom). *The ingenious device is set up so that if-and when the radioactive material decays, it will trigger the release of poison gas, which will kill the cat.*

will the cat be alive?

CRUCIAL QUESTIONS

* If you wait outside the chamber for a suitable length of time, there will come a moment when there is exactly a 50:50 chance that the radioactive sample has decayed in just the right way to trigger the diabolical device. *What, asks Schrödinger, is the state of the cat at that precise instant? And what will you see if you open the chamber door?*

* The second question is easier to answer. If you look, you will see either a dead cat or a live cat, with equal probability. Or to put it another way, if you were to do such an experiment a thousand times, half the time you would find a dead cat and half the time you would find a live one.

Erwin Schrödinger

Erwin Schrödinger (1887-1961)

The man who came up with the most widely used version of quantum theory, wave mechanics, thought he was restoring sanity to a subject that had got out of control. A physicist of the old school, he was nearly 40 when he did this work. By expressing quantum physics in terms of waves, Schrödinger planned to bring it in line with classical ideas. When this proved impossible, he was deeply upset—and had little more to do with quantum theory, except to point out what he believed to be its flaws.

will the cat be dead?

OR

Schrödinger's cat experiment shows the weirdness of quantum physics. I think it shows the weirdness of Schrödinger...

I'm not going to look..
I'm not going to look.

OPENING THE DOOR

* According to the Copenhagen Interpretation, the collapse of the wave function *only occurs when you look*—so *just before* you open the door of Schrödinger's hypothetical chamber and look inside, the radioactive sample is still hovering in a state of uncertainty, not sure whether it has decayed or not.

DISCLAIMER

It is usual to comfort the reader by stressing that no experiment like the one in Schrödinger's puzzle has ever been carried out and no cats have been mistreated in this way. The idea of a thought experiment is that it is literally all in the mind.

DEAD OR ALIVE?

* At this point its wave function still contains both possibilities, like the unobserved electron in the two-hole experiment going through both holes at once. *So the poison both has and has not been released, and the cat is both dead and alive.* Everything inside the chamber is supposed to be described by an uncertain wave function, which only collapses when somebody looks at it. Nobody believes the inside of the chamber is really like that—but the trouble is that nobody has come up with a better way, mathematically, to describe what is going on.

thank goodness for the disclaimer

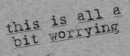

this is all a bit worrying

LETTING THE CAT DECIDE

* One seemingly obvious way
to resolve Schrödinger's paradox is
to say that the cat is quite capable of
deciding whether or not it is alive, and
can collapse the wave function all by
itself. But then where do you draw the
line? Can you do the same sort of thing
with a rat, or a flea, or a microbe?

* *Some people just say that it is the
number of atoms (or other particles)
involved that makes more complicated
systems behave in accordance with
classical physics, while simpler systems
(that is, ones having fewer atoms) obey
quantum rules.*

well I'm not going to do it

* But again, where do you
draw the line? DNA
molecules obey quantum
rules. Fleas don't. Where in
between is the boundary?

*Can there really be a system
that obeys quantum rules
but which if you added
just one more atom
to it would start to
behave classically?
Nobody can say.*

DNA molecules WILL obey quantum rules

What is life?

Schrödinger left Germany
in 1933, when the Nazis
came to power, and turned
up in Oxford with both a
wife and a mistress, but
he didn't stay long. After
several moves, he settled
in Dublin, where an
institute was set up to
give him a base. There
he wrote a book about
the molecular basis of
life, entitled *What is
Life?* This encouraged a
generation of physicists
to turn to molecular
biology after the Second
World War. One of
them was Francis Crick,
codiscoverer of the
structure of DNA.

MANY WORLDS

* To some people,
Schrödinger's puzzle is
so worrying that they
have come up with all
kinds of alternative
"interpretations" of the
quantum world. But in
their own ways they
are all just as weird
as the Copenhagen
Interpretation; for instance
the "Many Worlds" Interpretation, which
will be familiar to science-fiction fans.

but that's the next door universe mate

are all kinds of
things happening in a
parallel Universe?

First, but not best?

Some people find the
'Many Worlds' idea
easier to accept than
the Copenhagen
Interpretation. Some
don't. But more people
use the Copenhagen
Interpretation than any
other interpretation,
simply because it came
first and was established
in the marketplace by
Niels Bohr's powerful
advocacy of it.

SEPARATE REALITIES

* According to the "Many Worlds"
Interpretation, every time the quantum world
is faced with a choice (such as whether or
not the radioactive sample in the chamber
with the cat decays), the entire universe
splits into two—or into however many
copies are required to cover every possible
outcome of the quantum event.

* In the case of Schrödinger's cat, instead of
hovering in a state of uncertainty, the
radioactive atom both decays and doesn't
decay, creating two separate realities—which
in some sense coexist alongside each other.

* *These separate realities are complete
copies of each other in every detail except for
the outcome of the particular quantum
choice.* So there is one universe in which you

open the door and find a dead cat, and a Universe next door in which an exact copy of you opens the door and finds a live cat.

MULTIPLE INTERPRETATIONS

* The thing is, all of the different interpretations of quantum mechanics give you exactly the same answers about

computer chip

things you can actually measure. They have exactly the same value in designing computer chips, or tinkering with DNA for the purposes of genetic engineering, or whatever. If there was any practical way to tell them apart at this level, it would be clear which one was best—*but because they are all mathematically identical, you are allowed to choose which one you like (or which you find least unacceptable).*

the "Many Worlds" theory says there are parallel worlds, one where the cat is dead and one where it is alive

MATHEMATICAL TRUTH

Don't worry if you can't understand how the quantum world works. In the words of Richard Feynman (who won the Nobel Prize, in 1965, for his work in quantum physics and knew what he was talking about), "nobody knows how it can be like that." ***What matters is the truth about the way the world works, expressed in mathematics.*** The truth lies in the equations—and all the physical images are just mental crutches, designed to help inadequate human minds get a picture of what is going on by using analogies drawn from the world of everyday experience. And that, surely, is all anyone without a degree in physics needs to know about quantum mechanics.

CHAPTER 4

EVEN NEWER PHYSICS

how does the world work?

* The latest physics forms a two-pronged attack on the puzzle of how the world works. One line of attack continues the approach developed by the quantum pioneers, probing deeper and deeper into the structure of matter in an attempt to find the ultimate building blocks. The other takes a different route entirely, and concentrates on the way large numbers of building blocks (whatever they may be) behave. The suggestion is that the whole may be greater than the sum of its parts—or at least, that it would be a good idea to find out whether or not this is true.

FIELD QUANTA

The old physics said that particles are carried from one particle to another by waves in a field of force. The new physics says they are carried by other particles, called field quanta.

FERMIONS AND BOSONS

* The everyday world is made of atoms, and the behavior of the entities that make up atoms is very well described by the rules of quantum physics. Although we should remember that all particles are also waves, and all waves are also particles, it is still convenient to think of the material world as made of particles and to talk about the interactions between particles as being associated with fields like the electromagnetic field.

* But there is a fundamental difference between the two ways of looking at things. The things we are used to thinking of as particles, such as electrons, are conserved (there is always the same number of electrons in the universe). While the things we are used to thinking of as field quanta —such as photons—are not conserved (you make billions of them when you turn on a light, but they disappear when they are absorbed by your eye). For historical reasons, the first kind of particles are called FERMIONS, while the latter (the photonlike particles) are called BOSONS.

there is always the same number of electrons in the Universe

QUANTUM ELECTROMAGNETISM

* The particles that make up atoms are the protons and neutrons in the nucleus and the electrons surrounding the nucleus. The interactions between the electrically charged particles (the protons and electrons) and between atoms themselves are described by the quantum version of electromagnetism— a theory known as QUANTUM ELECTRODYNAMICS, or QED.

All change

Instead of describing electromagnetic interactions in terms of waves, in QED these interactions are described in terms of photons being exchanged between charged particles. *In quantum theory, because all waves can be described as particles, it follows that all forces can be described in this way (as the exchange of field quanta). The photon is the quantum of the electromagnetic field.*

I'll trade you a couple of photons for that

a force of
strength
keeping
them
together

GRAVITY AND GRAVITONS

We don't have to worry about gravity when thinking about the forces between atoms and molecules at the level of chemistry, because gravity is very much weaker than electromagnetism. To be precise, the electrical force of repulsion between two protons is about 10^{36} (a 1 followed by 36 zeros) times stronger than the gravitational force trying to pull them together. That is why stars are so big. They have to be, in order for gravity to overwhelm those electromagnetic forces and make protons fuse together in their cores, releasing energy as they do so. *But gravity can also be described as operating by the exchange of field quanta, which in this case are called* GRAVITONS.

NUCLEAR INTERACTIONS

* In order for nuclei of atoms to hold together despite the fact that they are filled with positively charged protons, there has to be a force much stronger than electromagnetism— and much, much stronger than gravity— to do the trick. It is called the strong nuclear force.

proton

electrons moving around the nucleus

nucleus

neutron

inside the atom

THE STRONG NUCLEAR FORCE

* *The strong nuclear force has a very short range. In fact, it cannot be felt at a distance bigger than the diameter of a nucleus, which is why nuclei have the diameters they do.* But, in fact it is very much stronger than the electromagnetic force (about a hundred times stronger) and holds the nucleus together in spite of the repulsion of all that positive charge. This situation is also helped by the presence in the nucleus of neutrons, which also feel the strong force, but have no electric charge.

THE WEAK NUCLEAR INTERACTION

* There is one other interaction that affects nuclei. This is called the weak nuclear interaction—because it is weaker than the strong nuclear interaction and weaker than electromagnetism (although it is still 10^{25} times stronger than gravity). *It operates in a subtly different way from the other interactions and makes itself known by causing the process of radioactive decay, when an unstable nucleus splits (or fissions) into two or more pieces.*

BETA DECAY

The weak interaction is also the driving force behind a related process known as beta decay. This happens when a neutron left on its own spontaneously spits out an electron (electrons used to be known as beta rays), plus a particle called an electron <u>ANTINEUTRINO</u>, and transforms itself into a proton. That is allowed by the quantum rules —even though electrons are conserved—because the electron antineutrino balances the books. For the purposes of this kind of bookkeeping, the neutron and proton can be regarded as different versions of the same particle, which is sometimes dubbed the <u>NUCLEON</u>.

KEY WORDS

GRAVITON:
the field quantum of the gravitational field

NEUTRINO:
a particle in the same family as the electron that has no electric charge and only a tiny mass (possibly no mass at all)

ANTINEUTRINO:
antimatter counterpart to the neutrino

NUCLEON:
either of the two kinds of particle found in an atomic nucleus—the proton and the neutron

atomic bookkeeping is all about keeping the positive and negative charge balanced

PARTICLES AND ANTIPARTICLES

* ANTIPARTICLES are a kind of mirror-image counterpart to everyday particles: they possess reversed properties. For example, the antiparticle counterpart to the electron, the anti-electron, has positive charge instead of negative charge. For this reason, it is often called the POSITRON.

the antiparticles are a mirror image

THE DISCOVERY OF QUARKS

* There is no experimental evidence that electrons have any internal structure (they behave as if their mass and electric charge were concentrated at a point). But in the 1960s several lines of experimental evidence indirectly suggested that there might be structure inside protons and neutrons. *George Zweig and Murray Gell-Mann independently came up with an explanation for*

we call it a quark!

the experiments by proposing that there were particles inside both kinds of nucleons. Gell-Mann gave these particles the name "QUARKS." Although he intended the name to rhyme with "pork," most physicists pronounce it to rhyme with "bark"—but either pronunciation is acceptable.

Murray Gell-Mann

INSIDE NUCLEONS

✱ In the 1970s a team at the Stanford Linear Accelerator, in California, probed the structure of nucleons by firing beams of electrons at solid targets—in much the same way that Rutherford's team had probed the structure of the atom by firing alpha particles at gold foil in 1909 (see page 88). The electrons bounced off something inside the nucleons, and James Bjorken and Richard Feynman showed that the properties of the particles inside nucleons matched the expected properties of quarks.

✱ *The picture that emerged of the structure inside nucleons is that the proton and the neutron are each composed of three quarks. But only two different kinds of quark are needed to describe them.* These quarks were given the whimsical names "UP" and "DOWN"—but the names don't mean anything, they could just as well have been called Tom and Jerry. *A proton is made up of two up quarks and one down quark, while a neutron is made up of two down quarks and one up quark.*

COUNTING PARTICLES

When we are working out how many particles are involved in an interaction, each particle counts as +1 and each antiparticle counts as –1. *There must always be the same number of particles coming out at the end of the interaction as went in at the beginning.* In this sense, when a neutron decays into a proton and releases an electron and an antineutrino, these two entities cancel each other out. We start with a single particle, the neutron, and a count of +1. We end up with three "particles," but the count is +1 for the proton, +1 for the electron, and –1 for the antineutrino. So the total is still +1.

Huey   Dewey   Louie

The name given to the property of quarks analogous to electric charge is totally arbitrary. It doesn't mean that quarks are colored in the everyday sense of the word, any more than calling a child Rose means she is rose-colored. It is just a name. It might have been better if the color charge and color field had been called the glue charge and glue field, especially since the term "glue force" is used. Although there are only two types of electric charge (positive and negative), there are three kinds of color charge: <u>RED, GREEN</u> and <u>BLUE</u>. They could just as well have been called Huey, Dewey, and Louie.

THE COLOR FORCE

* The quarks are held together inside nucleons by what seems at first sight to be another force (or interaction), which behaves in a similar way to the strong nuclear force. But it turned out that this is really the underlying interaction responsible for the strong nuclear force itself—so there are still only four fundamental forces of nature.

now take the glue and the 3 quarks you made earlier and assemble the model

COLOR CHARGE

* Quarks carry an electric charge (the up quark has a charge of $2/3$ of the charge on a proton, and the down quark has a charge of $1/3$ of the charge on an electron), but

they also have another property very similar to electric charge. It is called color charge, but the name is entirely arbitrary. It doesn't mean that quarks are actually colored.

QUANTUM CHROMODYNAMICS

* *Quarks are held together by the exchange of particles called* GLUONS *(because they "glue" quarks together), which play the role in the context of the* COLOR FIELD *that photons play for the electromagnetic field.*

* The quark/gluon theory that describes this behavior is modeled on QED (see page 119) and is called QUANTUM CHROMODYNAMICS, or QCD. Some of the color force that holds quarks together inside nucleons leaks out of the nucleon, and can hold onto the nucleon next door. *And this is what we perceive as the strong nuclear force.*

quantum physics is full of whimsical names

KEY WORDS

GLUONS: the field quanta of the color field

Strange duplication

The two kinds of quarks needed to make protons and neutrons are neatly balanced by the electron and its partner the neutrino, which is involved in processes like beta decay (see page 121). *There are just four kinds of particle needed to describe all of the observed material world, and just four kinds of force. Strangely, though, it turns out that the particles are duplicated in nature—not once, but twice.*

ACCELERATED PARTICLES

* Particle accelerators are machines used to speed particles like electrons and protons to very high energies and smash them together. We talk about high energies, rather than high speeds, because no particle can move faster than the speed of light. As the speed of the particles in accelerators gets close to this limit, the energy put in (from electromagnetic fields) increases the mass of the particles, instead of making them go faster.

new particles
are created in
the collisions

Charm and strange, top and bottom

As well as the up and down quarks, there are heavier, unstable, versions that can be manufactured in particle collisions— namely, a pair known as CHARM and STRANGE, and a pair known as TOP and BOTTOM. Nobody knows why nature should have triplicated the fundamental particles in this way, making three "generations" of the fundamental particles. But, for most purposes, all we need to worry about are the up and down quarks, the electron and its neutrino, and the four fundamental interactions.

CREATING NEW PARTICLES

* New particles are created in the collisions. *These are literally new, not just pieces of colliding particles that have broken off.* The new particles are made out of pure energy—in line with Einstein's famous equation $E = mc^2$, which can be turned around to read $m = E/c^2$. The more energy (E) you put in, the more mass (m) you can get out (as ever, c is the speed of light). *Most of the particles made in this way are unstable, and soon decay into familiar forms such as electrons and protons.*

three types of
electrons

HEAVY VERSIONS

* *As well as the electron and its neutrino, it is possible by using a particle accelerator to manufacture a heavier version of each particle, and a third, even heavier, version.*

* A heavy electron is called a <u>MUON</u>. Its mass is just over 200 times bigger than the mass of an electron (for comparison, the mass of a proton is about 2,000 times the mass of an electron, and the neutron has much the same mass as a proton), but otherwise it is identical to an electron. Although it can be made in accelerators, it decays into an electron in just two-millionths of a second.

brother... these muons are hard to shift

just you wait until we get to the tau particles

SPLIT-SECOND LIVING

The even heavier electron is called a <u>TAU PARTICLE</u> (sometimes tau-minus), or <u>TAUON</u>. It has a mass 70 percent bigger than a proton, but its lifetime is only 30-thousandths of a billionth of a second. The muon and the tauon each have their own kind of neutrino to accompany them in particle interactions (neutrinos have only tiny masses). All these electronlike particles and neutrinos are collectively known as <u>LEPTONS</u>.

KEY WORDS

MUON:
a heavier version of the electron
TAUON:
an even heavier version of the electron
LEPTONS:
collective name for the electron, muon, tauon, and their respective neutrinos

THE WEINBERG-SALAM THEORY

* One of the greatest achievements of theoretical physics in recent decades came in 1967, when two researchers, Abdus Salam and Steven Weinberg, each independently found a way to combine the electromagnetic interaction and the weak nuclear interaction in one package. They showed that both interactions could be regarded as manifestations of a single force, which became known as the ELECTROWEAK INTERACTION.

physicists are on a quest for a universal theory of everything

POPULAR PHYSICIST

Outside the field of theoretical physics Steven Weinberg, the American physicist who played a major role in the development of the electroweak theory in the 1960s, is known to a wide audience as the author of a best-selling book about the Big Bang, entitled *The First Three Minutes*.

ELECTROWEAK AT WORK

* *The crucial feature of the electroweak theory is that it includes four field quanta.* There is the familiar photon, which mediates the electromagnetic interaction; and there are three other bosons, called W^+, W^- and Z^0, which between them mediate all possible weak interactions.

* There are three of these bosons because weak interactions, unlike electromagnetic interactions, can involve the particles concerned in changing their electric charge

—as when a neutron (which is electrically neutral) decays into a positively charged proton and a negatively charged electron, plus an electron antineutrino. According to the new picture, what happens is that the neutron spits out a W⁻ particle, leaving a proton behind, and the W⁻ then decays into the other two particles.

* More generally, the charged quanta of the electroweak field can carry either negative electric charge or positive electric charge from one particle to another. But since some weak interactions do not involve a change of charge, there also has to be a neutral boson, the Z particle.

PREDICTIONS FULFILLED

* Unlike photons, though, the two Ws and the Z particle have to have mass. *The great triumph of the electroweak theory was that when these particles were first manufactured in accelerator experiments, at CERN in the early 1980s, the masses predicted for the particles turned out to be exactly correct.* The two Ws each have about 83 times the mass of a proton, while the mass of the Z is about 93 times a proton's. All three particles are, of course, highly unstable and quickly decay into other things.

it's about 83 or could it be 93 times the mass

ELECTROWEAK INTERACTION: unified version of electromagnetism and the weak interaction, described by a single set of equations

Quest for a universal theory

What physicists would like to have is a single theory that can describe all of these entities in one set of mathematical equations, in the same way that Maxwell's equations described everything known to 19th-century science about electromagnetic interactions. This is a good analogy, because Maxwell showed that electricity and magnetism could be unified in one mathematical package. If two forces can be unified in this way, why not all of them?

MADE FROM PURE ENERGY

* How can a particle like a neutron spit out a particle that is 80 or 90 times heavier than itself? Because the particle that is being spat out has been made out of pure energy, not out of the mass of the neutron. It was never "inside" the neutron in any sense.

Abdus Salam (1926–96)

Devoted to encouraging the development of science in the Third World, Salam worked in Pakistan, where he was born, then in Cambridge, before becoming Professor of Theoretical Physics at Imperial College, London (1957–93). Besides his pioneering work on electroweak theory, he set up the International Center for Theoretical Physics, in Trieste, where young scientists from developing countries work alongside visiting experts.

Abdus Salam

ENERGY FROM UNCERTAINTY

very strong forces have a short range but less strong forces have an enormous range

* *The energy comes from* QUANTUM UNCERTAINTY. *Like the uncertainty that relates position and momentum, there is an uncertainty that relates time and energy. It says that for a brief instant of time, a packet of energy can pop into existence out of nothing at all.* The shorter the time involved, the more energy is allowed to appear in this way. But it has to disappear again within a time limit determined by its equivalent mass, which is given by that familiar equation $E = mc^2$.

PROMPT DISCARD

* Enough energy to make a W or a Z particle can appear in this way, provided it promptly disappears. In beta decay, a little extra energy comes from the mass of the neutron ($E = mc^2$ again)—so when the W particle is forced to disappear, it turns the extra energy it stole from the neutron into an electron and its antineutrino partner, instead of leaving behind nothing at all. Protons are therefore a bit less massive than neutrons.

* *The amount of energy involved determines how far a particle made in this way (called a* <u>VIRTUAL PARTICLE</u>*) can travel before it has to decay. The more mass, the shorter the distance it can go. This limits the range of the bosons involved and explains why the strong and weak nuclear forces only operate on a tiny scale, while the electromagnetic interaction and gravity—which are mediated by massless photons and gravitons respectively— have an enormous (in principle, infinite) range.*

can I borrow a bit of energy until Tuesday

a packet of energy can appear from nothing at all, provided it promptly disappears

KEY WORDS

QUANTUM UNCERTAINTY: Phenomenon of the quantum world that applies to various pairs of properties, such as position-momentum and energy-time. The more accurately one member of the pair is known, the less accurately the other is known.

VIRTUAL PARTICLE: A particle that only exists as a result of quantum uncertainty. It "borrows" energy from the vacuum to make itself, but quickly has to give it back and disappear. Empty space is a seething froth of virtual particles.

ELASTIC BANDS AND GLUE

* Unlike gravity and electromagnetic forces, the glue force is *strongest* when it operates on pairs or triplets of quarks that are far apart. This sounds utterly bizarre, until you realize that we are all familiar with something that acts in a similar way—an elastic band. If the two ends of the band are close together, the elastic is loose and floppy; but if you move the ends apart, the elastic stretches and resists the movement by pulling back.

it's the glue force

HOW THE GLUE FORCE WORKS

* The glue force is like that. If you try to move two quarks apart (perhaps by hitting one of the quarks inside a proton with a high-speed electron), they can only go so far before being snapped back to where they belong—in this case inside the proton. This is why the glue force only has a short range in practice, even though gluons have no mass.

the glue force will snap if you hit it hard enough

QUARK PLUS ANTIQUARK EQUALS PION

* If you pull an elastic band hard enough, it will break. With a pair or triplet of quarks, if you hit one hard enough it will eventually break free, in a sense.

* But this can only happen if you put so much energy in that there is enough to manufacture not one but *two* new quarks (strictly speaking, a quark and an ANTIQUARK) at the point where the break occurs. One of the new quarks snaps back into place inside the proton, and the other new quark (actually the antiquark) escapes alongside the first quark, in a quark–antiquark pair known as a PION. *No experiment has ever shown the existence of an isolated quark, but when matter is bombarded by high energy electrons it is possible to see streams of pions emerging.*

I've got a GUT feeling about this

Three interactions or four?

Strictly speaking, even today we really only have three fundamental interactions (the electroweak interaction, QED, and gravity) to worry about, not four. However, many people have tried to take things a stage further by bringing QCD into the fold. There are several different ideas about how this might be done, and they are generally known as GRAND UNIFIED THEORIES, or GUTs.

133

I'm working on the grand unified theory

GRAND UNIFIED THEORIES

* Nobody has quite succeeded in finding a grand unified theory that works perfectly—largely because QCD is a much more complicated kind of interaction than QED or the weak interaction.

QED AND QCD

* In QED (see page 119) there is only one kind of boson to worry about—the photon—and it doesn't have any mass. In the weak interaction there are three bosons to worry about, and they have mass as well. But at least none of these bosons interact with each other.

* In QCD (see page 125) there are eight different kinds of bosons—the gluons—to worry about. They don't have mass (which is one less thing to worry about) but they can interact with each other, even forming entities known as GLUEBALLS. Which makes things a lot more complicated.

EQUALITY FOR LEPTONS

* *If a grand unified theory could be developed, it would have to include quarks and leptons on an equal footing.* This is similar to the way the electroweak theory puts electrons and neutrinos on an equal footing, with the appropriate bosons able, thanks to their electric charge and other

these glueballs are great fun

KEY WORDS

GLUEBALL:
(sometimes called a gluonium) hypothetical particle that would be made up solely of a ball of gluons

X-BOSON:
hypothetical particle required to unify electroweak theory and QCD

properties, to change electrons into neutrinos, and vice versa. (This is essentially what happens in the second stage of beta decay, after the neutron has spat out a W⁻ particle.)

FAMILY LIKENESS

* The equality of quarks and leptons seems likely, because, as we have seen, there are three generations of quarks and three generations of leptons, hinting at some sort of family connection.

* *So there would have to be a kind of boson that could transform quarks into leptons, in the same way that the weak interaction can transform a neutrino into an electron – or turn itself into an electron plus an antineutrino, which is the same thing.* The various approaches that have been developed toward a grand unified theory predict the mass of this field quantum, which is called the X-BOSON.

A difficult test

Since different GUTs predict different masses for the X-boson, why don't we test the theories by measuring the mass of real X-bosons? Unfortunately, all the masses predicted by the candidate GUTs are so high (around a million billion times the mass of a proton) that there is no hope of manufacturing them in any particle accelerator that could be built on Earth. In fact the energies required to make such massive particles would only have existed in the first split second of the existence of the universe—in the Big Bang.

135

TOWARD A THEORY OF EVERYTHING

I have found the theory of everything

* Gravity is even harder to bring into the fold, because gravity is so much weaker than all the other interactions. But during the last two decades of the 20th century theoretical physicists found a way to circumvent all the difficulties with QCD and gravity, and jump straight to a complete theory of all of the particles and forces of nature—a true "THEORY OF EVERYTHING" **(or** <u>TOE</u>**), operating at a much deeper level than anything we have considered so far.**

Canceling out the infinities

In theories like QED, the infinities are got rid of by a trick called <u>RENORMALIZATION</u>. This amounts to dividing one infinity by another one to make them cancel out. It works, but the cleverest physicists, such as Paul Dirac and Richard Feynman, were always deeply unhappy about it.

ZERO SIZE

* The prehistory of this new idea—which goes by the prosaic name of <u>STRING THEORY</u>—takes us back to the 1960s. *Not surprisingly, up to the end of the 1960s particle physicists had pictured fundamental particles like electrons simply as particles.*

* Some (such as protons, which have a measurable size) were thought of as tiny objects like miniature billiard balls.

billiard balls

Others, such as electrons (which have no size measured by any experiment to date), were thought of as points with literally zero size. But there were always problems with this picture.

ZERO PROBLEMS

★ The main problem is that entities with zero volume allow infinite quantities to come into the equations. For example, the electric force associated with the charge on an electron is inversely proportional to the distance, from the electron, of the object being affected. The closer you are (if you are another charged particle), the bigger the force. If the electron has zero size, you can get to zero distance from it—and one divided by zero (let alone by zero squared) is infinity.

it's to do with string

Gabriele Veneziano was one of the first string theorists

KEY WORDS

RENORMALIZATION: trick used by particle physicists to get rid of infinities in their equations

The birth of string theory

At the end of the 1960s new results were coming out of the particle accelerators, and different kinds of "new" particle were being made there (and promptly decaying into the familiar particles). There were many suggestions as to what might be going on. A particularly intriguing one came from **Gabriele Veneziano**, in the form of a set of equations (a mathematical model) designed to describe the patterns made by the interactions. *When physicists looked at the implications of these equations, they were surprised to realize that they didn't describe pointlike particles—but tiny lines, like bits of string.*

137

TANGLING WITH STRING

* The first proper string theory came from Yoichiro Nambu, who tried to describe particles in terms of spinning and vibrating lengths of string, each one only about one ten-thousandth of a billionth of a centimeter long. The idea was that one kind of string could vibrate in different ways, like different notes being played on a guitar string, to produce states corresponding to different particles. Some properties of the strings (like charge) were thought of as being stuck to the ends of the spinning strings.

I can't get out!!

I can't get out!!

EXTRA DIMENSIONS

KEY WORDS

STRING THEORY: theory of the quantum world that describes particles such as electrons and quarks (and field quanta such as photons) in terms of the vibration of tiny loops of "string"

* To most people, the strangest thing about this kind of string is that it involves many more dimensions than the ones we are used to. *In order to explain the properties of different kinds of "particle" entities, the kind of string we are talking about has to vibrate in at least ten dimensions. This is straightforward to describe mathematically. But what does it mean physically? Where are the other six dimensions? And why don't we see them?*

a few people played with the equations that describe string

SUPERSTRING THEORY

superstring is a lot better than ordinary string

* The latest variation on string theory goes by the name of "SUPERSTRING." This is not just because physicists think it is better than ordinary string theory, but because it uses an idea called SUPERSYMMETRY, or SUSY. *According to SUSY, there ought to be an exact correspondence between fermions and bosons. Because none of the known bosons correspond to the known fermions in the appropriate way, this calls for a new kind of fermion to partner every known kind of boson, and vice versa.* These are termed SUPERSYMMETRIC PARTNERS, or SUSY PARTICLES. We can't see SUSY particles today because they only existed in the Big Bang, then quickly decayed. But they have been given names. The new bosons have names arrived at by adding an "s" to the appropriate fermion name (so the partner to the electron is the selectron), while the names of the new fermions end in "ino" (such as photino). Supersymmetry explains many features of the particle world. So physicists at CERN, in Geneva, and at Fermilab, near Chicago, are now busy conducting high-energy experiments in search of the elusive SUSY particles.

STRING IN THE 1970S

The first, accidental, version of string theory, which came out of Veneziano's equations, was readily explained in terms of quarks. So quark theory became the main line of research for particle theorists in the 1970s—and only a few people, mainly out of interest in the mathematics, played with the equations that describe string, which are not for the faint-hearted.

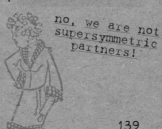

no, we are not supersymmetric partners!

UNWANTED DIMENSIONS

* To get rid of unwanted dimensions, mathematicians use a trick called COMPACTIFICATION. If you view a watering hose from a very long way away, it looks like a one-dimensional line or thin string. But viewed more closely, it reveals itself to be a two-dimensional sheet wrapped around a third dimension. Similarly, a line is just a string of points, one after the other—but what looks like a single point on the line from a distance is really a little circle, or closed loop. This is compactification.

I thought this was a one-dimensional line, but it's really a watering hose

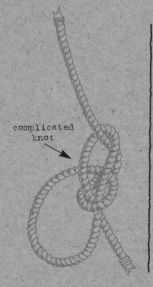

complicated knot

MULTIPLE ROLL-UP

* If you do the trick repeatedly, rolling up six or more dimensions in a more complicated knot, what you are left with looks—from a distance—like a sphere, or a line, or a little loop of string, depending on how you roll the dimensions up.

* *There are two important things about compactification. The first is that it will always work to hide dimensions from view—provided you apply it on a small enough scale, compared with the things you are actually measuring. The second is that*

who needs string?

although the distances involved are small, they are not zero. So the problems with infinities do not arise, at least not in the best versions of string theory.

BOTH BOSONS AND FERMIONS

* Nambu's version of string theory worked, after a fashion. *But it only described bosons, the field quanta that carry forces.* It didn't describe fermions—which was embarrassing, since Nambu had set out with the intention of describing fermions, not bosons. *But another physicist, Pierre Ramond, found a way to adapt Nambu's equations to describe both bosons and fermions in general terms, and this was developed into a theory describing bosons and fermions in terms of vibrating strings in ten dimensions.*

hey presto! compactification

$$2000 - A^2$$
$$M^2 = \Box \parallel$$

KEY WORDS

COMPACTIFICATION: trick used by mathematicians to "roll up" unwanted dimensions and hide them from view

HOLDING ON TO STRING

Hardly anybody took much notice of these developments in the 1970s, because quark theory was causing so much excitement. The big buzz was QCD. Who needed string? By the early 1980s, just about the only two people still working at string theory seriously were **John Schwartz**, in the United States, and **Michael Green**, in England. They decided that if string theory was to be of any use to anyone, it would eventually have to describe all particles and all the forces of nature, gravity included. *In fact, it would have to be a quantum theory of gravity.*

if you take a closed
loop of string
it's more
likely to
shrink

QUANTUM GRAVITY

Quantum gravity had been a dream of physicists ever since the 1920s. *Because gravity is so weak, quantum effects only become important for gravity on a tiny distance scale, known as the PLANCK LENGTH.* This is virtually impossible to picture since it is only 10^{-33}cm or 0.000000 00000000000000000 0000000001cm (the nucleus of an atom is a hundred billion billion times bigger than the Planck length). *If quantum theory applies to gravity, then on this scale spacetime itself is grainy, or granulated, so that the universe can be thought of as a vast checkerboard made up of tiny squares (or cubes) measuring just one Planck length across.*

SHRINKING STRING

* Any thoughts of bringing gravity into the quantum fold were still just a dream in the early 1980s, but Schwartz and Green knew they would take a step toward quantum gravity if they could shrink Nambu's string theory to the Planck length. At first, they did this with open strings, like Nambu's. Then they came up with another idea—closed loops of string.

NEAT LOOPS

* *Closed loops turned out to be a particularly neat idea—because different ripples running around the loop one way correspond to different kinds of bosons, while different ripples running around the loop the other way correspond to different kinds of fermions.*

the universe ca
be thought of a
a vast checker
board made up o
tiny squares

* But it was very difficult to make the properties of these "particles" match up with the properties of known particles—even though the closed-loop versions of string theory did away with the infinities that plague theories like QED and did so in a pleasingly straightforward way.

Among other difficulties, the string theories seemed to be predicting too many particles—not just too many individual particles, but too many varieties as well.

STRING THEORY TAKES OFF

* *One problem had been particularly worrying. It turned out that compactification only works if you start out with an odd number of dimensions in the first place. And ten is definitely not an odd number.* But in spite of the difficulties, interest in string theory suddenly took off in the middle of the 1980s, when it turned out that one of the puzzling things in the theory that Schwartz and Green had been worrying about was actually just what they had been looking for.

> but there are too many particles

PLANCK LENGTH:
the quantum of length —the smallest length that has any meaning

Schwartz and Green

The American physicist John Schwartz was appointed to a professorship at Caltech in 1989. He has also worked in Paris and London, and at other American institutions. British physicist Michael Green has worked at several universities and research institutions in Britain and the United States, and at CERN in Geneva. In 1993 he took up a professorship at the University of Cambridge. It was almost solely thanks to Schwartz and Green that the idea of string theory was kept alive between the mid-1970s and the mid-1980s.

THINKING ABOUT GRAVITY

* To understand why string theory turned out to be of such importance to physicists, let's take another look at ideas about gravity. Einstein's theory of gravity is in essence a "classical" theory, like Maxwell's theory of electromagnetism. It describes interactions between massive particles (which means any particles that have mass, not necessarily very heavy ones) in terms of the gravitational field, just as Maxwell's equations describe interactions between charged particles in terms of the electromagnetic field.

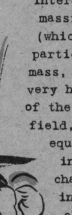

now the trouble with gravitons is...

Belated recognition

In the 1960s nobody took much notice of Feynman's ideas about gravity, but in the 1990s his way of looking at gravity became very popular and successful—not least because of the connections with string theory that we are about to consider.

THE TROUBLE WITH GRAVITONS

* In QED, quantum theory developed this idea for electromagnetism, by describing the field in terms of quanta—in the form of bosons (or more specifically, photons)—that are exchanged between charged particles. *It is easy to see that a proper theory of quantum gravity would do the same sort of thing by describing interactions between massive particles in terms of the exchange*

Richard Feynman

of the appropriate field quanta—again bosons (in this case, gravitons).

* Any quantum theory of gravity would be bound to be more complicated than QED, because the equations tell us that *gravitons, like gluons, can interact with each other (even though they each have zero mass) as well as with massive particles*. But in principle it could be done, and this was the traditional route followed by most people who tried to find a quantum theory of gravity.

FEYNMAN AND GRAVITY

* There was one notable exception. **Richard Feynman**, who had invented quantum electrodynamics, became intrigued by gravity. In the early 1960s, even though he could not find a complete theory of quantum gravity, he was able to prove mathematically that *if you started out with a quantum field theory involving the exchange of gravitons, then at an everyday level this would be indistinguishable from the general theory of relativity.*

Feynman explained superfluidity when very cold liquids flow without friction

Richard Feynman (1918–88)

Arguably the greatest physicist since Newton (certainly on a par with Einstein), Feynman achieved wider fame with his memoirs and when he pinpointed the cause of the Challenger disaster. But many people do not appreciate the scale of his contributions to physics. In addition to developing QED (the work for which he won the Nobel Prize), he made major contributions to our understanding of the weak interaction, QCD, and gravity, each also worthy of a Nobel Prize, and almost as an aside explained a strange quantum phenomenon called superfluidity (when very cold liquids flow without friction). An inspiring teacher, he produced a series of textbooks still influential today.

145

TWO UNITS OF SPIN

* In the mid-1980s Schwartz and Green were trying to get their string theory to describe the known fermions and bosons. They expected it to be very difficult to include gravity, so at first they tried to make the particles predicted by their theory match things like photons and gluons, quarks and leptons. But their equations kept throwing out a different kind of particle—one with zero mass and spin 2. Eventually, they worked it out. Their string theory was predicting the existence of gravitons. And that meant, according to Feynman, that it was predicting the general theory of relativity. They had arrived at a "Theory of Everything"!

KEY WORDS

SPIN:
A quantum property which is subtly different from the way something like a spinning top, or Earth, spins. In the quantum world, sometimes you have to rotate through 360 degrees *twice* to get back to where you started.

VARIATIONS ON THE STRING THEME

* Schwartz and Green had, in fact, discovered that there were only a handful of candidates for this Theory of Everything —*just one particular family of variations on the string theme that worked in this way and had no infinities troubling it.*
* Before the mid-1980s, there had been lots of variations on the theme. Because there is no way to test these ideas directly

you can't test the equations, so you can dream up whatever you like

Zero mass, spin 2

The key properties of the graviton are that it has no mass, and has two units of a property quantum physicists call <u>SPIN</u>*.* This is not like the spin of a spinning top, or the spin of the Earth on its axis. It's just one of those quantum labels you have to get used to. *Feynman had shown that if you had gravitons with zero mass and spin 2, then you would automatically get the general theory of relativity.*

by experiment, you could dream up anything allowed by the maths and it might be a way of describing the real world.

MATHEMATICALLY CONVINCING

* It's a bit like what would happen if it was impossible to test theories of gravity by looking at things like the orbits of the planets around the Sun. You might guess that there was an inverse-square law, or an inverse-cube law, or some other kind of law that you could describe mathematically. But you wouldn't be able to prove which version was the right one. And nobody would take much notice of such a vague theory.

* *So when it turned out that only one kind of string theory was free from infinities, it was as if mathematics, not experiments, was saying that the only true law of gravity would have to be an inverse-square law. And then people had to start taking it seriously.*

TWO NOTHING TWO NOTHING

the graviton has no mass and two units of spin

THE POWER OF MATHEMATICS

* It may seem strange that mathematics alone can be used to tell us which sort of string theory applies to the real universe, without ever doing experiments. But in fact the analogy with a theory of gravity based on an inverse-cube law really works, at this level.

THE ANTHROPIC PRINCIPLE

According to the anthropic principle, the very fact that we exist tells us what the universe at large is like. For example, life forms like us depend on the chemistry of carbon. So carbon must be made in the universe. In the 1950s, Fred Hoyle used this requirement of our existence to predict that certain nuclear reactions would be able to make carbon inside stars. Experiments in laboratories here on Earth then confirmed that those reactions are possible.

Fred Hoyle

it's all there in the equations

NO STABLE ORBITS...

* *If you try to describe (mathematically) an imaginary universe in which gravity obeys an inverse-cube law, it turns out that there are no stable orbits.*

* In our Universe, with an inverse-square law of gravity, if a planet like Earth is struck by a meteorite and nudged a tiny bit closer to or farther away from the Sun, then it automatically moves back toward its old trajectory. You don't have to do

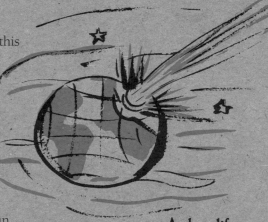

experiments to find this out—it is built into the equations.

* But the equations also tell us that in a universe obeying an inverse-cube law of gravity, a planet that moved a little closer to the Sun, for whatever reason, would keep falling inward toward the Sun. And a planet that moved a little farther out, for whatever reason, would keep spiraling out.

an inverse-square law of gravity tells us that Earth cannot be knocked out of its orbit

NO SOLAR SYSTEM...

* At a more subtle level, if you follow the mathematics of curved spacetime through in the way Einstein did in his general theory of relativity, the equations tell you that an inverse-square law of gravity is the natural law *only if there are three dimensions of space.* So if a universe existed with more or less space dimensions than three, there would be no stable planetary orbits and no planetary system like our solar system. So, presumably, no life as we know it.

life as we know it

...And no life on Earth

Some people argue that this is why we see that the extra dimensions of space have compactified to leave only three "visible" on the large scale. Other universes might exist, but there would be nobody in them to notice. So the very fact that we are around to wonder about these things means that we must live in a universe with three space dimensions. This sort of argument can be applied to other features of the visible universe and to other laws of physics. It is sometimes called the ANTHROPIC PRINCIPLE, and people still argue about whether it is more than a mere tautology.

149

PRINCETON STRING QUARTET

* One team that enthusiastically followed up the breakthrough made by Schwartz and Green was a group of four mathematicians based at Princeton University. They became known to their colleagues as the Princeton String Quartet, which gives you an idea of the kind of jokes mathematicians find amusing.

Princeton String Quartet

MORE DIMENSIONS STILL

The Princeton String Quartet's chief contribution to string theory was to write down the equations describing closed loops of string, using a different mathematical approach. You need a Ph.D. to understand the mathematics, but fortunately for us their variation on the theme corresponds to a very neat physical picture of what is going on (provided you are willing to accept a few more extra dimensions of space).

HETEROTIC STRING

* The quartet's version of string theory glories in the name of "HETEROTIC STRING." The name comes from the Greek root 'hetero' (as in heterosexual), implying two different varieties of something. *It is apt, because in heterotic string theory the kind of vibrations associated with fermions require ten dimensions, while those associated with bosons require no less than 26 dimensions. The ten-dimensional vibrations run one way around the loop of string, while the 26-dimensional vibrations run the other way.*

now smear the properties along the string

* It isn't really surprising that the bosonic vibrations require more dimensions, because there is a much greater variety of bosons (which range from photons to the W and Z particles, gluons, and gravitons) than there is of fermions. Admittedly, fermions include six quarks and six leptons, but there are only two basic "body plans" for each.

FOUR OUT OF TWENTY-SIX

* The equations that describe this richness of particles are interpreted as implying that 16 of the 26 dimensions have compactified as a set, providing the framework for the bosonic vibrations. The ten remaining dimensions provide scope for the fermionic vibrations, with six of these ten dimensions compactifying in a different way—leaving the familiar four dimensions of spacetime.

Smeared along the string

Properties like electric charge are also properly described by heterotic string theory, and can be pictured as being smeared out around the entire loop of string.

It's space Jim but not as we know it

the different vibrations run around the loop

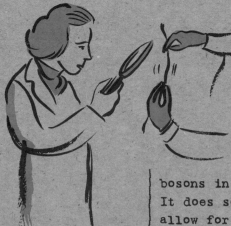

there is no way to test string theory

* There is one intriguing curiosity about heterotic string theory.

It doesn't just describe fermions and bosons in one complete package. It does so *twice*. The equations allow for two complete sets of everything—everything known to particle physics is described by one half of the equations, and the other half of the equations seems to describe another complete set of particles and fields.

Testing string

As already mentioned, there is no immediately available way to test string theory definitively. However, there is one test that would go some way towards proving its validity. *Most versions of the theory predict the existence of another kind of Z particle, as well as the one we already know. If experimenters found this particle, it would be powerful evidence in support of the theory.* But if they don't find it, that won't settle the issue, since absence of evidence is not the same thing as evidence of absence.

TWO OF EVERYTHING

* Some quantum theorists think this means that at the birth of the universe, in the first split-second of the Big Bang, two completely independent sets of particles and fields were created. These duplicate worlds would only interact at all through gravity. *According to this picture, there could be another universe of stars, planets, and even people occupying the same four-dimensional spacetime as our universe. This hypothetical ghostly duplicate universe is called the* "SHADOW UNIVERSE."

do we all have our counterpart in the shadow universe?

hello there shadow

no you're the shadow

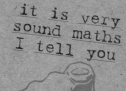

it is very sound maths I tell you

ELUSIVE SHADOWS

* The idea is that there would be shadow particles (the equivalent of quarks, photons, and all the rest) making the shadow stars and planets, all forever invisible to us. Except for the fact that we would notice its gravitational pull, a shadow star or planet could pass right through Earth, without either of them being affected.

Unfortunately (or fortunately?), short of a collision of this kind between a shadow object and ourselves, there seems to be no way to test the idea.

GREAT LEAP FORWARD

In the second half of the 1990s, despite all the difficulties, string theory took a great leap forward when the theorists found a way to get rid of the problem of having an even number of dimensions. Their suggestion looks outrageously obvious, almost silly. But you have to remember that it is backed up by very sound mathematical physics. It isn't just wishful thinking.

INTO THE 21ST CENTURY

* The great idea of the late 1990s was that, instead of thinking in terms of one-dimensional strings, we ought to be adding in another dimension—so as to produce two-dimensional sheets, usually referred to as MEMBRANES.

Membranes or magic

Remember how in basic string theory (see page 140) a hose is treated as a two-dimensional sheet (membrane) rolled up to give the appearance of a line? In membrane theory, although you are dealing with 11 dimensions (at one level, 27 at the other), one of them is immediately rolled up—so that the membrane behaves like a ten-dimensional string. The resulting mathematical package is called M-THEORY because the M stands for membrane, mystery, or magic—the experts say you can choose whichever name you like!

bringing M-Theory out of the hat

THE CASE FOR M-THEORY

* The reason why people take this idea seriously is that there are still, even after the breakthrough made by Schwartz and Green in the 1980s, several different versions of basic string theory—and it would be nice to have just one single theory, a unique Theory of Everything. *It turns out, however, that all these variations on the theme can be expressed*

it would be nice to have one single theory

in terms of a single M-theory. This is rather like the way electromagnetism and the weak interaction turned out to be different facets of a single mathematical package, the electroweak theory.

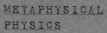

THE END IS NOT NIGH

* As we enter the 21st century, many physicists are convinced that M-theory provides the ultimate description of the way the universe works at the deepest level, down on the Planck scale. But this does not mean the end of physics, because they are just beginning to realize how much remains to be explained at higher levels— when huge numbers of particles are involved, working together to produce the complexity of a breaking ocean wave, the pattern of orbital motions of the planets in the solar system; the complexity of a living creature, or the workings of the weather.

physics has a lot to explain about the interactions of large numbers of particles

CHAPTER 5

BACK TO THE FUTURE

> I'm sowing the seeds of the new physics

* The seeds of the newest physics were sown in the mid-1880s, when a maths professor in Stockholm announced a competition to honor the si^xtieth birthday of the king of Sweden and Norway, Oscar II, due in 1889. A generous prize was offered for the best piece of work on one of four specified puzzles, one being the question of whether or not the solar system is stable—a topic that, in a sense, dated back to Isaac Newton's work on gravity.

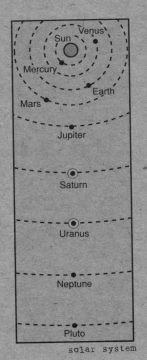

solar system

NEWTON AND GRAVITY

* Newton's inverse-square law of gravity describes the orbit of a single planet around a single star perfectly. It affirms that the orbit is an ellipse, exactly matching both the observations made by **Tycho Brahe** and explained by **Johannes Kepler** (see page 7) and all the observations made ever since. *But if you have two or more planets orbiting the same star, they tug at each other, so that their orbits are no longer perfect Keplerian ellipses.*

Isaac Newton

UNSOLVABLE EQUATIONS

* Using his own equations of gravity and orbital motion, Newton could not find a way to describe the resulting orbits accurately. This wasn't because he was incompetent, or because it was impossible without computers. *It's simply that the equations cannot be solved.*

* An elliptical orbit can be described by a very simple <u>DETERMINISTIC FORMULA</u>—called an <u>ANALYTICAL SOLUTION</u> to the equations of motion—which can be used to tell us where a planet will be in its orbit at any time in the future, and where it was at any time in the past. *But if three or more objects are involved, all affecting each other by gravity, there are no analytical solutions to the equations. In fact, there's no option but to laboriously work through the complete calculation, starting from the equations of motion and the law of gravity, for each individual case.*

the orbit is
an ellipse,
observes
Tycho Brahe

how can we solve
the three-body
problem?

TAKING IT
STEP BY STEP

The only way to 'solve' the three-body problem is step by step. Pretend two of the bodies do not move and calculate the orbit of the third one. Then move it a tiny bit forward in its orbit. Now hold that body still, plus one of the others, and calculate a tiny move in the orbit of the remaining one. Repeat for the third body and continue *ad infinitum*. (This is all done on a computer of course, not in the real world.)

157

CELESTIAL PREDICTABILITY

surely God will intervene

* **What troubled Newton**
was that if a planet were
tugged even slightly out of
orbit by the gravitational
influence of another planet,
it might not go back where
it belonged. He feared that
Earth, or another planet,
might one day start to
spiral in toward the Sun or
out into the depths of
space. However, he was a
deeply religious man and
consoled himself (and his
readers) by suggesting that
God would intervene to nudge
the planet back again into its
proper orbit.

Newton believed that God
controlled the Universe

COMPLEX TIMING

* In the 1780s the French mathematician
and astronomer Pierre Laplace took a
careful look at the problem that had
worried Newton, concentrating on the
orbits of Jupiter and Saturn—the two
largest planets in the solar system, with
the strongest gravitational influence after
the Sun itself.

* He found that the orbit of Jupiter was
expanding slightly, while the orbit of
Saturn was shrinking slightly. He linked

God will not be necessary

When Laplace's work was
published in book form,
Napoleon commented
that there was no mention
of God anywhere in its
pages. To which, Laplace
proudly replied **"I have no
need of that hypothesis."**

Jupiter

these changes to the gravitational influence of the two planets on each other. This operates in a particular rhythm: Saturn makes two orbits of the Sun while Jupiter journeys around the Sun five times, so they are close to each other roughly every 59 years. Using Newton's laws, Laplace calculated that the change in the orbits would reverse after about 929 years—with the orbit of Jupiter shrinking and the orbit of Saturn expanding—and this cycle would be repeated roughly every 929 years.

REGULAR AS A CLOCK

Saturn

* Laplace was so impressed by the habits of Jupiter and Saturn that he wrote: "*The irregularities of these two planets appeared formerly to be inexplicable by the law of universal gravitation—they now form one of its most striking proofs.*" And he went on to show that the same kind of stability applied, as far as he could tell, to the orbits of all the planets—so that the whole solar system was as stable and regular as a clock.

Pierre Laplace (1749–1827)

The son of a magistrate in a small town in Normandy, Laplace studied under the Benedictines at a local college, then moved on to Caen and from there to Paris, where he became a professor of mathematics in 1768. One of the few members of the Paris elite who held government posts both before and after the French Revolution, he was a member of the committee that introduced the metric system of weights and measures. Laplace served in the Senate and briefly as Minister of the Interior, but voted for the restoration of the monarchy in 1814. This didn't help his prospects when Napoleon returned to power, but he got his reward when Louis XVIII made him a marquis.

Pierre Laplace

THE QUESTION OF STABILITY

* Why the stability of the solar system figured in the competition honoring Oscar II wasn't because mathematicians thought Laplace had been wrong. Quite the reverse. In 1858 Peter Dirichlet had worked out a new method of solving differential equations—which, he claimed, could prove that the Solar System is stable. Dirichlet died in 1859, and nobody had succeeded in reconstructing his calculation. Hence the question included in the competition.

is the solar system stable?

Peter Dirichlet (1805–59)

German mathematician who became a professor in Berlin in 1828, then moved to a similar post in Göttingen in 1855. His predecessor there was the great mathematician Karl Gauss, and one of his most notable contributions to mathematics was to clarify Gauss's work and make it more accessible. Dirichlet set great store by conceptual clarity in mathematics. Although shy and modest, he had a major influence on the way the subject developed.

DAWN OF A NEW ERA

* The prize was won by a French mathematician, **Henri Poincaré**, for a paper that didn't really answer the question. But it was clearly a profound new development in mathematics— "of such importance," the judges wrote to the king, "that its publication will inaugurate a new era in the history of celestial mechanics."

* *Poincaré had come up with a new way of looking at problems like orbital motion that did not depend on working out the orbit (or whatever it was you were interested in) step by step.* He pointed out that if any kind of system starts out from a particular state and does something complicated, then gets back to exactly the same state it started in, then it is bound to repeat its whole complicated pattern of behavior.

CYCLICAL BEHAVIOR

★ Take the (very simple) case of a planet orbiting around the Sun. If you notice that at a particular point in its orbit the planet is moving in a certain direction at a certain speed and later see the same planet in the same place traveling in the same direction at the same speed, then you know it must be in an orbit that will repeat indefinitely. *Poincaré realized that there is therefore no need to carry out a calculation of every step of its orbital motion, or even to discover what it does in the rest of its orbit.* You know that whatever it was it did, it got back to exactly where it started.

Poincaré had found a new way of looking at the complexities of the solar system

KEY WORDS

DIFFERENTIAL EQUATION: equation that describes how something affects the rate of change (often over a period of time)

I'm back where I started

BEGINNING

Henri Poincaré

Henri Poincaré (1854–1912)

Poincaré qualified as a mining engineer, but he was always keenly interested in mathematics and in 1881 became a lecturer at the Faculty of Sciences of the University of Paris, where he spent the rest of his career. He made many contributions to many areas of science, including the understanding of probability theory and planetary orbits. In the 1890s, when Einstein was still at school, Poincaré thought and wrote about the implications of relative motion. As early as 1900 he pointed out that Maxwell's equations require that nothing can travel faster than light, but never followed this up with a complete theory of relativity.

WAITING FOREVER

* If you have a box divided in two, with gas in one half and empty space in the other, when you pull the partition out the gas spreads to fill the box. You never see all the gas congregating at one end. But Poincaré argued that if you were able to wait long enough you could see this happen, because the atoms of gas bouncing off the walls of the box must eventually pass through every state allowed by the laws of physics—including a stage where all the gas is at one end of the box.

I've been waiting here for ages!

MORE ZEROS THAN STARS

★ *The key words here are "long enough"* *and "eventually."* A small box of gas might contain 10^{22} atoms (a 1 followed by 22 zeros, or 10,000 billion billion atoms), and there is an enormous number of different ways in which so many atoms can be arranged. The time it would take for so many particles to pass through every possible state is much greater than the age of the universe. *Typical Poincaré cycle times have more zeros after the 1 than there are stars in all the known galaxies in the universe put together—numbers so big that it hardly matters whether you are counting in seconds, hours, or even years.*
★ *Poincaré had found the key to chaos, but nobody used it to unlock the box.* All the mathematical tools needed to develop chaos theory were in the hands of scientists at the beginning of the 20th century, but they did nothing about it for half a century. *This turned out to be one of the biggest oversights in science.*

so what are the odds then?

watch the orbits

THE THREE-BODY PROBLEM

* If you have two bodies (planets, for example) with equal mass alone in space, they will orbit around each other in exactly predictable elliptical orbits. Now extend this picture by adding in a single tiny particle of dust, so small that its gravitational influence on the two planets can be ignored. What is the orbit that this dust particle follows around the two larger objects?

Poincaré and orbital dynamics

Poincaré thought his approach could, in a much more rigorous mathematical form, be used to prove the stability of the Solar system. But he was wrong. Not surprisingly perhaps, because even the simplest version of the classic "three-body problem" shows just how complicated orbital dynamics is.

the orbit of the tiny particle around the larger particles is completely random

INTERMINABLE CALCULATIONS

* There is just no simple answer to this question, unless the dust particle is far enough away from the two planets for it to be able to orbit around the pair of them. Otherwise, it sometimes follows a complicated looping orbit, like a tangled ball of string, around one of the objects.

I'm going to score in a minute

the orbit is like a tangled ball of string

NO RETURN TO SQUARE ONE

The crucial thing about the three-body problem is that you **never** get back to a point where the particle is moving in the same direction at the same speed as before, with the two planets also in their original places and moving at the same speeds and in the same directions as before. *The orbit does not repeat—and there is no simple formula describing it, like the formula that describes an ellipse.*

Then, at other times, it crosses over and orbits in the same sort of complicated way around the other planet. And sometimes it follows a confused kind of figure-of-eight pattern, orbiting around each of the planets in turn.

* The only way to work out the path of the orbit is to trace it step by step using a computer (or, much more laboriously, a pencil and paper). At each instant, you can work out all the forces involved and see how the dust particle will move a tiny bit. *But all the forces immediately change as a result, because the dust particle is now in a different position relative to the two planets (which have also moved in their own orbits). So you then have to calculate all the forces again and work through the next step.*

I'll never get back to square one

Tiny changes can make big differences

The ultimate form of the orbit followed by the dust particle in the three-body problem depends on where it starts from and at what velocity. If you were to make a tiny change to the Earth's speed or direction through space, it would still follow almost exactly the same orbit as before because its motion is almost entirely dominated by the gravity of the Sun. *But if you give the dust particle a tiny nudge, altering its speed or direction ever so slightly, at some points in its orbit that would be enough to make it veer off onto a completely different, though equally complicated, looping orbit.*

COMETS AND CHAOS THEORY

* There are, in fact, things in our solar system that behave very much like the dust particle in the three-body problem. And, like the dust particle in the problem, they are small objects—things like comets and asteroids, much smaller than planets.

A CRITICAL NUDGE

* Comets are basically chunks of icy material, a few miles or tens of miles across. Many of these icy chunks can be seen in what seem to be stable orbits, in the outer part of the solar system, near

comets are very sensitive to the gravitational influence of the planets

the Sun is the dominant body in the Solar System

CHAOS:
Term used to describe the behavior of systems that are very sensitive to initial conditions. A tiny change in the starting conditions makes a big difference to where you end up. Chaotic systems are essentially unpredictable, because you can never specify the starting conditions accurately.

the giant planet Jupiter. But computer calculations tell us that a tiny nudge at certain points in their orbits could switch objects such as comets onto a completely different trajectory, perhaps tumbling past Earth and in toward the Sun. Just such a nudge is provided from time to time, by the gravity of Jupiter, or Saturn, or something else.

* What matters is that these orbits are extremely sensitive to small changes, if those changes are applied at certain times. And this "sensitivity to initial conditions" is what CHAOS THEORY *is all about.*

I didn't touch it!

there are factors in the solar system apart from the Sun that affect planetary orbits

Planetary influences

In the solar system, the Sun is so much bigger than any of the planets that its gravity dominates and is by far the most important factor in deciding what orbits the planets follow. But it isn't the only factor. The planets themselves have an effect on each other.

167

FROM RAINDROPS TO CASCADES

* It's easy to appreciate how a tiny difference at the outset can have a big influence on how or where you end up. Think of a drop of rain falling on a high mountain range such as the Rocky Mountains. Rainfall that lands on one side of the mountains will flow westwards and end up in the Pacific, while rain landing on the other side is likely to end up in the Atlantic or the Gulf of Mexico.

well what the heck started that?

sometimes a tiny cause can have a big effect

THE IMPACT OF INITIAL CONDITIONS

"A very small cause that escapes our notice determines a considerable effect that we cannot fail to see, and then we say that the effect is due to chance. If we knew exactly the laws of nature and the situation of the universe at the initial moment, we could predict exactly the situation of that same universe at a succeeding moment. But even if it were the case that the natural laws had no longer any secret for us, we could still only know the initial situation approximately. If that enabled us to predict the succeeding situation with the same approximation, that is all we require, and we should say that the phenomenon had been predicted, that it is governed by laws. But it is not always so; *it may happen that small differences in the initial conditions produce very great ones in the final phenomena. A small error in the former will produce an enormous error in the latter. Prediction becomes impossible, and we have the fortuitous phenomenon.*" Henri Poincaré

CRITICAL POINT

* Somewhere high in the mountains, there must be a point or a line where a tiny difference (maybe only a fraction of an inch or so) in where the raindrop lands will make a difference of thousands of miles in where it ends up.

* Which ocean it ends up in may not matter to the raindrop, but it certainly matters to us. *And sometimes such a tiny initial difference can trigger a cascade of events with dramatic consequences.*

CHAINS OF EVENTS

* Domino effects of this kind are hardly new to human experience. Indeed, there is a well-known old rhyme that makes the point forcefully:

> For the want of a nail, a shoe was lost;
> For the want of a shoe, a horse was lost;
> For the want of a horse, a rider was lost;
> For the want of a rider, a battle was lost;
> For the want of a battle, the kingdom was lost.

"It may happen that small differences in the initial conditions produce very great ones in the final phenomena. A small error in the former will produce an enormous error in the latter. Prediction becomes impossible and we have the fortuitous phenomenon."

HENRI POINCARE

What is new is the realization that this kind of magnification of small events, culminating in major influences, applies in the world of science. And this kind of phenomenon can be described, by mathematics, in a scientific way. Chaos may not be predictable but it *is* scientific.

for the want of a nail my kingdom was lost

169

it's absolute chaos in here

IMPRECISE CONDITIONS

* It wouldn't matter that systems are sometimes sensitive to initial conditions if you could always specify the initial conditions completely accurately. But even apart from the question of quantum uncertainty, sometimes it is impossible to specify even such a simple thing as the position of an object with complete precision.

RATIONAL NUMBERS

* Suppose you are only trying to specify the position of an object at a particular point on a line, without worrying about its position in three-dimensional space. Label one end of the line "0" and the other end "1," and divide it into any units you care to use. It is then easy to specify the position of *some* points on the line, using fractions such as $1/2$ or $3/7$ or even $2573/6937$.

I knew all of that already

* These fractions are ratios of one number to

NOTHING UNCERTAIN

"Assume an intelligence that at a given moment knows all the forces that animate nature as well as the momentary positions of all things of which the Universe consists, and further that it is sufficiently powerful to perform a calculation based on these data. It would then include in the same formulation the motions of the largest bodies in the Universe and those of the smallest atoms. To it, nothing would be uncertain. Both future and past would be present before its eyes."
Pierre Laplace

another, which is why they are called "rational" numbers. You can find a rational number that is as close as you like to any point on the line—even the ancient Greeks knew this.

IRRATIONAL NUMBERS

* But there are points on the line that can never be labeled precisely by any fraction that is a ratio of two ordinary numbers. These points correspond to irrational numbers, which are expressed as an infinitely long string of numbers after the decimal point, with no repeating sequence to it. The word "irrational" doesn't mean they are illogical—just that they are not ratios. *The lack of a repeating pattern in these numbers is very similar to the way the orbit of the dust particle in the three-body problem never repeats itself.*

```
to spell out an
irrational number
precisely is beyond
the capacity of any
computer
```

Asking too much

If the position on the line you need to specify corresponds to an irrational number, then to spell it out precisely you would need a decimal expression with an infinite number of digits in it. This would require an *infinite* amount of information—so no computer, or intelligence of the kind envisaged by Laplace, could work it out precisely. *This is where Laplace's vision of a perfectly predictable universe falls down. The only computer powerful enough to describe the behavior of the entire universe would be the entire universe itself.*

171

CHAPTER 6

TOMORROW'S PHYSICS

* The first person to notice chaos at work in a practical context was not a physicist but an American meteorologist, Edward Lorenz. **The effects of chaos suddenly confronted him while he was working with one of the first computers used to tackle the problems of weather forecasting, in the early 1960s.**

Science in the 20th century

The reason why scientists didn't turn their attention to phenomena such as chaos sooner was that they were busy solving all the things that could be solved using Newton's approach to science. They achieved so much, so quickly, by concentrating on equations amenable to analytical solutions that there was no incentive to tackle the much messier situation of equations they couldn't solve analytically—until the importance of such situations was rammed home by a series of discoveries in the second half of the 20th century.

computers in the 1960s were quite primitive

PREDICTING THE WEATHER

* The idea behind this kind of weather forecasting is that the laws of physics governing how winds move around the globe and how the temperature changes, and so on, can be described by sets of equations that can be solved using a computer. The computer simulations are fed with numbers corresponding to things like the temperature and pressure of the atmosphere at different points—maybe on

a tiny change in where you
start makes a big difference
to where you end up

a grid with points separated by 100 miles over the surface of Earth, and at 100 miles intervals up through the atmosphere. Then you plug the numbers into the equations and run the computer to calculate how the weather will change.

SURPRISE FORECAST

* One day, Lorenz decided to extend an earlier run. To save time, he started in the middle of the old run, typing in the numbers corresponding to the weather taken from the printouts of the first run. He assumed that the computer would duplicate the second half of the old forecast, then extend it. But to his surprise, it didn't. *Instead, the forecast weather gradually diverged from the previous run, until there was no resemblance at all between the two forecasts.*

what a surprise!!

the computer's forecast could change drastically with only tiny changes in the initial data

FEEDING IN THE DATA

The computer Lorenz was using, back in 1961, was much more primitive than modern supercomputers, and he wasn't trying to predict the real weather but merely looking at how the computer handled some of the simplest equations that would be needed in real forecasting. It seemed to work. When sensible numbers were fed into the computer, plausible "forecasts" of things like temperature came out. You could start the machine off in a certain way, and get numbers out corresponding to things like the temperature variation day by day, for weeks ahead—as far as you wanted to run it. Or so everyone assumed.

THE BUTTERFLY EFFECT

* Lorenz's discovery that weather systems and forecasts suffer from chaos explains why accurate forecasts today are limited to a few days ahead (at most a week or two), and will never get any better. No matter how good your computer is, the effects of chaos begin to show up after about that time.

The discovery of chaos

Why Lorenz's computer presented him with such a divergent forecast was that Lorenz had rounded off one of the numbers he typed into the computer. Numbers used in the computer were kept to six decimal places —in this case, 0.506127. When he started his second run, Lorenz omitted the last three digits and typed in 0.506. *This tiny difference was enough to drastically alter the forecast that came out of the machine.*

DISTANT FLUTTER

* Forecasters can see this by feeding very slightly different numbers into their computers and running a forecast again. For the first few days, the alternative forecasts will be almost identical; but after a week they look very different (unless the weather happens to be in an unusually stable pattern). No matter how accurate the equations are, and no matter how good the data you feed in are, after a week tiny effects that are too small for us to notice can exert a significant influence on the results. Lorenz called this "THE BUTTERFLY EFFEC." *He imagined that a butterfly fluttering its wings in the jungle*

the figures just don't add up!

of Brazil could set up little eddies in the atmosphere that might change the weather in London months later.

I've discovered chaos!

CHAOS NAMED

* One reason why Lorenz's discovery didn't change the course of science immediately was that it was published in the *Journal of the Atmospheric Sciences*. The meteorologists who read it seem not to have realized that it had universal significance—and the physicists and mathematicians who might have appreciated the importance of the discovery didn't read weather journals. *The person who gave chaos its name was indeed a mathematician,* James Yorke, *who came across Lorenz's paper in the early 1970s and realized that it gave a physical basis for a whole host of things that mathematicians had been playing with in the 1960s.*

TUNING IN TO CHAOS

* When Yorke and other
mathematicians publicized Lorenz's
discovery, physicists began to see
that chaos was all around them
and that by concentrating their
attention on regular things (like
planetary orbits) they had been missing something
crucial, literally for centuries. Ever since
Newton, physicists had trained themselves to look
for order in nature—and to disregard disorder as a
kind of unwanted noise, like the distortions you
hear when you tune in to a radio station with a
weak signal. Now, they began
to realize that the noise
might be more important
than the signal.

do-it-
yourself
chaos

Just like Lorenz

By the way, should you
use the same starting
number on your
calculator and on your
desktop computer or
another calculator, don't
be surprised if you end
up with two different
sequences of numbers.
This is because the
machines may round off
the numbers in slightly
different ways—*just like
the rounding-off process
that led Lorenz to
discover chaos in the
first place.*

DO-IT-YOURSELF CHAOS

* You can see chaos at work
mathematically using a calculator, or
program your computer to do all the work
for you. Start with a simple mathematical
expression, $(2x^2 - 1)$. You can work out a

doing the same calculation on
different computers will give
different answers

ITERATION

Iteration is a
mathematical process
that goes around and
around in a loop,
starting out with some
input (usually just a
number), then carrying
out a series of
mathematical
manipulations, and
coming up with an
output (another
number) which is then
used as the input to
the next run around
the cycle.

iteration is a
process that
goes around and
around in a loop

value for this expression, for any number
you choose (x), by squaring x, doubling
the result and then subtracting 1.

* Now do the same with the number you
are left with, and repeat the whole process
again and again (this is called ITERATION).
You might expect that if you start out with
two very similar numbers, after a few
iterations you will end up with two similar
numbers. But you don't.

* Try it with 0.51234, and make a note of
each number you get at each step in the
iteration. Now try it again, starting with
0.51235, again writing down the numbers
at each step of the iteration. *After about
50 iterations, the two sequences of
numbers will be completely different. This
is chaos. A simple deterministic formula
leads to very different places from very
similar starting conditions.*

177

CHAOS AT WORK

* You can see chaos at work, physically, in executive toys based on the principle of a double pendulum. A double pendulum is essentially two equal rods joined by a hinge in the middle. The double pendulum is set swinging by a motor that gives it a little nudge from time to time, or by being given a poke with your finger. Depending on just how it is nudged, the pendulum behaves in very different ways.

Galileo's
pendulum

What is chaos?

To a scientist, chaos is not the kind of incomprehensible and messy situation that the word means to most people. Instead, it is a special kind of messy behavior that results from entirely predictable physical laws, such as the ones formulated by Newton. *It is unpredictable behavior obeying predictable laws.*

IMPERCEPTIBLE DIFFERENCES

* Sometimes it swings as one piece, like a clock pendulum. Sometimes the bottom part swings wildly back and forth, while the top half hardly moves. And sometimes

this toy is
completely
chaotic

the bottom hardly moves, and the top hardly moves, but the joint in the middle part of the pendulum swings wildly back and forth. The pendulum seems to switch from one kind of oscillation to another for no reason, even though it has been given apparently identical nudges.

* *The crucial point is that the nudges are very slightly different to each other, and even though these differences are too small to notice they make a very noticeable difference in the behavior of the pendulum. This is a form of chaos.*

* The same pendulum will also go through its entire repertoire of gyrations as it slows down, because although its speed is only changing gradually as it slows, at some points a small change in speed will flip it into a different pattern of oscillations.

KEY WORDS

SELF-ORGANIZED CRITICALITY:
the way patterns appear in a system just before it tips over into chaos

CHAOS, COMPLEXITY, AND LIFE

The most dramatic implications of chaos are only beginning to be investigated as we enter the new millennium. They link all of these ideas to the appearance of complexity in the universe, and to the mystery of life and evolution. *The key new discovery is that complex things exist "on the edge of chaos," at the border between stability and chaotic behavior.* The neatest analogy to demonstrate this comes from PER BAK, a Danish physicist who describes complex systems as being in a state of "SELF-ORGANIZED CRITICALITY."

evolution and everything is living on the edge of chaos

chaos can be found throughout the natural world

SELF-ORGANIZED CRITICALITY

* All you need to demonstrate self-organized criticality is a tray of sand. If sand is spread out all over the tray, it is in a stable—and boring—state. Nothing interesting happens to it. But if you drop grains of sand onto the middle of the tray, one by one or in a slow stream, they build up a pile.

hang on Mom,
I want to
reach the
critical
point

SCALE-FREE PHENOMENA

Earthquakes, large and small, are all generated by the same process, just like the avalanches produced by adding grains to a pile of sand. There's nothing special about large earthquakes, except for their size. This is good news for physicists, because it means you only need one theory to describe all kinds of earthquakes, *whatever their size.* Another way of describing this kind of phenomenon is to say that it is "SCALE FREE."

DRAMATIC BUILD-UP

* At first, this is just as stable and almost as boring as the rest of the sand. But at a critical point, little landslides and avalanches start to occur in the growing pile of sand. You reach a stage where adding just one grain of sand triggers a lot of avalanches, rearranging the sand pile into an interesting and complicated structure. Then, as you keep adding sand to it, it will build up again, before collapsing in the same dramatic fashion.

chaos is scale-free

But even when the sand pile is on the edge of stability, it doesn't always collapse completely—adding that extra grain of sand may merely trigger a small or medium-sized avalanche. It is impossible to predict in advance which kind of avalanche will happen next.

FREQUENCY AND SIZE

* The collapsing sand pile is an example of a very common kind of pattern in nature—where similar events can occur on many different scales, but bigger events are less common than smaller events. Not just less common, but less common in a very precise way.

an earthquake is the same thing as the collapsing sand pile, only bigger

* The frequency of an event of a certain size is inversely proportional to its size—or, turning this around, the size of an event is inversely proportional to its frequency (f). This is therefore known as 1/f noise. 1/f noise turns up all over the place, in avalanches, earthquakes, traffic jams, and even in evolution.

KEY WORDS

SCALE-FREE PHENOMENA: things that are the same except for their size are scale-free (a bonsai tree is a tree, even though it is small)

Pure 1/f noise

A striking example of 1/f noise at work in the real world is the occurrence of earthquakes of different sizes.

On the Richter scale, a magnitude 5 event is 10 times bigger than a magnitude 4 event, a magnitude 6 event is 10 times bigger still (and 100 times bigger than magnitude 4), and so on. It turns out that for every 1,000 earthquakes of magnitude 4 on the Richter scale, there are 100 with magnitude 5, 10 with magnitude 6, and so on. This is pure 1/f noise.

FEEDING OFF ENERGY

As we have just seen, a pile of sand can become a complicated and interesting structure on the edge of chaos. Yet each individual grain of sand automatically falls into place, in obedience to the laws of gravity and friction. A very simple set of physical rules has produced a relatively complicated pattern. There is, crucially, one other vital ingredient. We have been putting sand in from outside. *This corresponds to a flow of energy through the system. What Bak and a few other physicists are saying is that simple laws feeding off a flow of energy can produce very complicated systems, without any other help at all.*

PUNCTUATED EQUILIBRIUM

* Some of the most exciting applications of these ideas involve life itself. Charles Darwin's theory of evolution by natural selection describes a gradual process, with tiny changes accumulating from one generation to the next. But some evolutionary biologists—notably the Americans Niles Eldridge and Steven Jay Gould—argue that the fossil record seems to show long periods with little change going on, alternating with short intervals in which a lot of evolutionary change takes place. This is known as PUNCTUATED EQUILIBRIUM.

it's all falling into place

each individual grain of sand obeys the laws of gravity and friction

DARWIN'S VIEW OF EVOLUTION

Darwin

* According to Darwin, evolution by natural selection occurs because of two things. First, genetic information is passed on slightly imperfectly from one generation to the next—so that the offspring of plants and animals resemble but are not exactly the same as their parents. Secondly, there is competition within any population for things like food or a chance to mate, so the individuals best "suited" to their environment are more successful and pass on more copies of their genes to later generations. The more copies of your genes you pass on, the more successful you are in evolutionary terms.

* Darwin's theory works beautifully to explain how organisms get progressively better at coping with the kind of environment they live in (which includes how they coexist or compete with other living things). *But it is much harder to see how Darwin's theory on its own can account for the dramatic changes that occur from time to time, when many species disappear and then new species evolve (punctuated equilibrium).*

the evidence is in the fossil record

Something extra?

Punctuated equilibrium does not mean that Darwin was wrong. But if what we are seeing in the fossil record is an accurate portrayal of what really happened, it means that something else needs to be added to Darwin's theory. *That something else may be what we see in a growing sand pile, or in the historical record of earthquakes—the edge of chaos.*

KEY WORDS

PUNCTUATED EQUILIBRIUM: when something stays the same for a long time, then undergoes a sudden change before resuming a state of stability

THE RED QUEEN EFFECT

* Darwin's view of evolution implies that the whole web of life on Earth is constantly poised in an unstable state, like a growing sand pile. Everything in the ecosystem has to keep on evolving, to preserve its own niche, because everything else is evolving. This is known as the Red Queen effect, from the character in Lewis Carroll's *Through the Looking-Glass* who has to keep running as fast as she can in order to stay in the same place.

the Red Queen has to move as fast as she can to stay in the same place

The peacock's tail

The splendid tail of the peacock may be a result of instability and the Red Queen effect. If— for whatever reason— peahens start to favour peacocks with large tails, then those peacocks will have more offspring than their less well-endowed brothers. Over many generations, this can produce the tails we see today.

EQUILIBRIUM RESTORED

well it's not eating me

* To see what biologists mean by the Red Queen effect, think of two different species living alongside one another. Suppose there are frogs that eat a certain kind of fly, which they catch by flicking out their tongues. If the frogs evolve a particularly sticky tongue, they will be adept at catching flies. The frogs will do well, and the flies badly, in the evolutionary stakes.

sticky-tongued frog

* But if the flies evolve a particularly slippery body surface, they will be able to escape from the sticky tongue more easily —and the original balance will be restored. Both species have evolved in the way Darwin envisaged, but neither species has benefited as a result. *Overall, nothing has changed. There are still the same number of frogs, each of them eating the same number of flies.*

STABILITY, THEN INSTABILITY

* *The Red Queen effect is in evidence all around us, all the time—involving many species interacting with each other and their physical environment simultaneously, not just pairs of species.* Per Bak built a computer model of this kind of behavior. As you might expect, competitive evolution encourages the spread of individuals that are best fitted to their environment (including the effect on them of other species). *But once the happy situation is reached where all the species are well adapted, the system turns out to be unstable—in exactly the same way that happens with the growing pile of sand.*

the fossil record shows the patterns of extinction

PATTERNS OF EXTINCTION

When Bak made a small change to his model, removing just one species from his computer ecosystem, he found that sometimes this produced a small ripple effect as the other species adapted, sometimes it produced a big effect, and sometimes the ripples spread dramatically— with many species disappearing and others evolving to take their place. *He had produced a model of punctuated equilibrium, a scale-free model obeying the 1/f law. What makes this discovery so special is that if you look at the fossil record and make a note of how often extinctions of a certain size have occurred, you find that this pattern follows a 1/f law, too.*

185

extinctions of
all sizes can be
triggered by the
same events

THE WEB OF LIFE

* According to Bak, life
on Earth is an integrated
web—the failure of one
part of the system may
have repercussions that
affect the whole system.
Maybe the flies that frogs
feed on become so good at
escaping that the frogs
starve. So the fish that eat the
frogs' eggs and tadpoles starve. Then the bears that
feed on fish go hungry and start to eat rabbits
(say) instead. And so on, in a series of widening
ripples. It may be that the change is triggered by
a change in the physical environment—a new rainfall
pattern, or a burst of volcanic activity, or
whatever. The important point is that extinctions of
all sizes can be triggered by the *same* events.

Scale doesn't matter

As with earthquakes,
there's no need for a
different theory to
explain extinctions on
different scales. All you
need is for something to
trigger a small change in
the web of life, which
may or may not spread.
Small meteorites hitting
Earth every so often
could explain extinctions
in the fossil record of life
on Earth on **all** scales.

I'm bound to catch
something here if
I wait long enough

DINOSAURS, METEORITES, AND CHAOS

* Some people think that the catastrophic
extinction that occurred 65 million years
ago was caused by a meteorite striking
Earth from space. Because this was a
particularly big extinction, in which a huge
number of species (including the
dinosaurs) died, it is natural to think that
it was caused by the impact of a
particularly large meteorite. It's then logical
to assume that smaller extinctions, in

which only a few species died, must have been caused by the impact of smaller meteorites. *But Bak's insight says that this need not be the case. Even a small meteorite crashing into the Earth is capable of triggering a massive extinction, in just the same way that adding a single grain of sand to the growing pile can trigger a catastrophic collapse. And it happens for the same reason—because both systems, the growing sand pile and life on Earth, are in a state of self-organized criticality, on the edge of chaos.*

THE EDGE OF CHAOS

Bak's computer models do not yet reflect the complexity of the real world. A lot more work needs to be done, building on his discovery. But it may mean that all the puzzling extinctions in the fossil record, the punctuation marks of evolution, are no more than the biological equivalent of adding another grain of sand to a pile in a critical state. When just one or two species become extinct, or develop a mutation that changes their place in the web of life significantly, the results may be small-scale, or medium-scale, or dramatic. *Because life itself is poised on the edge of chaos.*

187

Jim Lovelock

Jim Lovelock

British chemist and inventor best known as the originator of the Gaia hypothesis, Lovelock also designed instruments used by NASA in the search for life on Mars and the highly sensitive detectors that revealed the way CFCs spread around the globe. Lovelock is that rare phenomenon, a truly independent scientist. Since 1964 he has lived off the income from his inventions and books while carrying out fundamental research in his own laboratory, at his home in the south of England.

THE GAIA HYPOTHESIS

* Per Bak's view of life on Earth as a complex web of interacting species, intimately affected by changes in the environment, provides an intriguing underpinning for Jim Lovelock's idea of Earth as a single living organism, called Gaia.

Earth is alive

A QUESTION OF ATMOSPHERE

* In the 1970s, when he was working for NASA on the experiments intended to search for life on Mars, it occurred to Lovelock that Earth is in effect a single superorganism. Mars, he argued, must be a dead planet, because it is in a state of chemical equilibrium, with an atmosphere of inert carbon dioxide. *The atmosphere of our planet, on the other hand, is in an unstable state, since it is rich in oxygen, a highly reactive gas.*

POISED ON THE EDGE

lung

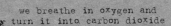

we breathe in oxygen and turn it into carbon dioxide

* Earth is maintained in this state—on the edge of chaos—by life, which both produces the oxygen and depletes it. The process by which we breathe in oxygen and turn it into carbon dioxide is like a slow burning; and this prevents a major conflagration of the planet, which would occur if the oxygen level increased.

the energy from the Sun is what sustains the self-organized criticality of life on Earth

* *As with the growing sand pile, and all systems involving self-organized criticality on the edge of chaos, the whole Earth "feeds" off a stream of energy from outside, in the form of heat and light from*

THE END OF PHYSICS?

Some people claim the end is in sight for physics, because we have discovered all the simple rules by which the universe operates. This is like saying that because you've learned the rules for moving chess pieces, you are ready to take on a grandmaster. ***The truth is that, as the 21st century dawns, physicists are only just starting to understand the universe.*** It has taken a little over 300 years, from the time of Isaac Newton to the present day, to work out the rules of the game. Now, we have to learn how to play it and to appreciate that complexity arises from simple beginnings in a universe governed by simple laws.

plants change carbon dioxide into oxygen

189